Lecture Notes in Business Information Processing 229

Series Editors

Wil van der Aalst
Eindhoven Technical University, Eindhoven, The Netherlands
John Mylopoulos
University of Trento, Povo, Italy
Michael Rosemann
Queensland University of Technology, Brisbane, QLD, Australia
Michael J. Shaw
University of Illinois, Urbana-Champaign, IL, USA
Clemens Szyperski
Microsoft Research, Redmond, WA, USA

More information about this series at http://www.springer.com/series/7911

Raimundas Matulevičius · Marlon Dumas (Eds.)

Perspectives in Business Informatics Research

14th International Conference, BIR 2015
Tartu, Estonia, August 26–28, 2015
Proceedings

 Springer

Editors
Raimundas Matulevičius
University of Tartu
Tartu
Estonia

Marlon Dumas
University of Tartu
Tartu
Estonia

ISSN 1865-1348   ISSN 1865-1356   (electronic)
Lecture Notes in Business Information Processing
ISBN 978-3-319-21914-1   ISBN 978-3-319-21915-8   (eBook)
DOI 10.1007/978-3-319-21915-8

Library of Congress Control Number: 2015944201

Springer Cham Heidelberg New York Dordrecht London

Printed on acid-free paper

Springer International Publishing AG Switzerland is part of Springer Science+Business Media
(www.springer.com)

Preface

The international conference series on Perspectives of Business Informatics Research (BIR) was established 15 years ago. Its goal has been to provide a forum where researchers in business informatics, both senior and junior, can share and discuss their ideas and projects in order to forge stronger ties within the business informatics research community in Europe and elsewhere. Previous BIR conferences have been held in Rostock (Germany – in 2000, 2004, 2010), Berlin (Germany – 2003), Skövde (Sweden – 2005), Kaunas (Lithuania – 2006), Tampere (Finland – 2007), Gdańsk (Poland – 2008), Kristianstad (Sweden – 2009), Riga (Latvia – 2011), Nizhny Novgorod (Russia – 2012), Warsaw (Poland – 2013), and Lund (Sweden – 2014). The 14th International Conference on Perspectives in Business Informatics Research (BIR) was held in Tartu (Estonia), during August 26–28, 2015, at the Institute of Computer Science of the University of Tartu.

This year, the BIR conference attracted 49 submissions from 16 countries, including the core countries and regions traditionally represented at the conference (Germany, Northern, and Eastern Europe) but also from Italy, The Netherlands, Turkey, and Colombia among others. All papers were rigorously reviewed by the Program Committee consisting of 47 members representing 23 countries. The selected 16 full papers and four short papers are included in this volume. The volume also includes abstracts of the keynote talks by Manfred Reichert and Marcello La Rosa.

Papers presented at the conference cover manifold aspects of business informatics research, underscoring the boundary-spanning and inclusive nature of the conference series. This year the conference theme was "making business information systems interoperable and adaptive in highly interconnected and changing contexts." The theme is reflected in several of the accepted papers. Other topics covered in this year's edition are business and information systems development, business intelligence, knowledge management, and contextualized evaluation of business informatics. Furthermore, workshops and a doctoral consortium complemented the program of the conference itself.

We would like to thank everyone who contributed to the BIR 2015 conference. We thank the authors for contributing and presenting their research. We appreciate the invaluable contribution of the members of the Program Committee and external reviewers. Thanks also go to all the members of the local organization team from the University of Tartu for their dedication in ensuring a successful conference. We acknowledge the EasyChair development team for providing a convenient tool for preparing these proceedings and Springer for their continued collaboration in publishing the proceedings of BIR. Last but not the least we thank the Steering Committee. We are confident that BIR 2015 was a valuable addition to the development of the BIR conference series.

June 2015

Raimundas Matulevičius
Marlon Dumas

Organization

Program Co-chairs

Raimundas Matulevičius	University of Tartu, Estonia
Marlon Dumas	University of Tartu, Estonia

Program Committee

Esma Aimeur	University of Montreal, Canada
Eduard Babkin	State University - Higher School of Economics (Nizhny Novgorod), Russia
Per Backlund	University of Skövde, Sweden
Marko Bajec	University of Ljubljana, Slovenia
Ilia Bider	Stockholm University/IbisSoft, Sweden
Rimantas Butleris	Kaunas University of Technology, Lithuania
Cristina Cabanillas	Vienna University of Economics and Business, Austria
Sven Carlsson	Lund University, Sweden
Raffaele Conforti	Queensland University of Technology, Australia
Massimiliano de Leoni	Eindhoven University of Technology, The Netherlands
Marie-Christine Fauvet	University of Grenoble, France
Peter Forbrig	University of Rostock, Germany
Bogdan Ghilic-Micu	Bucharest University of Economic Studies, Romania
Claude Godart	University of Lorraine, France
Jānis Grabis	Riga Technical University, Latvia
Markus Helfert	Dublin City University, Ireland
Björn Johansson	Lund University, Sweden
Anna Kalenkova	National Research University Higher School of Economics, Russia
Mārīte Kirikova	Riga Technical University, Latvia
John Krogstie	Norwegian University of Science and Technology, Norway
Michael Le Duc	Mälardalen University, Sweden
Barbara Livieri	University of Salento, Italy
Irina Lomazova	National Research University, Higher School of Economics, Russia
Charles Møller	Aalborg University, Denmark
Jacob Nørbjerg	Aalborg University, Denmark
Grzegorz J. Nalepa	AGH University of Science and Technology, Poland
Alexander Norta	Tallinn University of Technology, Estonia
Boris Novikov	St. Petersburg University, Russia

Michael Petit	University of Namur, Belgium
Tomáš Pitner	Masaryk University, Czech Republic
Nava Pliskin	Ben-Gurion University of the Negev, Israel
Václav Řepa	University of Economics, Prague, Czech Republic
Manuel Resinas	University of Seville, Spain
Kurt Sandkuhl	University of Rostock, Germany
Flavia Santoro	UNIRIO, Brazil
Stefan Seidel	University of Liechtenstein, Liechtenstein
Andrzej Sobczak	Warsaw School of Economics, Poland
Pnina Soffer	University of Haifa, Israel
Chris Stary	Johannes Kepler University of Linz, Austria
Janis Stirna	Stockholm University, Sweden
Bernhard Thalheim	Christian Albrechts University Kiel, Germany
Peter Trkman	University of Ljubljana, Slovenia
Anna Wingkvist	Linnaeus University, Sweden
Stanislaw Wrycza	University of Gdańsk, Poland
Jelena Zdravkovic	Stockholm University, Sweden
Iryna Zolotaryova	Kharkiv National University of Economics, Ukraine

External Reviewers

Pavel Andreev, Israel
Isaac-Bernardo
Caicedo-Castro, France
Leona Chandra, Liechtenstein
Kuan-Lin Chen, Denmark
Zippy Erlich, Israel
Marko Janković, Slovenia
Kestutis Kapočius, Lithuania
Sagit Kedem-Yemini, Israel
Krzysztof Kluza, Poland
Michal Kuciapski, Poland

Bartosz Marcinkowski, Poland
Lina Nemuraitė, Lithuania
Gali Naveh, Israel
Elan Sasson, Israel
Tara Shahim, Denmark
Ofira Shmueli, Israel
Anna Plekhanova, Ukraine
Fatemeh Rahimi, Denmark
Sanja Tumbas, Liechtenstein
Slavko Žitnik, Slovenia

BIR Steering Committee

Kurt Sandkuhl	University of Rostock, Germany (Chair)
Eduard Babkin	State University - Higher School of Economics (Nizhny Novgorod), Russia
Rimantas Butleris	Kaunas Technical University, Lithuania
Sven Carlsson	Lund University, Sweden
Peter Forbrig	Rostock University, Germany
Björn Johansson	Lund University, Sweden
Mārīte Kirikova	Riga Technical University, Latvia
Andrzej Kobyliński	Warsaw School of Economics, Poland

Keynotes

The Next Wave of Research in Business Process Management

Manfred Reichert

Ulm University, Institute of Databases and Information Systems, Germany
manfred.reichert@uni-ulm.de
www.uni-ulm.de/dbis

Abstract. Business Process Management (BPM) has been evolving as a research discipline for more than a decade and a multitude of innovative concepts, methods and techniques have been suggested, e.g., related to process modeling languages, process model analyses, process enactment infrastructures, process flexibility, and process mining. Although BPM has matured as a research discipline, there is still a gap between its promises and its actual achievements in practice. This keynote speech reflects on this gap, discusses emerging challenges, and relates BPM research to current waves like "Big Data", "Big Software" and "Cloud Computing", which provide new prospects for future BPM research.

Keywords: Process science · Next-generation process management tools · Big processes · Real-world aware processes · Process flexibility

References

1. Reichert, M., Weber, B.: Enabling Flexibility in Process-Aware Information Systems: Challenges, Methods, Technologies. Springer, Heidelberg (2012)
2. Dadam, P., Reichert, M.: The ADEPT project: a decade of research and development for robust and flexible process support - challenges and achievements. Comput. Sci. - Res. Dev. **23**(2), 81–97 (2009). Springer
3. Weber, B., Reichert, M., Mendling, J., Reijers, H.: Refactoring large process model repositories. Comput. Ind. **62**(5), 467–486 (2011)
4. Ayora, C., Torres, V., Weber, B., Reichert, M., Pelechano, V.: VIVACE: a framework for the systematic evaluation of variability support in process-aware information systems. Inf. Softw. Technol. **57**, 248–276 (2015)
5. Lanz, A., Weber, B., Reichert, M.: Time patterns for process-aware information systems. Requir. Eng. **19**(2), 113–141 (2014)
6. Kolb, J., Reichert, M.: A Flexible approach for abstracting and personalizing large business process models. ACM Appl. Comput. Rev. **13**(1), 6–17 (2013)
7. Künzle, V., Weber, B., Reichert, M.: Object-aware business processes: fundamental requirements and their support in existing approaches. Int J. Inf. Syst. Model. Des. **2**(2), 19–46 (2011)
8. Fdhila, W., Indiono, C., Rinderle-Ma, S., Reichert, M.: Dealing with change in process choreographies: design and implementation of propagation algorithms. Inf. Syst. **49**, 1–24 (2015). Elsevier

Liquid Process Model Collections:
How to Get There?

Marcello La Rosa

Queensland University of Technology, Australia
NICTA Queensland Lab, Australia
m.larosa@qut.edu.au

Business processes are multimillion dollar assets in large firms. Explicit representations of these processes in the form of process models are used to inform strategic decision making by various stakeholders and as blueprints for automation.

However, the large number of business processes within an organization, their frequent changes and the variety of process stakeholders and related purposes, lead to significant challenges in keeping these models aligned with corporate reality. It is not uncommon that different teams of analysts within the same organization work on different sets of process models with little to no cooperation between the teams, resulting in inconsistencies between the models being created or updated. The problem is exacerbated by the lack of a proper governance structure for managing process model collections within organizations. In the worst case, the entire collection of process models becomes out-of-date and is slowly deprecated, as new models are created from scratch. This puts under question the value of process modeling, as managers struggle to see the benefits of active process management.

This keynote explores the idea of a "liquid" process model collection, i.e. a collection of process models that can self-adapt to organizational changes in order to remain synched with real-world processes, as these evolve over time. These changes, or *process drifts*, are observed from process execution logs (event logs) that are recorded by common IT systems within an organization, such as an enterprise resource planning system for a sales company or a claims management system for an insurance company. The keynote will show that the cornerstone techniques required to render process model collections liquid already exist, and stem from the combination of techniques from process mining with those from the management of large process model collections. However, there are still open challenges related to scalability and accuracy when dealing with large process model collections and large event logs, that call for the attention of the research community.

Contents

Business Information Systems Development

Research in Progress

Business Information Systems
Interoperability

Creation of Smart-Contracting Collaborations for Decentralized Autonomous Organizations

Alex Norta[✉]

Department of Informatics, Tallinn University of Technology,
Akadeemia Tee 15A, 12816 Tallinn, Estonia
alex.norta.phd@ieee.org

Abstract. Electronic communities of decentralized autonomous organizations (DAO) that engage in agile business-network collaborations, are enabled by recent blockchain-technology related innovations using smart contracting. DAOs utilize service-oriented cloud computing in a loosely-coupled collaboration lifecycle that commences with the setup phase. The latter supports the selection of services provided and used by DAOs in combination with smart contract negotiations. Such setup phases for DAO-communities use blueprints of business-network models that DAOs populate with tentative service offers. The negotiation phase may result either in a consensual agreement, a counteroffer, or a disagreement. In the latter case, the smart contract negotiation collapses and the lifecycle returns to the beginning of the selected collaboration blueprints. To the best of our knowledge, such a smart-contracting setup lifecycle has not been formalized so far. The paper fills the gap and evaluates the model with means of model-checking methods.

Keywords: Decentralized autonomous organization · Smart contract · Open cloud ecosystem · Governance-as-a-Service

1   Introduction

A trend emerges for so-called decentralized autonomous organizations (DAO) [3] to engage in the formation of electronic communities that smart contracts [31] cast together. A smart contract is a computerized transaction protocol [30] to execute contract terms. Consequently, for achieving non-repudiation and fact-tracking of a consensual smart-contract agreement, blockchain technology [17,26] is suitable. The blockchain is a distributed database for independently verifying the chain of ownership of artefacts [25] in hash values that result from cryptographic digests. As a further means to realize electronic communities of DAOs, the emergence of service-oriented cloud computing (SOCC) [33] promises for companies an acceleration of seamless, ad-hoc integration and coordination of information- and business-process flows [10] to orchestrate and choreograph [21] heterogeneous legacy-system infrastructures.

While research results emerge for cross-organizational business collaboration, a gap exists with respect to a formalized exploration of DAO-collaboration setup

© Springer International Publishing Switzerland 2015
R. Matulevičius and M. Dumas (Eds.): BIR 2015, LNBIP 229, pp. 3–17, 2015.
DOI: 10.1007/978-3-319-21915-8_1

lifecycles. This paper fills the gap by investigating the research question how to set up in a dependable way electronic communities of business collaborating DAOs to the point of a consensually agreed upon smart contract? Here, dependable [2] means the components that are part of the setup lifecycle are relied upon to perform exclusively and correctly the system task(s) under defined operational and environmental conditions over a defined period of time. Based on this main research question, we deduce the following sub-questions to establish a separation of concerns. What is the top-level setup-lifecycle and which business data flows along it? When exceptional scenarios occur, what mechanisms exist for an orderly compensation-rollback and partial-, or complete lifecycle termination? What are the relevant system properties for successfully realizing the startup-lifecycle with transactionality platform as Governance-as-a-Service (GaaS) in a Cloud?

The remainder of the paper is structured as follows. Section 2 provides additional information relevant for understanding the business-collaboration context. Section 3 shows the top-level of the formalized startup-lifecycle in which service protocols are visible with their data-exchanges. Furthermore, in Sect. 4 we show the successful rollbacks of smart-contracting semantics within a startup-lifecycle. Section 5 lists the results from model checking that are aiding the application-system implementation of a sound startup-lifecycle. Section 6 discusses related work and finally, Sect. 7 concludes this manuscript by summarizing the research work, giving the contributions achieved and showing directions for future work.

2   Conceptual Collaboration Context

For comprehending the setup-lifecycle in the sequel, the following frameworks are important to comprehend. We explain a peer-to-peer (P2P) collaboration model for DAOs in Sect. 2.1. Furthermore, as contracts are the foundation of business collaboration, we also show in Sect. 2.2 concepts and properties for smart contracting.

2.1   P2P-Collaboration Model

Pertaining to DAO-collaboration, Fig. 1(a) conceptually depicts a configuration. The blueprint for an electronic-community formation is a so-called business-network model (BNM) [27]. The latter captures choreographies that are relevant for a business scenario and it contains legally valid template contracts that are service types with affiliated organizational roles. The BNMs are available in a collaboration hub that houses business processes as a service (BPaaS-HUB) [22] in the form of subset process views [10]. The latter enable a fast and semi-automatic discovery of collaboration parties for learning about their identity, services, and reputation.

On the external layer of Fig. 1(a), service offers identically match with service types contained in the BNM with the contractual sphere of collaborating parties. Additionally, a collaborating partner must match into the specific partner roles

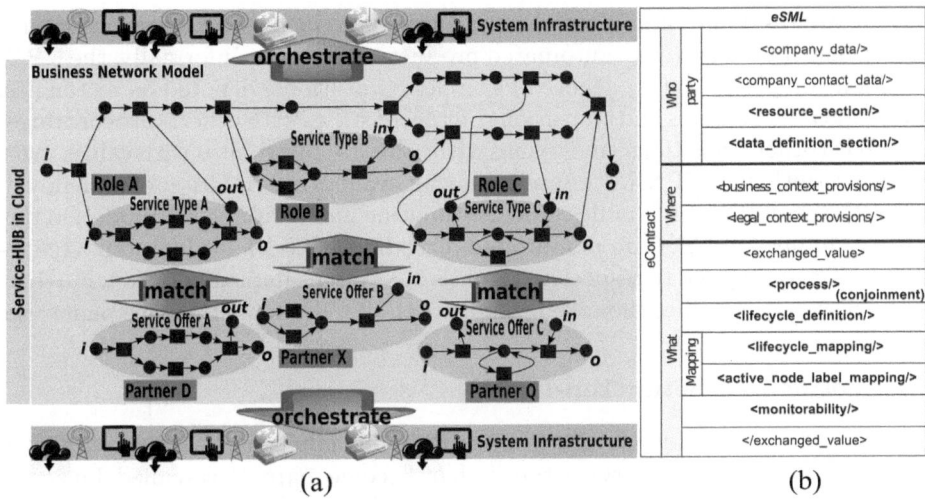

Fig. 1. P2P-collaboration using the eSourcing framework.

associated with a respective service type. We refer the reader to [10] for details about the tree-based process-view matching to establish a DAO-configuration into a contract-based collaborations.

2.2   Smart Contract

The top-level structure shows a smart contracting language termed eSourcing Markup Language (eSML) [23] in Fig. 1(b). The bold typed definitions in the eSML-structure are extensions and modifications that are not part of the Electronic Contracting Markup Language (ECML) [1] foundation.

The core structure of a smart contract we organize according to the interrogatives *Who* for defining the contracting parties together with their resources and data definitions, *Where* to specify the business- and legal context, and *What* for specifying the exchanged business values. For achieving a consensus, we assume the *What*-interrogative employs matching process views that require cross-organizational alignment for monitorability. We refer to [23] for more information about the smart-contracting ontology.

Next, we discuss first the DAO-lifecycles for the top-level collaboration-setup stages. Note, from here on we use eCommunity for a community of collaborating DAOs and eContract for an electronic contract.

3   Top-Level Setup-Lifecycle

First, Sect. 3.1 shows the formalized top-level of the setup lifecycle[1] using Coloured Petri Nets (CPN) [13]. The latter is a graphical oriented language for the design,

---

[1] Full CPN-model: http://tinyurl.com/ofae8gn.

specification, simulation and verification of systems such as communication protocols, distributed systems, automated production systems. Informally, the CPN-notation comprises states, denoted as circles, transitions, denoted as rectangles, arcs that connect states and transitions but never states with other states or transitions with other transitions, and tokens with color, i.e., attributes with values. Arcs carry inscriptions in CPN-ML expressions that evaluate to a multiset or a single element. We use CPNtools[2] for designing, evaluating and verifying the models in this paper. Modules in CPN are non-atomic place-holder nodes for hierarchic refinements that correspond to respective services in a system-implementation. Furthermore, Sect. 3.2 describes the token colours that all CPN-models of this paper use.

3.1   Formalized Setup Top-Level

The lifecycle of Fig. 2 shows that a nested module labelled *BNM selection* is an ecosystem for breeding service types that become part of so-called business-network models (BNM). For establishing such an eContracting preliminary, the so-called eSourcing Markup Language eSML [23] is a candidate for BNM-specifications. The latter is a cross-enterprise collaboration blueprint to insert service types and roles for the next step in the lifecycle, namely the population with service offers and eCommunity-partners. The BNMs that emerge from the breeding ecosystem exist permanently for repeated use in the subsequent populating stage, i.e., conformance-validated service offers and BNMs. The *populate*-module validates the inserted service offers against the service types of the BNM as it emerges from the breeding ecosystem.

Such a breeding ecosystem in the form of service brokers citation [11] investigates in a state-of-the-art comparison since this is identified as a key concern for future cloud technology development and research. In [6,7], the authors introduce service value brokerage between service consumers and service providers that crosscuts business modeling, knowledge management and economic analysis. The research in [22] describes a lifecycle of finding and matching service requests with service offers for collaboration enactment in a Business-Process-as-a-Service (BPaaS) HUB.

At the end of the *populate*-phase in Fig. 2, a proto-contract exists for a *negotiate* step that is carried out by the eCommunity-partners. The negotiation of the proto-contract has three different outcome options. An agreement of all eCommunity-partners establishes the eContract for subsequent rollout and enactment; a counter-offer from only one eCommunity-partner triggers a business-semantics rollback to the inception of the *negotiate*-module; finally, a disagreement of only one eCommunity-partner results in a complete termination of not only the contract negotiation but additionally, the startup-lifecycle also suddenly terminates with the identification ending in the state labelled *terminated eCommunity*.

According to [15], agent-based negotiation is progressing fast and enables semi- to fully automated negotiation. In [5], an agent-based coordinated-negotiation

---

[2] http://cpntools.org/.

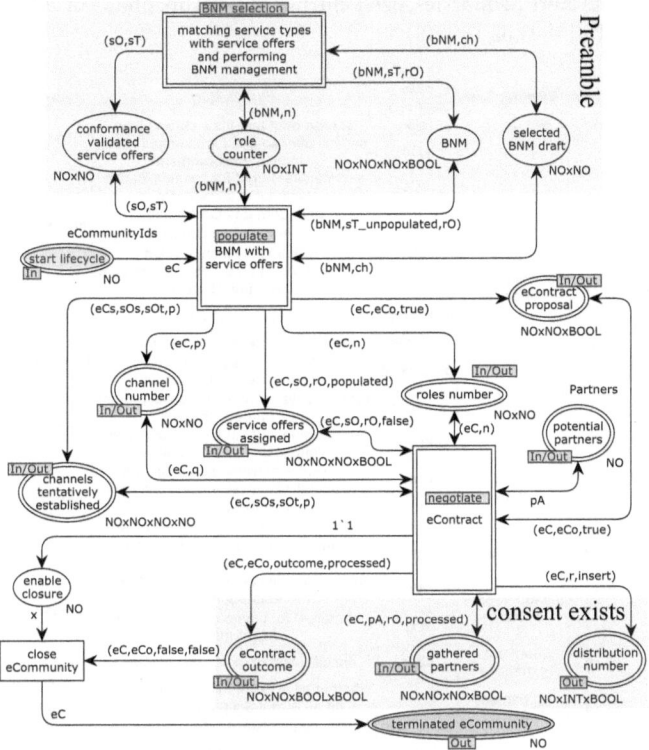

Fig. 2. Top-level formalized setup-lifecyle for electronic community establishment.

architecture ensures adherence to service-level agreements and the stateful coordination of complex cross-organizational services.

3.2 Related Business-Collaboration Data

In the left column of Table 1 showing 1 is the top-level and 4 the lowest refinement of the setp-lifecycle components. Data-flow properties listed for availability in a certain refinement-hierarchy level are present for all lower- but not for any higher hierarchy levels. The fourth column of Table 1 textually explains the purpose of a data-flow property while the types are either integer, string or boolean. In the first case, the integer mostly represents a token identification number, a string is either an eContract-negotiation outcome or an eContract-proposal extracted from a business-network model and boolean represent decision points. The data-flow properties of Table 1 either represent in concrete implementations more elaborate database tables, or XML-schemata with more refining properties.

Next, we show what rollback mechanism are in place on a refined setup-lifecycle level for flexibly responding to exceptional situations.

Table 1. Concepts and properties used during the setup phase of an electronic community of DAO (full details in [20]).

level	CPN module	data property	description	type
1	eCommunity lifecycle	sO	service offer that fits a service type	integer
		sOs	service offer source for communication channel establishment	
		sOt	service offer target for communication channel establishment	
		pA	partner of an eCommunity	
		rO	role a partner can fill	
		eC	eCommunity identification	
		eCo	eContract based on which partners of an eCommunity transact	
		n,r,k,p,l,q,s	counter variables	
		assigned	service offer assigned to a service type	boolean
		processed	partner prepared for eContract counteroffer re-distribution	
		decision	for negotiated contract proposal (agree|disagree|counter)	string
		outcome	like decision, but input for eCommunity continuation or termination	
2	create	bNM	business network model that get populated with service types and roles	integer
		m	counter variable	
		sT	service type that populates a bNM	
3	populate	ch	channel of communication between services	integer
4	interoperability checking	rOt	role source for communication channel establishment	integer
		rOs	role target for communication channel establishment	
4	contract extraction	spec	specification of extracted eContract	string
4	agreement finalizing	result	whether all eCommunity partners agree on an eContract proposal or not	boolean
		distributed	contract distributed to partner	
4	disagreeing	z	counter variable	integer
		eCo_new	new eContract from a counteroffer to be negotiated	

4   Compensation Rollbacks

To study the rollback types in detail, the following CPN-models are all refinements of Fig. 2 and we commence with Sect. 4.1 for discussing the establishment of an eContract-preamble. Next, Sect. 4.2 shows rollbacks that occur during the BNM-population phase and finally, Sect. 4.3 comprises detailed rollbacks furing the negotiation-lifecycle.

4.1   BNM Selection

This module functions as an ecosystem to breed BNMs. For that, a repository exists in the *BNM selection* for which we assume users insert service types over time that they specify themselves. The same assumption holds for the repository of service offers in *BNM selection* that is correspondingly a state in the CPN-module labelled *repository service offers*.

To be considered as a service offer for populating a BNM, beforehand the passing of a conformance validation is necessary. The actual BNM-selection involves choosing a BNM-draft for adding validated service offers and roles to be filled subsequently with respective eCommunity-partners.

Research in [16] focuses on finding service providers that minimizes the total execution time of a business process based on cost and execution time constraints. Work in [8] gives a Web service selection algorithm that satisfies not only user preferences and functional requirements but also takes into account transactional properties and service-level-agreement characteristics.

4.2   The BNM-population

In this service depicted in Fig. 3, an unique eCommunity number identifies the entire transaction lifecycle. The service types in the chosen BNM draft specification are populated with conformance-validated service offers. Next, an interoperability check of those service offers ensures the channels are capable of exchanging data that matches semantic expectations. When the proto-contract with tentatively established channels is ready, the population stage is ready for the next BNM population.

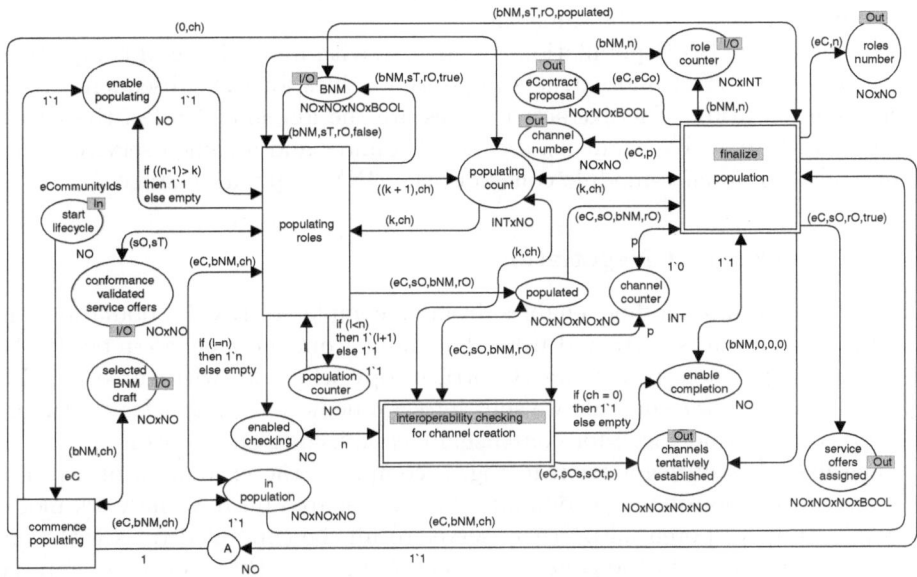

Fig. 3. Populating a BNM with service offer, roles, and checking interoperability (module *populate* in Fig. 2).

The service offers chosen for populating a BNM are in the state labelled *populated*. For the tentatively established channels between service offers, a dedicated token color contained in the BNM indicates the required amount of channels. Consequently, a chosen service offer becomes a channel source and another one a channel target that must adhere to given channel requirements and data-semantics matching. The interoperability checking ends when the number of required tentative channels exists that enables the completion stage of BNM-population.

Populating the BNM with roles touches on many open issues in the state of the art [4]. The open issues pertain to hiding business details in the process that, e.g., constitute a competitive advantage; the lacking expressiveness of existing resource-assignment languages to meaningfully automate role population; remaining in control over the allocation of outsourced activities; different vocabulary in the respective domains of the parties involved; and so on. For interoperability checking in Fig. 3, citation [34] gives many aspects. When checking the interoperability abilities within a populated BNM, the categories involved [9] comprise collaboration knowledge, models and standards, business processes, services, information and data.

To complete the population of BNMs, the *finalize*-module empties the *populate*-module of remaining tokens. In an application-system implementation, this emptying corresponds to emptying an instantiation of not needed database entries and abandoned computing processes that lead to a collapse of the overall system. Such a collapse and restart is undesirable if many eCommunities are active to transact at the same time.

Finalizing the BNM-population commences with an enabling of completion, continues with a reset and extracts important values for the subsequent proto-contract negotiation. The extracted values are the amount of roles, the proto-contract with tentative channels, a channel counter and assigned service offers. Eventually, the *finalize*-module concludes the BNM-populating stage.

4.3   The eContract Negotiation

Once the *negotiate*-module enables from a completed BNM population, an eContract-proposal is extracted from that input from the *populate*-module. All eCommunity-partners receive an eContract copy who vote with three possible options. The *negotiate*-module we split into two depictions, Fig. 4 for extracting a proto-contract and Fig. 5 for consensually establishing an eContract.

The first part of negotiation in Fig. 4, comprises the extraction of a proto-contract. After choosing an eCommunity for a prepared business-network model (BNM), a pool of potential partners serves to fill the contained roles with concrete partners. Next, in the *contract extraction* module, the eContract-proposal emerges from the *population*-module, extending specifications of the tentatively created service-offer channels. The created eContract-proposal is ready for the subsequent steps of negotiation.

The *negotiate*-module in Fig. 5, caters in an ideal case for an *agree* of all eCommunity partnersthat establishes a consensus to make an eContract come into existence. Secondly, one eCommunity-partner decides on a modification and proposes a *make counteroffer* for an eContract. The counteroffer instantaneously disables all voting options, removes the already casted votes and redistributes a copy of the modified contract for every respective eCommunity-partner. Thirdly, in the case of only one *disagree*, the voting process halts, again, it triggers the

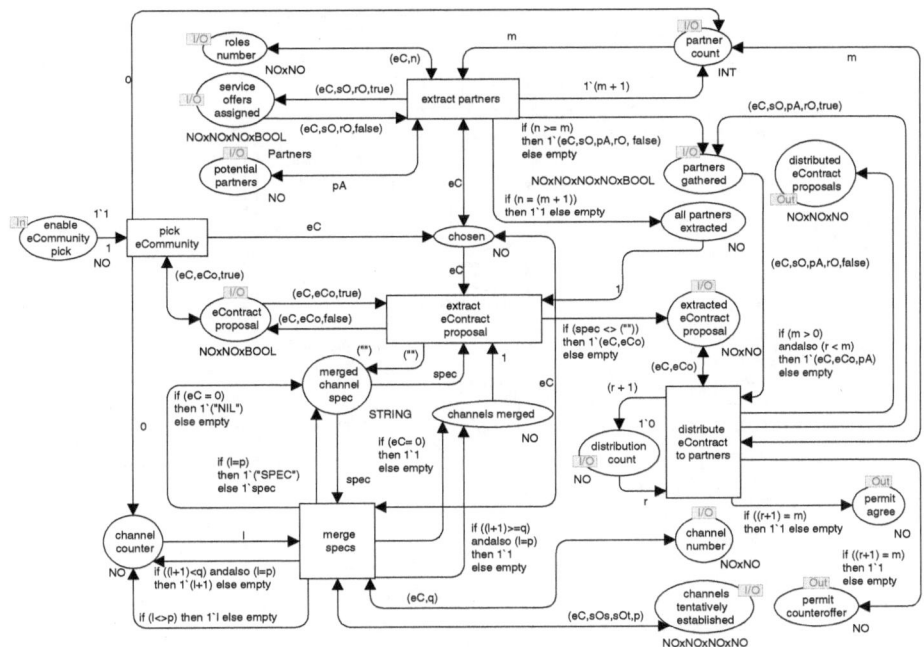

Fig. 4. Extracting a proto-contract (in module *negotiate* of Fig. 2).

removal of already casted votes and terminates the entire CEC-lifecycle. Subsequently, the eCommunity identification comes to rest in the state labelled *terminated eCommunity*.

When all eCommunity-partners vote on an eContract-proposal, the objective is to achieve a consensus by all agreeing. In that case, the nested module *agreement finalizing* empties the *negotiation* of eCommunity-partner instances and the offered services are reset for the next negotiation phase. Finally, the negotiation outcome is set to *true*. For both cases of an eContract-proposal disagreement and also for the issuance of a counteroffer by an eCommunity-partner, the calculated number of eCommunity-partners serves as input to empty the *negotiate*-service.

A disagreement leads to the removal of all eCommunity-related tokens, the lifecycle termination and the identification token moves to its final state labelled *terminated eCommunity*. However, with a new counteroffer, the existing eCommunity-partners must cast votes again and as such, each partner must receive a contract-proposal copy of the counteroffer. All other eCommunity-related tokens remain in their respective states.

When an eCommunity-partner casts a vote in a negotiation phase indicating a disagreement, this module performs the final clearance preparation for the subsequent enactment that is *disagreement finalizing*. Setting the negoti-

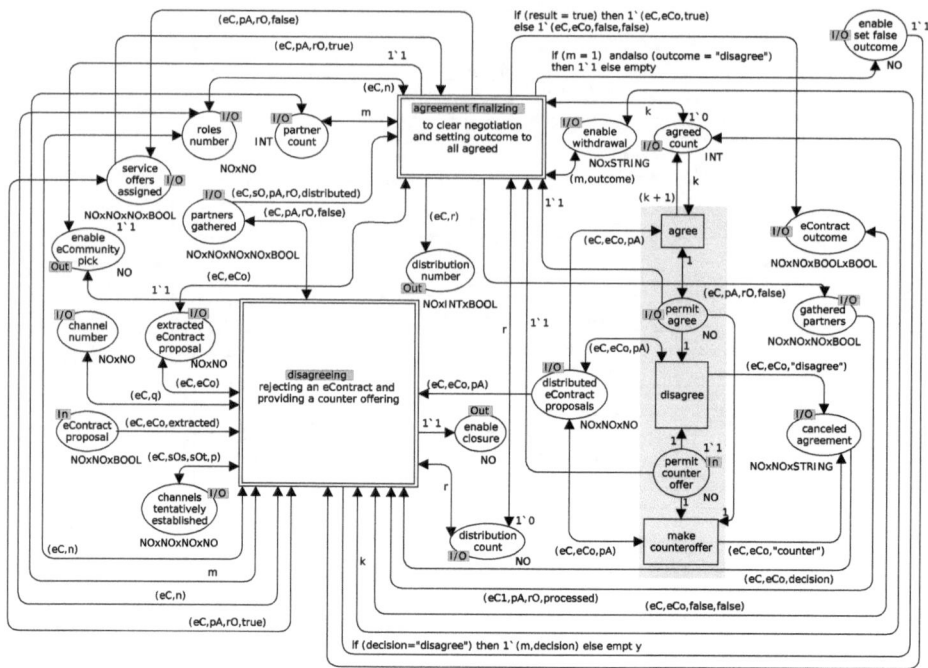

Fig. 5. Deciding on an eContract to complete a negotiation (in module *negotiate* of Fig. 2).

ation outcome to *false* starts the removal of the eCommunity-partners, followed by a removal of service offers and channelsthat completes the disagreement finalization.

For eContract negotiation, the citation [14] defines a knowledge-based negotiation procedure where specific separate protocols and strategies enable agent participation in interaction processes between collaborating parties. In [28], contributions are a discussion of core elements in an eContract negotiation such as role, properties of electronic services and contract models; the definition of the actual negotiation process; and a conceptual model to support the negotiation of web service. In [32], the authors give features of an eContract metamodel they connect with quality-of-service (QoS) for being taken into account during a negotiation and renegotiation process a feature-based toolkit supports as a proof-of-concept prototype. Finally, the contribution [18] propose a lifecycle to support the management of eContracts comprising proposal, configuration, publication, negotiation, operation, and closure. A broker enables automatic configuration and deployment of web services.

Next, we perform a formal- and also proof-of-feasibility evaluation of the startup lifecycle.

5 Model Properties

We employ CPN Tools [13] for correctness and performance checking, especially on aspects relevant for system developers: reachability of CPN-modules end states in manual, or fully automated simulation token games as state explosion means full computational verification is challenging for this size of models; detection of loops as a potential source of livelocks that prevent desired termination reachability; loops require specific attention with respect to effectiveness of exit conditions, such as elements of business-level policy control; performance peaks during runtime either for the design of sufficient resources or for restricting the load with business-level policy control; full system utilisation for ensuring that each part of the modelled system actually is used in some scenario; and consistent termination, i.e., consistent home markings that ensure simple testing of a real system.

Table 2. Model-checking results for the setup-lifecycle.

| module | loops | module property | | | home marking | dead marking |
		performance peaks	liveness	Utilization		
BNM selection	no	evenly balanced	ND/NL	yes	no	multiple
populate	no	populating roles, interoperability checking	ND/NL	yes	no	no
negotiate with forced agreement	yes	contract extraction, agreement finalizing	D*/NL	yes*	no	multiple
negotiate with forced counteroffer	yes	contract extraction, distribute eContract to partners	D*/NL	yes*	no	no
negotiate with forced disagree	yes	contract extraction, agreement finalizing	D*/NL	yes*	no	multiple

The model-checking results in Table 2 focus on CPN-modules where the generated state-space is computationally feasible. For the *negotiate*-module there are three outcomes. Either all collaboration partners agree on a contract proposal, or a counteroffer negotiation unfolds, or one partner disagrees and collapses the proposal.

Loops exist in all three outcomes of the *negotiate*-module. The contract negotiation loop is self-restricting as it only processes the collaboration partners respectively. However, finalising the negotiation comprises loops because of a counteroffer issuance. The test results for remaining modules in Table 2 show they do not contain loops.

Performance peaks in Table 2 represent places in the startup-lifecycle that are potential performance bottlenecks. Peaks exist in all but the module *BNM selection*. For the *populate*-module, peaks occur for populating roles and also for checking if channel requirements and data-semantics match. Pertaining to the latter modules we refer the reader to [20] for details. For all three *negotiate*-run cases, peaks exist for counteroffers and negotiation finalisation. All these elements are effectively dependent on the amount of populations and negotiations performed, and therefore, stay limited.

While no module listed in Table 2 have any home marking, the model-checking results for dead markings differ. Multiple dead markings and no home markings means for practitioners the testing of implementations is more demanding as many test cases are required. $D*$ means the model-checking results show the dead markings result from intentional disabling of marking paths for the purpose of focusing in specific marking paths under investigation. The latter means for practitioners the testing of implementations is more demanding as many test cases are required. Finally, pertaining to utilisation tests, Table 2 shows no unused subsets exist in the models. We refer to [20] for full details about the model-checking results. Pertaining to utilisation tests, Table 2 shows no unused subsets exist in the models. Entries yes* state a subset of the CPN-module is intentionally disabled as an available runtime path to manage state-space explosion issues, or for allowing an analysis to focus on specific enactment paths.

Finally, due to page limitations, we refer the reader to [23] for details about the feasibility of an application-system implementation.

6   Related Work

As noted earlier, it is necessary to cross-organizationally establish collaboration frameworks in a way that does not force companies into disclosing an undesirable amount of business internals [10]. Different research efforts address this issue. In [12], the authors investigate tool support for cross-organizational collaboration design. Similarly in [29], research results present an integrated specification language and a user interface for collaborating government organizations to specify events of common interest, policies, constraints and regulations in the form of different types of knowledge rules, manual and automated services, and sharable workflow processes.

In [19], a framework facilitates the understanding of major cross-organizational collaboration challenges. For example, supporting process-level collaboration, and protection of shared IP and data with various enterprise-level and regulatory policies, including flexible and policy-aware process collaboration among people from different enterprises. Also [24] points out the need for agility of business operations in a collaborative services ecosystem of partners and providers by proposing Work-as-a-Service that a collaboration hub facilitates. A cross-organizational architecture in [12] specifies the features and their composition at a higher level that abstracts the internal implementation mechanisms of the organizations involved.

7   Conclusion

We investigate the setup-lifecycle of cross-organizational business-process aware collaboration for decentralised autonomous organizations. During the collaboration setup, the parties must consent to establish a smart contract. The setup-lifecycle commences with equipping a business network model with service types and assigned partner roles. Candidate partners with their service offers populate the service types and a negotiation follows that results either in a dissent, counter-offer issuance, or a consent. We model-check the setup lifecycle to reveal formal properties that have practical implications for application-system implementations.

For exploring the setup-lifecycle in a dependable way, we choose CPN Tools that has a graphical modelling notation backed with formal semantics. Exceptional scenarios that may occur are mismatches during the service-endpoint creation during the population stage. Additionally, exceptions may occur in the negotiation state of a smart contract when either parties disagree, or when a counteroffer issuance occurs. In the first case a loop back to the population stage occurs while a counteroffer issuance remains contained within the negotiation loop. The relevant model properties we check for are loops, performance peaks, liveness, utilization, home markings and whether dead markings exist in the setup-lifecycle.

For future work, we plan to apply the setup-lifecycle in projects for cyber-physical system governance in the realm if Internet-of-Things. Consequently, we plan to explore how blockchain-technology can realize non-repudiation in process-aware collaboration missions. Additionally, we plan to investigate how blockchain technology can enable novel approaches for effective management of trust, reputation, privacy and security in cross-organizational cyber-physical system collaboration scenarios.

Acknowledgments. This work was funded by the Estonian IT Akadeemia and also partly the research project SF0140013s10 "Model-based Creation and Management of Evolutionary Information Systems" by the Estonian Ministry of Education and Research.

References

1. Angelov, S.: Foundations of B2B electronic contracting. Dissertation, Technology University Eindhoven, Faculty of Technology Management, Information Systems Department (2006)
2. Avizienis, A., Laprie, J.C., Randell, B., Landwehr, C.: Basic concepts and taxonomy of dependable and secure computing. IEEE Trans. Dependable Secure Comput. **1**(1), 11–33 (2004)
3. Butterin, V.: A next-generation smart contract and decentralized application platform (2014)
4. Cabanillas, C., Norta, A., Resinas, M., Mendling, J., Ruiz-Cortés, A.: Towards process-aware cross-organizational human resource management. In: Bider, I., Gaaloul, K., Krogstie, J., Nurcan, S., Proper, H.A., Schmidt, R., Soffer, P. (eds.) BPMDS 2014 and EMMSAD 2014. LNBIP, vol. 175, pp. 79–93. Springer, Heidelberg (2014)
5. Chhetri, M.B., Lin, J., Goh, S.K., Yan, J., Zhang, J.Y., Kowalczyk, R.: A coordinated architecture for the agent-based service level agreement negotiation of web service composition. In: Software Engineering Conference, p. 10. Australian, April 2006
6. Duan, Y., Huang, K., Kattepur, A., Du, W.: Towards value-driven business modelling based on service brokerage. In: Lomuscio, A.R., Nepal, S., Patrizi, F., Benatallah, B., Brandić, I. (eds.) ICSOC 2013. LNCS, vol. 8377, pp. 163–176. Springer, Heidelberg (2014)

7. Duan, Y., Wang, Y., Wei, J., Kattepur, A., Du, W.: Value-added modelling and analysis in service value brokerage. In: Lomuscio, A.R., Nepal, S., Patrizi, F., Benatallah, B., Brandić, I. (eds.) ICSOC 2013. LNCS, vol. 8377, pp. 209–222. Springer, Heidelberg (2014)
8. El Hadad, J., Manouvrier, M., Rukoz, M.: TQoS: Transactional and QoS-aware selection algorithm for automatic web service composition. IEEE Trans. Serv. Comput. **3**(1), 73–85 (2010)
9. Elvesæter, B., Taglino, F., Del Grosso, E., Elguezabal, G.B., Capellini, A.: Towards enterprise interoperability service utilities. In: EDOCW, pp. 224–229 (2008)
10. Eshuis, R., Norta, A., Kopp, O., Pitkanen, E.: Service outsourcing with process views. IEEE Trans. Serv. Comput. **8**(1), 136–154 (2015)
11. Fowley, F., Pahl, C., Zhang, L.: A comparison framework and review of service brokerage solutions for cloud architectures. In: Lomuscio, A.R., Nepal, S., Patrizi, F., Benatallah, B., Brandić, I. (eds.) ICSOC 2013. LNCS, vol. 8377, pp. 137–149. Springer, Heidelberg (2014)
12. Hahn, C., Recker, J., Mendling, J.: An exploratory study of IT-enabled collaborative process modeling. In: Muehlen, M., Su, J. (eds.) BPM 2010 Workshops. LNBIP, vol. 66, pp. 61–72. Springer, Heidelberg (2011)
13. Jensen, K., Michael, L., Wells, K.L., Jensen, K., Kristensen, L.M.: Coloured petri nets and cpn tools for modelling and validation of concurrent systems. Int. J. Softw. Tools Technol. Transfer **9**(3–4), 213–254 (2007)
14. Kravari, K., Papavasileiou, C., Bassiliades, N.: Knowledge-based e-contract negotiation among agents using semantic web technologies. In: Bădică, C., Nguyen, N.T., Brezovan, M. (eds.) ICCCI 2013. LNCS, vol. 8083, pp. 215–224. Springer, Heidelberg (2013)
15. Lin, R., Kraus, S.: Can automated agents proficiently negotiate with humans? Commun. ACM **53**(1), 78–88 (2010)
16. Menasce, D.A., Casalicchio, E., Dubey, V.: On optimal service selection in service oriented architectures. Perform. Eval. **67**(8), 659–675 (2010). Special Issue on Software and Performance
17. Nakamoto, S.: Bitcoin: a peer-to-peer electronic cash system. Consulted **1**(2012), 28 (2008)
18. Neto, J.B., Hirata, C.M.: Lifecycle for management of e-contracts based on web service. In: Proceedings of the World Congress on Engineering and Computer Science, vol. 1 (2013)
19. Nezhad, H.R.M., Bartolini, C., Erbes, J., Graupner, S.: A process- and policy-aware cross enterprise collaboration framework for multisourced services. In: 2012 Annual SRII Global Conference (SRII), pp. 488–493, July 2012
20. Norta, A.: Safeguarding trusted eBusiness transactions of lifecycles for cross-enterprise collaboration. TBT SOCC.pdf (2012). http://www.cs.helsinki.fi/u/anorta/publications/
21. Norta, A., Grefen, P., Narendra, N.C.: A reference architecture for managing dynamic inter-organizational business processes. Data Knowl. Eng. **91**, 52–89 (2014)
22. Norta, A., Kutvonen, L.: A cloud hub for brokering business processes as a service: a "rendezvous" platform that supports semi-automated background checked partner discovery for cross-enterprise collaboration. In: 2012 Annual SRII Global Conference (SRII), pp. 293–302, July 2012
23. Norta, A., Ma, L., Duan, Y., Rull, A., Kõlvart, M., Taveter, K.: eContractual choreography-language properties towards cross-organizational business collaboration. J. Internet Serv. Appl. **6**(1), 1–23 (2015)

24. Oppenheim, D., Bagheri, S., Ratakonda, K., Chee, Y.M.: Agility of enterprise operations across distributed organizations: a model of cross enterprise collaboration. In: 2011 Annual SRII Global Conference (SRII), pp. 154–162, March 2011
25. Panikkar, B.S., Nair, S., Brody, P., Pureswaran, V.: Adept: an iot practitioner perspective (2014)
26. Patron, T.: The Bitcoin Revolution: An Internet of Money. Travis Patron, London (2015)
27. Ruokolainen, T., Ruohomaa, S., Kutvonen, L.: Solving service ecosystem governance. In: 2011 15th IEEE International Enterprise Distributed Object Computing Conference Workshops (EDOCW), pp. 18–25. IEEE (2011)
28. Silva, G.C., de Souza Gimenes, I.M., Fantinato, M., de Toledo, M.B.F.: Inter-organizational negotiation of web-services. Int. J. U-E-Serv. Sci. Technol. **6**(5), 97–114 (2013)
29. Su, S.Y.W., Xiao, X., DePree, J., Beck, H.W., Thomas, C., Coggeshall, A., Bostock, R.: Interoperation of organizational data, rules, processes and services for achieving inter-organizational coordination and collaboration. In: 2011 44th Hawaii International Conference on System Sciences (HICSS), pp. 1–10, January 2011
30. Swan, M.: Blockchain thinking: the brain as a dac (decentralized autonomous organization). In: Texas Bitcoin Conference, pp. 27–29 (2015)
31. Szabo, N.: Formalizing and securing relationships on public networks. First Monday, 2(9) (1997). http://dx.doi.org/10.5210/fm.v2i9.548
32. Vecchiato, D.A., Toledo, M.B.F., Fantinato, M., Gimenes, I.M.S.: A feature-based toolkit for electronic contract negotiation and renegotiation. Proc. IADIS Int. Conf. WWW/Internet **2010**, 3–10 (2010)
33. Wei, Y., Blake, M.B.: Service-oriented computing and cloud computing: challenges and opportunities. IEEE Internet Comput. **14**(6), 72–75 (2010)
34. Zelm, M., Sanchis, R., Poler, R., Doumeingts, G.: Enterprise Interoperability: I-ESA'12 Proceedings. Wiley, New York (2012)

Reliable Customers and Credible Fixed-Price Contracts for Software Development Projects: A Study of One Supplier's Contracts

Cornelia Gaebert[(⊠)]

Research Group on Strategic Information Management,
European Research Center for Information Systems, C/O University of Muenster,
Leonardo Campus 11, 48149 Muenster, Germany
Cornelia.Gaebert@uni-muenster.de,
Cornelia.Gaebert@indal.de

Abstract. A fundamental tenet of the information systems discipline holds that changing requirements in software development projects (SDP) are the main reason for failure; therefore, in case of such uncertainties, fixed-price contracts (FPC) are not suitable for success. Our empirical research, informed by economic theories, compellingly illustrates that the FPC is an appropriate contractual form. However, we claim that there is a need to optimize its use. With this paper, we show that reliable customers allow credible FPCs enhancing project success, whereas sophisticated contract provisions do not have this effect. Customer reliability reflects whether the customer uses stable methods and regulations for information processing regarding goal definition, belief generation, and decision-making. Our findings offer managers important insights into how they can design and enact FPCs to manage SDPs successfully. Further, we show how economic theories can enhance understanding of SDP success.

Keywords: Customer reliability · Credible contract · Software development project · Failure reasons

1 Introduction

For decades, the information systems (IS) discipline holds that changing requirements in software development projects (SDP) are the main reason for failure [1–5]. The central argument posits that changing requirements of the information system generate uncertainty for the concerned customer and supplier in terms of budget and time; the goal of the SDP shifts by changing requirements. Researchers claim that in this situation a predetermined price for the software system - defined in a fixed-price contract (FPC) - is not suitable for completion of the SDP in line with the expectations of the contracting parties [6, 7]. Indeed, the contract influences the success or failure of SDPs [8]. However, the budget of the organization is limited. In addition, the legislator forces public authorities to carry out a Request for Proposals to find the supplier with the best price. Consequently, the parties mostly sign an FPC for the SDP. Therefore, the central challenge is to govern a project with an inevitably incomplete contract (in terms of specification of tasks and outcomes), which however has a fixed price.

© Springer International Publishing Switzerland 2015
R. Matulevičius and M. Dumas (Eds.): BIR 2015, LNBIP 229, pp. 18–32, 2015.
DOI: 10.1007/978-3-319-21915-8_2

We claim that the customer's reliability and the credibility of the contract with its provisions influence the effectiveness of the contract and thus the project success. We argue that researchers need to consider the settings of the contracting parties themselves when the effect of the contract on the SDP is the focus of the investigation. It is widely accepted that customer and supplier pursue at the transaction level different economic targets and outcome goals [9]. Savolainen [9] elaborated after a comprehensive literature review that the customer's attention is on cost, time, and quality, whereas the supplier's attention is on customer satisfaction, short-term business success for the supplier, and long-term success for the supplier. Ultimately, an SDP is not an anonymous or unassisted transaction in the market [10, 11].

In this paper, we study one supplier's contracts regarding (a) the contract provisions of the FPCs, (b) the customers' properties and (c) the SDPs characteristics. We show that reliable customers allow credible FPCs enhancing project success, whereas sophisticated contract provisions do not have this effect. Economic theory can improve our understanding of reasons for failure of SDPs. However, there is a paucity of research on how the contracting parties can improve SDP's performance or outcome by the use of a credible FPC.

We develop our argument, in particular our understanding on reliable customers and credible contracts, in Sect. 2 of this paper. In Sect. 3, we review the theoretical background of our empirical investigation. After a description of our results, we discuss some findings in Sect. 4. In Sect. 5, we summarize our results. We end up with the limits of our paper and with suggestions for further research.

2 Credible Contracts and Reliable Customers

A first typology of the contracts under uncertainty found its way into economic theory in the late 1970s [10]. Transactions with asset specificity and uncertainty need assistance by contractual control [11]. Such relational contracts provide long-term relationships more than short-term projects. Relational contracts are designed for the continuation of the relationship between the contractual parties. The researchers suggested for long time to carry out transactions with asset specificity and uncertainty internally or under customers' hierarchical control. However, the contracting parties of software development outsourcing (SDO) projects need contracts for short-term projects. Therefore, Williamson took up this topic again in 2008 [12]. Hybrid contracts for transactions not feasible in the market or in hierarchy need a mediating style. He argued the three leading styles are (1) muscular, (2) benign, and (3) credible.

(1) Often large customers do business with smaller suppliers. The *muscular* customer asks the supplier only for the best price for the services. If for whatever reason the service fails, the customer will refuse payment. However, the supplier cannot easily redeploy the assets (customized code) if such unexpected developments arise. Therefore, suppliers will ask the customers to provide safeguards to mitigate the risks, or they will try to increase their price to consider the additional risk. This exploitation is myopic and inefficient for a long-term relationship. For a short-term project, it is very risky for the supplier.

(2) In case of *benign contracts*, trust in reputation replaces the concept of power. However, if conflict arises, "defection from the spirit of the contract can be projected" (cf. [12]).

(3) This study builds on Williamsons pioneering work when adopting his call for *credible contracts*. This approach is hard-headed, but not mean-spirited. The parties look ahead and work out the mechanisms managing potential hazards. Credible according to a sentence form 1750 BC: „When you ask us for troops, we will not answer you with evasions, we shall brandish our maces and strike down your enemy. ..."(cf. [12]). In earlier time, kings intermarried their children for this. However, this is not an option in context of an FPC for the SDP. Therefore, this study will look for conditions making the FPC credible to effect hazard mitigation. Being willing to agree upon such conditions, is a sign of the reliability of a contractual party. Thus, we want to assess the customer's reliability. We use the term reliability here not in a moral sense, but with a technical meaning [13]. A market partner is reliable, if he acts in a comprehensible way, if he makes rational decisions due to his transparent interests and earlier promises. Economic theories developed for the description and understanding of rational actors use this construct implicitly [14–16]. Therefore, being reliable is connected with rationality. Organizations have the ability to generate their own rationality through stable methods and regulations for information processing regarding goal definition, belief generation, and decision-making [17–19]. These characteristics determine the *customer reliability*.

For our empirical investigation, we are in need of measureable attributes, which we draw from existing studies. Numerous studies examined contract design choices and contracts. However, we must be careful when considering the interpretation of results of these studies. One example of contract research is the study by Fink and Lichtenstein [7], giving a suggestion for contract choice. Typically, two basic contract types are used in practice: FPC, and time and material (T&M) contract. The T&M contract requires that the customer pays the costs plus a profit to the supplier. The authors deemed FPCs incompatible with short-term SDPs under uncertainty. The study by Gopal et al. [20], cited by Fink and Lichtenstein [7], did not distinguish project types. The cited studies had all together in focus: development, re-engineering, and maintenance. However, the asset specificity and uncertainty of these project types are not comparable. Therefore, our focus is on development.

The second example is the study of Søderberg et al. [21]. The contracting parties establish a long-term business relationship. Mostly, researchers consider long-term business relationships between customer and supplier when considering SDO (e.g. [20, 22, 23]). In this paper, we refer to short-term development projects. Therefore, we hook up on two recent studies. First, the study of Eckhard and Mellewight [24], having contractual functions under investigation. Second, the study of Benaroch et al. [14] building on it. These researchers identified measurable attributes in the categories of contractual functions. We address these studies in the next section.

3   Research Methodology

We conducted our empirical analysis using an abductive approach [25, 26]. In the first stage, we referred to the contractual functions, identified in an extensive literature study by Eckhard and Mellewight [24]. The authors carried out a systematic analysis of 22 top-ranked management and economics journals to identify all articles dealing with the contractual form of inter-firm relationships between 1993 and 2005. As a result, they identified contractual functions, which they classified under one of the following three categories: safeguarding of parties investments, coordination of the exchange process and contingency adaptability to cope with future disturbances. *Safeguard provisions* should protect the investments of the contracting parties. In particular, intellectual investments require sensitivity and confidentiality. Furthermore, this includes the protection against performance risks for reaching the goal of the project as well as the risk of premature termination of the SDP after one party has achieved his own goal. Therefore, dispute resolutions belong to this category. In conclusion, safety risks are opportunism-driven relational risks. *Coordination provisions* include the definition of a project schedule and of roles and responsibilities for the time of project execution. In addition, reporting specifications and the assignment of specific personnel belong to this category. These provisions provide the subsequent collaboration and address performance risks stemming from the task itself. *Contingency adaptation provisions* concern future circumstances. The contracting parties need to map technical changes as well as changes in the business environment when they become known. Therefore, the contracting parties have to define price adjustments. These provisions address risks arising in the future.

From this preliminary work and after a comprehensive literature review, Benaroch et al. [14] carefully identified measurable attributes for these contractual categories. The authors studied pure SDO contracts to improve the understanding of contract design in SDO. As a result, they substantiated that SDO contracts require a different mix of contract provisions than other ITO arrangements. Fortunately, they studied the mix of provisions in two contract subsamples, FPCs, and T&M contracts. Therefore, we can hook on this research. However, we have only the FPCs under investigation.

Benaroch et al. [14] focused on drivers of contract complexity and on "how the transaction attributes and the effect of learning to contract impact the complexity of specific contract functions". The researchers analyzed 270 SDO contracts of a leading international bank. In detail, they analyzed 181 FPCs. The remaining 89 contracts were T&M contracts. Some results they found are: (a) Asset specificity generally lowers reliance on safeguards in SDO contracts. (b) Asset specificity increases reliance on contingency adaption provisions, at least in FPCs. (c) Transaction uncertainty does not increase reliance on contingency adaption provisions in FPCs. (d) In standard contracts, safeguard provisions are more standardized than coordination and contingency adaption provisions. This holds most notably for contingency adaption provisions in FPCs. The authors believe that the contract manager perceive these provisions as less important. We will come back to these results when discussing our findings in Sect. 4.

Benaroch et al. [14] investigated the contracts of a customer. We could observe opportunely the opposite side, one supplier working for different customers in

Germany such as a bank, insurance companies, public authorities, a wholesaler, a machine manufacturer, and others. In total, we identified 49 different customers. This German software development company has been developing software systems since 1994, based on the individual requirements of their customers. The supplier employs 10 software developers.

For our empirical analysis, we used the written contracts from the last twenty years. All associated contracts were stored in a database we could use. Additionally, many contracts were available in email form. We used the 152 FPCs for software system development. Their values range from 550 € to 270,000 €, with an average of 17,011.40 €. Their durations range from 1 to 491 days, with an average of 30.9 days.

3.1   The Measurement Model

We started our empirical investigation with the identified and just discussed attributes of the contractual categories. After a first iteration step, we decided to adjust the attributes of our investigation. In particular, we were in need of further details about the customers and their processes. Therefore, we defined three sections: customer constructs, contract constructs, and project constructs (Table 1).

For the first *customer construct*, we wanted to know the market segment (construct 1). Private companies have business goals, whereas public authorities have to solve administrative tasks. We assumed that different types of goals results in different behavior and contractual provisions. Furthermore, we wanted to know the company size (construct 2). We assumed that different sized companies work differently. Since we classified the observed supplier as a small company, we wanted to examine if there are differences in SDPs with customers of different sizes. With the last customer construct item customer reliability, we could measure to which extend the customers follow clear and comprehensive rules during the negotiation phase and the project phase (construct 3), so that he can be seen as a reliable customer. We asked whether the customer has standardized processes, whether he follows them and whether he cannot bypass them during the contract negotiation. For the project phase, we asked whether the customer has standardized processes, and whether little changes in requirements result typically in little changes in the goals and the behavior. We asked whether the customer communicated the business objectives in the contracting phase as well as in the project phase. For the measurement of reliability, we counted all fulfilled attributes. Therefore, we classified customer reliability in the range from 0 up to 7. For the collection of the attributes, we interviewed the supplier's chief negotiator.

The *contract constructs* we draw from Benaroch et al. [14]. In detail we draw the safeguard, coordination, and contingency adaptation provision (construct 5-7). Furthermore, we added a question about the contract type, as we assumed customers and suppliers have their own standard contract (construct 4). We wanted to find out who determines the contractual provisions.

For the *project constructs*, we draw from Benaroch et al. [14] the constructs project size, prior interaction, and transaction uncertainty (construct 8-10). Furthermore, we added some questions about project failure, customer satisfaction, and supplier satisfaction. We consider an SDP as being definitely failed if the parties are not able to

Table 1. Items in the measurement model

Customer constructs*	Item
(1) Market segment	-Private company or public authority
(2) Company size	-Small (<50 employees), medium (>=50 and <500 employees) or large (>500 employees)
(3) Customer reliability	-Customer has standardized processes in contracting phase (yes/no)
	-Customer follows his standardized processes in contracting phase (yes/no)
	-This process cannot be bypassed in contracting phase (yes/no)
	-Business objectives communicated in contracting phase (yes/no)
	-Customer has standardized processes in project phase (yes/no)
	-Little requirement change results in little project change in project phase (yes/no)
	-Business objectives communicated in project phase (yes/no)
Contract constructs	Item
(4) Contract type	-Follows the whose standard contract: customers' standard contract [CSC], supplier's standard contract [SSC], supplier's standard contract changed by the customer [SSC +], or not formal [-]
(5) Safeguards	-Penalty amount payment defined for a breach of confidentiality, data protection, or employment of staff (yes/no) [P]
	-Customer acceptance test specified (yes/no) [CAT]
	-Warranty: period of post project completion defined (yes/no) [W]
	-Intellectual Property Rights protection specified (yes or no) [IP]
(6) Coordination	-Delivery milestones, identified points of delivery (number), Payment milestones, identified points of payment (number), Additional milestones without payment defined (yes/no) [MS]
	-Meetings or reports frequency specified (yes/no) [MR]
(7) Contingency adaptation	-Contingency adaptation changes clause specified (yes/no) [CA]
Project constructs	Item
(8) Project size	-Duration in days
	-Price in €
(9) Prior interaction	-Prior SDP (yes/no)
(10) Transaction uncertainty	-Business objectives specified and functional and technical outcomes provided (yes/no)
(11) Failure	-Came the project to court (yes/no)
(12) Customer dissatisfaction	-Was the customer dissatisfied with the SDPs' outcome (yes/no)
(13) Supplier dissatisfaction	-Was the supplier dissatisfied with the SDPs' outcome (yes/no)
(14) Start date	-Contract signing date

*recorded by interview

come to an amicable agreement regarding arising problems without a third party and so it comes to the court (construct 11). Furthermore, a project is not completely successful, if one of the parties is not satisfied with the result.

As already mentioned, the customers and the suppliers have different economic targets and outcome goals with an SDP. The supplier observes the customer because he is interested in customer satisfaction. Therefore, we could ask him for both, customer dissatisfaction and his own dissatisfaction with an SDP (construct 12-13). For the sake of completeness, we added the start date of the SDP (construct 14).

3.2 Hypotheses

We ordered the constructs in a way that we could study the dependencies between these constructs (marked with X) in a systematic way (Table 2). Dependencies, from which we derived our hypotheses, are marked with a reference to the hypotheses.

Table 2. Examined dependencies.

Customer constructs	(3)	(4)	(5)–(7)	(8)–(10)	(11)–(13)
(1) Market segment	H1a	X	X	X	X
(2) Company size	H1b	H2a	X	X	X
(3) Customer reliability		H2b	H3a	X	H4a
Contract constructs					
(4) Contract type			H3b, H3c	X	H4b
(5) Safeguards				X	H4c
(6) Coordination				X	H4c
(7) Contingency adaptation				X	H4c
Project constructs					
(8) Project size					X
(9) Prior interaction					X
(10) Transaction uncertainty					X
(11) Failure					
(12) Customer dissatisfaction					
(13) Supplier dissatisfaction					
(14) Start date					

We expected a connection between market segment and customer reliability as well as between customer size and customer reliability. Public authorities do not depend from short-term changes in a market environment, they can make planes for a longer time, and they have by law stronger rules for their decisions as private companies have. Furthermore, bigger-sized organizations develop more internal rules for decision-making then smaller ones. Therefore, we hypothesized that:

Hypothesis H1a. Public authorities act more reliable than private companies do.
Hypothesis H1b. Customer reliability is positively associated with customer size.

We expected that big-sized customers have the power to enforce the usage of own standard contracts. Furthermore, we assume that a customer with high reliability has developed own standard contracts. In addition, he should have rules that demand the enforcement of the usage of these contracts. Therefore, we hypothesized that:

Hypothesis H2a. Large customers mostly enforce the use of their standard contracts.
Hypothesis H2b. Customers with a higher reliability mostly enforce the use of their standard contracts.

We assumed that the customer reliability affects the provisions of its standard contract. Therefore, we hypothesized that:

Hypothesis H3a. Customer reliability is positively associated with the contract's provision number.
Hypothesis H3b. Customers' standard contracts include more safeguard provisions than supplier's standard contracts do.
Hypothesis H3c. Supplier's standard contracts include more contingency adaption provisions than customers' standard contracts do.

We expected a connection between customer reliability and project failure. In addition, we assumed that it is relevant, which standard contract is used. Therefore, we hypothesized that:

Hypothesis H4a. Customer reliability is negatively associated with project failure.
Hypothesis H4b. Customers' standard contracts rarer result in project failure than supplier's standard contracts do.
Hypothesis H4c. The number of contract provisions is negatively associated with project failure.

We collected all contract information in a database for further analysis and interpretation, which we discuss in the next section.

4 Data Analysis and Interpretation

Our sample consists of 152 data sets with the constant FPC. For our statistical analysis, we calculated for each hypothesis the proportion of data sets with the respective value of the dependent variable for each value of the leading variable. We present one analysis for each hypothesis followed by an interpretation.

4.1 Dependencies Between Customer Constructs

Our sample consists of 22 contracts with public authorities and 130 contracts with private companies. There are 78 contracts with large customers, 60 contracts with medium customers, and 14 contracts with small customers.

There is no significant difference between the reliability of public authorities and private companies (Our sample consists of 22 contracts with public authorities and 130 contracts with private companies. There are 78 contracts with large customers, 60 contracts with medium customers, and 14 contracts with small customers. Table 3) Most of the customers have an intermediate or high reliability level.

Table 3. Market segment and customer reliability (H1a)

Market segment	0	1	2	3	4	5	6	7
Public authorities	0 %	0 %	0 %	36 %	14 %	50 %	0 %	0 %
Private companies	5 %	5 %	5 %	32 %	19 %	32 %	0 %	0 %
In total	5 %	5 %	6 %	35 %	21 %	38 %	0 %	0 %

Table 4. Customer size and customer reliability (H1b)

Customer size	0	1	2	3	4	5	6	7
Large	1 %	0 %	1 %	12 %	18 %	**68 %**	0 %	0 %
Medium	0 %	12 %	3 %	**62 %**	23 %	0 %	0 %	0 %
Small	**43 %**	0 %	29 %	29 %	0 %	0 %	0 %	0 %
In total	5 %	5 %	6 %	35 %	21 %	38 %	0 %	0 %

We found a strong dependency between reliability and customer size (Table 4). Most of the big customers are highly reliable. Nearly half of the small customers show a reliability level of Zero.

Hence, hypothesis H1b is supported in the entire sample, but not H1a.

4.2   Dependencies Regarding Contract Constructs

In the case of small customers, mostly the supplier's standard contract is used. However, for medium and large customers, the chosen contract type does not depend on customer size (Table 5). For large customers, the quota of supplier's standard contract is nearly the same as of customers' standard contracts.

Table 5. Customer size and contract type (H2a)

Customer size	[-]	[SSC]	[SSC+]	[CSC]
Large	3 %	**45 %**	10 %	**42 %**
Medium	10 %	50 %	10 %	30 %
Small	14 %	79 %	0 %	7 %
In total	7 %	50 %	9 %	34 %

For the interpretation of dependencies from the customer reliability, it is remarkable that the sample is not evenly distributed over the reliability levels. There are only seven contracts with a customer reliability of 0, 1, or 2, respectively. There is no contract with a customer reliability of 6 or 7.

If the customer's reliability is high, he mostly provides his own standard contract (Table 6). At first glance, one can assume that this is only an implicit dependency from the connection between customer size and reliability. On the other hand, only 42 % of the contracts with large customers base on their own standard contract, although in 80 % of contracts with large customers the customer reliability is high (4 or 5). For medium-sized customers the situation is similar (cf. Tables 4 and 5). Therefore, using the customers' standard contract is not a matter of size (of pressure from the customer as the stronger party). Consequently, the connection between customer's reliability and the provision of customer's standard contracts is independent from the customer size.

Table 6. Customer reliability and contract type (H2b)

Customer reliability	[-]	[SSC]	[SSC+]	[CSC]
0	43 %	57 %	0 %	0 %
1	0 %	57 %	43 %	0 %
2	0 %	**86 %**	0 %	14 %
3	12 %	**74 %**	6 %	8 %
4	0 %	32 %	0 %	**68 %**
5	2 %	30 %	15 %	**53 %**
6	0 %	0 %	0 %	0 %
7	0 %	0 %	0 %	0 %
In total	7 %	50 %	9 %	34 %

Hence, hypothesis H2b is supported in the entire sample, but not H2a.

Only if the reliability of the customer is high, we found a high proportion of contracts with safeguard provisions (about 50 %, Table 7). We found additionally in mostly all of these cases, the customer enforced the use of his standard contract. This means: If a high-reliable customer enforced the use of his standard contract, it contained mostly always safeguard provisions. However, independently of the contract type, the customers with high reliability do not accept change provisions. We did not find a continuous growth of the contract's provision number with customer reliability, but a singularity for high-reliable customers.

Table 7. Customer reliability and contract provisions (H3a)

Customer reliability	(1)	(1)	(1)	(1)	(2)	(2)	(3)
	[P]	[CAT]	[W]	[IP]	[MS]	[MR]	[CP]
0	0 %	0 %	0 %	0 %	14 %	0 %	14 %
1	14 %	0 %	14 %	29 %	14 %	0 %	14 %
2	14 %	14 %	14 %	14 %	0 %	0 %	0 %
3	4 %	0 %	0 %	4 %	10 %	0 %	4 %
4	7 %	4 %	4 %	4 %	4 %	0 %	4 %
5	**49 %**	**47 %**	**51 %**	**49 %**	13 %	47 %	2 %
6	0 %	0 %	0 %	0 %	0 %	0 %	0 %
7	0 %	0 %	0 %	0 %	0 %	0 %	0 %
In total	21 %	18 %	20 %	20 %	10 %	16 %	4 %

With few exceptions, only standard contracts delivered by customers define safeguard provisions (Table 8). About 50 % of them include such provisions. The situation regarding coordination provisions is ambiguous. For provisions regarding meetings and reporting the quota is as high as for safeguard provisions, whereas the quota for milestones is lower.

Table 8. Contract type and contract provisions (H3b, H3c)

Contract type	(1)	(1)	(1)	(1)	(2)	(2)	(3)
	[P]	[CAT]	[W]	[IP]	[MS]	[MR]	[CP]
[-]	10 %	10 %	10 %	10 %	0 %	10 %	0 %
[SSC]	4 %	0 %	1 %	0 %	7 %	0 %	5 %
[SSC +]	0 %	0 %	7 %	29 %	7 %	0 %	0 %
[CSC]	**54 %**	**50 %**	**52 %**	**50 %**	17 %	**46 %**	4 %
In total	21 %	18 %	20 %	20 %	10 %	16 %	4 %

Only 5 % of the supplier's standard contract and 4 % of the customers' standard contracts contain change provisions.

Hence, hypothesis H3b is supported for in the entire sample, but not H3a and H3c.

4.3 Dependencies Regarding Project Failure

If the customer reliability was high, no project completely failed (Table 9). In addition, both the customers and the supplier are more satisfied with the result if the customer reliability is high. There is a small sign in the figures that there is a higher risk for supplier satisfaction if the customer reliability is extreme high.

Table 9. Customer reliability and project failure (H4a)

Customer reliability	Failure	No Customer satisfaction	No Supplier satisfaction
0	12 %	0 %	14 %
1	29 %	29 %	43 %
2	43 %	14 %	43 %
3	2 %	2 %	2 %
4	0 %	0 %	4 %
5	0 %	2 %	8 %
6	0 %	0 %	0 %
7	0 %	0 %	0 %
In total	5 %	3 %	9 %

There is a weak indication in the figures that supports the hypothesis H4b (Table 10). The highest quota of failing or not satisfying projects we found when supplier's standard contract with changes by the customer [SSC+] is used.

We can confirm that the risk of a complete failure is low in projects with contracts containing safeguard provisions (Table 11). On the other hand, the quota of projects

Table 10. Contract type and project failure (H4b)

Contract type	Failure	Customer dissatisfaction	Supplier dissatisfaction
[-]	0 %	0 %	10 %
[SSC]	7 %	4 %	7 %
[SSC+]	**14 %**	0 %	**14 %**
[CSC]	0 %	4 %	10 %
In total	5 %	3 %	9 %

that finish without success for the supplier is higher than the overall quota of 9 %. However, because of the low number of contracts with contingency adaptions and milestones provisions, the figures for these provision types are not significant.

Hence, hypothesis H4a and H4c are supported for in the entire sample, hypothesis H4b is weakly supported.

Table 11. Contract provisions and project failure (H4c)

Contract provisions	Failure	Customer dissatisfaction	Supplier dissatisfaction
(1) [P]	0 %	9 %	19 %
(1) [CAT]	0 %	7 %	15 %
(1) [W]	0 %	10 %	20 %
(1) [IP]	3 %	6 %	13 %
(2) [MS]	0 %	20 %	27 %
(2) [MR]	0 %	4 %	12 %
(3) [CP]	17 %	0 %	0 %
In total	5 %	3 %	9 %

4.4   Answers to Benaroch et al.

In direct comparison to Benaroch et al. [14] and their results (Sect. 2), our empirical analysis delivers the following results:

(a) The first finding is that the supplier invests in each SDP specifically. From the suppliers' point of view, the asset specificity is high. We could detect only two projects for different customers based upon the same software code. Moreover, both these customers are public authorities and expressly agreed. Both these public authorities perform the same function. Aggravating this situation, we could detect safeguard provisions only unilaterally in the interest of the customer. Therefore, we cannot notice any reliance between suppliers' asset specificity and safeguards in the FPCs.

(b) We did not find any sustainable contingency adaption provision. At the most, the supplier might have been able to incorporate a payment provision for additional, unforeseen requirements. Only in 6 contracts (4 %) we found a clause regarding payments for change requests. However, there were now rules for detecting change requests. Therefore, we cannot notice any reliance between suppliers' asset specificity and contingency adaptions in FPCs.

(c) Mostly the customer gives a general overview about his business objectives. In 95 % of the contracts, the customers communicated their economic goals clearly and stable before the parties signed the contract. We could not detect a significant dependency from customer type, customer size, or contract type. However, the supplier has to develop the detailed specification on functional and technical outcomes during the SDP. Therefore, uncertainties exist about projects outcome. However, as mentioned, we did not find contingency adaption provisions covering these suppliers' risks.

(d) We can confirm that customers' own standard contract often include standardized safeguard provisions. For contracts based on customers' standard contracts, we found in about 50 % such provisions. On the other hand, in contracts based on suppliers' standard contracts, we found these provisions only in less than 10 %. However, for coordination and contingency provisions we found another situation. Only 12 % of the contracts based on customers' standard contracts contain milestone definitions unless the delivery of the final software system. Although 46 % of these contracts contain clauses regarding meetings and reporting, in fact they all contain only the suppliers' obligation to deliver weekly status reports. None of the contracts based on suppliers standard contracts contain such a clause. Benaroch et al. [14] believe the contract managers perceive both types of provisions as less important. We discovered that customers' legal departments generate the standard contract. However, they cannot (yet) standardize project-dependent coordination or contingency provisions in detail.

5 Conclusion

Our empirical analysis shows first, that the project's failure risk for SDPs with FPCs significantly decreases if the customer reliability increases. Customer reliability reflects whether the customer uses stable methods and regulations for information processing regarding goal definition, belief generation, and decision-making. In particular, if the customer reliability is high, the risk of failure is low. Therefore, a high customer reliability is an important success factor for SDPs with FPCs. As a first result, a reliable customer makes the FPC credible.

Second, reliable customers tend to bring safeguard and coordination provisions into the contract. However, only the half of contracts bases on customers' standard contracts (in line with Benaroch et al. [14]). Therefore, for the project's success these provisions are obviously in this case not necessary, because this holds even if the supplier's standard contract is chosen and the customer has a high customer reliability. However, if a customer's standard contract with a high number of safeguard provisions is agreed, the risk of supplier's dissatisfaction increases. Furthermore, we investigated the contracts of only one supplier. For two decades, this supplier has signed contracts with customers very different in size, structure, age, and market area. The overall failure quota is low in comparison with the results of the cited studies [2–4]. Most of the projects this supplier has carried out were SDPs under FPCs. The overall success of this supplier allows us to state, that contracts as signed by this supplier do not hinder the project's success in general. Not the FPC itself is the challenge but if the customer influences the suppliers' safeguard provisions. In this case, the customer's reliability is low. Our interpretation is that the customer demonstrates his low reliability by tightening the authoritarian FPC. The FPC itself is an authoritarian contract; in addition, the customer stresses his authoritarian position. Therefore, such a contract is muscular in the sense of Williamson. As a second result, safeguard provisions have more coordinating role and should not be too clever (as discussed already by Axelrod [27]), the fixed-price itself is the customer's best safeguard. The customer assets are obviously not in danger.

Third, contingency provisions are not in use. As a third result, a fixed-price project has a budget limit, which the customer is encouraged not to weaken.

At this point, we recognize the limits of our investigation. We used the contracts only from one supplier. Furthermore, we did not find credible contract provisions in the sense of Williamson [12]. Customers can suspense the payment. In addition, the supplier has the risk of repayment if for whatever reason the project fails. However, he invests in each SDP specifically. Further research can start here. We expect that regardless of customers' reliability non-repayable deposits can make a contract itself credible.

References

1. Dijkstra, E.W.: The humble programmer. Assoc. Comput. Mach. **15**(10), 859–866 (1972)
2. Standish Group: CHAOS Report (1995). http://www.projectsmart.co.uk/docs/chaos-report.pdf, (21 June 2011)
3. El Emam, K., Koru, A.G.: A replicated survey of IT software project failures. IEEE Softw. **25**(5), 84–90 (2008)
4. Al-Ahmad, W., Al-Fagih, K., Khanfar, K., Alsamara, K., Abuleil, S., Abu-Salem, H.: A taxonomy of an IT project failure: root causes. Int. Manage. Rev. **5**(1), 93–104 (2009)
5. Dwivedi, Y.K., Ravichandran, K., Williams, M.D., Miller, S., Lal, B., Antony, V., Muktha, K.: IS/IT Project Failures: A Review of the Extant Literature for Deriving a Taxonomy of Failure Factors. In: IFIP Advances in Information and Communication Technology, 402, pp. 73–88. Springer, Heidelberg (2013)
6. Dey, D., Fan, M., Zhang, C.: Design and analysis of contracts for software outsourcing. Inf. Syst. Res. **21**(1), 93–114 (2010)
7. Fink, L., Lichtenstein, Y.: Why project size matters for contract choice in software development outsourcing. ACM SIGMIS Database **45**(3), 54–71 (2014)
8. Chen, Y., Bharadwaj, A.: An empirical analysis of contract structures in it outsourcing. Inf. Syst. Res. **20**(4), 484–506 (2009)
9. Savolainen, P.: Why do software development projects fail?: emphasising the supplier's perspective and the project start-up. Jyväskylä. Stud. Comput **136**, 1456–5390 (2011)
10. Williamson, O.E.: The Economic Institutions of Capitalism: Firms, Markets, Relational Contracting. Free Press, New York (1985)
11. Macneil, I.: Contracts: adjustment of long-term economic relations under classical, neoclassical, and relational contract law. Northwest. Univ. Law Rev. **72**, 854–905 (1978)
12. Williamson, O.E.: Outsourcing: transaction cost economics and supply chain management. J. Supply Chain Manag. **44**(2), 5–16 (2008)

13. Heiner, R.A.: The origin of predictable behavior. Am. Econ. Rev. **73**, 560–595 (1983)
14. Benaroch, M., Lichtenstein, Y., Wyss, S.: Contract design choices in IT outsourcing: New lessons from software development outsourcing contracts. Available at SSRN 2137174 (2012)
15. Gaebert, C.: Dilemma structures between contracting parties in software development projects. In: Proceedings of the 9th International Conference on Software Engineering and Applications, 29–31 August 2014, pp. 539–548. SCITEPRESS – Science and Technology Publications (2014)
16. Gaebert, C.: Contract design and uncertainty in software development projects. In: Johansson, B., Andersson, B., Holmberg, N. (eds.) BIR 2014. LNBIP, vol. 194, pp. 217–230. Springer, Heidelberg (2014)
17. List, C., Pettit, P.: Aggregating sets of judgments: an impossibility result. Econ. Philos. **18** (01), 89–110 (2002)
18. Goldman, A.I.: Group knowledge versus group rationality: two approaches to social epistemology. Episteme **1**(01), 11–22 (2004)
19. Tollefsen, D.: Groups as rational sources. Collective Epistemology **20**, 11–22 (2011)
20. Gopal, A., Sivaramakrishnan, K., Krishnan, M.S., Mukhopadhyay, T.: Contracts in offshore software development: an empirical analysis. Manage. Sci. **49**(12), 1671–1683 (2003)
21. Søderberg, A.M., Krishna, S., Bjørn, P.: Global software development: commitment, trust and cultural sensitivity in strategic partnerships. J. Int. Manag. **19**, 347–361 (2013)
22. Rajkumar, T.M., Mani, R.V.S.: Offshore software development: the view from indian suppliers. Inf. Syst. Manag. **18**(2), 63–73 (2001)
23. Khan, S.U., Niazi, M., Ahmad, R.: Barriers in the selection of offshore software development outsourcing vendors: an exploratory study using a systematic literature review. Inf. Softw. Technol. **53**, 693–706 (2011)
24. Eckhard, B., Mellewigt, T.: Contractual Functions and Contractual Dynamics in Inter-Firm Relationships: What We Know and How to Proceed, University of Paderborn Working Paper No. 88, 8 January 2006. SSRN: http://ssrn.com/abstract=899527 or http://dx.doi.org/10.2139/ssrn.899527
25. Klein, H.K., Myers, M.D.: A set of principles for conducting and evaluating interpretative field studies in information systems. MIS Q. **23**(1), 67–94 (1999)
26. Osei-Bryson, K.M., Ngwenyama, O.: Using decision tree modelling to support Peircian abduction in IS research: a systematic approach for generating and evaluating hypotheses for systematic theory development. Inf. Syst. J. **21**(5), 407–440 (2011)
27. Axelrod, R., Hamilton, W.D.: The evolution of cooperation. Science **211**(4489), 1390–1396 (1981)

Life Events: A Crucial Point of e-Government

Vaclav Repa[✉]

Faculty of Informatics and Statistics, University of Economics, Prague,
W. Churchill Sqr. 4, 13067 Prague, Czech Republic
repa@vse.cz

Abstract. Life events (life situations) are usually understood as a specific view on public administration activities which is close to their clients: citizens. This view usually helps to effectively and client-friendly organize the web platform of the public authority. However, the real meaning of life events is more essential. Such a view allows regarding the public administration activities as consequences of real events in real lives of the public administrations clients. This paper introduces an approach to the analysis of life situations in the context of life cycles of the public administration objects and the use of this approach in a real ongoing project. The relation of life events to the public administration processes as well as their relation to e-government are discussed and illustrated with examples from the project.

Keywords: Life event · Object life cycle · Public administration · Conceptual modeling · Process-driven management

1 Introduction

Effectiveness in the field of public administration always has been a hot topic for politicians. It seems that what is called the 'black hole for public finances' is a natural attribute of this area. The advances in technology paradoxically even worsen the situation; so called e-government often leads to large investments without an adequate effect which would justify them. However, these problems are first of all a great challenge for the management theory researchers. It is obvious that the problem is rooted not in the infrastructure (IT) but in the management itself. E-government is defined in [1] as: 'the use of ICTs as a tool to achieve better government'. The impact of e-government at the broadest level is simply better government 'e-government is more about government than about 'e' ' [10]. This idea became widespread as noted in many other sources: [9,11]. Once we accept this idea, we need to answer the consequential question: what are the changes that e-government should offer in order to 'achieve better government' and how to make them? The origin of this question is the same as in case of business process re-engineering in market oriented companies as defined in [3]. It is about how to use technology to make the public authority flexible enough to be able to change its internal behavior to conform to the changes in the environment. Thus, it seems that to achieve the ideal effects of

© Springer International Publishing Switzerland 2015
R. Matulevičius and M. Dumas (Eds.): BIR 2015, LNBIP 229, pp. 33–47, 2015.
DOI: 10.1007/978-3-319-21915-8_3

e-government as stated in [10], the concept of process-oriented management in the field of public administration should be applied.

Unlike in market-oriented businesses, the application of general management principles in public administration poses considerably harder problems. The cause is in particular the absence of the market. The absence of the market causes the need for using a great amount of abstraction to implement general management principles in this field. Questions as 'who is a customer?' or 'what is the customer's interest?' are typically not easy to answer here. The difficulty of using general management practices in this business is visible best in the context of business processes, especially in their re-engineering. These problems manifest themselves specifically in identifying core processes.

While implementing process-driven style of management, the critical success factors of the public administration are:

- Primary function of public administration (what are the main 'strategic' goals of public administration activities?) is very abstract. The best illustration of the needed amount of abstraction are the following questions:
  - Who is a 'customer' of public administration? Obviously it is not only a citizen. The community itself or enterprise and other 'actors' in the field of the community life are additional specific types of customers.
  - What are a 'customer needs' in the area of public administration? There are often more interconnected 'needs' that may be mutually in conflict in this area.
  - How do these 'customer needs' manifest themselves?
    As many needs are not in the form of explicitly expressed 'requirements', it is necessary to systematically analyze different factors of the situation to uncover them. Moreover, the precise knowledge of the general context is often necessary to uncover the needs in this area.
- The field of public administration is typically tied to the legislation which is neither perfect, nor consistent. At the same time, the legislation is traditionally regarded as an expression of basic values, in other words as a substitution of the primary function. This fact makes the analysis of the roots of the strategic values in this area very complicated and cumbersome especially if there exists some resistance against possible changes ('You are not allowed to revise the legislation!', 'It is against the law!').

The consequence of both aforementioned factors is the fact that the idea of main strategic values of a community is not commonly accepted and that there are strong mental as well as legislative barriers which have to be overcame while uncovering the primary function of public administration. On the other hand, to shift the conception of management activities from the traditional to the process-oriented one we need in the first place to define its primary function - 'what should be the main purposes and goals of public administration activities'.

The main purpose of this paper is to introduce the specific approach to overcome the crucial problems of public administration and e-Government as stated above based on the fundamental analysis of life events (situations).

Life events of the public administration objects are analyzed in the context of their life cycles. Life cycle describes the universal context of the group of life events that characterizes the given object in terms of their causal and time dependencies. It brings the essential information about what may (and may not) happen in the life of the given object in the given context. We use this information as a basis for the analysis of the essence of the needed public administration actions. The result of this analysis is intended to be used for the conception of essential public administration processes, i.e. processes which are undoubtedly necessary for objective reasons. The approach introduced in this paper has been used in the real analysis project managed by the Czech Ministry of Interior. We use the experience from this project for the discussion of the crucial features of the concept of application of the process-driven management in the field of public administration as well as its consequences. We argue that life events should be regarded as a crucial point of the analysis in the field of public administration for the purpose of the application of e-government.

The paper is organized into the five sections. In the second section, immediately after this introduction, we explain the methodology background. We briefly characterize the MMABP methodology as the basic source of the main principles and techniques for information organizational modeling as well as the PARMA project as a source of the approach to the application of the process-driven ideas in public administration. Finally, the concept of life events and its relationships to other basic public administration aspects are explained. It the third section we describe the project, its context, and the way in which this methodology approach has been used there. Fourth section contains the main discussion of the experience from the project and some generalization of this experience. In the conclusion section we summarize the main ideas of this paper and point out the needed future work.

2   Methodology Background

In the project described in the following section we use two main methodology resources:

- MMABP (Methodology for Modeling and Analysis of Business Processes)
- PARMA (Public Administration Reference Model and Architecture)

MMABP is a methodology for information modeling of organizations. Its goal is to create a precise model of the 'Real World' as the basis for any consequent infrastructure (such as the information or organization system). The methodology has been originally developed for the purpose of the application of the ideas of processes -driven management (see [3]). Nevertheless, it covers all important dimensions of the information model of an organization (see Fig. 1).

MMABP uses four basic types of models derived from the combination of two basic organizational viewpoints:

- *Ontological view* focused on the description of the causality in the Real World. Models in this view express the main objects which the Real World consists of, their relationships and rules for their dynamics.

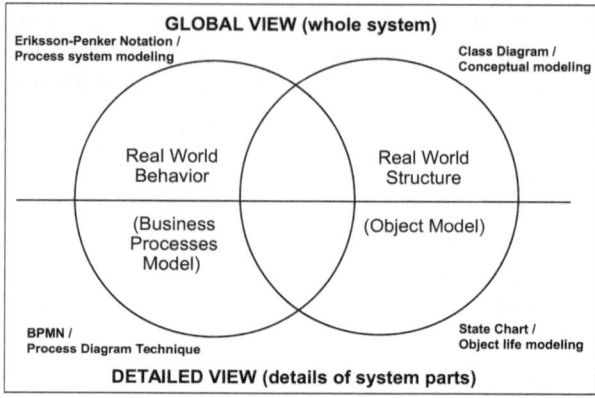

Fig. 1. Types of particular models in the MMABP

- *Behavioral view* focused on the description of the intentionality in the Real World. Models in this view express the main processes of the Real World and their relationships.

Each view is represented by two types of models:

- *Global (system) view* that look at the system as a whole. This type of models is oriented on the static aspects of the system its parts and their relationships.
- *Detailed view* looking at just one essential part of the system in the proper detail. This type of models is oriented on dynamic aspects of the system. Such aspects can sufficiently describe just one part of the system.

Only the ontological models are relevant for the purpose of this paper. Therefore, the methodology uses two essential UML diagrams for the two basic types of models:

- *Class Diagram* for the description of the global contextual view on objects in the given area.
- *State Chart* for the description of how one particular object can change during its life cycle.

MMABP applies these two models is based mainly on the following theoretical resources: the conceptual modeling with the UML [7] and the work of M. Jackson [5,6]. More detailed information about the MMABP methodology can be found in [12].

PARMA (Public Administration Reference Model and Architecture) [13] is a long-term project aimed at the application of the process-driven management concepts in the field of public administration. This project resulted in a set of essential principles where the central point are life events as described in the following sub-section.

2.1   Life Events

The concept of Life Events is often used in the context of the process-oriented view of public administration. This concept represents the view of public administration activities in their natural relations. These 'natural consequences' are always given by the situation in the life of the public authoritys 'customer' a citizen. Life situations of a citizen are in fact very close to the main goal of the public administration activities and objective reason for its existance. It is obvious that such view has very much to do with the main principle of business process re-engineering ordering activities according to the main goals, which have to be directly connected with the natural strategic goals of the organization consequently always follow from the customer needs.

Life events became one of the most important subjects of the e-government activities. Several standard classifications of life events emerged as a reaction to the fact that standardization is very natural in the area of public administration. These standards are of different quality from simple description of routine activities of clerks to the lists of life events carefully analyzed as core representations of the public administration activities. One of the most interesting classifications stems from the LEAP project. LEAP (Life Events Access Project) [8] is a partnership project among British Councils. According to its mission statement, 'LEAP aims to utilize knowledge management in order to improve service provision to customers. The LEAP consortium will use new information and communication technologies to develop services to best meet the needs of customers and clients.' In this project, life events are derived from the conception of the standard life cycle of a citizen. Despite the fact that 'citizen' is not the only crucial type of public administration objects it is obvious that such an approach is a good basis for constituting the interface between the authority and its customers as it is very closely aligned with the real life and, consequently, with the essence of public administration itself.

Figure 2 shows the general context of the concept of life situations (life events) consisting of other important public administration concepts. Public administration object (such as 'citizen') always exists in some external environment that is a source of basic rules, necessities, possibilities, obligations and other limitations which the object has to respect because they are objective from its point of view. The objective factors are always commonly valid for all public administration objects.

At the same time, the object is limited even by its internal factors dependent on the overall context of its life: its current life situation, its past history as well as its possible future. This context of internal factors is called the 'life cycle' of the object. These factors can be called subjective as they are specific, private for every object. These factors are subjective and valid specifically for the given object nevertheless the object has to respect them in its behavior as well.

In its life the object is experiencing different life situations that follow from the external, objective situation as well as from the internal state of the object's life. The objective, environmental factors are driven by objective logic of the external world. There are three basic sources of crucial life events (see Fig. 2):

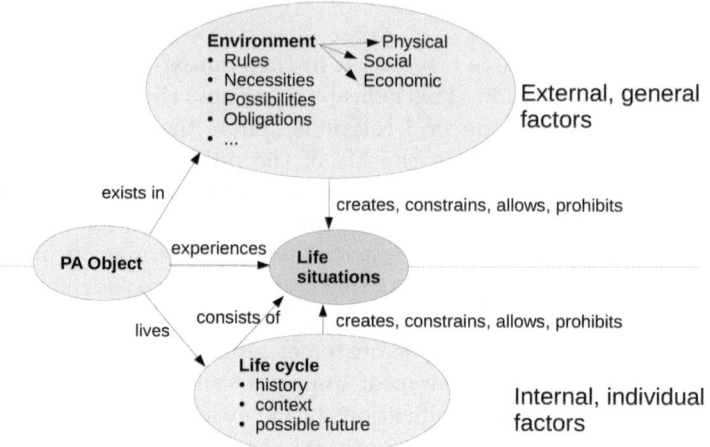

Fig. 2. General context of life situations

- *Physical environment* which represents the natural and other physical values of the given territory. It consists of the natural and physical attributes of the territory such as raw materials, nature and its values for recreation and tourism, and also infrastructure and other values of physical environment important for people as well as for business.
- *Social Environment* which consists of people and their personal, cultural, and social values. It includes not only the individual personal characteristics of people but also global attributes of the society itself often called the culture' of the society.
- *Business environment* including organizational and cultural values necessary for realization of opportunities. This area includes all business entities: enterprises, entrepreneurs and their quality, employees and their qualification, as well as legislation and quality of public administration services supporting the business.

Similarly, even the internal life cycle factors are driven by the general logic of the life cycle. This general logic of the object's life is objective in the same way as the logic of the external world. This fact is the reason for describing life cycles on the same level of preciseness and regarding them as being as important as the logic of the external world.

3   The Project

The aforementioned methodology has been used in the analysis project managed by the Czech Ministry of Interior. This project is focused on the revision of the current official view of life events (life situations) in order to make it consistent with the Czech e-Government Architecture and its intended future development [4]. According to the Chief e-Government Architect Office this architecture should consist of:

- Countrywide catalog of Public Services supported by Information Systems Services catalog.
- Key Agenda Information Systems redesign, re-engineering and consolidation.
- National Architecture Standards.
- EU interoperability standards and gateways.
- Compliance with Cyber Security standards.
- Data orchestration via common service bus called 'eGon Service Bus'.
- and other important features and tasks.

From the point of view of the project, the most important feature of the architecture is the interface between the public administration processes and 'public administration services' which is called the 'service bus'. At the current state of the architecture, which is mostly technically oriented, this service bus is viewed just as an issue of data, and its meaning is interpreted as 'data orchestration'. However, the meaning of the orchestration should be conceived in a much wider scope. The concept of orchestration is often used in the context of process-driven management and its IT support. Not just data but even the actions in information systems should be orchestrated the same way as the events in the real world are naturally synchronized. From this point of view the service bus has the crucial meaning for the contents and the quality of e-government as it is a direct interface between what is happening in the real life and between the public administration processes. Therefore, it has to take into the account all the essential rules and restrictions of the real life and cover them within its functionality. We posit that the analysis based on the description of life events is the best way to fulfilling these requirements.

The methodology used in the project is based on the conceptual analysis in the area of public administration that includes even the analysis of life cycles of crucial objects, i.e. those objects whose life events are critically important for the public administration activities.

The methodology uses two essential UML diagrams for two basic types of models:

- *Class Diagram* for description of the global contextual view on objects in the given area.
- *State Chart* for description of the life cycle of one particular object.

Both types of models are used in close mutual dependency.

Figure 3 shows a fragment of the contextual model of public administration objects and their life cycles. The model describes concepts and their relationships which characterize the context of the crucial object types in public administration. In this project we primarily need to identify the crucial objects in the field and all relevant roles which these objects have. Each role represents the specific life cycle. Life cycle is an algorithmic structure of actions driven by events. We primarily need to identify all important algorithmic dependencies connected

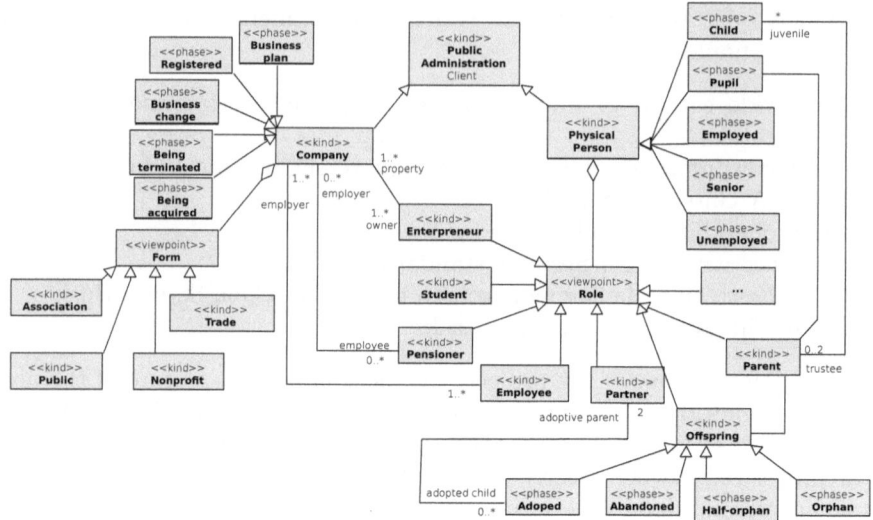

Fig. 3. Contextual model of public administration objects and their life cycles a fragment

with each given object. In other words we need to find all possible roles of this object where each of the roles represent a specific life cycle a set of algorithmic dependencies. As the object can have a number of different roles in one moment, it has typically different life cycles (i.e. algorithmic structures of relevant actions) valid at the same time. From the methodological point of view we need to solve the problem of parallel dynamic structures tied to the same object. This theoretical problem is outlined in [2] and its general solution in the form of special pattern is described in [14]. This pattern is used as the main technique in our model. Concepts are classified according to their meaning as follows:

1. Stereotype *kind* is used for the concepts which define the basic physical objects and their types.
2. Stereotype *phase* is used for the concepts which express the states (phases) in the life cycle of given basic physical object that is a super-type of this set of life phases.
3. Stereotype *viewpoint* is used for the concepts which express the element of the aggregation structure that represents the set of different points of view from which the given physical object can be seen.

This way we can describe any physical object as a set of parallel lives, each one from a specific point of view. All objects in the model are sub-types of the object Public Administration Client. This generic object is an abstract concept existing in two possible forms (sub-types) Physical Person and Company. Both Physical Person and Company are generalizations of the sub-types that represent their life phases. At the same time, each of these objects is an aggregate of the possible

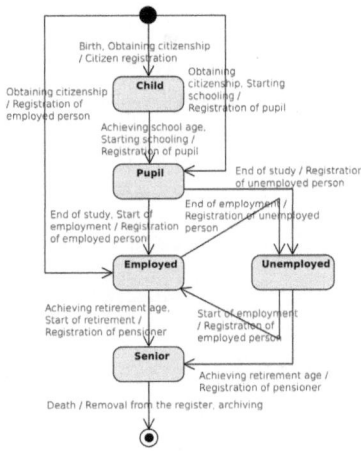

Fig. 4. Physical person life cycle

viewpoints (roles of person, respectively forms of company), and each of them represents a possible specific life cycle.

Figures 4 and 5 describe the life cycles of object classes Physical Person and Company. Each model represents the specific set of states and possible transitions among them. Every transition is described by its reason (alias some Real World event) and the action taken as a reaction to the reason (the relevant reaction of the public administration). From the contents of both models it is obvious that the same object instance cannot have both life cycles at the same time as it can be either Physical Person or Company, but not both. Their mutual exclusivity follows from the fact that they both are different sup-types of the same abstract type PA Client. Nevertheless, at the same time each of them can have a number of parallel lives in different roles (of Physical Person) or forms (of Company) since both are the aggregate of a number of possible viewpoints that represent different sub-types, each of them living its specific life.[1]

4   Discussion of the Lessons Learned

During the project we have uncovered many important aspects, specific features, and problems to overcome which originated form the objective of applying the process-driven management in the field of public administration by means of life events. The most important aspects can be structured into two main groups of actual needs:

---

[1] This is visible in the contextual model (class diagram) of the role Offspring of Physical Person which has several life phases (see Fig. 3). Similarly, any other sub-type of viewpoint can have its own life cycle (which are not described by the model in this figure).

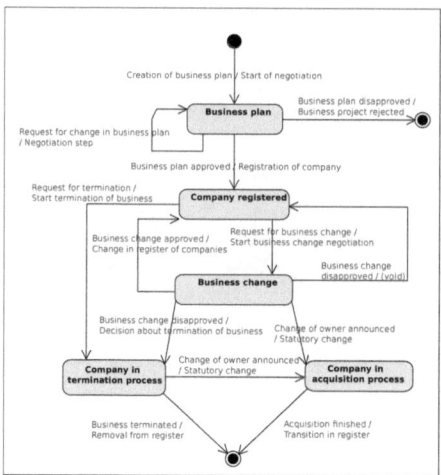

Fig. 5. Company life cycle

1. *Need for distinguishing between essential life events and those events which are forced by public administration:*

   - Essential life events are those regarded as objective, natural factors. Events of this type represent the happenings in the real life no matter whether they are influenced by the public administration actions or not. Examples of essential life events are such natural events as 'birth', 'marriage', 'material poverty', and even personal intention events like 'starting a business' or 'building a house'.
   - On the other hand, 'forced' life events are those which can (and should) be potentially overcome or eliminated by the means of future technology development in terms of M.Hammer's argumentation for process-driven management [3]. The main reason for such forced events is the need to support the public administration activities. 'Obtaining the ID' or 'filing tax return statement' are examples of such forced events. In public administration, the 'forced' life events are represented exclusively by the legislation. The legislation sets the rules which force all actors to respect them - whether they are essential for the support of public administration activities, or whether they are arguably irrelevant. Thus, we cannot fully accept the idea, widespread especially in the field of public administration, that the legislation is the highest authority expressing the essence of the real life, and therefore it has to be respected without a doubt. If we were respecting such an understanding of the legislation we would never be able to eliminate even a single 'forced' life event. This means in turn that we would never be able to make any positive change in the public administration practice, in terms of the idea of process-driven management, using the possibilities provided by the new technology. On the other hand, we cannot ignore the forced events as they are a regular part of the current

state of the real life. For most people the legislation is the basic view that determines their understanding the public administration activities and their conceptual meaning. However, from the practical point of view, the respect for the legislation rules is mandatory including even the rules which represent the forced events.

Based on from the above argument it seems necessary to distinguish not only between essential and forced life events but also between the similar two kinds of models. This finding led us to maintain two types of public administration ontology models:

- *Full current state ontology models* that contain all life events: the essential as well as the 'forced' ones. These models allow us to communicate with people from the public administration in the manner that is very close to their understanding of their business. This mutual understanding is very important for our need to make all models complete, i.e. to incorporate in them all the important, and necessary events as well as the consequent public administration actions. Only such complete models create a sufficient basis for understanding all necessary e-government services which is the ultimate original goal of the project.

- *Essential ontology models* that contain only the essential life events. The main value of these models lies in the fact that they express the essential reasons for the public administration acts which have to be respected anyway. In other words, these models express the extent to which the processes of the public administration can be reduced without simultaneously reducing their essential meaning the borderline between what can and what cannot be actually eliminated by means of technology.

2. *Need for shifting the understanding of life events and their role in public administration.*

Figure 6 shows the fragment of the public administration ontology that emphasizes the difference between the public administration and the citizen points of view on life situations. It also shows in which direction the traditional understanding of life events should be shifted. In the traditional understanding (represented by the bold association between the concepts 'PA Agenda' and 'Life situation'), life situations are regarded as a specific view of the public administration official processes (so-called 'PA agendas'). Agendas are defined by legislative documents and fixed in the organizational structure of PA authorities. Thus, the meaning of a particular life situation is defined by the PA agenda(s) connected to this situation. From this point of view the life situation is nothing more than just a specific view of the agenda, the view which is close to the client's perception of such agendas. Even though it represents a significant difference in the presentation of PA agendas, this point of view is still far away from the natural meaning of life situations and from the real value of this approach to the PA development.

The needed new understanding of the concepts (represented by the bold association between the concepts 'Employee' and 'Life situation') is substantially different. For the PA authority employee, as a provider of PA agendas, the life

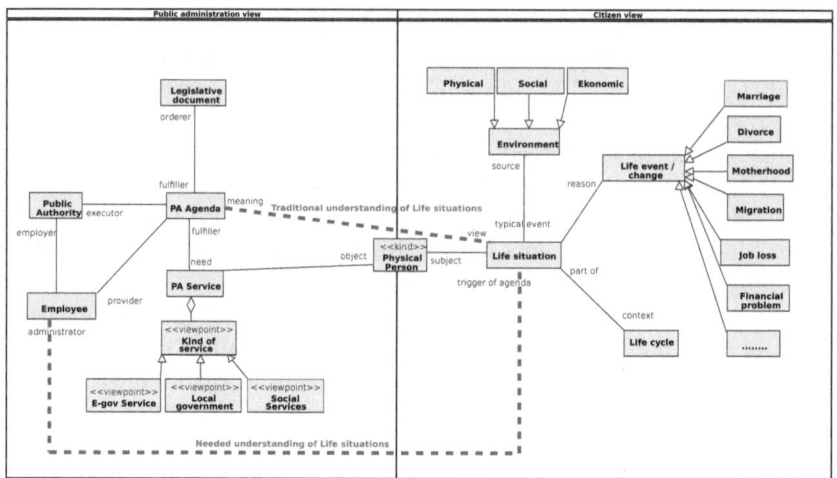

Fig. 6. Public administration versus person's views on life situations

situation represents the trigger of the particular agenda. Agendas are regarded as tools for solutions of life situations. Given the fact that life situations are naturally dynamic (as the environment is changing, the new life situations emerge and the meaning of current situations mutates as well, etc.), even the agendas acquire different meaning from this viewpoint. Therefore the agendas should be regarded as something dynamic, continuously changing. This understanding of the meaning of the agenda contrasts with the original meaning of this concept and consequently leads to a dramatically different view on the public administration processes which is close to the process-driven management ideas as expressed in [3]. Further consequences can be deducted from the aforementioned literature: the need for changing of the public administrations organizational structure as well as redefining the role of legislation, etc.

Although, at the first look, this view does not seem to be much different from the traditional one, the proposed enhancement of the life situation concept naturally leads to a substantially different perception of the meaning of PA agendas. Consequently, it also naturally leads to a substantially different perception of the traditional roles in public administration it starts fulfilling the original purpose of e-government: a client-oriented public administration.

5   Conclusions and Future Work

As follows from the previous section, the use of the life events concept as the root of the public administrations activities naturally invokes many related essential changes and uncovers many important problems to be solved in the field of public administration and e-government. The experience gained from the project mentioned in this paper led us to the following main conclusions:

– Looking at the public administration in terms of life events and their needed solutions allows a comprehensive analysis of the requirements for so-called e-government based on the essential nature of the public administration: the situations in lives of the crucial objects and their natural consequences. This point of view is an analogy of the idea of the process-driven management. In fact, it expresses exactly the same idea.
– At the same time, this point of view naturally leads to an essential change of the approach to the understanding of the public administration role. Public administration actions have to be understood not as the purpose but as the consequence of the life of society and its elements (called in our project 'public administration clients').
– Moreover, this point of view is closely connected to the essence of the so-called e-Government, i.e., as the application of the information technologies in public administration. Semi-formal models of life cycles completed with the ontology model of their mutual context can serve as a precise definition of the contents of the central common part of the public administration IT applications' logic. It expresses the essence of the real world logic together with the basic contents of the legislation. In the Enterprise Architecture and connected terminologies, this central common part of the applications' logic is usually called 'enterprise service bus' or 'common request broker', etc.
– The main actual problems connected with above described paradigmatic change, as uncovered in the project, are:
  • The need for distinguishing between essential life events and those events which are forced by the public administration.
  • The need for shifting the understanding of life events and their role in public administration.

Overcoming these two kinds of actual problems is an essential condition for successful application of the process-driven management concepts in the field of public administration. At the same time, given how substantial is the connection between information technology and process-driven management, it is as well an indispensable condition for successful application of e-government per se.

Future work should have two main directions:

– The completion the model of life events to achieve the state in which it will express *all substantial events that require some reactions from the public administration bodies*. This model then will be used as a basis for the definition of the need for essential public administration processes. Further analysis of these processes will lead to their standardization and to the specification of the basic central public administration agendas. This way the border between the mandatory standard activities and the space for individual creativity in managing public administration processes in various public administration bodies will be exactly defined.
– The use of the definitions of life cycles (state charts) together with the contextual information from the connected global ontology models (class diagrams) as a basis for the development of the *central public administration service*

bus - a crucial part of the e-government architecture framework. This element of the framework represents the essence of the interface between the public administration activities and their central support by the information systems in several dimensions:

- From the technical point of view, the bus is a central broker ensuring the interchange between the process requests (representing real events) for the information support and suitable information systems that offer the corresponding IS services. It also contains the mechanism assuring general correctness of the reactions as well as of the requests based on the knowledge of the context of every event in the life cycle models.
- At the same time, this meeting point represents the standard interface for all possible information systems for their connection with the corresponding information requests from the public administration processes. In other words, this standard represents the market place that allows the integration of public administration processes with the information services market supply in terms of opening as wide as possible public-private cooperation. Public-private cooperation in terms of the open market for information services is the only warranted way to decreasing the public expenses for IT support towards their optimal value.

Acknowledgments. The paper was processed with contribution of long term institutional support of research activities by Faculty of Informatics and Statistics, University of Economics, Prague.

References

1. eGovernment, Information Society Commission, Dublin, Ireland. http://www.isc.ie
2. Guizzardi, G.: Ontological Foundations for Structural Conceptual Models, Telematica Instituut, Fundamental Research Series No. 15 (2005). ISBN 90-75176-81-3 ISSN 1388-1795
3. Hammer, M., Champy, J.: Reengineering the Corporation: A Manifesto for Business Revolution. Nicholas Brealey Publishing, London (1993)
4. Hrabe, P.: The proposal of czech government enterprise architecture implementation. In: CONFENIS-2013, 7th International Conference on Research and Practical Issues of Enterprise Information Systems, Prague, Trauner Verlag, Linz (2013)
5. Jackson, M.A.: Principles of Program Design. Academic Press, London (1975)
6. Jackson, M.A.: System Development. Prentice-Hall Inc., Englewood Cliffs (1982)
7. Kobryn, C.: Introduction to UML: Structural Modeling and Use Cases, Object Modeling with OMG - UML Tutorial Series (2000). www.omg.org
8. LEAP Project. http://www.leap.gov.uk/
9. McKendrick, J: Making e-government more than a glorified service-delivery platform, SmartPlanet (2009). http://www.smartplanet.com/blog/business-brains/making-e-government-more-than-a-glorified-service-delivery-platform/2964
10. The e-government imperative: main findings, OECD Observer, March 2003
11. The Obama Administrations Commitment to Open Government, status report (2012)

12. OpenSoul, 2000–2015. http://opensoul.panrepa.org
13. PARMA: Public Administration Reference Model and Architecture Project. http://parma.vse.cz
14. Repa, V.: Modeling life cycles of generic object classes. In: Linger, H., Fisher, J., Barnden, A., Barry, C., Lang, M., Schneider, C., et al. (eds.) Building Sustainable Information Systems, pp. 443–454. Springer, New York (2013). ISBN 978-1-4614-7539-2

A Linked Data Model for Web API-s

Svetlana Omelkova$^{(\boxtimes)}$ and Peep Küngas

University of Tartu, Tartu, Estonia
{svetlana.omelkova,peep.kungas}@ut.ee

Abstract. Web APIs (Application Programming Interface) provide means for rapid enterprise integration. The progress in Web API-s has reached the level of maturity where the impact of new advances can and should be validated in practical setting. Usage of various datasets have been reported in the literature of Web API-s. These datasets could allow systematic validation of methods such as composition, selection and recommendation, just to mention a few. However, we have seen that there are obstacles in using these datasets. More specifically, sometimes the datasets are not publicly available and the authors cannot be easily contacted. Furthermore, although some data is available in unprocessed format, the data processing steps are often not completely revealed to facilitate replication of experimental results. Finally, although there are multiple datasets available, there is no common metamodel, which would allow building a unified view to the data and thereby allow efficient development of Web API evaluation suites. In this paper we extend Linked USDL model to embrace a variety of available Web API datasets using linked data principles. Applicability of the metamodel is validated via encoding two Web service's datasets, which are made available for community use.

Keywords: Linked data · Semantic Web Services · Web services · Web API · USDL · RDF

1 Introduction

Web services technology has reached the level of maturity where standardized benchmarking methodologies, methods and datasets will provide a basis for systematic comparison of proposed advanced. In the past years several studies have been conducted in the field of Web services and Web API-s, where specific datasets have been composed and applied. More specifically, OWL-TC family of datasets has been used in studies related to semantic Web services [1,2], ProgrammableWeb dumps have been used in analysis of API ecosystem evolution [3,4], collections of WSDL files have been used for schema matching and network analysis [5,6], and measured Quality of Service (QoS) metrics of specific Web services endpoints have been used in evaluation of Web services selection methods or QoS studies in general [7,8]. A common characteristic of these studies is that they all apply some data harvesting and/or pre-processing steps before

© Springer International Publishing Switzerland 2015
R. Matulevičius and M. Dumas (Eds.): BIR 2015, LNBIP 229, pp. 48–63, 2015.
DOI: 10.1007/978-3-319-21915-8_4

the real analysis is performed. Furthermore, the intersection of datasets or their corresponding conceptual metamodels is not empty, meaning that there are great possibilities to combine these datasets into a coherent cleansed dataset with a unified metamodel for more effective and efficient benchmarking and studies.

Initial attempt in that direction has been taken by Wittern et al. [9] who proposed a generic linked data metamodel for representing the key features of (Web) APIs, users and applications plus relations between them. The authors also revealed some realization details (partial Resource Description Framework (RDF) vocabulary) of the model. Unfortunately, the proposal has three main deficiencies. First, the proposed metamodel does not consider already existing standards and representations, such as services ontologies. Second, the realization of the model is not documented in large extent, neither is it available for download. And third, the constructed dataset, which was encoded by using the proposed metamodel, is not available. Nonetheless, the paper presents a good example of potential benefits of a unified metamodel and reusable data in studies, such as analysis of Web services ecosystems.

At the same time there have been initiatives for systematic representation of services. The recent proposal is Unified Service Description Language (USDL), advocated by Oberle et al. [10]. A qualitative evaluation [11] of USDL indicates that the concepts provided by the USDL to specify software services are in many aspects superior to the current state of the art or at least comparable wrt languages and models such as WSDL, OWL-S, SOAML, SysML and WS-Specification.

USDL language has been elaborated further into a model, called Linked USDL, for representing service descriptions as linked data [12]. Linked USDL builds upon the experience gained from USDL and prior research on semantic Web services, business ontologies and Linked Data. Although Linked USDL covers well the business aspects of Web services, it lacks means for technical integration, such as schema definitions and schema matching details plus it does not define specific Service Level Agreement(SLA) variables which are needed for representing services networks and QoS details of services. Complementary to this approach Cardoso [13] proposes a computational model to model service networks and goes beyond Linked USDL wrt modelling causal relations and KPIs. However, it does not model the business aspects, SLA-s nor technical details.

In this paper we extend Linked USDL while adopting the same requirements to the vocabulary as Pedrinaci et al. [12] outlined for Linked USDL. We add vocabulary and RDF encoding schemes for representing service networks, QoS metrics such as availability, performance and reliability in addition to some minor enhancements. Our contribution provides an enhancement to an existing industrially-driven standard wrt Web services network aspects for which there does not exist a widely used metamodel although majority of Web services ecosystem studies use such data models.

In addition, to validate the proposed metamodel and to accelerate research in Web API ecosystem analysis, we will describe 2 datasets which we encoded by using the proposed metamodel. The first dataset represents all governmental Web services provided by an EU country together with SLA, service provider and service user data. This dataset allows conducting research in evolution of governmental information systems. The second dataset is a subset of global Web API dataset with schema-matching degree data for benchmarking Web API selection and composition algorithms.

2 Background

2.1 Models of Semantic Web Services

Relatively mature SWS conceptual models include Web Service Modeling Ontology (WSMO) [14], OWL-S [15], SA-WSDL [16] and WSMO-Lite [17]. While the first two models allow expressing a top-down view over services, the latter two are bottom-up models where semantics is added to Web service's elements by adding semantic annotations to their syntactic descriptions. A more recent model is *Linked usdl*[1], which is a vocabulary [12] for capturing and sharing service descriptions. Analogously to WSMO and OWL-S this vocabulary is used to describe services. The main difference is the focus on business characteristics of the service offered. *Minimal Service Model* (MSM) vocabulary[2] has aim to support semantic annotations of both "classical" WSDL Web services, as well as Web APIs and RESTful services [18]. The MSM vocabulary suits well for semantic Web API description, apart from the possibility to express different types of relationships between distinct APIs.

2.2 Models of Web Services Networks

With the advent of social networks and Web technologies network analysis has become a popular technique in understanding a variety of phenomena. Network theory provides effective means to understand dynamics in constantly changing complex systems. Network analysis techniques are also applicable in the field of Web API-s. In contrast to complex systems such as the Web and biological networks, Web API networks emerge, evolve and behave differently. There is no unified way to combine Web API-s into a network. One can envision links between Web API-s, API providers, domains of Web API-s, data structures of messages and other domain entities. A heterogeneous Web API network model has been proposed by Zhou et al. [19]. In their approach services, attributes and associated entities, such as providers and consumers, are modeled as vertices connected by multiple types of edges. Kil et al. [20], Cherifi and Santucci [5], Oh et al. [7], Mokarizadeh et al. [21] considered operations and parameters, or more generally Web services, as interacting entities at various levels of granularity. Figure 1 illustrates how a bipartite labelled graph of three Web services using bipartite graph projection [22] can be converted into three types of networks: parameter-parameter network, operation-operation network and service-service network, where nodes are either parameters, operations or web services.

---

[1] http://linked-usdl.github.io/.

[2] http://iserve.kmi.open.ac.uk/ns/msm/msm-2014-09-03.html.

Typically such networks have been constructed from semantic annotations of Web services [23] or Web API-s. Semantic annotations can be constructed either manually, which is complicated by the annotation cost [24], or by using existing techniques for semi-automatic Web service interface annotations such as the ones developed by Zhou [25], Heß et al. [26] or Mokarizadeh et al. [23]. In our previous work [6] we evaluated applicability of schema matching for automated construction of Web Service networks. The empirical results from this work show that automatically constructed Web services network exhibit similar properties as manually crafted ones.

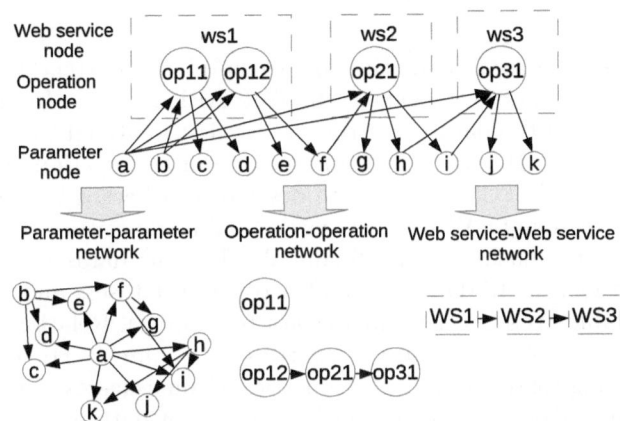

Fig. 1. An example of Web API network formation patterns.

2.3   Requirements to Web API Metamodels

We adopt the same requirements to the vocabulary as Pedrinaci et al. [12] outlined for Linked USDL.

- **Should be Open** — service descriptions needs to rely on a conceptual model with formal foundations that can enable automated processing. In order to support engagement of any other concerned parties the technological approach should be open. Moreover, the solution should be highly interoperable and scalable in terms of data sharing, data processing and communication protocols.
- **Reuse of Existing Models** — linked data principles promote and support reuse of existing conceptual models and datasets.
- **Wide Coverage** — majority of exposed Web API meta-data should be covered by proposed model
- **Suitability for Tasks and Applications** — the solution has to be applicable for solving existing issues.

3   Web API Metamodel

3.1   Requirement's Fulfilment

Should Be Open Web-Based Solution. In order to facilitate capturing, sharing and interlinking Web API's meta-data and relationships of highly heterogeneous nature, the proposed model is designed following Linked Data standards [27,28]. Best practices of Linked Data suggest usage of URIs, more specifically URLs, as identifiers of objects. In our case we use namespace http:// deepweb.ut.ee/ontologies/api-network# (*api-network*) for Web API description objects. We also use this namespace to describe our extensions.

Wide Coverage. Essential motivation to build the current model was the structural diversity and heterogeneity in Web API datasets. In order to grasp the wide overview of the dataset's structure we first analyzed the set of publicly available datasets on the Web. We summarize our observations in Table 1. X-ROAD and SAWSDL-TC3 datasets are described in Sect. 4.1. Third dataset is well-known ProgrammableWeb (PW) - largest online repository of Web APIs and their corresponding mashups. And finally WS-Dream[3] dataset, which provides wide variety of QoS meta-data. We analyzed listed datasets and outlined main classes of available Web Service's meta-data (column 1). Relationships between detected classes denoted as object properties in column 2. For conciseness we omit the wide range of different data properties of some classes, e.g. WebApi class in Programmable Web dataset has about 35 different data properties according to PW API documentation. In Table 1 "+" symbols depict presence of a class or property in a given dataset. It is clear that PW dataset has richest meta-data available, however working with it is out of the scope of the current work. In this work we are focus on covering first two datasets keeping in mind that there are also other datasets available.

Reuse of Existing Models. Considerable effort was devoted to identify well-adopted ontologies that can be reused. Below we provide the list of used ontologies, their usage in the extended model is outline by using different colors. The model is build upon a set of widely used vocabularies, which have been designed to capture particular domains. Namely, the model has been build using following vocabularies:

- **Good Relations (GR)** is a popular vocabulary to describe products (or services) and offers. In our model the Web Service itself is a subclass of *gr:ProductOrService*. The Dataset is a bundle of Web Services and is a subclass of *gr:Offering*.
- **Linked USDL (USDL-*)** [12] is a vocabulary for capturing and sharing rich service descriptions. The kinds of services targeted for coverage by

---

[3] http://www.wsdream.net.

Table 1. Structural comparison of datasets.

Class	Object property	X-ROAD	SAWSDL-TC3	Programmable Web	WSDream
:Dataset		+	+	+	+
	gr:include <:WebAPI>	+	+	+	+
:WebAPI		+	+	+	+
	:hasOperation	+	+	+	
	:hasProvider	+		+	
	:hasConsumer	+		+	
	:hasClassification	+	+	+	
	:hasSLA	+	+	+	+
:Mashup				+	
	gr:include <:WebAPI>			+	
:Operation		+	+	+	
	:hasInput	+	+	+	
	:hasOutput	+	+	+	
:Parameter		+	+	+	
	:modelReference		+		
:Actor		+		+	
	gr:seeks	+		+	
	gr:offer	+		+	
:SLA		+			+
:Match		+	+	+	
	:hasSource	+	+	+	
	:hasTarget	+	+	+	

USDL include human services (e.g., consultancy), business services (e.g. purchase order requisition), software services (e.g., WSDL and RESTful services), infrastructure services (e.g., CPU and storage services), etc. We utilized this vocabulary in order to fully cover Business part of the proposed model.
- **Minimal Service Model (MSM)** is a simple integration ontology which captures the maximum common denominator between existing conceptual models for services. MSM supports publication and discovery of Web services and Web API.
- **SKOS Core** provides support for capturing knowledge organisation systems (e.g., classifications and thesauri) in RDF. We defined business role and SLA variable individuals using this vocabulary.

Suitability for Tasks and Applications. We provide an example of application of existing model in Sect. 4. We chose two publicly available Web API datasets and mapped them into semantic representation utilizing the proposed model.

3.2   Metamodel Description

Motivated by aforementioned issues and model requirements we present a Linked data model for Web APIs. Proposed model takes advantage of using formal ontology representation languages. The proposed model is publicly available[4] and exposed using Turtle serialization format for better readability. It aims at covering such essential aspects as Web Services, service's bundles (i.e. datasets, mashups), business entities involved in service's lifecycle, possible relationships between services, which may serve as a cause of network formation. Figure 2 depicts the model's structure. Blue-colored classes are defined within *api-network* namespace, while the rest of classes are adopted from other suitable vocabularies. Three essential components of a model are the Functional part, Business part and the SLA part. Two latter parts are imported from Linked USDL vocabulary. The reader is expected to refer to *usdl-core* and *usdl-sla* Linked USDL modules documentation for more details. The Functional part aims to cover structural and dynamic aspects of a Web Service.

Most important classes introduced in the model are:

– **Dataset** and **Mashup** classes represent a bundle of APIs. Both classes are extensions of *gr:Offering* and enable binding multiple services together. Usually the set of APIs in the *Dataset* is characterized by the common set of object and datatype properties. But the *Mashup* is a collection of APIs bound together in order to provide wider functionality.
– **WebAPI** or Services class is a general representation of Web services, information systems and other collections of methods, which are exposed over the Web. *WebAPI* class represents services from functional perspective.
– **WebService** is a subclass of *WebAPI*. We defined *api-network:WebService* as an equivalent class to *msm:Service* in order to be able to reuse predicates from *msm* vocabulary.
– **Match** class describes functional matches between components of Web API-s. The illustration of mapping of matching property to the independent class is provided in Fig. 3. We defined three subclasses of a *Match* class. Each subclass is aimed to restrict the type of connected nodes. For instance *OperationMatch* class represent link between two *msm:Operations*, while *ParameterMatch* is link together two *msm:MessageParts*. Class *Match* and all it's subclasses has two object properties: *hasSource* and *hasTarget*. The range of those properties depends on the type of *Match* node. Moreover we define data properties such as *similarityDegree* to reflect the conformity between two nodes. Another data property is a *rdf:type* of matching, which can be defined as "schema matching similarity" or "semantic similarity" or any other link's type the user wants to express. The list of data and object properties of a *Match* class is extensible.

---

[4] http://deepweb.ut.ee/ontologies/api-network.ttl.

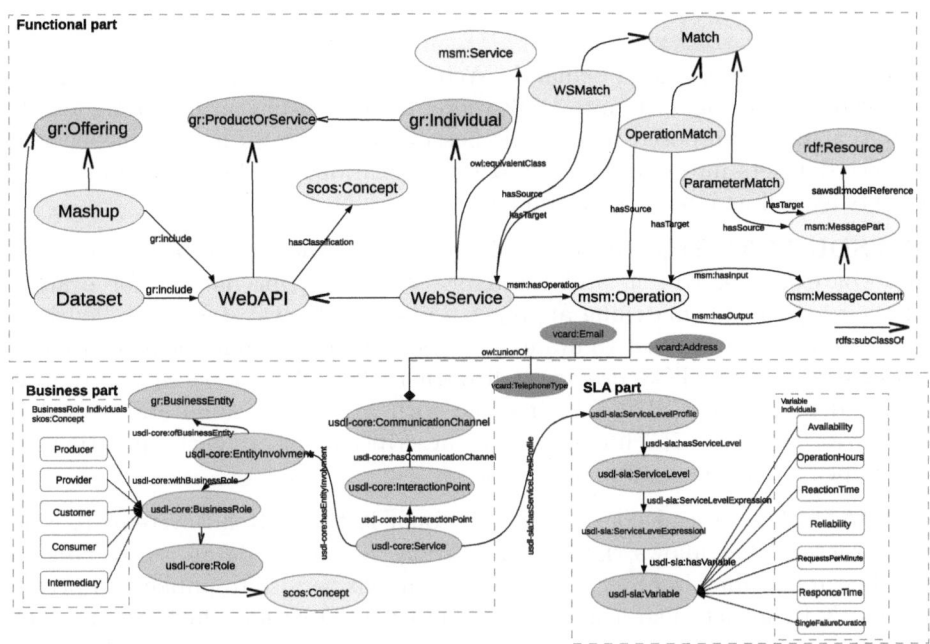

Fig. 2. Ternary Web services network model: functional, business and SLA parts.

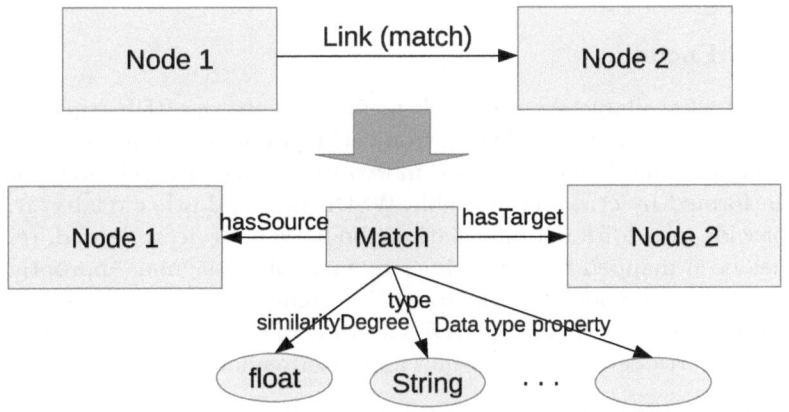

Fig. 3. Mapping of matching property to Match class.

4   Application of the Metamodel

4.1   Data

We evaluated the proposed Semantic Web Services network model by mapping two Web Services datasets into RDF representation using proposed model. We show that using proposed model it is possible to integrate heterogeneous Web Services datasets into one, to mark existing relationships between model components as well as infer potential links.

SAWSDL-TC3[5]: This dataset is widely used by the Semantic Web community. For example, Klusch and Kapahnke [29] used this dataset for evaluating their logic-based matching approach and text retrieval strategies, Pedrinaci et al. [30] used the dataset to evaluate services discovery functionality of iServe platform. SAWSDL-TC3 provides altogether 1080 Web services descriptions from 9 domains in WSDL 1.1 language with SA-WSDL annotations of data structures. We chose 753 unique service descriptions where each operation has non-empty input and output messages.

X-ROAD: The crucial core of the e-Estonia is the X-Road system. It is an infrastructure that allows the nation's various e-services databases to co-work together in harmony in order to provide a complex service to public and private sectors. X-Road acts like a mediator to 170 databases for which around 2000 services are used by over 900 organizations. More then 50 % of the inhabitants of Estonia use X-Road through the information portal eesti.ee. X-Road offers a wide range of services to be conveniently consumed, i.e. presenting a registration of residence electronically, checking personal data from the national database, declaring taxes electronically and many more. Our X-Road dataset consists of 118 Web service descriptions from 40 domains and was fetched from http://riha. eesti.ee.

4.2   RDF Encoding

We mapped all available Web service's meta-data into the RDF triples[6,7] by re-using existing vocabularies and the introduced metamodel extension (see Sect. 3).

The mapping has been performed in two steps. First, the relational database has been formed by crawling available WSDL files and other related resources which provide an additional information about Web services. Second, relational tables has been mapped to RDF triples by manually assigning appropriate concept from proposed model to each atom of information in the relational database.

In this chapter we explain the RDF encoding of datasets. All the RDF data is presented in Turtle serialization format for better readability. We defined our own

---

[5] http://projects.semwebcentral.org/projects/sawsdl-tc/.
[6] The SAWSDL-TC3 is available at http://deepweb.ut.ee/services/api-network-sawsdl-tc3.rdf.
[7] The X-Road dataset is available at http://deepweb.ut.ee/services/api-network-x-road.rdf.

namespace http://deepweb.ut.ee/ontologies/api-network# to isolate our contribution from the existing advances. Prefix mappings are provided in Listing 1.

The description of the structure of dataset's RDF representation starts from the root element of type *api-network:Dataset* (Listing 2). The rest of elements are linked to the root element directly or indirectly. This bundle helps to identify Web service's and operation's origin, while lots of other semantic links form a diverse ties with other datasets.

```
1  @prefix api-network: <http://deepweb.ut.ee/ontologies/api-network#> .
2  @prefix gr: <http://www.heppnetz.de/ontologies/goodrelations/v1#> .
3  @prefix msm: <http://iserve.kmi.open.ac.uk/ns/msm#> .
4  @prefix rdfs: <http://www.w3.org/2000/01/rdf-schema#> .
5  @prefix sawsdl: <http://www.w3.org/ns/sawsdl/> .
6  @prefix xs: <http://www.w3.org/2001/XMLSchema#> .
```

Listing 1. Prefix mapping

```
1  api-network:sawsdl-tc3
2      a api-network:Dataset .
```

Listing 2. Root node

The *api-network:Dataset* node can contain multiple *api-network:WebAPIs*. While the *api-network:WebService* is a subclass of *api-network:WebAPI* we can directly link it to *api-network:Dataset* using predicate *include* from GoodRelation vocabulary (Listing 3).

```
1  api-network:sawsdl-tc3
2      gr:include
3          api_network:novel_person_Reserverservice.wsdl ,
4          api-network:adventure_ruralarea_service.wsdl, <...> .
```

Listing 3. WebService inclusion

```
1  api_network:novel_person_Reserverservice.wsdl
2      a api-network:WebService;
3      api_network:hasClassification
4          api-network:education;
5      msm:hasOperation
6          api-network:novel_person_Reserverservice-get_PERSON.
```

Listing 4. Service's object properties

Since we defined a *api-network:WebService* as equivalent class to *msm:Service* we can use the predicate *hasOperation* from same vocabulary in order to express relationships between *api-network:WebService* and it's *msm:Operations* (Listing 4).

Figure 4 explains message structure of Web API operations. Each operation has input and output messages. Normally the message is aimed to represent an abstract definition of the data being transmitted. A message consists of parts, each of which is associated with type definition provided within type element of WSDL file. Types described using XSD as a canonical type system. WSDL defines several message-typing attributes for use with XSD, such as *element* and *type*. We didn't map message-typing attributes into current RDF mapping, but the user have to keep in mind that every message part can have extensible type definition which is not included into current RDF document. In order to get this information user have to refer to *types* element of a WSDL file.

The next set of triples is aimed at describing mappings from the operation's structure to RDF. The URI of the operation is constructed as a conjunction of names of service and operation using dash. Example in Listing 5 comes from SAWSDL-TC3 dataset, which benefit is a SA-WSDL annotations of data elements. Each annotated element refer to separated ontological concept described in domain specific ontology and stored in separate file. The Input and Output Message nodes (showed in Fig. 4) are mapped into *msm:hasInput* and *msm:hasOutput* predicates respectively in RDF representation in Listing 5. All triplets in square brackets refer to the information about message parts, which constitute input and output messages. In the example in Listing 5 the operation itself does not have a SA-WSDL reference, while both it's message parts has a reference to ontological concept (lines 12 and 21).

```
1   api-network:novel_person_Reserverservice-get_PERSON
2       a msm:Operation ;
3       rdfs:label
4           ''get_PERSON''^^xs:string ;
5       msm:hasInput
6           [ a msm:MessagePart ;
7           rdfs:label
8               ''_NOVEL''^^xs:string ;
9           api-network:type
10              <http://deepweb.ut.ee/services/services/sawsdl_wsdl11/NovelPerson/NovelType>
                    ;
11          sawsdl:modelReference
12              ''http://deepweb.ut.ee/services/ontology/books.owl#Novel''
13          ] ;
14      msm:hasOutput
15          [ a msm:MessagePart ;
16          rdfs:label
17              ''_PERSON''^^xs:string ;
18          api-network:type
19              <http://deepweb.ut.ee/services/services/sawsdl_wsdl11/NovelPerson/PersonType
                    > ;
20          sawsdl:modelReference
21              ''http://deepweb.ut.ee/services/ontology/books.owl#Person''
22          ] .
```

Listing 5. Operation's structure

The main contribution of the model proposed in Sect. 3 is an ability to express relationships (or links) between Web Service's network nodes. We already described link's representation in Sect. 3 on Fig. 3. On Listing 6 the match is a blank node connected to the root element via *api-network:hasMatch* predicate. This blank node is of a type *api-network:OperationMatch* and it serves as a connection between two *msm:Operations*. The match node has two data properties - *api-network:hasSource* and *api-network:hasTarget*, which bind together two nodes. The set of object properties is extensible, in this model we defined an *api-network:similarityDegree* predicate, which indicates the degree of schema similarity between two nodes. Match class also can be used in order to establish links between nodes in different datasets. This fact facilitates four's Linked data principle, which encourage to include links to other related things.

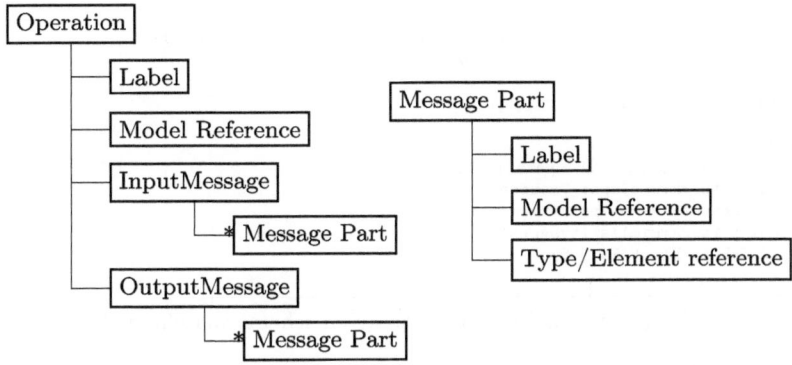

Fig. 4. Web Service's operation structure

```
1  api-network:sawsdl-tc3
2     api-network:hasMatch
3        [ a api-network:OperationMatch ;
4        api-network:hasSource
5           api-network:title_comedyfilmmaxpricequality_service-
                 get_COMEDYFILM_MAXPRICE_QUALITY ;
6        api-network:hasTarget
7           api-network:title_mediataxfreepricequality_service-
                 get_MEDIA_TAXFREEPRICE_QUALITY ;
8        api-network:similarityDegree>
9           ''0.408242''^^xs:float
10       ] ;
```

Listing 6. Node's relationship representation

All preceding RDF triple examples refer to SAWSDL-TC3 dataset and cover the functional part of a model on Fig. 2. In order to cover two remaining parts (Business and SLA) we now refer to X-ROAD dataset described in Subsect. 4.1. According to the Table 1 X-ROAD dataset has meta-data about Web service's providers and consumers as well as about SLA details. In order to see examples of RDF triples user can refer to Linked data representation of X-ROAD dataset.

4.3 Queries

After data aggregation and mapping we are evaluating obtained dataset by showing flexible search queries and result analysis possibility. First query example is driven by the use case to support user to retrieve network with given characteristics. SPARQL query in Listing 7 is aimed to return the network in edge list format enriched by the edge weight, where the similarity degree between source and target nodes should be above 0.9 threshold.

```
1  PREFIX api_network: <http://deepweb.ut.ee/ontologies/api-network#>
2  PREFIX rdf: <http://www.w3.org/1999/02/22-rdf-syntax-ns#>
3
4  SELECT ?source ?target ?threshold
5
6  WHERE {
7  _:x rdf:type api_network:OperationMatch ;
8     api_network:hasInput ?source ;
9     api_network:hasOutput ?target ;
10    api_network:similarityDegree ?threshold .
11    FILTER (?threshold>0.9)
12 }
```

Listing 7. Query WS Network with given schema matching threshold

Another SPARQL query on Listing 8 allows us to answer specific question such as "whether there exists such edges that takes a source from service of Education class and gives an output to Medicine class no matter the similarity degree between those edges?". Such restrictions also can be applied to any SLA parameters or to specific provider or consumer.

```
1  PREFIX api_network: <http://deepweb.ut.ee/ontologies/api-network#>
2  PREFIX rdf: <http://www.w3.org/1999/02/22-rdf-syntax-ns#>
3  PREFIX msm: <http://iserve.kmi.open.ac.uk/ns/msm#>
4
5  SELECT ?inputOp ?outputOp ?threshold
6
7  WHERE {
8  ?inputOp rdf:type api_network:WebService ;
9     api_network:hasClassification api_network:education ;
10    msm:hasOperation ?input .
11 ?outputOp rdf:type api_network:WebService ;
12    api_network:hasClassification api_network:medicine ;
13    msm:hasOperation ?output .
14 _:z rdf:type api_network:OperationMatch ;
15    api_network:hasInput ?input ;
16    api_network:hasOutput ?output ;
17    api_network:hasWeight ?threshold .
18 }
```

Listing 8. Query WS Network with specific restrictions

SPARQL query language gives unlimited possibilities for model querying. Relatively simple queries, like aforementioned, have been executed in affordable time. However more complex queries with diverse restrictions and conditions can raise graph traversal complexity. Nevertheless we would say that using presented RDF data representation allows effectively store and query meta-data about Web APIs and their relationships.

5   Conclusion and Future Work

In this paper we described a metamodel, an extension of MSM and Linked USDL vocabularies, for encoding Web API descriptions as linked data. Applicability and validity of the proposed metamodel is demonstrated on encodings of two datasets - one encoding governmental Web services of an entire country and another encoding a SAWSDL-TC3 dataset of Web services. Although not demonstrated, the metamodel suits well for describing also other Web API-s than Web services. Furthermore, the described metamodel provides a model for efficient development of Web API evaluation suites. The demonstrated datasets lower the barriers of systematic validation of Web API methods such as composition, selection and recommendation since they are publicly available, already pre-processed and ready to use for evaluation purposes. As a feature work we will concentrate our efforts to widening the set of available datasets, which are encoded by using the metamodel and developing standardized benchmark environments where the datasets can be used.

The main limitation of current approach concerns our restrictions to the operation's message structure. Since we did not map message-typing system into the RDF graph we can consider obtained graph as partially incomplete. We actually missing message's structural information along with semantic annotations of some message's schema elements(i.e. in SAWSDL-TC3 dataset). On the other hand this information can overload resulted RDF graph with redundant information. In order to get this information user can refer to *types* element of a WSDL file, however it remains unavailable for RDF graph analysis. This issue will be tackled in our future enhancements.

References

1. Wang, G., Xu, D., Qi, Y., Hou, D.: A semantic match algorithm for web services based on improved semantic distance. In: 4th International Conference on Next Generation Web Services Practices, NWESP 2008, pp. 101–106. IEEE (2008)
2. Fernández, A., Cong, Z., Baltá, A.: Bridging the gap between service description models in service matchmaking. Multiagent Grid Syst. **8**(1), 83–103 (2012)
3. Huang, K., Fan, Y., Tan, W.: An empirical study of programmable web: a network analysis on a service-mashup system. In: 2012 IEEE 19th International Conference on Web Services (ICWS), pp. 552–559 (2012)
4. Huang, K., Yao, J., Fan, Y., Tan, W., Nepal, S., Ni, Y., Chen, S.: Mirror, mirror, on the web, which is the most reputable service of them all? In: Basu, S., Pautasso, C., Zhang, L., Fu, X. (eds.) ICSOC 2013. LNCS, vol. 8274, pp. 343–357. Springer, Heidelberg (2013)
5. Cherifi, C., Santucci, J.F.: On topological structure of web services networks for composition. Int. J. Web Eng. Technol. **8**(3), 291–321 (2013)
6. Omelkova, S., Küngas, P.: Schema matching similarity threshold detection for automated web services network construction. In: Haav, H.-M.A.K., Robal, T. (eds.) Databases and Information Systems: Proceedings of the 11th International Baltic Conference on DB and IS, Baltic DB&IS, pp. 101–112. Tallinn University of Technology Press, Tallinn (2014)
7. Oh, S.C., Lee, D., Kumara, S.R.: Effective web service composition in diverse and large-scale service networks. IEEE Trans. Serv. Comput. **1**(1), 15–32 (2008)
8. E, H., Jin, X., Tong, J., Song, M., Zhu, X.: Measure method and metrics for network characteristics in service systems. In: Zu, Q., Hu, B., Elçi, A. (eds.) ICPCA 2012 and SWS 2012. LNCS, vol. 7719, pp. 180–193. Springer, Heidelberg (2013)
9. Wittern, E., Laredo, J., Vukovic, M., Muthusamy, V., Slominski, A.: A graph-based data model for api ecosystem insights. In: Proceedings of the 21 IEEE International Conference on Web Services (ICWS). IEEE Computer Society, June 2014

10. Oberle, D., Barros, A.P., Kylau, U., Heinzl, S.: A unified description language for human to automated services. Inf. Syst. **38**(1), 155–181 (2013)
11. Birkmeier, D., Overhage, S., Schlauderer, S., Turowski, K.: How complete is the usdl? In: Barros, A., Oberle, D. (eds.) Handbook of Service Description, pp. 521–538. Springer, New York (2012)
12. Pedrinaci, C., Cardoso, J., Leidig, T.: Linked USDL: a vocabulary for web-scale service trading. In: Presutti, V., d'Amato, C., Gandon, F., d'Aquin, M., Staab, S., Tordai, A. (eds.) ESWC 2014. LNCS, vol. 8465, pp. 68–82. Springer, Heidelberg (2014)
13. Cardoso, J.: Modeling service relationships for service networks. In: Falcão e Cunha, J., Snene, M., Nóvoa, H. (eds.) IESS 2013. LNBIP, vol. 143, pp. 114–128. Springer, Heidelberg (2013)
14. Roman, D., Keller, U., Lausen, H., de Bruijn, J., Lara, R., Stollberg, M., Polleres, A., Feier, C., Bussler, C., Fensel, D.: Web service modeling ontology. Appl. Ontol. **1**(1), 77–106 (2005)
15. Martin, D., Burstein, M., Hobbs, J., Lassila, O., McDermott, D., McIlraith, S., Narayanan, S., Paolucci, M., Parsia, B., Payne, T., et al.: Owl-s: Semantic markup for web services. W3C member submission 22 (2004) 2007–04
16. Kopecky, J., Vitvar, T., Bournez, C., Farrell, J.: Sawsdl: semantic annotations for wsdl and xml schema. IEEE Internet Comput. **11**(6), 60–67 (2007)
17. Vitvar, T., Kopecký, J., Viskova, J., Fensel, D.: WSMO-lite annotations for web services. In: Bechhofer, S., Hauswirth, M., Hoffmann, J., Koubarakis, M. (eds.) ESWC 2008. LNCS, vol. 5021, pp. 674–689. Springer, Heidelberg (2008)
18. Pedrinaci, C., Domingue, J.: Toward the next wave of services: Linked services for the web of data. J. UCS **16**(13), 1694–1719 (2010)
19. Zhou, Y., Liu, L., Perng, C.S., Sailer, A., Silva-Lepe, I., Su, Z.: Ranking services by service network structure and service attributes. In: 2013 IEEE 20th International Conference on Web Services (ICWS), pp. 26–33. IEEE (2013)
20. Kil, H., Oh, S.C., Elmacioglu, E., Nam, W., Lee, D.: Graph theoretic topological analysis of web service networks. World Wide Web **12**(3), 321–343 (2009)
21. Mokarizadeh, S., Kungas, P., Matskin, M., Crasso, M., Campo, M., Zunino, A.: Information diffusion in web services networks. In: 2012 IEEE 19th International Conference on Web Services (ICWS), pp. 488–495. IEEE (2012)
22. Zhou, T., Ren, J., Medo, M., Zhang, Y.C.: Bipartite network projection and personal recommendation. Phys. Rev. E **76**(4), 046115 (2007)
23. Mokarizadeh, S., Küngas, P., Matskin, M.: Ontology learning for cost-effective large-scale semantic annotation of web service interfaces. In: Cimiano, P., Pinto, H.S. (eds.) EKAW 2010. LNCS, vol. 6317, pp. 401–410. Springer, Heidelberg (2010)
24. Kungas, P., Dumas, M.: Cost-effective semantic annotation of xml schemas and web service interfaces. In: IEEE International Conference on Services Computing, SCC 2009, pp. 372–379. IEEE (2009)
25. Zhou, L.: Ontology learning: state of the art and open issues. Inf. Technol. Manage. **8**(3), 241–252 (2007)
26. Heß, A., Johnston, E., Kushmerick, N.: ASSAM: a tool for semi-automatically annotating semantic web services. In: McIlraith, S.A., Plexousakis, D., van Harmelen, F. (eds.) ISWC 2004. LNCS, vol. 3298, pp. 320–334. Springer, Heidelberg (2004)
27. Bizer, C., Heath, T., Berners-Lee, T.: Linked data-the story so far. Int. j. Seman. Web Inf. Syst. **5**(3), 1–22 (2009)

28. Berners-Lee, T., Hendler, J., Lassila, O., et al.: The semantic web. Sci. Am. **284**(5), 28–37 (2001)
29. Klusch, M., Kapahnke, P.: Semantic web service selection with sawsdl-mx. In: The 7th International Semantic Web Conference, p. 3. Citeseer (2008)
30. Pedrinaci, C., Liu, D., Maleshkova, M., Lambert, D., Kopecky, J., Domingue, J.: iServe: a linked services publishing platform. In: CEUR Workshop Proceedings, vol. 596 (2010)

Business Information System
Requirements and Architecture

Requirement Elicitation Using Business Process Models

Sander Valvas[(✉)] and Fredrik Milani[(✉)]

University of Tartu, Tartu, Estonia
sander.valvas@gmail.com, milani@ut.ee

Abstract. Oftentimes, when eliciting requirements for system development, the input of domain experts is of great importance. Domain experts are not familiar with artifacts predominantly used by system analysts but rather more attuned to models representing the flow of their work such as business process models. However, these models are rarely used as basis for requirement elicitation. As such, there is a communication barrier, which can cause misunderstandings that translate into imprecise requirements. To address this gap, we propose a systematic approach for eliciting functional requirements using business process models as artifacts in discussion with domain experts. We call this method for Requirement Elicitation from Business Process Models (REB). Based on a mapping of requirement components and elements of business process models, the method guides the discussion between system analysts and domain experts around process models for the purpose of eliciting requirements. The method is validated with a case study and the results show that the REB method was successful in eliciting higher number of relevant requirements with less time required.

Keywords: Requirement elicitation · Business process models

1 Introduction

One of the initial tasks of requirement elicitation is to uncover and extract needed information to specify a requirement [1]. One main source of valuable information is documentation currently being used by an organization [2]. Such information is commonly captured as written text and as graphical models [3]. Oftentimes, graphical representations of the work being conducted, such as business process models, are used for communicative purposes between various stakeholders, for understanding how work is being performed and where improvements can be made. Business process models, and in particular models following the Business Process Model and Notation (BPMN) language, are widely used as it has been designed to accommodate the needs of domain experts, business analysts and system analysts.

These business process models are valuable sources of information for requirements elicitation. In fact, these models are not only used to understand the environment [4] but increasingly becoming an important part of the requirements specification process [5]. Although there is an abundance of modeling techniques for representing processes, they have their origin in software engineering and therefore, difficult for

© Springer International Publishing Switzerland 2015
R. Matulevičius and M. Dumas (Eds.): BIR 2015, LNBIP 229, pp. 67–81, 2015.
DOI: 10.1007/978-3-319-21915-8_5

domain experts to use. To remedy this gap, extensions of existing software modeling methods (e.g. Activity Diagram in UML) have been developed to also accommodate the needs of the business side. However, business oriented modelers have not adopted such languages and rather prefer to use languages such as BPMN for capturing their business processes as graphical models.

Business process models, while being widely used, are rarely utilized as the main artifact when discussing requirement with domain experts. The lack of a method for systematic elicitation of requirements from business process models might be one reason for such models not being used more. In light of this context, this paper aims at presenting and validating a systematic method for eliciting requirements that are complete (include all the data needed for a requirement), consistent (with no internal contradictions), bounded (include relevant data for the software engineering project) and at the appropriate level of detail. The research question is therefore "*how can requirements be systematically elicited from business process models when engaging with domain experts?*"

The REB method provides a template, which includes the data needed for a requirement, and a set of questions that will guide the elicitation of requirements in collaborative discussions, based on business process models, with the domain experts. For each relevant activity, questions are asked of the domain experts that allows for eliciting the intended requirement. The method is validated with a case study for eliciting requirements for customizing and implementing a standard enterprise system.

The rest of the paper is structured as follows. Section 2 introduces the conceptual foundation of our method and Sect. 3 describes the proposed method. Next, Sect. 4 introduces the case study and the findings. Section 5 discusses related work while Sect. 6 draws conclusions and outlines future work.

2   Conceptual Foundation

In this section, we first define the necessary components of a requirement and discuss the elements of a business process model. In order to show that necessary components of a requirement are, either explicitly or implicitly, present in business process models, we use BPMN to map the requirement components with business process elements.

2.1   Components of a Requirement

Generally, the definition of a requirement is that it describes what a product must do and how it should be done [3]. However, such a definition is general and therefore, many attempts have been made to specify or decompose in more detail the components of a requirement [6]. The decomposition offered by Domain Theory for Requirements Engineering [7] is considered as complete [8] and is widely accepted within the field of requirement engineering [9].

Domain Theory for Requirements Engineering [7] provides a structure of knowledge types (see Fig. 1) present in RE and suggests domain knowledge to be represented in two types of generic models: Object System Models (OSM) and Information System

Models (ISM). OSM describes the essential transaction of the application in terms of a set of cooperating objects and their behavior whereas ISM contains processes that provide information about an OSM.

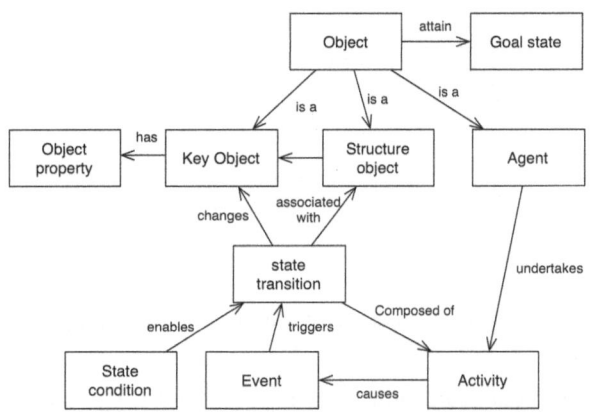

Fig. 1. Meta-schema of knowledge types for domain modeling [7]

The knowledge types that form the basic components of a requirement are *"object"*, *"state transition"*, *"goal state"*, *"activity"*, *"event"*, and *"stative condition"*.

An *object* can be of type *"key object"*, *"structure"* or *"agent"*. A *"key object"* is the subject matter of the essential system transaction. A *"structure object"* is a passive objects that are approximations for real entities, which normally do not appear in data models (e.g. a warehouse or a library). They are therefore persistent, have spatial properties and express containment or possession of *"key objects"* (such as a library contains books). An *"agent"* carries out *"activities"*, which may then create *"events"* initiating *"state transitions"*. A *"state transition"* changes the state of an *"object"* by transferring its membership between *"structure objects"* to achieve a desired *"goal state"* (e.g. a borrowed book moves from the library to the borrower).

A *"goal state"* describes a future, required state, which the system should satisfy, maintain or in some cases, avoid. A goal is specified by describing the state, which is to be achieved, or by describing the algorithms/processes that must be carried out. An *"activity"* is a process, which normally runs to completion and resulting in a state change. An *"activity"* is carried out by actors and triggers the state changes and cause *"events"*. An *"event"* is a single point when something happens.

2.2   Business Process Model and Notation

BPMN provides a modeling notation for designing and managing business processes [10]. A business process is a collection of related, structured activities or tasks that produce a specific service or product for a particular customer [11].

Dumas *et al.* [12] decompose business processes into elements as depicted in Fig. 2.

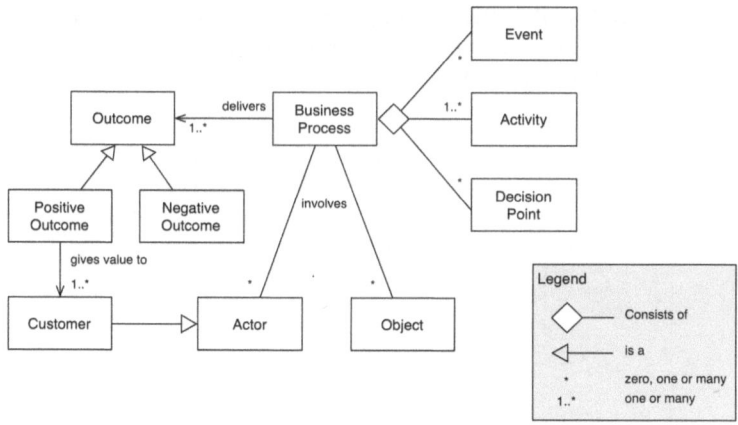

Fig. 2. Ingredients of a business process [12]

An "*event*" represents something that happens and triggers a series of activities. An "*activity*" is a task that takes places for the purpose of fulfilling an operational contract [13]. A "*decision point*" is a point at which a decision is taken that affects the way the process is executed. An "*actor*" is someone or something that performs an "*activity*" or benefits from the output of a process. An "*object*", be it physical or immaterial, is a thing consumed or produced by an "*activity*". A process results in "*outcome*" which can be desirable ("*positive outcome*") or undesirable ("*negative outcome*").

The above listed elements are represented in BPMN by using a core set of elements (see Fig. 3). These are "*flow objects*" that capture "*events*", "*activities*" and "*decision points*" (called "*gateways*" in BPMN) as described above. The "*actor*" is represented with "*swimlanes*" that capture "*pools*" and "*lanes*". The "*artifacts*" represent the "*objects*" and are of either "*data objects*" (data required as in- or output) and "*data store*" (data retrieval or data update) and finally, "*connecting objects*" of BPMN represents the relationship between "*objects*" and "*actors*" with "*activities*". The core elements of BPMN can be supplemented with different additional markers that specify certain attributes or behaviors of the core elements.

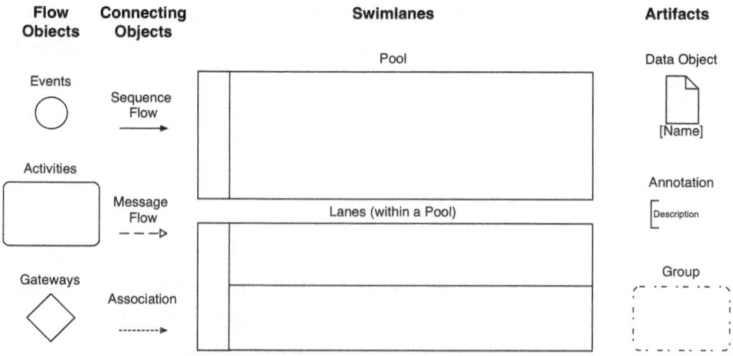

Fig. 3. Core set of BPMN elements [14]

2.3   Mapping a Requirement to BPMN

Here, we compare the components of requirements to the elements of a business process model. The mapping, as seen in Table 1, shows that all necessary information required for a requirement, can be represented in process models represented in BPMN. In Table 1, the first column lists the components of a requirement; the second shows its corresponding element in BPMN and finally, the third column offers a brief comment.

Table 1. Mapping of requirement and BPMN components

Requirement	BPMN	Comment
Key Object	Artifact Events Gateways	Information about a key object can be found in artifacts (data objects, data stores, annotations) or in event types (such as input or output of an event) or in gateways.
Structure Object	Artifact Events Gateways	A structure object is a type of property of a key object and this information in BPMN can be found in the same form as in the case of key objects.
Agent Object	Swim lane (Pool, Lane)	In BPMN, the agent or resources are represented with pools and lanes.
Object Property	Artifact Events Gateways	Key, structure and agent objects have properties that are relevant for requirements definitions. This information can be found in the same form as in the case of key object.
Goal State	Artifact	A goal state is a set of key object properties and is related to structure objects when the process has reached a positive outcome. Since the information about the key and structure objects is found in artifacts, events and gateways, the goal state is also described in the same way as BPMN.
Activity	Activity	Represented as activities in BPMN.
Event	Event	Represented as events in BPMN.
Stative Condition	Artifact, Events and Gateways	Stative condition consists of object properties and therefore, found in artifacts and text annotations of a preceding event or an activity. Also, if the preceding element is a gateway, some of the conditions are described in the outgoing node of the gateway.
Relationship	Connecting objects	Represented as connecting objects in BPMN such as message flows and associations.

As can be seen from Table 1, the components of a requirement, has a corresponding counterpart in business process models as exemplified by BPMN. However, it should be noted that one component of a requirement could have its matching counterpart in several BPMN elements. Nevertheless, the information is either explicitly or implicitly available and therefore, it is possible to elicit functional requirements from business process models.

3   Description of the REB Method

In this chapter, we describe the REB method. The method aims at eliciting requirements and as such, its main artifact is a template for requirement specification. The template is filled for every relevant activity of the process model, covering all requirement components as discussed in Sect. 2. The REB method begins with a template, which is populated by asking a set of pre-defined questions from the domain experts while using the business process model as main artifact.

The requirement specification is gradually elicited for each relevant activity. The first step is to determine if the activity is relevant or not. An activity is considered as relevant if it requires some form of functionality support from an information system. If the activity is performed manually and does not require any support from any semi-automated or automated system, it is not relevant. As such, a specification is only elicited for activities that require some sort of support to be considered or developed.

The process of populating the requirement specification is practically achieved by eliciting information about the goal, actor, trigger, operational steps, alternative paths, failure conditions and their management for each relevant activity (see Fig. 4). The information required, is elicited by applying a set of questions that are designed to capture that specific information from the domain experts using business process models as common artifact. As such, the requirement specification template is gradually defined until it forms a complete specification. The process is then repeated for each activity of the business process that is relevant.

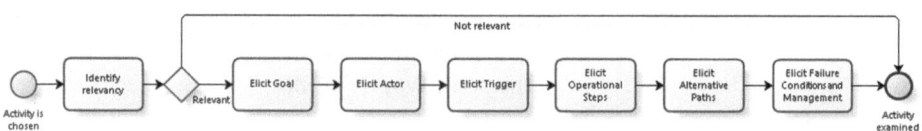

Fig. 4. The REB method.

The REB method requires a set of business process models as input. Access and availability of domain experts are necessary as requirements are being elicited from them by sets of questions related to each step of the elicitation process. The extent, to which the domain experts are engaged, depends on the level of detail in the business process models. If the process models have been modeled in great detail, most of the information is already captured in the models. In such cases, the input of the domain experts is of a more confirmatory nature. However, if the models are not of such detailed level, the REB method will elicit that "hidden" information from the domain experts. For instance, if the model lacks artifacts, the REB method will, through its questions, inquire about the objects and thus capture the information from the domain experts. As such, the REB method can identify incompleteness's in business process models and assist in capturing the business processes in greater detail.

Activities are the focal point of the method. Each requirement specification corresponds to at least one activity. The requirement specification (see Table 2) consists of two columns, where the first one states what data is to be captured in the second column of each row. The data required are "*id*" (a unique id for the requirement specification), "*business process*" (name of the process model in which the main activity of the requirement specification belongs to), "*activity*" (the name of the focal activity that is the object of requirement elicitation), "*goal*" (the expected outcome of the activity), "*actor*" (the performer of the activity), "*trigger*" (what initiates the actor to perform the activity), "procedures of the activity" (the operational steps taken to perform the activity, both desired steps and alternative steps required when the desired steps cannot be executed), and "*failure conditions and handling*" (cases where the activity cannot be executed or interrupted in its execution and actions to handle the failures). The requirement specification template, which is inspired by use case specification of Cockburn [15], covers all components necessary for a requirement as aligned with their corresponding business process model elements.

Table 2. Requirement specification template

Requirement Specification	
ID:	
Business Process:	
Activity:	
Goal:	
Actor:	
Trigger:	
Steps of Activity (positive scenario)	Operational steps:
	Alternative paths:
Failure conditions and management:	

A requirement specification is populated for each activity. However, in some cases, several activities are so connected that they should be treated as one from the perspective of requirement specification. To determine if two or more adjacent activities should be included in one requirement specification, the following questions as inspired by Cockburn [15] are asked: (1) Are the consecutive activities executed by one person, in one place and at the same time? (2) Is it possible or reasonable to have a break between the activities? If the answers to both questions are "yes", the execution of the activities are tightly connected and there is no reasonable reason to separate them. They should therefore, be treated as one requirement for the system being built.

When eliciting requirements from process models, it is reasonable to assume that the processes are not captured with enough details needed for the elicitation process. If the information is not captured in the model, the REB method will highlight it and leave it to domain experts to add it to the models. The purpose and phase of the project of the requirement specification determines the level of detail that the requirement is specified. In early stages of an IT project, the requirements do not need to be at the same level of detail as in later stages. The REB method allows the elicitors to determine the level of detail by deciding when the template contains enough detail about the requirement. It should be noted that the questions have the purpose of securing the required information but further discussions and follow up questions that enrich the discussion and clarify the requirements further are expected.

Step 1 – Identify Relevancy of Activity: The first step is to determine if the activity is relevant. If the activity requires some form of system support, there is a need for having its functional requirements specified. In order to determine the relevancy of the activity, the following questions are asked:

1. Does the execution of the activity require any support from any computer-based system?
2. Is the system under construction to be involved by providing, executing or receiving data during the execution of the activity?
3. Are there any connections to external systems involved in the execution of the activity that need to be considered for interfacing with the system under construction?

Step 2 – Elicitation of Goal: An executed activity serves to fulfill a certain predefined outcome or goal. In this step, the outcome of the activity is elicited by asking the following questions:

4. What changes after the activity has been executed?
5. What is required to be achieved or accomplished with the execution of the activity?
6. In what form and/or format are the results in?

Step 3 – Elicitation of Actor: In this step, the executor of the activity is elicited. The actor can be either human such as a role, department or organizational unit or a non-human resource such as an information system. The actors are elicited by asking the following question:

7. Who are the actors, human and non-human, who are involved in the execution of the activity?

Step 4 – Elicitation of Trigger: Triggers determine when an activity is to be executed. Activities are generally triggered by either an actor receiving a message, a specific predefined time or by the end of a preceding activity. The following questions assist in eliciting the triggers:

8. How does the actor (human or non-human) know when to start the execution of an activity?

9. If it is a message, what kind of message is it and how does the actor become aware of receipt of the message?
10. If the activity is time-dependent event, how is the actor notified about when to start the execution of the activity?
11. If it is complete execution of the preceding activity that is the trigger, is the actor responsible for the execution of the preceding activity and if not, how is the actor informed about it?

Step 5 – Elicitation of Operational Steps: An activity usually consists of procedural or operational steps, i.e. the individual steps that need to be carried out in order to execute the activity. In this step, the preferred or desired operational steps are elicited by asking the following questions:

12. What are the operational steps required for the execution of the activity?
13. Who performs the operational steps?
14. What tools or aids does the actor engage or use in carrying out the operational steps (such as human or non-human actors, internal or external systems)
15. How are these tools or aids used?
16. Are verifications required in carrying out the operational steps?

Step 6 – Elicitation of Alternative Paths: Alongside the standard set of operational steps, there are alternative paths taken when the standard cannot be executed. This could be for instance, entering an order when the customer is not registered and an alternative path is required before the order can be registered. These alternative paths are elicited by asking the following questions:

17. Are there cases (when carrying out the standard operation steps) where additional or alternative steps need to be taken in order to reach the goal of the activity?
18. What are the conditions of these cases?
19. What complementary or replacing steps need to take place in such cases?

Step 7 – Elicitation of Failure Conditions and Failure Management: Activities cannot always successfully be executed and reach its goal as they might be interrupted or disrupted. In this step, such conditions that hinder an activity from being initiated, interrupted or disrupted are elicited. Furthermore, such failure situations require additional steps to be taken in order to solve the disruption. These failures and steps to manage them are elicited with the aid of the following questions:

20. What can hinder the initiation of an activity?
21. What can cause to interrupt or disrupt an activity?
22. What activities or steps are needed to limit the loss, handle or resolve issues so an activity can be initiated?

4   Case Study

The case study method allows researchers to investigate a phenomenon within its real-life context [16], particularly when the boundaries between what is studied and its context are unclear [17]. Case studies are often used for exploratory purposes, but they are also suitable for testing a hypothesis in a confirmatory study [16, 18] or to evaluate a method within the software and systems engineering domain [19]. These features make the case study method applicable to validate our proposed method.

Our research question is: *"how can requirements be systematically elicited from business process models when engaging with domain experts?"* The purpose of our method is to elicit requirements that are complete (covering the required set of requirements for a system to be constructed) and relevant (requirements that the system being constructed need to have in order to support the business process it was designed to support).

4.1   Setting and Design

The case study is on the quality assurance process of a mid-sized electric engine manufacturing company. The company completed a full implemented an ERP system including process modeling, requirement elicitation, configuration, testing and implementation of the final system. As such, the process models had already been modeled, all requirements elicited and implemented. Furthermore, as the project, at the time of the execution of this case study, had been fully operational for 2 months, all major requirements that had been missed during the elicitation process but implemented in the project were identified. As such, the project had a (1) list of requirements elicited prior to the implementation of the system and (2) a final set of requirements that were implemented including those that were discovered during the implementation of the system. A system analyst, an expert on the ERP system, elicited the requirements of the project. The analyst did not apply any formal method but rather relied on his own expertise and extensive knowledge of the system and expertise from previous implementation of similar projects.

The design of the case study consists of 3 parts. The first part consisted of a series of meetings with the business analyst who headed the implementation project. In this part of the case study, the REB method was introduced followed by meetings where the requirements were elicited with the REB method. The second part was converting the requirements to make them comparable with the two sets of requirements elicited prior to and during the project implementation. The final part of the case study consisted of analysis and comparison of the results.

4.2   Execution

The first author conducted the case study with the lead domain expert of the implementation project. The first part of the case study began with a description of the REB method including the template for requirement specification, its components, some of the questions and an illustrative example. Following the introduction, the elicitation process began. For each activity of the process model, a requirement specification was created. Table 3 illustrates the requirement specification for *"check and update order confirmation"*.

Table 3. Example of a populated requirement specification (abridged due to space limitation)

Component	Description
ID:	003
Business Process:	Supply chain security (purchase)
Activity:	Check and update order confirmation
Goal:	Updated order (suggested delivery date and order status updated)
Primary Actor:	Purchase department
Trigger:	Order confirmation received by e-mail
Steps of Activity (positive scenario)	**Operational steps:**
	1. Open PDF format order confirmation received by email
	2. Find the relevant purchase order
	3. Check that ordered materials are the same as on the order
	4. Enter suggested delivery date and change the status to "Confirmed"
	5. Reply the email confirming the order confirmation
	6. Save the order
	Alternative paths:
	1. If order confirmation differs from the order (e.g. quantity smaller than ordered), contact the person who created the order and ask for advice; If changes OK follow the normal flow.
	2. If suggested delivery date is later than the needed delivery date, take same actions as in alternative path 1.
Failure conditions and management:	1. If order confirmation differs from the order and is not acceptable, the order will be deleted and the process will be interrupted.

The activity, "check and update order confirmation" was determined as relevant (step 1) as it requires some interaction with a system support (not a purely manual task). Then, the goal of the activity was elicited (step 2). With the aid of the questions, it became clear that the goal of this activity is to achieve an updated order. After this, the actor was determined (step 3) which was someone from the purchasing department. The next set of questions aim at eliciting the trigger of the activity (step 4). In this case, a message event preceded the activity indicating that an incoming message from the supplier is the trigger. This was further clarified (with the aid of the questions) that the trigger is an email from the supplier with an attachment. Further discussion revealed that there is no need for any automation or an interface. Next, the operational steps of the activity were elicited (step 5). By using the questions, the operational steps were elicited and clarified. Some steps, such as the second step, "find the relevant purchase order" were elaborated as to what parameters are used to find an order. Following the operational steps, the alternative paths (step 6) were elicited. The discussions based on the questions of the method, revealed that two alternative paths exist, one for when the confirmation differs from the order and when the suggested delivery date is later than the customer needs the goods. The final step of the method (step 7) is eliciting failure conditions and management. In this step, situations that prevent the activity from starting or that interrupts/disrupts the activity and the measures needed to be taken are discussed. Naturally, the failures are connected with the operational steps and alternative paths. For instance, the alternative path of order confirmation differs from the order and it is not acceptable, the management of this situation is clarified here. In this case, it is to delete the order and the process is interrupted.

5 Findings

In order to make the requirements elicited with the REB method (REB set) comparable with the set of requirements elicited (baseline set) prior to the project start and the set after the project was implemented (final set), they were converted. The final set included elicited requirements that had been discarded during the project implementation and requirements that had been missed in the elicitation process prior to project start. The baseline and the final set of requirements were not documented in the same way as the REB set. For instance, an ERP system provides a certain set of functionalities per default and therefore, such requirements were not recorded in the baseline and the final set. These were added, as they are valid requirements in order to make the sets of requirements comparable. The domain expert verified all converted requirements to ensure comparable results.

5.1   Comparison

With the implementation of the REB method, a total of 128 versus 121 (baseline set) requirements were elicited. Number of requirements, valuable as it may be, is not enough but needs to be complemented with the quality of the requirements.

The ratio of irrelevant and incorrect requirements to the total number of requirements is used as approximation for the quality of the requirements elicited. The baseline set of requirements had 6 irrelevant or incorrect requirements out of 121 which gives ratio of 4, 9 %. The corresponding ratio for the REB method was 5, 4 % (7 out of 128).

The REB method resulted in the elicitation of more requirements of equal quality as compared to the baseline set. However, the final set consists of 128 relevant and correct requirements including requirements that had not been elicited prior to the start of the project but identified as relevant during the implementation. The final set included 19 requirements that the baseline had not elicited, thus the ratio of "missed" requirements is (as compared to the final set) 14, 8 %. The corresponding ratio for the REB method is 9, 4 %. It should be noted that the REB method elicited 4 requirements out of 6 that was discovered during the project implementation and an additional 2 that were not included in the final set but were considered as both relevant and correct. These have been put on the list of enhancements to be developed.

The baseline set of requirements took 60 man-hours to elicit whereas the application of the REB method took 46 man-hours.

5.2 Threats to Validity

Case studies come with several inherent threats to validity, particularly regarding external validity [16]. External validity concerns the extent to which the findings can be generalised beyond the setting of the study. The REB method has been applied on a small size project of ERP implementation. As such, results are limited in the extent they can be generalised but it should be noted that the case study is from a fully implemented industry example. Furthermore, the case study included a learning effect, as the project was implemented prior to the application of the REB method. Although this risk is very difficult to practically combat, we reduced the risk to the extent possible by instructing the domain experts to only answer the questions and not volunteer additional information. As such, the requirements elicited were discovered through the set of questions included in the REB method.

6 Related Work

Luis et al. [20] describes a method to elicit requirements from process models in three stages. First, organizational modeling is done in BPMN, then the model is validated by purpose analysis and finally functional requirement specifications are created from the refined BPMN models. It creates use-cases like specifications and suggests the elements of the model to be used in order to fill in the specification. However, the method and the requirement specification are not systematic and do not specify requirements in detail.

Use-cases and scenarios also describe the business. Maidens *et al.* [21] research aim at improving the completeness of requirements by analyzing scenarios. This process uses the existing use case model as a starting point and derives new scenarios, taking into account situations, which have not yet been considered (alternative courses). It proposes a technique to validate the completeness of models and concentrates more on the alternative paths and failure conditions. However, this approach does not hold the models as a central artifact in the elicitation process as it concentrates on the improvements and classification of requirements already gathered. However, no systematic method for eliciting requirements form a system level use-case or scenario, which was the aim of the method created in this thesis, can be found.

Meziane *et al.* [22] propose a system that generates natural language specifications from UML class diagrams. The main focus is on automatically converting models into natural language specifications. Pavlovski and Zou [23] propose a method how to formally verify informal UML Activity Diagrams. While both use UML diagrams, they concentrate on formal methods. The requirements will be in accordance with the source of elicitation and as such, inconsistent or incomplete models will result in requirement specifications of lower quality. The REB method focuses on eliciting with the aid of domain experts and therefore, produces complete requirements despite the inconsistency or incomplete models.

Some approaches include using process models in the elicitation process. For instance Demorörs et al. [24] see process models as a way to define business requirements and for creating visibility and consensus among different stakeholders.

Abeti et al. [25] suggest to use SI*, UML and BPMN models to model organizational knowledge and use the knowledge in the RE process. These approaches recognize the usefulness of various process models but view them more for communicative purposes rather than sources of requirement elicitation.

7 Conclusion

The involvement of domain experts is critical when eliciting requirements. However, models used by IT are often alien and hard to understand by domain experts. On the other hand, business process models are more aligned to how domain experts see their workflows but oftentimes, such models are not complete. This paper introduces a systematic approach to elicit requirements from process models. In reality, however, such models are usually not complete. The REB method circumvents this deficiency by systematically going through different aspects of each relevant activity and thus extracting the information from the domain experts needed for a complete requirement specification. The REB method, built on mapping of components required for a complete requirement and business process models, is evaluated on a real-life case study. The results show that with less effort in terms of man-hours, the REB method results in more relevant and correct requirements being elicited as compared to the baseline set of requirements.

While other elicitation approaches value process models as communicative tools in the elicitation process, the REB method uses the process models that the domain experts understand and are comfortable with, as the foundation of systematic elicitation or requirements. As such, the elicitation process is brought much closer to the artifacts domain experts use.

Currently the REB method elicits functional requirements while non-functional requirements are not supported. Therefore, one direction for future work is to extend the method to include elicitation of non-functional requirements as well. Furthermore, the REB method would benefit from a semi-automated supporting tool that supports for instance categorization of requirements. Development of such a tool is also considered for future work.

Acknowledgement. This research was supported by the European Social Fund via the Doctoral Studies and Internationalisation Programme – DoRa.

References

1. Zowghi, D., Coulin, C.: Requirements elicitation: a survey of techniques, approaches, and tools. In: Aurum, A., Wohlin, C. (eds.) Engineering and Managing Software Requirements SE - 2, pp. 19–46. Springer, Heidelberg (2005)
2. Coulin, C.R.: A Situational Approach and Intelligent Tool for Collaborative Requirements Elicitation (2007)

3. Adam, S., Riegel, N., Gross, A., Uenalan, O., Darting, S.: A conceptual foundation of requirements engineering for business information systems. In: Bider, I., Halpin, T., Krogstie, J., Nurcan, S., Proper, E., Schmidt, R., Soffer, P., Wrycza, S. (eds.) EMMSAD 2012 and BPMDS 2012. LNBIP, vol. 113, pp. 91–106. Springer, Heidelberg (2012)
4. Nuseibeh, B., Easterbrook, S.: Requirements engineering : a roadmap. In: ICSE 2000 Proceedings of Conference on Future of Software Engineering, vol. 1, pp. 35–46 (2000)
5. Li, J., Jeffery, R., Fung, K.H., Zhu, L., Wang, Q., Zhang, H., Xu, X.: A business process-driven approach for requirements dependency analysis. In: Barros, A., Gal, A., Kindler, E. (eds.) BPM 2012. LNCS, vol. 7481, pp. 200–215. Springer, Heidelberg (2012)
6. Zapata, C.M., Losada, M.B., González-calderón, G.: An approach for using procedure manuals as a source for requirements elicitation. In: CLEI (2012)
7. Sutcliffe, A., Maiden, N.: The domain theory for requirements engineering. IEEE Trans. Softw. Eng. 24, 174–196 (1998)
8. Sutcliffe, A., Papamargaritis, G., Zhao, L.: Comparing requirements analysis methods for developing reusable component libraries. J. Syst. Softw. 79, 273–289 (2006)
9. Naish, J., Zhao, L.: Towards a generalised framework for classifying and retrieving requirements patterns. In: 2011 First International Workshop on Requirements Patterns, pp. 42–51 (2011)
10. Object Management Group Inc. Business Process Model and Notation (BPMN)
11. Wikimedia Foundation Inc. Business process
12. Dumas, M., La, R.M., Mendling, J., Reijers, H.: Fundamentals of Business Process Management. Springer, Heidelberg (2013)
13. Wikimedia Foundation Inc. Activity (UML)
14. Dunstan, T.: BPMN Explained, a guide to the Business Process Modeling Notation (2014)
15. Cockburn, A.: Writing Effective Use Cases, The Crystal Collection for Software Professsionals. Addison-Wesley Professionals, Boston (2000)
16. Runeson, P., Höst, M.: Guidelines for conducting and reporting case study research in software engineering. Empir. Softw. Eng. 14(2), 131–164 (2009)
17. Yin, R.: Case study research: Design and methods. Sage Publication, New York (2008)
18. Flyvbjerg, B.: Five misunderstandings about case-study research. Qual. Inq. 12, 219–245 (2006)
19. Kitchenham, B., Pickard, L., Pfleeger, S.L.: Case studies for method and tool evaluation. IEEE Softw. 12(4), 52–62 (1995)
20. de la Vara, J.L., Sánchez, J., Pastor, Ó.: Business process modelling and purpose analysis for requirements analysis of information systems. In: Bellahsène, Z., Léonard, M. (eds.) CAiSE 2008. LNCS, vol. 5074, pp. 213–227. Springer, Heidelberg (2008)
21. Maiden, N.A.M., Minocha, S., Manning, K., Ryan, M.: CREWS-SAVRE : Systematic Scenario Generation and Use 1 2 : The CREWS-SAVRE Software Tool, pp. 1–9
22. Meziane, F., Athanasakis, N., Ananiadou, S.: Generating natural language specifications from UML class diagrams. Requir. Eng. 13, 1–18 (2007)
23. Pavlovski, C.J., Zou, J.: Non-functional requirements in business process modeling. In: APCCM, vol. 79, pp. 103–112 (2008)
24. Demirörs, O., Gencel, Ç., Tarhan, A.: Utilizing Business Process Models for Requirements Elicitation, pp. 1–4 (2003)
25. Abeti, L., Ciancarini, P., Moretti, R.: Business process modeling for organizational knowledge management. In: Degano, P., De Nicola, R., Meseguer, J. (eds.) Concurrency, Graphs and Models. LNCS, vol. 5065, pp. 301–311. Springer, Heidelberg (2008)

Elements and Characteristics of Enterprise Architecture Capabilities

Matthias Wißotzki[1(✉)] and Kurt Sandkuhl[1,2]

[1] Institute of Computer Science, University of Rostock, Rostock, Germany
{matthias.wissotzki,kurt.sandkuhl}@uni-rostock.de
[2] ITMO University, St. Petersburg, Russia

Abstract. Enterprise Architecture Management (EAM) is expected to contribute to strategic planning and systematic development of enterprises by
capturing the essential structures and processes of an enterprise on different
architectural levels (e.g. business, data, application, technology) and showing
inter-dependencies. Capabilities in EAM are among the subjects in research
which have received substantial attention during the last years, but still are not
thoroughly defined regarding their characteristics, elements and lifecycle processes. Many different definitions of the term capability exist and different views
on what the elements of capabilities are have been presented. The main contributions of the paper are (a) an analysis and discussion of the literature on
capabilities in EAM, (b) a conceptualization of EAM capability identifying the
core elements and characteristics, and (c) the results of expert interviews for
validating this conceptualization.

Keywords: Capability management · Capability engineering · Enterprise
architecture management · Business-IT alignment · Business capabilities

1 Introduction

Adaptability of business models, quick-responsiveness to market changes and continuous business and IT-alignment are among the acknowledged factors for competitiveness on a globalized market [1]. Changes in market environments of enterprises are
triggered by new technologies like big data, cloud computing, social business or
cyber-physical systems. When adapting to these changes or pro-actively implementing
new business models, enterprises have to be aware of their existing organizational and
technical infrastructures which are manifested, e.g., in value creation and business
processes, resources, information systems, devices, applications, networking and
communication systems. Enterprise Architecture Management (EAM) is expected to
contribute to the above challenges by capturing the essential structures and processes of
an enterprise on different architectural levels (e.g. business, data, application, technology), showing dependencies and supporting strategic planning and systematic
development (see also Sect. 2).

In the last decade, EAM has attracted a lot of interest in industry and a lot of
activity in the research community. This is confirmed by surveys among companies
regarding the use and importance of EA (see, e.g., [2]) and by literature studies

R. Matulevičius and M. Dumas (Eds.): BIR 2015, LNBIP 229, pp. 82–96, 2015.
DOI: 10.1007/978-3-319-21915-8_6

investigating research topics under consideration (e.g., [3]). Capabilities in EAM are among the subjects in research which have received substantial attention during the last years, but still are not thoroughly defined regarding their characteristics, elements and lifecycle processes. Many different definitions of the term capability exist and different views on what the elements of capabilities are have been presented (see Sect. 3).

The aim of this paper is to contribute to the field of EAM by investigating the concept "capability" and identifying the most significant characteristics and elements of EA capabilities. The main contributions of the paper are (a) an analysis and discussion of the literature on capabilities in EAM, (b) a conceptualization of EAM capability identifying the core elements and characteristics, and (c) the results of expert interviews for validating this conceptualization.

Research work in this paper started from the following research question: *In EAM, what elements and characteristics should a capability have which need to be taken into account in capability development and maintenance?* The research approach underlying this work is an abductive approach, i.e. a combination of (a) deduction from the body of knowledge in the field of EAM what theoretical basis applies to EA capabilities and (b) development of a conceptualization of "EAM capability" and induction from work with experts in the field to what extent our conceptualization is sound and would work in practice.

The remainder of the paper is structured as follows: Sect. 2 summarizes the background for our work from EAM and from previous projects motivating the work. Section 3 investigates the use of the term EAM capability in scientific literature which includes a systematic literature analysis in the area. Based on the background work and the results from Sects. 3, 4 proposes a conceptualization of EAM capability identifying the elements and characteristics. Section 5 evaluates the conceptualization with the means of applying it in an industrial case and a survey among experts and practitioners. Summary and conclusions are presented in Sect. 6.

2 Research Background

Enterprise architecture (EA) denotes the fundamental conception or representation of an enterprise—as embodied in its main elements and relationships—in an appropriate model. EA models have evolved over the last decade from pure IT architecture models into control instruments that can be used by the management as a tool for their business decisions and allow an integrated view on an enterprise. An EA supports the understanding and documenting of an organizational structure with all dependencies of artifacts and information objects necessary for business performance [5].

EA management (EAM) provides an approach for a systematic development of an enterprise's architecture in line with its goals by performing planning, transforming, and monitoring functions. The reasons for implementing an EA via EAM are manifold. On the one hand, it enables and supports the adaptation of IT to the business goals, the identification of problems or assistance coping challenges and on the other hand, it allows a detailed description of the conjunction between business and IT. This type of joint interaction results in creation of a common and consistent vocabulary for business processes and objects anon as well as for business functions and skills in the technical departments and the IT [6].

Starting points for the research work presented in this paper were studies of the use of EA capabilities in industrial practice. Two of these projects will be briefly presented in this section. In both projects, we discovered the lack of a consistent conceptualization of "EAM capability" and the need for developing such a conceptualization as a basis for structured and systematic EAM capability management. How could you manage and EAM capability if you do not know exactly what it consists of?

(P1) EACN Project[1]: The idea of constructing an EAM capability maturity model called Enterprise Architecture Capability Navigator (EACN) was triggered by a project between University of Rostock and alfabet AG (now Software AG, Berlin). In cooperation with alfabet AG, the goal is to develop an instrument suitable for assessing and improving the EA capabilities of an enterprise. The main focus of the research was to identify EAM capabilities and their use in a flexible, feature-related measurement system which contains a methodology for determining the maturity of certain capabilities and concepts for the enhancing relevant EAM capabilities of an enterprise. The project resulted in challenges to EAM and an initial structure of an EAM capability catalogue [4].

(P2) OpenGroup Capability Improvement Project[2]: The primary objective of this project is to support elaboration of a high-functioning Enterprise Architecture capability approach as well as identifying and executing improvements to the capability benchmarking by validating purpose-based capability approaches that use a standard Enterprise Architecture service model, capability model and/or maturity model. In the course of this project, existing approaches within EAM capability management were analyzed (see also Sect. 3). One of the main conclusions was the need for a more precise definition and conceptualization of the term EAM capability.

Both projects also showed that capabilities should be considered as specific or at least adaptable to enterprise needs, i.e. there might be generic capabilities for EAM in certain domains but how to interpret them in practice and how to establish them in an enterprise substantially depends on the enterprise context. As a consequence, we developed the hypothesis that the "lifecycle" of an EAM capability including identification of capabilities in enterprises, differentiation of capability types (e.g. regarding the EA layers), implementation of capabilities, improvement, evaluation and benchmarking etc. should be supported by a systematic process. Table 1 summarizes requirements identified in the projects relevant for capability conceptualization.

3   The Term "Capability" in EA Literature

A capability is defined as the organization's capacity to successfully perform a unique business activity to create a specific outcome [8, 9]. First of all, the term capability has to be distinguished from other related terms. Possible terms with a similar or even

---

[1] http://www.wirtschaftsinformatik-rostock.de.

[2] http://opengroup.org.

Table 1. Requirements from projects (P1 + P2) regarding capability conceptualization

Lifecycle Pgases and Requirements	(1) EACN	(2) EACapImp
Differentiation of Capability Types	x	
Identifying Capabilities	x	
Improvement of Capabilities	x	x
Benchmarking of Capabilities	x	x
Capability vs. Service, Process, Function	x	x
Description of Capability Elements	x	x

synonymous meaning are competency, capacity and skill. Vincent worked on differentiating capability from these three terms in [10]. According to [10], a competence is characterized by the fact that something is functionally adequate. It has sufficient knowledge, strength and skill. "Competence is another word for an individual's know-how or skill". Capacity, describes the power to hold, receive or accommodate something. Capacity is really about 'amount' or 'volume'. In contrast to these terms, a capability is used in the context of features, faculties, processes, functions and much more that should be developed or improved. Moreover, it is a collaborative term that can be deployed and through which individual competences can be applied an exploited" All in all, while competency is the knowledge of an individual and capacity is rather a dimensional unit, capability addresses the implementation of strategies and has more organizational character. According to [11], capabilities belong to elements being strategically relevant for an enterprise even though just a few studies about features and criteria for demarcation of the capability idea are existing.

In order to identify relevant work on EAM capability in scientific literature, we performed a systematic literature review following the principles and steps defined in Kitchenham's approach [7]. After having defined the research question to be investigated (see Sect. 1), one of the first steps in this approach is to define which publication sources will be taken into account during the systematic analysis. In order to identify these sources, we searched AISeL, SpringerLink and IEEE Xplore and selected those journals and conference series offering publications regarding capabilities or EA capabilities. Table 2 shows the publication resources analyzed during the process of the literature review and the number of hits within the papers published between 2005 and 2014 (10 years).

As the result of the process of searching, 23 papers were classified as relevant in the context of aforementioned investigations. When analyzing these papers, we directed our attention specifically on information about used capability definitions and types, research methods and capability frameworks. It is recalled that both the selection of relevant resources and the method of analysis [7] have an influence on the results found. Furthermore, we are aware that this kind of review procedure comes along with limitations. For instance, the literature review was conducted based on 3 conferences and 4 journals that published a high amount of data on a regular basis in the defined period of time. Number of the relevant papers should rise when taking other journals, conferences and books into account.

Table 2. Resources of the systematic literature analysis

Publication source	Search results	Relevant after proving	Share
European Conference on Information Systems (ECIS)	24	13	54,2 %
Enterprise Computing Conference (EDOC)	28	3	10,7 %
International Conference on Advanced Information Systems Engineering (CAiSE)	15	1	6,7 %
Journal on Information Systems	25	1	4 %
Journal on Software and Systems Modeling	19	1	5, 3 %
Journal of Management	13	3	23,1 %
Strategic Management Journal	65	3	4,6 %
Total	189	23	12,2 %

However, 14 of 23 publications, i.e. more than half of the search results, featured case studies as preferred method of analysis. Second most frequent research method was an argumentative-deductive analysis used by six authors. In addition, two papers contained a literature review.

Besides the research methodology, different concepts of capabilities were investigated. As "Dynamic Capabilities" appeared in 9 of 23 publications, it has been the most frequently applied concept. However, universal "Business Capabilities" as well as these capabilities restricting themselves to information technologies of an enterprise (IT Capabilities) are approached in eight and seven papers, respectively. In addition to aforementioned concepts, two publications addressed so called "Core Capabilities" (either core or basic) of an enterprise. Residual concepts represent a specific object of research as they simply appear in individual papers. Respective concepts focus on the lifecycle of capabilities (1), capabilities in the context of BPM (Business Process Management), innovation (1) capabilities as well as strategic capabilities (1).

In addition to specified capability concepts, both scientific and industrial approaches were examined in order to assess their value of support for the process of developing and evaluating capabilities. Consequently, a distinction is made between methods of *assessment* and *development*. Tools that are applied to map those capabilities being already available in enterprises onto either interval or ordinal scale fall within the scope of assessment. Such an evaluation is proceeded for instance in the form of specific questionnaires or expert interviews. In contrast, methods of development support the identification as well as progression of existing capabilities. Within the 23 examined papers, nine approaches that addressed the introduced subject were identified. In detail, seven publications occupied themselves with the *development of capabilities* whereas the other two dealt with *methods of assessment*.

Three [11–13] out of the seven papers that covered the development of capabilities refer to a framework of Teece and Pisano [25] (Dynamic Capabilities) from 1998 of which the foundations were already released in 1990 by Pisano and Shuen [26, p. 3]. Respective conceptual framework is applied to develop Dynamic Capabilities which relate to unique elements of an enterprise [11, p. 3], [12, p. 4]. Sun and Chen [13] adapts of a phase-based model of Montealegre from 2002 (Capability Development

Process Model) in order to focus on the determination of important resources and capabilities in SME.

A more generic approach is pursued by the framework of [14] as a general pattern and possible way of proceeding for developing capabilities is introduced. While the framework is formulated in a very general manner, an implementation of all forms of capabilities inside an enterprise is possible [14, p. 4]. In consequence of the universal applicability, an approximate outline instead of a detailed development is provided. The two stages of respective framework is briefly introduced hereafter [14, p. 5–7]:

- The *Development Stage*: This stage begins after a team is both organized and assigned to a capability being developed. The development is supported by the search of achievable alternatives as well as the accumulation of team experience.
- The *Maturity Stage*: The maintenance of a certain capability is performed within this stage involving measures such as revising a capability in order to keep it in the memory of an enterprise. Repeating these measures helps to embed a capability within internal structures.

In contrast, the "CPX Capability Framework" introduced in [15] supplies more details. This framework pursues a new and innovative approach applied to combine the domains of "Dynamics", "Systems", "Cognition", and "Holism" having a focus on knowledge-based SME. "Dynamics" relate to both the market an enterprise appears on and capacities required to be responsive to shifts on the market. "Systems" depict relationships between resources and stakeholders of a company. "Cognition" is the responsibility of managers to effectively organize corporate processes. "Holism" represents the gained knowledge about these stakeholders contributing resources to valued-added processes [15, p. 4].

Hereinafter, the papers related to *Capability Assessment* are explained in detail. The two identified papers gathered data with the aid of case studies in order to provide results in the context of capability assessment. Even though the results are presented, a description of the evaluation was absent. International case studies are used in [16] for the purpose of investigating relationships between the different strategy types of the so called "*Miles and Snow Strategic Frameworks*", strategic capabilities, environmental factors and the success of an enterprise.

However, derived from the introduced analyses, it appears that terms of capabilities, business functions and processes are applied as synonyms. Consequently, several criteria that help to clarify the differences between these terms are identified and illustrated in Table 3.

4 Elements of an EAM Capability

Based on the findings from the literature analysis presented in Sect. 3, this section develops a conceptualization for EA capabilities, i.e. identifies the descriptive elements of a capability and their relationships. Based on the review similarities of definitions, capability elements and theoretical principles were identified. Furthermore, already available frameworks and assessment methods, which are being used to identify and refine capabilities, were investigated.

Table 3. Classification: capability, eusiness function and process

	Capability	Function	Process
Decomposition	Business by strategic goals	Business by tasks/objectives	Business by activities
Extension	Enterprise wide	Unit specific	Task specific
Solidity	Enduring and stable		Change frequently
Purpose	What		How
Focus	Strategically	Tactically	Operatively
Layer	Business execution		
Modelling approaches	e.g. Figures, Text, Archimate 2.0	e.g. 4EM, Archimate 2.0	e.g. BPMN, EPC etc.

Different types of capabilities are explained, concepts applied in the identified papers are observed and corresponding approaches are outlined. A detailed analysis of the relevant papers including their subject and concepts was created, but is not presented in the context of this paper due to space limitations. The investigated papers revealed four types of capabilities that partially feature a certain subtype (Fig. 1).

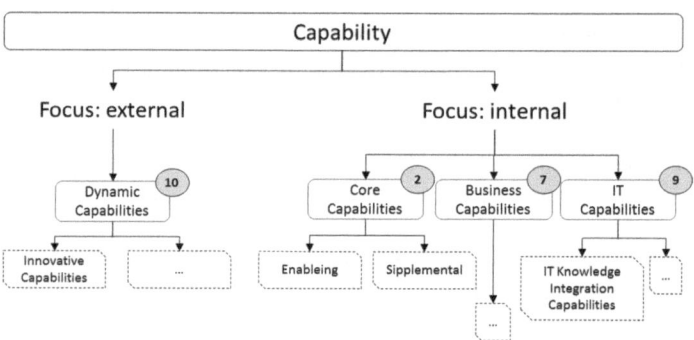

Fig. 1. Differentiation of capability subtypes

A separation of the focus areas was made in consequence of individual characteristics these capability types acquired. Instead of being dependent on specific definitions, the characteristics that are explained in detail below developed from similarities of investigated papers. The number in brackets is the number of papers a characteristic appears in:

- *Dynamic Capabilities (10):* These are the only capabilities focusing primarily on the business environment. In case an enterprise acquired dynamic capabilities, it has the ability to be responsive to alterations of enterprise environment by e.g. recombining resources. The identification of existing opportunities and potentials belongs to this type of capability as well. The Innovative Capability subtype refers to the development and supply of both new products and services [17–19].

- *IT Capabilities (9):* This is where the focus is on technical aspects. IT capabilities enable an enterprise to both internally and externally provide IT services. Moreover, an advanced output of different IT resources is obtained. The IT Knowledge Integration Capability represents a subtype that concatenates knowledge management and IT resources [20–22].
- *Business Capabilities (7):* These capabilities permit an enterprise to deploy resources specifically in activities to achieve certain goals. The focus is on superior business goals [14, 23].
- *Core Capabilities (2):* Core capabilities are described in general terms. They represent the execution of core competencies within a business process for the purpose of providing either products or services. In addition, Core Capabilities are supported by both Enabling (these capabilities that are necessary but not sufficient) and Supplemental (even though they create an added value, they are replaceable) capabilities [11].

The different types of capabilities are combinable, e.g. Dynamic and IT Capabilities. Correspondingly, the focus is on the IT supported adjustment to environmental alterations. For the purpose of creating an overview of similarities as well as differences the subject of "Capability" shares, identified papers were analyzed with regards to descriptive elements. Accordingly, it was examined whether the individual concepts are either a permanent feature of the definition (if provided) or simply get a mention in the context of "Capabilities". Subsequent figure illustrate the frequency of identified elements (Fig. 2).

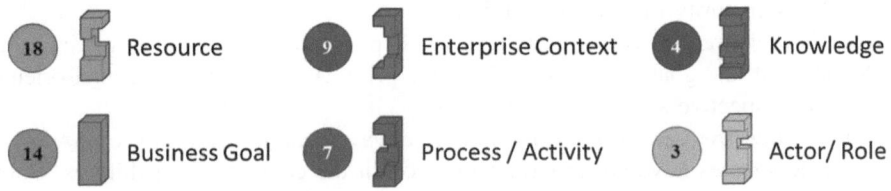

Fig. 2. Found descriptive elements of analyzed capability types

The characterization of descriptive elements presented below is essentially based on the authors' perception of the papers' intentions as most papers do not provide an explicit definition or exact explanation. Nevertheless, an overview arises as a result that is helpful to understand the later introduced Integrated Capability Approach:

- *Resource (18):* Aggregates all material and immaterial goods of an enterprise.
- *Business Goal (15):* As an enterprise represents a goal-oriented system, every capability is attended to a certain business goal from a logical perspective. It was examined whether a reference was made to the goal concept (e.g. competitive advantages, satisfying customer wishes, provide services).
- *Enterprise Context (9):* The enterprise context is an issue in the context of Dynamic capabilities as their focus is on dynamic enterprise environments.

- *Process (7):* Represents a sequence of activities in order to achieve a certain objective.
- *Knowledge (4):* Even though Knowledge might be classified as immaterial resource, there exist a distinct concept due to its multiple references.
- *Actor/Role (4):* Capabilities are assigned to a certain actor. Though, an actor does not only imply a single person but rather an organizational unit that is defined by its roles and corresponding responsibility, authority to decide and financial capital.

Subsequent to the investigation of descriptive elements, different perspectives or attitudes of the paper authors in regard to the capability concept were observed. In consideration of the analyzed literature, the following list presents capability characteristics that were identified during literature work and explicitly supported by at least one of the papers:

- *Core Capabilities lead to competitive advantages* [11, p. 4]: Capabilities do not per se give lead to competitive advantages but only if capabilities are successfully implemented within the organization in order to provide an increase in value.
- *Capabilities have to be difficult to imitate* [11, p. 2]: Enterprise might have general as well as special abilities whereas the latter should be hard to imitate.
- *A capability represents a process that uses resources* [17, p. 3]: According to obtained experience, a capability is not a process as it represents a sequence of individual activities. Instead, a capability specifies a general framework for the activities being performed.
- *The result a capability yields is sufficient* [20, p. 9]: A capability neither considers items of input nor output. Accordingly, these are not comparable with each other in the context of satisfaction. In order to evaluate the quality of a capability, e.g. capability maturity models are applied.
- *Capabilities are adjusted to user needs* [11, p. 3]: Satisfying a user's need corresponds with the goal orientation of an enterprise. As capabilities are goal-oriented as well, respective statement is supported.
- *Capabilities are used for coordination of activities and utilization of resources* [20, p. 3]: Resources have an important function in the context of capabilities. Correspondingly, both the utilization of resources and the combination with activities represent an essential feature of capabilities.
- *A capability is the ability of a structural unit to use a resource in order to achieve a certain goal* [27, p. 2]: The aspect of the ability has priority in this context as it indicates that a capability has to be initiated by a human instead of being proceeded automatically.

According to the definition, recourse to the six aforementioned descriptive concepts was made. The concept of "Knowledge" was aggregated with the concept of "Information" in order to create a more universally valid statement. Furthermore, the "Business Goal" was converted into "Strategic Goal" for the same reason. The concept of "Enterprise Context", characterizing the environment of an enterprise, is an inherent part of the definition for the purpose of seizing a relationship to Dynamic Capabilities. As a consequence of the fact that only three of the investigated papers had a business unit featuring a capability and considering that the remaining papers define capabilities from an enterprise's point of view, the concept of "Actors" did not have an influence on the definition on the first thoughts. Still, the investigation of the EAM sector [3] reveals that the allocation of functional and financial responsibilities is an inherent part of the organizational development/alteration. Consequently, the respective element, whose influence is recognizable in the terms of "join resources" or "ability", was integrated in the definition as well. The essential point of the definition is the combination of resources and information as this progress is iterated on the execution of every capability. Depending on the current conditions as well as circumstances of an enterprise, there could emerge similar capabilities from different kind of combinations. Moreover, these processes a combination is inserted into might alter in the course of time as well. Nevertheless, a capability remains in a stable and steady condition.

The definition below is predicated upon the identified concepts as well as the presented projects. The aim is to provide a general definition that copes with the requirements of projects:

> **Capability**: *Represents the ability of an enterprise to join information and roles able to execute a specific activity with available resources in order to support strategy goals under consideration of its context.*

Consequently, a capability generally describes the ability to combine information relating to a specific context like architecture objects and management functions for e.g. an *EAM Capability* or business objects and management functions for a *Business Capability*. The context elements merged with a combination of information relating to e.g. information about architecture models or standards, roles with corresponding competences to create a specific outcome that should be applicable in an activity, task or process with appropriate available resources such as technologies, HR, Budget, Personnel will form our artefact for validation: an *EAM Capability* (Fig. 3).

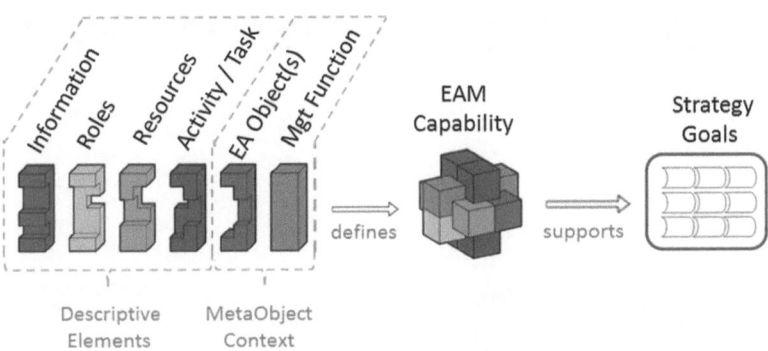

Fig. 3. Elements of an EAM capability (Colored cube image is provided by Corso Ltd.) (Colour figure online)

5 Validation

As the conceptualization presented in Sect. 4 is based on scientific literature only, we decided to validate suitability for practical application and soundness of the approach using a two-step procedure. In a first step (Sect. 5.1) we applied the conceptualization within the EACN project (see Sect. 2); the second step was a survey among EAM experts (Sect. 5.2).

5.1 Application in the EACN Project

As a first validation step, we put the conceptualization to a kind of feasibility test by describing a concrete capability from the EACN project with the elements of an EAM capability identified in Sect. 4. The EAM capability selected for this feasibility test is *"Impact Analysis IS Architecture"*. Its elements are illustrated in Fig. 4 and will be introduced in the following. The selected EAM capability assumes a formulated enterprise specific IS strategy that aims to ensure the "implementation of high-quality data management" processes in order to guarantee information supply within the IS department (layer: strategy). To implement this strategic objective different initiatives have to be started within strategy implementation plan (layer: initiatives). From these initiatives, we select *"Implement a central IS Architecture Inventory"* for our example. Key goal of this initiative is the establishment of a practice to sustain a reliable documentation of the enterprise architecture by focusing on identifying the data stewards and data requirements stored in a central inventory. Based on this goal and the fact that the required inventory did not exist needed EAM capabilities were derived. One of these capabilities is reflected in our selected example: *Impact Analysis IS Architecture* (layer: capabilities). The Impact Analysis IS Architecture capability is characterized by the ability to analyze the impact of change needs/business requirements against the current state IS architecture under consideration. In order to satisfy

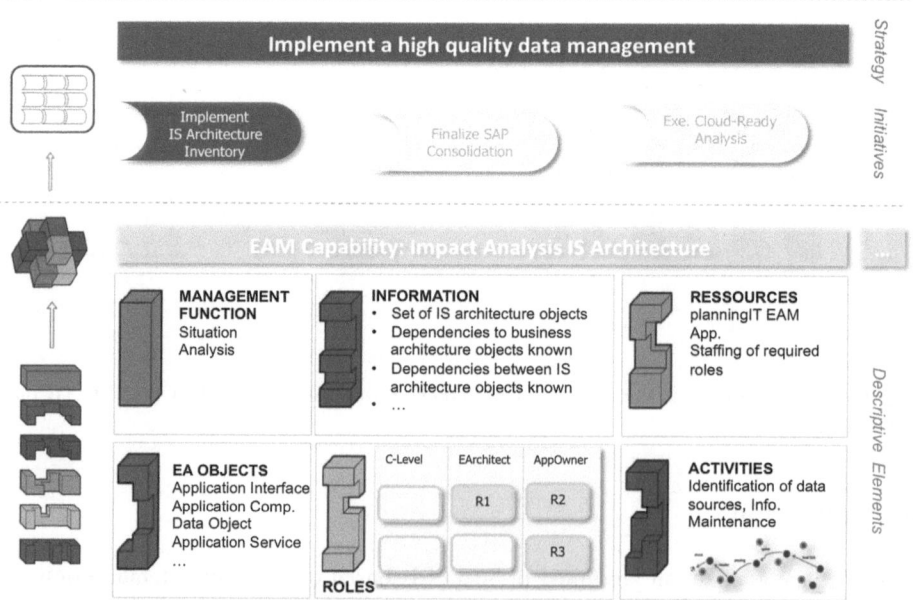

Fig. 4. Example of an EAM capability: impact analysis IS architecture

the information demand of this capability, information like: set of IS architecture objects, dependencies between IS architecture objects, technology architecture objects, etc. should be provided by existing source (layer: descriptive elements, red element: information). The green and purple objects represent the two meta-object dimensions (management functions, EA objects) and shows how the example EAM capability arises from. The management functions *situation analysis* represents a sub- function of the defined planning phase, the EA objects are components of *alfabet's EA meta-model*. The activity/process (*identification of data sources, information maintenance process*) element combined with the turquoise role element including the roles *enterprise architect* and *application owner* and the yellow resource (e.g. *EAM software planningIT*) represent necessary components of our EAM capability example.

5.2   Expert Survey

The second validation step aimed at evaluating soundness and completeness of the conceptualization from the perspective of experts in the field of EAM. For this purpose we performed a survey among experts and practitioners from the field of EAM. We performed two separate survey sessions and analyzed the results using quantitative survey analysis [24]. The first survey took place at the beginning of November 2013. In context of a master class[3] with academic practitioners at the 6th IFIP WG 8.1 Working conference on the Practices of Enterprise Modeling (PoEM2013) in Riga, Latvia we evaluated the EAM capability conceptualization and parts of the EAM capability type. Before elaborating on the result some design parameters of the first survey. Basic population n = 11, 7 participants answered, that they are well familiar with EAM (intermediary level of expertise) whereas 4 were just beginners in the field. The capabilities experience level of the audience can be described as follows; 1 expert, 3 intermediates and 7 beginners. Due to the fact that the basic population is not very big, an interpretation according correlation of the different groups (expert, intermediate, beginner) will not be presented here. Table 4 shows the distribution of answers (in percentage of total) for all three groups concerning the question *"In your opinion, which of the following aspects are needed to describe an EAM capability?"*

The second survey session was executed in cooperation with alfabet AG in Boston, US, at the end of November 2013. We evaluated EAM capability conceptualization as well usability and feasibility of the capability management process (CMP). Basic population n = 15, 12 participants answered, that they are EAM experts as well as 3 are intermediate. The capabilities experience level of the audience can be described with 12 experts, 2 intermediates and 1 beginner. The fact that the basic population is not very big, an interpretation according correlation of the different groups (expert, intermediate, beginner) will not be presented here. Table 5 shows the distribution of answers (in percentage of total) for all three groups concerning the question *"In your opinion, which of the following aspects are needed to describe an EAM capability?"*

---

[3] http://poem2013.rtu.lv/invited-talks, accessed 13.05.2014.

Table 4. Academic audience: POEM 11/2013 survey

Capability elements	Answers	n	Frequency	
Information	9	11	81 %	Descriptive elements
Roles	8	11	72 %	
Resources	8	11	72 %	
Process	9	11	81 %	
EA object	8	11	72 %	EAM context elements
Mgt function	7	11	63 %	

Table 5. Industrial audience: alfabet Boston 11/2013 survey

Capability elements	Answers	n	Frequency	
Information	13	15	86 %	Descriptive elements
Roles	12	15	80 %	
Resources	14	15	93 %	
Process	10	15	66 %	
EA object	13	15	86 %	EAM context elements
Mgt function	12	15	80 %	

All in all, 84 % of 26 respondents think that information and resources are needed to describe an capability. 76 % and 73 % answered that roles and a process should be included. For the specific EAM capability type, the context should be described by EA objects and management functions for 80 % and 73 % of the respondent.

6 Summary and Outlook

Motivated by experiences from two industrial EAM projects this paper investigated elements and characteristics of EAM capabilities. A systematic literature analysis was used to identify scientific literature addressing EAM capabilities. By analyzing the identified publications, descriptive elements, EAM capability types and characteristics of EAM capabilities were identified. These analysis results formed the basis for a conceptualization of EAM capabilities, which identified information, role, resource, EA object, and management function as elements of an EA capability. This conceptualization is validated by an empirical study in form of a quantitative survey analysis with academic and industrial respondents.

One of the biggest limitations of our work is the small number of participants in the quantitative survey analysis sessions. Although we performed two such sessions, the current validation is based on a quite small group, which needs extension. As part of the future work, we plan additional validation activities. Another survey is planned to be executed within The Open Group and its capability project *EA Capability Improvement Project*. The project members already were provided with corresponding information (*Academic and Industrial Audience*: The Open Group, planned mid 2014). In order to perform another validation cycle we run a qualitative survey analyses in form of five expert interviews within the EACN project. These interviews have been performed already and are currently in the transcribing- and evaluation phase.

Another part of the future work will be application of the conceptualization in practice. We plan a project of EAM capability modeling which captures selected capabilities of an enterprise using the developed conceptualization. Furthermore, the result of this work forms the basis for another investigation "*The Integrated Capability Approach*". Classification of capability types and its integration into process of strategy implementation represents the main goal of this investigation.

References

1. Gunasekaran, A.: Agile Manufacturing: The 21st Century Competitive Strategy: The 21st Century Competitive Strategy. Elsevier, Amsterdam (2001)
2. Niemi, E.: Enterprise architecture benefits: perceptions from literature and practice. Evaluation of enterprise and software architectures: critical issues, metrics and practices. University of Jyväskylä, IT Research Institute (2008). ISBN: 978-951-39-3108-7
3. Wißotzki, M., Sonnenberger, A.: Adoption of EAM in small and medium enterprises. Rostock University (2013). ISBN: 978-3-00-042608-7
4. Wißotzki, M., Koç, H., Weichert, T., Sandkuhl, K.: Development of an enterprise architecture management capability catalog. In: Kobyliński, A., Sobczak, A. (eds.) BIR 2013. LNBIP, vol. 158, pp. 112–126. Springer, Heidelberg (2013)
5. Stirna, J., Grabis, J., Henkel, M., Zdravkovic, J.: Capability driven development – an approach to support evolving organizations. In: Sandkuhl, K., Seigerroth, U., Stirna, J. (eds.) PoEM 2012. LNBIP, vol. 134, pp. 117–131. Springer, Heidelberg (2012)
6. Becker, J., Knackstedt, R., Pöppelbuß, J.: Developing maturity models for IT management. Bus. Inf. Syst. Eng. **1**(3), 213–222 (2009)
7. Kitchenham, B.A.: Guidelines for performing systematic literature reviews in software engineering. EBSE Technical report, University of Durham (2007)
8. Scott, J., Cullen, A., An, M.: Business capabilities provide the rosetta stone for business-IT alignment: capability maps are a foundation for BA (2009). www.forrester.com. Accessed 08 Apr 2015
9. The Open Group. TOGAF® Version 9.1 (2014). http://pubs.opengroup.org/architecture/togaf9-doc/arch/chap32.html. Accessed 08 Apr 2015
10. Vincent, L.: Differentiating competence, capability and capacity. In: Innovating Perspectives 16, Nr. 3. June 2008
11. Butler, T., Murphy, C.: Unpacking Dynamic Capabilities in the Small- to-Medium Software Enterprise: Process, Assets, and History. University College Cork, Ireland (2013)
12. Butler, T., Murphy, C.: Integrating Dynamic Capability and Commitment Theory for Research on IT Capabilities and Resources. University College Cork, Ireland (2005)
13. Sun, C.M., Chen, R.S.: A study on the strategic alignment process with information technology for new ventures from a dynamic capability perspective. National Chiao Tung University, National Yulin University of Science and Technology, Taiwan (2006)
14. Helflat, C.E., Peteraf, M.A.: The dynamic resource-based view: capability lifecycles. Strateg. Manag. J. **24**(10), 997–1010 (2003)
15. Duhan, S., Levy, M., Powell, P.: IS Strategy in SMEs Using Organizational Capabilities: the CPX Framework. Oxford Brookes University, Oxford (2005)

16. Desarbo, W.S., Di Benedetto, C.A., Song, M., Sinha, I.: Song; Revisiting the Miles and Snow Strategic Framework Uncovering Interrelationships Between Strategic Types, Capabilities, Environmental Uncertainty, and 28 Firm Performance. University of Washington (2005)
17. Vitari, C.: Sources of IT dynamic capability in the context of data genesis capability, Italy (2009)
18. Barreto, I.: Dynamic Capabilities: A Review of Past Research and an Agenda for the Future. Universidade Católica Portuguesa, Lisboa (2010)
19. Teoh, S.Y., Shun, C.: Innovative Capability Development Process: a Singapore IT Healthcare Case Study. RMIT University, National University of Singapore, Australia, Singapore (2009)
20. Hecht, S., Wittges, H., Krcmar, H.: IT Capabilities in ERP Maintenance - a Review of the ERP Post-Implementation Literature. Technische Universität München, München (2011)
21. Tarafdar, M., Gordon, S.R.: How Information Technology Capabilities Influence Organizational Innovation: Exploratory Findings from Two Case Studies. University of Toledo, Babson Park (2005)
22. Basaglia, S., Caporarello, L., Magni, M.: The mediating role of IT knowledge integration capability in the relationship between team performance and team climate, Italy (2009)
23. Iacob, M.E., Meertens, L.O., Jonkers, H., Quartel, D.A.C., Nieuwenhuis, L.J.M., van Sinderen, M.J.: From enterprise architecture to business models and back. University of Twente, Bizzdesign, Netherland (2012)
24. Teece, D.J., Pisano, G., Shuen, A.: Dynamic capabilities and strategic management. Strateg. Manag. J. **18**(7), 509–533 (1997)
25. Teece, D.J., Pisano, G.P., Shuen, A.: Firm capabilities, resources, and the concept of strategy: four paradigms of strategic management. University of California at Berkeley, Center for Research in Management, Consortium on Competitiveness and Cooperation (1990)
26. Duhan, S., Levy, M., Powell, P.: IS Strategy in SMEs Using Organizational Capabilities: the CPX Framework. Oxford Brookes University, University of Warwick, Centre for Information Management, UK (2005)
27. Azevedo, C.L.B., et al.: An ontology-based well-founded proposal for modeling re-sources and capabilities in ArchiMate. In: 2013 17th IEEE International Enterprise Distributed Object Computing Conference (EDOC), IEEE (2013)

Governing IT Services for Quantifying Business Impact

Oscar González Rojas[✉]

Systems and Computing Engineering Department, School of Engineering,
Universidad de Los Andes, Bogotá, Colombia
o-gonza1@uniandes.edu.co

Abstract. This paper presents a method that comprises a metamodel and two processes created for quantifying the business impact associated with the behaviour of IT services. These artifacts define impact analysis models for evaluating the risks, service agreements, quality attributes and criticality associated with IT services. The defined models are integrated with traditional enterprise models to assess how an IT service affectation impacts the business in terms of its objectives, its performance indicators, and financial issues generating costs, penalties or the loss of income due to non-provision of business services. Once IT critical services are identified and governed, strategies can be defined to prevent IT service affectations in order to improve IT-business interoperability.

Keywords: IT-business interoperability · Impact analysis models · IT services · Enterprise modeling · Quantification processes · Risk analysis

1 Introduction

Current business environments are highly dependent on Information Technology (IT) thus making Business-IT alignment a major concern among IT managers and researchers [1]. This alignment must be properly governed to improve the reliability and predictability of the performance of IT services in order to understand the current and potential business impact [2]. The aforementioned issue poses critical questions that are currently not easily answered by organizations: Is the organization able to operate properly with its current IT services?, Which IT services are critical to the organization?, What is the risk level of its IT services?, What would be the impact on the organization if an IT service suffers an affectation?. Therefore, modeling and understanding the impact of the dependencies between business and IT services lead to quantifying the delivery of business value.

In order to improve IT governance, multiple strategies [3,4] have emerged to quantify the impact of IT on business value by analyzing organizational impact variables or by modeling the events that could lead to a service failure. Other strategies [5–7] have incorporated Business-driven IT Management (BDIM) to optimize IT management processes. These strategies aim to guide IT so that

© Springer International Publishing Switzerland 2015
R. Matulevičius and M. Dumas (Eds.): BIR 2015, LNBIP 229, pp. 97–112, 2015.
DOI: 10.1007/978-3-319-21915-8_7

it is driven by the needs and expectations of the business. Nonetheless, most of these approaches do not define, simply and explicitly, the processes and the information that must be considered to interrelate the existing business and IT elements, nor a method for prioritization and decision making in regard to the selection of IT services. Moreover, the quantification of business impacts does not consider the analysis of critical models such as oversizing costs, service quality attributes, penalties on service agreements, and risks.

A method that comprises a metamodel and two processes is proposed in order to address the above problems. The metamodel characterizes and relates specific models that allow the specification of value metadata associated with the IT-business dependencies. A criticality model is used to evaluate the relevance of the business architecture elements and of the IT services architecture elements. Models for risks, quality attributes, and agreements are used to quantify the dependencies related to IT services. The quantification of dependencies with value metadata allows showing how an affectation in an IT service impacts the business in terms of financial issues arising from the materialization of risks, service agreements, or the loss of income due to non-provision of business services. The defined processes guide the modeling of IT-business dependencies and value metadata, as well as the quantification of their impact.

The paper is structured as follows. Section 2 summarizes an experiment performed to identify the need for the IT-business quantification approach that was created. Section 3 gives a brief overview of the general approach and terminology used by the author. It also shows the proposed metamodel and how IT-business dependencies are quantified. Section 4 shows the results of one of the four case studies for which the proposed method was used to quantify IT-business dependencies. Section 5 introduces multiple approaches for quantifying IT-business dependencies in order to position the research presented in this work. Lastly, conclusions and future work are presented in Sect. 6.

2   Open Issues for Quantifying IT-Business Dependencies

An experiment of identification and validation of the models and practices described by the BDIM [5] was performed to evaluate two aspects: (1) the complexity to establish dependencies between the IT solutions and business performance of an organization, and (2) the business impact of IT solutions for the optimal selection of a service portfolio. The Audiovisual Production IT Area from a Latin American University was used as a case study. This area was selected because its processes support most of the enterprise's core processes and also due to the availability of its IT service measures.

First, a survey was created to evaluate the importance of the ten IT services provided by this area (*cf.* BDIM practice [5]). A process leader of this IT area performed the assessment with regard to nine specific criteria: quality, cost, revenue generation capacity, reliance on staff, level of affectation by incidents, installed capacity, dependence on external factors, interaction with the customer, and time to perform specific tests. Each of the evaluation criteria was assigned a weight of 1 (low) to 10 (high) in order to determine the importance of the IT service. Second, the cost and loss models [6] associated with the prioritized IT services were analyzed. The cost model was defined by the interrelations among the components of each service. The loss model considered the income lost due to the unavailability of human resources caused by excessive requests in relation to the available capacity.

After applying BDIM to the case study, it was possible to establish which services were the most representative services regarding their contribution to the business impact (incomes and losses). Two open issues were found in this experiment as well as in related work (*cf.* Sect. 5).

Lack of Impact Analysis Models for Quantifying Dependencies. It was identified that the dependence between IT and business processes is highlighted from three points of view: the cost to the business, the losses caused by non-compliance to agreements, and the net revenue after minimizing losses and costs. Nevertheless, the following impact analysis models remain unconsidered: (a) impact upon the materialization of IT service risks, (b) oversizing costs, and (c) incidence of service quality attributes. It is then necessary to model and quantify these critical elements on IT-business dependencies so as to complement the business impact analysis when there is a change in an IT service. Moreover, alignment approaches do not define measures that relate IT behavior with the effects it has on different architectures: business motivation, business processes, and IT services. Therefore, the need arises to define specific analysis variables to be added on business-business dependencies, IT-IT dependencies, and IT-business dependencies.

Lack of Specific Processes and Procedures. Although it was possible to identify the dependencies between IT elements and business elements, the way to find these dependencies does not lead to a methodical and orderly approach but to an ad-hoc approach. It then becomes necessary to identify the elements that must be defined in the establishment of these dependencies. Specifically, how to follow the path from a business goal to an IT service and vice versa, as well as how to identify their level of importance along the way. Furthermore, a method for prioritization and decision making in regard to the selection of IT services under a criticality perspective (*e.g.,* contribution to IT and business elements) was not identified.

Based on the information presented above, a method for quantifying the impact of the dependencies between business elements and IT services was developed. The main features of this method are presented in the following section.

3   IT-Business Impact Quantification Method

The proposed method defines a metamodel as well as two different processes to model and quantify IT-business dependencies (Fig. 1 illustrates the general approach).

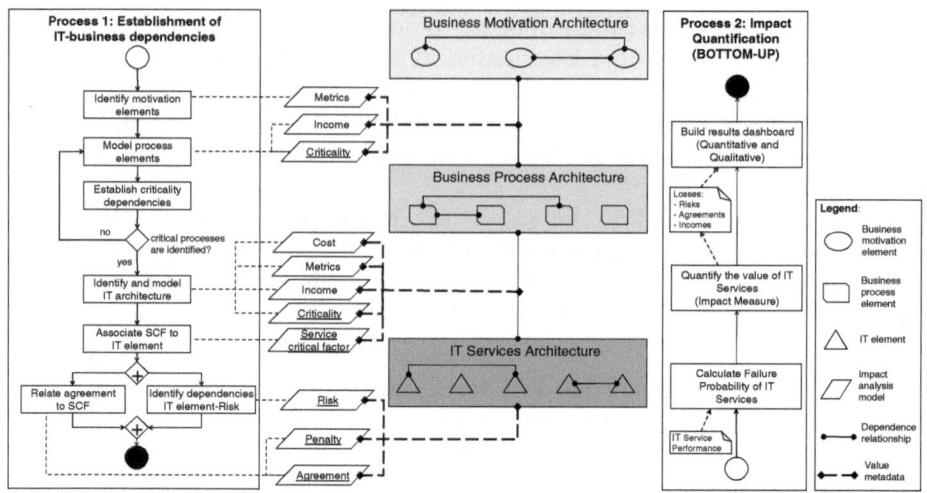

Fig. 1. Processes and impact analysis models to quantify IT-business dependencies

First, the metamodel represents impact analysis models on critical dependencies within the business architecture, within the IT services architecture, and between business and IT architectures. An architecture is defined as "the fundamental organization of a system embodied in its components, their relationships to each other, and to the environment" [8]. A business architecture involves the elements of a *Business Motivation Architecture (BMA)* (*e.g.*, goals, metrics, strategies) and of a *Business Process Architecture (BPA)* (*e.g.*, value chain activities, process specifications, tasks). An *IT services architecture* covers elements such as IT services, software components, data structures, etc. The elements and dependencies to be modeled in the BMA (first activity), BPA (second activity), and IT services architecture (fourth activity) are inspired by the alignment architecture defined by Aier et al. [9].

Second, the *configuration process* allows an architect to identify and model the IT-business dependencies and their related value metadata (TOP-DOWN approach). The proposed method defines value metadata as the analysis data (*i.e.*, cost, income, metric, risk, agreement, criticallity, quality attribute) added to particular architecture elements and to the dependencies defined among inter-architecture elements. Impact analysis metadata can be propagated and analyzed through the traceability of intra-architecture dependencies. Third, the *quantification process* allows IT-business managers to define the actual or expected values on Service Critical Factors (SCF) (*i.e.*, performance, availability, capacity, reliability) for each IT service. The latter process uses an algorithm to navigate the IT-business dependencies in order to quantify the impact (*i.e.*, losses) that IT services have on the business and which architecture elements are affected due to an IT service affectation (BOTTOM-UP approach). These three artifacts are detailed in the following subsections.

3.1   Proposed Metamodel

Figure 2 illustrates a simplified view of the metamodel that was created to model and quantify IT-business dependencies. This metamodel was described by using the Eclipse Modeling Framework (EMF) meta model (Ecore) due to its facilities for modeling and for generating code based on a structured data model. An instance of the metamodel (a model specification) was created to represent all IT-business dependencies for the case study presented in Sect. 4.1.

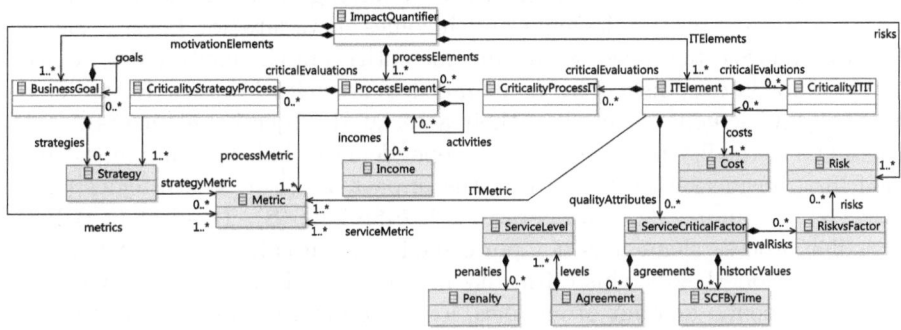

Fig. 2. Metamodel to configure and quantify IT-business dependencies

Impact analysis models such as criticality, risks, service agreements, and service critical factors are one of the main contributions. The three criticality entities enable many to many dependencies among IT and business elements. Costs, revenues, metrics, and losses impact analysis models are adopted from literature review [5,6]. The need to select critical services driven by the business elements (goals, processes) is adopted from literature review [10]. The value metadata of each of the proposed impact analysis models is described within the activities of the following processes.

3.2   Configuration Process: Creation of IT-Business Dependencies

The procedures of the activities involved in the configuration process are described below (*cf.* Process 1 in Fig. 1).

Identify the BMA. The first activity is to model the business elements supporting the value proposition of the organization by using inputs such as the strategic business plan, the business motivation model, and the balance score cards. The business motivation architecture includes elements such as competitive factors (*e.g.,* quality, access), their relationships with the business goals, the strategies defined to accomplish those goals, and the metrics to evaluate their performance (*cf.* BusinessGoal, Strategy, Metric entities in the metamodel). Value metadata is assigned to these elements to allow the quantification of dependencies: a relevance percentage is assigned to each competitive factor, the expected income is assigned to business objectives, and target performance objectives are assigned to the strategies. For example, a 5 % increase on sales represents a percentage on the revenues for the business. The output of this activity corresponds to the monetized strategic map of the organization.

Identify Criticality Dependencies in the BPA. The second activity is to model the BPA at different decomposition levels: Level0- Value Chain activities, Level1- Macro-processes, Level2-Process Groups, Level3- Business Processes, and Level4- Activities (sub-processes and tasks) (*cf.* ProcessElement in the metamodel). This BPA is built incrementally by adding value metadata: criticality metadata up to Level 2 elements and incomes metadata for Level 3 elements (*cf.* CriticalityStrategyProcess and Income entities in the metamodel). Criticality metadata is established by modeling dependencies between BPA elements and Strategy elements (including their associated Objective elements), and by assigning a criticality measure to these dependencies. This measure must be provided by a business expert based on the impact on business strategies (*i.e.*, 1-None (N), 2-Minor (M), 4-Moderate (O), 6-Serious (S), 10-Vital (V)) if that particular process element is not performed (*cf.* criticality on project management [11]). Nonetheless, this criticality measure could be associated with other concrete elements: amount of incomes, losses volume, number of affected users, business processes it supports, impacted business units, supported clients, impact on business indicators, and volume of transactions, among others.

Figure 3 illustrates how this criticality measure must be evaluated iteratively up to Level 2 of the BPA, but just for process elements that are classified by the model within a critical prioritization area. A process element is located within a prioritization area after calculating the criticality average between all its related strategy dependencies. The metamodel instance uses the following prioritization areas: Critical for averages higher than six, Important for averages between four and six, and Low for averages lower than four. Each organization can adjust these prioritization areas by considering its own availability of resources (*cf.* criticality margins [12]), and by evaluating not just the impact of the process element on motivation elements but also the execution frequency of processes (*cf.* risks assessment [13]). The output of this activity is the set of prioritized business processes for which the impact of the related IT services must be analyzed.

Identify Criticality Dependencies in the IT Services Architecture. The third activity is to model the IT services supporting the prioritized business processes and activities. This architecture must be specified at different decomposition levels (*cf.* ITElement in the metamodel): Level 1 − IT services (*e.g.*, enrollment management), Level 2 − IT systems (*e.g.*, authentication system), and Level 3 − IT components (*e.g.*, balancing cluster). Costs metadata associated with different concepts (*e.g.*, infrastructure, licensing, configuration) is assigned to Level 3 IT elements (*cf.* Cost in the metamodel). Criticality metadata is assigned to the dependencies between Level 1 IT elements and Level 3 process elements (*cf.* CriticalityProcessIT in the metamodel). This metadata allows identifying the potential points of failure on IT services that can impact

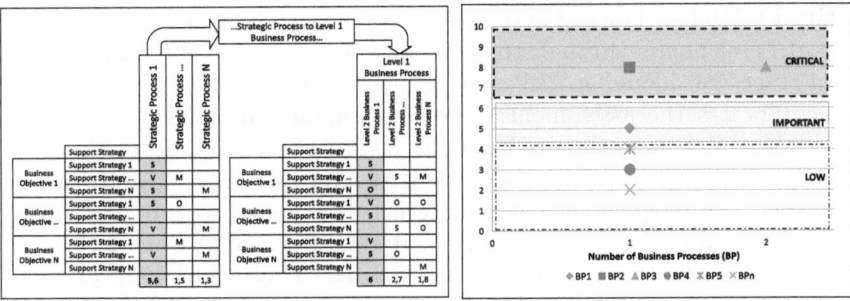

Fig. 3. Iterative prioritization of process elements based on dependencies criticality

the critical process elements. Criticality metadata is also assigned between Level 2 and Level 1 IT elements (*cf.* CriticalityITIT in the metamodel) by using the same scale and prioritization areas used for process elements. It is worth noting that the criticality-related entities are the main points of dependency and analysis between the different architectures (motivation, processes, IT). The output of this activity comprises the critical and monetized IT elements to be analyzed in terms of quality attributes, risks, and service agreements.

Associate SCF to IT Elements. The fourth activity is to model SCF metadata associated with the prioritized Level2 IT elements. A SCF represents a quality attribute (*i.e.,* capacity, availability, performance, reliability) in terms of three characteristics: minimum value, maximum value, and actual value (*cf.* ServiceCriticalFactor in the metamodel). Capacity refers to the percentage of transactions that can be processed by the IT element. Availability refers to the percentage of time that an IT element is working. Performance refers to the average response time of all operations using an IT element. Integrity refers to the probability of wrong transactions or a system failure. The actual value of a SCF is valuated by IT managers according to the behaviour of IT elements. These SCF were inspired when performing the experiment described in Sect. 2.

Relate Agreements. The fifth activity is to model the agreements metadata (service agreements, service levels, and penalties) associated with each SCF. A service agreement specifies the signing stakeholder (a customer, a business unit, a provider), the agreement type (*i.e.,* service-level (SLA), operational-level (OLA), underpinning contract (UC)), the service provider, and the service attendance time (*cf.* Agreement in the metamodel). Each agreement can be associated with multiple service levels which are specified by IT managers through a level type (*e.g.,* premium, standard), and with the lower and upper expected values to which the IT unit is committed (*cf.* ServiceLevel in the metamodel). A penalty must be associated with each service level by specifying the minimum and maximum percentage values that can be computed over services cost (*cf.* Penalty in the metamodel). When a service level is affected, the model takes the maximum computed penalty value as incomes (positive impact) for provider agreements, and as costs (negative impact) for client and inter-units agreements.

Identify IT Risks. The last activity is to model dependencies between business risks and IT elements through their SCF. This corresponds to the risk identification stage considered in risk management methods. The proposed method also incorporates the assessment stage by assigning the following value metadata to these dependencies: risk factor, its type (*i.e.,* operational, strategic, legal, reputational), the detection speed, the recovery speed, and the assessment value. The latter is specified in terms of impact (measured from 1-Very low to 5-Catastrophic), frequency of occurrence (measured from 1-Exceptional to 5-Frequent), and the cost if it is materialized. These values are provided by multiple business and IT experts.

3.3   Quantification Process: IT Services Behavior and Impact Results

This section presents the process that was defined to quantify the impact of IT services once the dependencies between the business and IT were identified, modeled, and rated. This configuration information is represented in a database that is generated from the ecore metamodel presented in Sect. 3.1. Most of the procedures associated with the three activities of the quantification process (*cf.* Process 2 in Fig. 1) were automated by implementing (a) an algorithm that calculates the value and the failure probability of IT Services, and (b) a web application in which the business and IT users quantitatively consult the business impact according to the actual or simulated performance of IT Services.

Calculate the Failure Probability of IT Services. A level 2 IT service must be selected within the web application in order to start the impact analysis. If the actual value of a SCF exceeds the predefined limits, the algorithm computes the failure probability as 1: the service is failing. If the actual value of the SCF is within the limits, historic SCF values (*cf.* SCFByTime in the metamodel) are used to perform an adjustment on the normal distribution to compute the mean value (μ) and the variance value (σ^2). Then, the quantification algorithm computes the failure probability (Fp) as the area under the curve within the normal distribution (the historic SCF behaviour) given by the difference between the probability of being in the range of the SCF limit value (l) defined at the service agreement and the probability of being in the range of the SCF actual value (a). The superior range of the integral (l or a) defines the limit for the independent variable (t), *i.e.,*

$$Fp = \int_{-\infty}^{l} \frac{1}{\sigma\sqrt{2\Pi}} e^{-\frac{1}{2}\left(\frac{t-\mu}{\sigma}\right)^2} dt - \int_{-\infty}^{a} \frac{1}{\sigma\sqrt{2\Pi}} e^{-\frac{1}{2}\left(\frac{t-\mu}{\sigma}\right)^2} dt. \tag{1}$$

Quantify the Value of IT Services. The quantification algorithm computes the monetary *value* of an IT service (ITSval) with the following formula:

$$ITSval = I + A + R + S. \tag{2}$$

- *I* represents the incomes expected from the IT services operation. These incomes are computed by summing the incomes metadata retrieved when querying the level3-processes associated with the selected IT service.
- *A* represents the maximum affectation on the incomes due to IT service degradation. An impact factor is computed for each process associated with the selected level2-service. This impact factor is the average of the monetary values of the strategies related to each process. For each prioritized level3-process associated to the selected IT service, a corresponding loss factor is computed by multiplying the weight of the services on the process, the failure probability, and the degradation factor for each SCF. A degradation factor (Df) is obtained as the relation between the SCF value estimated by the user (p) and the SCF actual value (a). For SCF such as integrity and performance, there can be a degradation on agreements if their values are closer to 1: $Df = (p-a)/a$. Values further away from 1 can denote a degradation for SCF such as availability and capacity: $Df = (a-p)/a$. The multiplication of the number of loss factors (n) with the costs metadata of the service components (k) is subtracted from the sum of all the loss factors obtained per process (m) in order to obtain the incomes affectation: $A = m - (n * k)$.
- *R* represents the costs of IT risks materialization. All SCF associated with the selected level2-service are queried so as to navigate to the risks related to them (*cf.* RiskvsFactor in the metamodel). The impact attribute of each IT risk and the impact magnitude of the SCF are multiplied to identify and prioritize the critical risks (over a predefined value). The cost metadata associated with all the prioritized risks is summed.
- *S* represents the costs of incomes for agreement violations. All agreements related to the SCF of the selected level2-service are queried in order to obtain their service levels. There is degradation when actual values on SCF differ from the target values defined on service levels. The maximum penalty value associated to the service levels is multiplied by the maximum affectation value on the incomes (A).

A and *R* represent negative magnitudes, whereas *S* can have a positive magnitude for UC agreements as well as a negative magnitude for SLA and OLA.

Build Results Dashboard The actual operation level for each identified SCF is established (*e.g.*, availability of 99,99 %) by the expert technical staff through the web application. This value is compared with the SCF levels that had been previously configured (*e.g.*, availability of 99,9 %) in order to compute the failure probability and degradation factor. Once the previous operation scenario has been established, a simulation scenario ("What If") must be presented by indicating the expected level for each SCF (*e.g.*, availability of 95 %). This value may correspond to a simulated or a real scenario depending on whether it is based on a forecast or if it responds to the measurement of the actual behavior of the IT service. Once these values are provided, the web application shows the income losses due to the degradation or absence of an IT service, losses due to risks materialization, and losses due to agreements violations. The web application also shows the impacted business goals, the affected metrics, the affected business processes, the risks that must be taken into account, and breached service level agreements. The use of the web application is illustrated in Sect. 4.2.

4 Impact Quantification Results: A Case Study

A Latin American University was used as a case study to evaluate the design of the proposed method by quantifying its critical IT-business dependencies. The data was collected in situ through the combination of interviews with the stakeholders involved in the Information Services Area, and the examination of institutional documentation (*e.g.*, integral development plan, value chains, etc.). The execution of the configuration process took approximately five months of which four months were required to gather, relate, and document the architecture and dependencies information. An additional month was required to instantiate the proposed metamodel in order to create the quantification model (an XMI specification). This quantification model contains approximately 13500 elements among business architecture elements, IT architecture elements, dependencies, and value metadata. The historic data of the SCF values was provided weekly during one year (2013–2014) by an IT Manager of the mentioned area.

4.1 Executing the Configuration Process (TOP-DOWN)

Business Motivation Architecture. Table 1 summarizes the strategic map that was identified and monetized. Each of the differentiating factors has an associated relevance for achieving the related strategic business goals. Associated metrics and their corresponding strategies were also defined.

Criticality Dependencies in the BPA. The criticality of the dependencies between the strategies above and the level1-business processes was established. The critical prioritization area was elaborated from this rating and the two processes that are closer to the criticality threshold were selected: Selection and Admission, and Teaching and Learning. Additional iterations of the criticality evaluation were performed to identify level2 critical elements (*i.e.*, Admission,

Table 1. Strategic map identified and monetized

Differentiating factor	Relevance	Goals	Measures	Value (USD)	Strategies	Metrics
Quality and differentiation	40 %	4	4	72.309.500	12	36
Administrative effectiveness	35 %	3	2	39.000.000	5	20
Environmental presence	25 %	2	2	10.100.000	3	8

Course registration) and level3 critical processes (*i.e.*, Undergraduate admission, Development of courses). Activities (BPA level 4) associated with the selected processes were determined: 19 activities were identified for the admissions process and 6 activities for the course registration process.

Criticality Dependencies in the IT Services Architecture. Each of the BPA activities was associated with the corresponding level 1 IT services. The organization does not have an official IT services catalog, so the mapping was done through a manager from the Information Services Area. The criticallity of level 1 IT services is evaluated in relation to the selected processes and to the level 2 IT services that support them. Three level1-services with the highest score within the critical prioritization area were selected: Database service, Authentication service and Banner System service; the latter being transversal to both processes. The costs of these selected services are given by the sum of all costs associated with their IT components.

IT Service Critical Factors. The IT business unit defined the actual and desired levels for each SCF on the selected IT services. A desired value between 0.75 and 0.91, and a actual value of 0.9 were defined for the *Capacity* SCF. A desired value between 0.7 and 0.99999, and a actual value of 0.7864 were defined for the *Availability* SCF. A desired value between 0.1 and 0.01, and a actual value of 0.0771 were defined for the *Integrity* SCF. A desired value between 0.3 and 0.01, and a actual value of 0.093 were defined for the *Performance* SCF.

Agreements and Service Levels for IT Services. No IT service level agreements are established between IT and the business units, however, these agreements were defined for critical IT services as an expected behaviour to be delivered. For example, a *standard* service level was defined on the availability SCF for the Banner IT service. If the measure for the % of availability of service components is between 88–90% the amount payed next month will be reduced by 30 %, between 85–88% the amount will be reduced by 50 %, and below 85 % the amount will be reduced by 100 %. The complete analysis involved the definition of 3 agreements with 3 service levels each.

IT Risks. Three risks were assessed on the capacity SCF for the Banner IT service. An application failure was assessed as low for impact and frequency, and therefore the cost of risk materialization was estimated as low (125 USD). A database failure was assessed with a high impact but with a low frequency, so the cost of risk materialization was estimated as medium (112.500 USD). The worst situation was estimated for a hardware failure (20.000 USD) which was assessed as high for impact and frequency. The entire analysis involved the identification and evaluation of 30 risks for 4 SCFs.

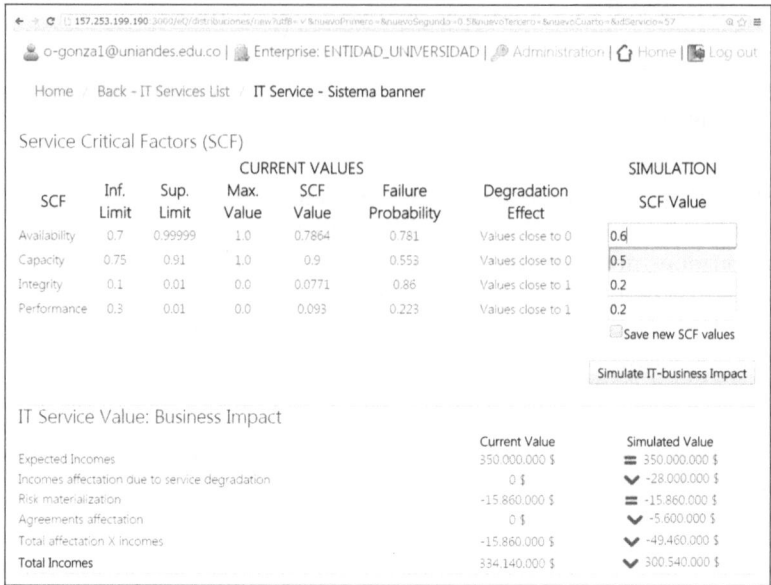

Fig. 4. Impact quantification results from the web application

4.2   Execution of the Impact Quantification Process (BOTTOM-UP)

In the above configuration process, dependencies and metadata between business and IT elements were established. Figure 4 illustrates the impact analysis results presented by the web application when comparing a simulated scenario ("What If") with the actual behaviour for the Banner IT service. The actual value of each critical IT service and the failure probability for each SCF associated with them are computed automatically by the algorithm implemented in the web application (*cf.* Sect. 3.3). The simulated SCF values on capacity, availability, performance and integrity were presented as estimates by the mentioned IT area. The business impact results correspond to the capacity simulation scenario.

The Capacity simulation scenario considers a peak in the number of transactions received concurrently so that the value supported by the SLA is exceeded. Since the installed capacity cannot meet all the transactions, around 90 % of the received transactions will be lost. The quantitative results show the maximum income losses due to Capacity SCF degradation (28.000.000 COP aprox. 14.000 USD), losses due to risks materialization (15.860.000 COP aprox. 7.930 USD), and losses due to agreements violations (5.600.000 COP aprox. 2.800 USD). Additional qualitative results showed the affected architecture elements: 4 business goals (*e.g.*, Attract and maintain quality students), 19 business processes (*e.g.*, Undergraduate admissions), 5 strategies (*e.g.*, Increase the number of student entries), 7 metrics (*e.g.*, Undergraduate positions filled), and 5 risks.

The Availability simulation scenario showed a lower income affection (18.430 USD) than the capacity scenario. The Integrity simulation scenario presented the most significant deviation (90.180 USD) from the expected income, which may be expected considering the affectation that wrong transactions may have on the system. The Performance simulation scenario showed a similar income affectation (23.680 USD) than the capacity scenario. Availability and Integrity are the most important SCF because their failure implies that the whole system stops working. On the other hand, Capacity or Performance are not as critical considering that the system may continue to operate despite service degradation.

Decision-Making Support. The actual or simulated failure probability allows IT-business analysts to support the decision making process regarding IT investments. This is achieved specifically through an explicit comparison of the losses generated by the failure against the opportunity of making an investment to mitigate it. The quantification results show the cost of business elements that are not adequately satisfied by IT services. Thus, IT-business decision makers can define continuity strategies and assign the required resources to keep business expectations aligned with IT operation. The method can be used to prioritize IT investments by assessing the criticality of their related IT services or components in relation to business elements (goals, strategies, metrics, processes).

5   Related Work

The alignment between business and IT can be analyzed from two perspectives: assessing the level of alignment, or quantifying the impact of its dependencies. In particular, dependencies quantification approaches assess the impact of IT on business elements. Gustafsson et al. [3] quantifies the impact of IT on business value (*e.g.*, flexibility, efficiency) through organizational impact variables (*e.g.*, functional structure, skills). Winker et al. [4] propose a model for defining and analyzing the dependencies (task-subtask, producer-consumer and simultaneity constraints) between the services and the compositions that may arise among them. This information can be used to simulate events that could lead to a service failure with measurable attributes (*e.g.*, time, location, resources), which could be used for adjusting SLA. These approaches do not quantify the impact of risks, service agreements, and criticality on IT services. The proposed method specializes the simulation of events on IT services by capturing the performance of their related SFC (*e.g.*, availability). The above measurable attributes and impact variables can be incorporated in the proposed method as additional impact analysis metadata.

BDIM uses different models and techniques to map and to quantitatively evaluate dependencies between IT solutions and business performance [5]. These techniques enable the design and constant optimization of IT processes (*e.g.*, incident management, capacity management) based on business needs [6,7]. The authors in [6] use BDIM to select SLA parameters (availability, maximum average response time) to design a servers farm to deploy the services. This approach analyzes SLA losses with regards to the costs and losses due to under or over capacity estimation of IT infrastructure. The proposed method complements this impact analysis on availability agreements with additional quality attributes (performance, reliability, capacity) and risks specified on IT services. Thus, a causal relationship between IT services performance and business elements can be established in quantitative terms (losses) as well as qualitative terms (traceability of processes, goals, strategies, and metrics). Bartolini et al. [7] prioritizes incidents by assigning urgency and impact parameters according to the level of importance of the solution with regard to the business objectives and the resulting costs when the business does not solve the incident immediately. The proposed method could be extended to link specific elements of IT processes with the performance of IT services to quantify business impact.

Risk management can be incorporated to analyze IT services [14]. Tohidi [15] includes risk management to support the evaluation of information systems within each stage of the development process. Bojanc et al. [16] analyze IT risks on information safety by identifying assets, threats, and vulnerabilities to further define quantitative risk metrics. These proposals identify IT risks in detail, however, they are missing support to quantify the business impact associated to the materialization of risks on IT operation. This can be done in the proposed method by associating risks to IT-business dependencies.

6 Conclusions and Future Work

The growing need for business and IT interoperability is forcing organizations to improve the management of their processes and IT services. This paper presents specific processes and models used to incorporate quantitative metadata on the existing IT-business dependencies. Quantitative analysis capabilities are achieved by modeling the criticality between business and IT elements, and the impact analysis models (risks, service agreements, and service critical factors) for IT services. In particular, the incorporation of risk analysis capabilities is an important supplement to better quantify IT-business dependencies.

However, there are a number of subtleties and limitations related to practical implications that arise when adopting the quantification method. First, the quantification of dependencies, criticality, and risk of each IT and business element cannot be done independently. Ongoing research is targeted to correlate and quantify these impact variables for IT and business elements that do not have an explicit dependency among them. Second, modeling and relating value metadata to IT-business dependencies can demand a considerable amount of effort from domain architects. Further research is required to define document configuration templates to automatically generate the metamodel instance or the web application database. A different approach is to extend an enterprise architecture tool with the impact analysis capabilities defined in the metamodel. Although the latter limitation is transparent for IT-business managers, who are the intended audience for executing the quantification process, it is also necessary to integrate the assets configuration tool with monitoring tools in order to capture the IT services performance continuously. Third, the method currently assumes business processes as the linking bridge between business and IT, however, it is necessary to incorporate the notion of business function to relate supporting IT services. Finally, the impact analysis capabilities of the method can be enriched by incorporating additional SCF (*e.g.*, maintainability).

The proposed method has been used in four case studies to quantify IT-business dependencies for three companies. Through the analysis of these implementations, it was found that the method can be used at different levels of detail to simplify the dependencies configuration. For example, the architect of one of these companies decided which were the critical business processes without establishing criticality dependencies for the complete BPA. However, once these business processes were selected, all the remaining activities were completely adopted to associate value metadata to IT-business dependencies. The proposed method should be applied iteratively and incrementally to cover the analysis of the different business and IT elements for the entire organization.

Acknowledgments. The author would like to thank Giovanny Torres and Guillermo Beltrán who collaborated in the validation of this work.

References

1. Luftman, J., Zadeh, H.S., Derksen, B., Santana, M., Rigoni, E.H., Huang, Z.D.: Key information technology and management issues 2011–2012: an international study. J. Inf. Technol. **27**(3), 198–212 (2012)
2. Maizlish, B., Handler, R.: IT (Information Technology) Portfolio Management Step-by-Step: Unlocking the Business Value of Technology. Wiley, Chichester (2010)
3. Gustafsson, P., Franke, U., Höök, D., Johnson, P.: Quantifying IT impacts on organizational structure and business value with extended influence diagrams. In: Stirna, J., Persson, A. (eds.) Practice of Enterprise Modeling. LNBIP, vol. 15, pp. 138–152. Springer, Heidelberg (2008)
4. Winkler, M., Springer, T., Trigos, E.D., Schill, A.: Analysing dependencies in service compositions. In: Dan, A., Gittler, F., Toumani, F. (eds.) ICSOC/ServiceWave 2009. LNCS, vol. 6275, pp. 123–133. Springer, Heidelberg (2010)
5. Moura, A., Sauve, J., Bartolini, C.: Business-driven IT management - upping the ante of IT : exploring the linkage between it and business to improve both IT and business results. IEEE Commun. Mag. **46**(10), 148–153 (2008)
6. Sauvé, J., Marques, F., Moura, A., Sampaio, M., Jornada, J., Radziuk, E.: SLA design from a business perspective. In: Schönwälder, J., Serrat, J. (eds.) DSOM 2005. LNCS, vol. 3775, pp. 72–83. Springer, Heidelberg (2005)
7. Bartolini, C., Salle, M., Trastour, D.: IT service management driven by business objectives: an application to incident management. In: 10th IEEE/IFIP Network Operations and Management Symposium, pp. 45–55. IEEE, Vancouver (2006)
8. Group, I. A. W.: IEEE Std 1471–2000. Recommended practice for architectural description of software-intensive systems. Technical report, IEEE (2000)
9. Aier, S., Winter, R.: Virtual decoupling for it/business alignment-conceptual foundations, architecture design and implementation example. Bus. Inf. Syst. Eng. **1**(2), 150–163 (2008)
10. Wei, X., Zhiqiang, Z.: Service portfolio selection driven by multiple business objectives. In: International Conference on Information Management, Innovation Management and Industrial Engineering, pp. 146–149. IEEE Computer Society, Washington (2011)

11. Kuchta, D.: Use of fuzzy numbers in project risk (criticality) assessment. Int. J. Project Manage. **19**(5), 305–310 (2001)
12. Markowski, A.S., Mannan, M.S.: Fuzzy risk matrix. J. Hazard. Mater. **159**(1), 152–157 (2008)
13. Ni, H., Chen, A., Chen, N.: Some extensions on risk matrix approach. Saf. Sci. **48**(10), 1269–1278 (2010)
14. McNaughton, B., Ray, P., Lewis, L.: Designing an evaluation framework for IT service management. Inf. Manage. **47**(4), 219–225 (2010)
15. Tohidi, H.: The role of risk management in IT systems of organizations. Procedia Comput. Sci. **3**, 881–887 (2011)
16. Bojanc, R., Jerman-Blai, B.: An economic modelling approach to information security risk management. Int. J. Inf. Manage. **28**(5), 413–422 (2008)

On Design Research – Some Questions and Answers

Pertti Järvinen[✉]

School of Information Sciences, University of Tampere, Tampere, Finland
pj@sis.uta.fi

Abstract. Design research is needed in building a new information system or information technology artifact for business informatics and its research. Our literature does not have a common view on design research. In this paper we are interested in a variety of ways how a research problem is stated, which kind of knowledge and innovations does design research produce, and how will a goodness of design research be specified. The variety of solutions to those problems will be found by using a particular method, phenomenography. A successful application of phenomenography is demonstrated. The results found in the information systems literature will be compared and supplemented.

Keywords: Information systems · Design research · Phenomenography

1 Introduction

Walls et al. [1] developed a design theory and motivated their readers by writing that ".. design is central to such varied fields as engineering, architecture, and art. It is also clearly an important topic within the Information Systems (IS) discipline." We, IS researchers must build and evaluate new information systems or information technology (IT) artifacts because researchers in other disciplines cannot do them. Lee [2] emphasized this as follows ".. research in the information systems field examines more than just the technological system, or just the social system, or even the two side by side; in addition, it investigates the phenomena that emerge when the two interact".

Iivari [3] advocates Design Science Research (DSR) by paying attention to conceptual mess and stating that "The idea of DSR in IS is still in its formative stage. As new members join the DSR research community, each of them may bring in his or her own interpretation of what DSR is. While the plurality of ideas is definitely beneficial, especially at this early stage, it is also good for people to understand what they are talking about." To this end, it is important to know a variety of ways how the design research process has been conceptualized.

We recognize some essential phases in the design research process: its beginning (problem definition), actual research project, its end (various outcomes, e.g., knowledge and instantiations) and its evaluation. Concerning the first phase of the design research process we like to ask: Question A: What is a research problem of design research and how it can be stated?

In analysis of outcomes of design research we found many kinds of knowledge and instantiations and hence we like to ask: Question B: Which kind of knowledge does

© Springer International Publishing Switzerland 2015
R. Matulevičius and M. Dumas (Eds.): BIR 2015, LNBIP 229, pp. 113–125, 2015.
DOI: 10.1007/978-3-319-21915-8_8

design research produce? Question C: Which kind of innovations design research will produce?

Design research seems to differ from traditional research that it emphasizes utility of innovation, not truth of theory describing a certain phenomenon. But are the traditional evaluation principles still valid for design research or not? To this end we ask: Question D: How can we specify a goodness of design research?

2 Methodology

In order to study the questions above we like to apply phenomenography [4] as a research method. According to Tesch [26] research interest in phenomenography is in the discovery of regularities discerning of patterns in conceptualization. Phenomenography [4] is intended to describe, analyze and understand conceptions: the aim is to describe the qualitative different ways in which various aspects of reality are seen and conceptualized and to search for logical relations between the categories of description arrived at. A conception in phenomenographic terms is a very starting point from which a person views some aspect of reality. The aim with the phenomenographic research is to show the *qualitative variation* in which persons understand a certain phenomenon. Researchers using phenomenography are thus not so interested in why persons think as they do. The idea of phenomenography is to describe the variation of how persons view something, not to explain the reasons for the variation. Kaapu [27] performed a literature review of phenomenography in IS and 5 specific phenomenographic studies in her doctoral dissertation.

To give a more concrete view on activities of the phenomenographic study we take an example [28]. A Järvinen asks interviewees: Please, define a conception of health by using your own words. The researcher will receive free-form answers that she classifies into a few classes. The researcher must not criticize the truthfulness of answers. She first differentiates the definitions described with a set of properties of health from the definitions where some relationships of health with other concepts were used (cf. Bunge's class and relation concepts [29]). She then tries to find similar definitions, she groups such ones together and finally forms five categories as in Grounded Theory [30]. Thereafter she puts the categories into order from the simple to more multi-faceted ones: (1) no illness, organism in good condition, (2) a physical and psychical balance or steady state, (3) interaction between mind and organism in good condition, (4) interaction between mind, organism and environment is without dysfunctions and (5) an individual is functioning, active and target-oriented. - From the short example above we can find the following phases of phenomenographic study: (I) Collect raw data, (II) formulate a definition per each person, (III) formulate categories from similar definitions (conceptual cluster analysis) and (IV) try to find a certain structure of categories (if such one exists).

Phenomenographic studies usually use interview or questionnaire to collect raw data. Instead of that we are using scientific articles as raw data in phenomenographic study (cf. literature review). A single author is a 'person' in phenomenographic sense and a group of authors of a particular article, too. In order to collect our raw data, some articles, we partially used our set of articles read in our doctoral seminar during years

1991–2015, on an average 30 new articles per year. (The titles of articles read during years 1991–2009 are in [31] and more recent ones under title IS Reviews 201n on web pages of our school). A major part of the articles read is method articles, because every doctoral candidate needs to select an appropriate research method. Readings were collected into a method book [32]. Concerning this study we selected highly ranked journal articles that have played a leading role in a progress of design (science) research (Phase I). In order to give a critical reader a chance to check our results we use direct citations from the articles to describe the author(s') definitions (Phase II).

In addition of phenomenograhic analysis of scientific articles we shall bring our own comments and frameworks to amend a discussion when it is possible. We shall structure our paper according to the four questions above and in each question we present the material found in the chronological order of publications.

3   Question A: What Is a Research Problem of Design Research and How It Can Be Described?

In this section we shall first try to find how various authors defined a building problem in design research. Our purpose is to pick up the problem formulation as it is or try to interpret and write it into a form of question, if it does not be written as such a form. The formulations will be collected into Table A. We shall comment the results thereafter and present how the authors have described a context of design problem. We shall also propose a framework of a problem-solving situation.

Nunamaker et al. [5] guide a systems development: "Formulate first a concept (i.e., a framework) that is found useful in organization of ideas and suggesting actions." Walls et al. [1] "take a position that design commences immediately after problem identification and terminates when the customer signs off on the system." According to March and Smith [6] ".. we *build* an artifact to perform a specific task." (They mean IT artifact.) Iivari [7] likes to ".. emphasize more the nature of Information Systems as an applied, engineering-like discipline that develops various 'meta-artifacts' to support the development of IS artifacts." According to Hevner et al. [8] "The objective of research in information systems is to acquire knowledge and understanding that enable the development and implementation of technology-based solutions to heretofore unsolved and important business problems. ... Design science approaches this goal through the construction of innovative artifacts aimed at changing the phenomena that occur." Van Aken [9] is a researcher who in Management Science emphasizes the role of design research, and he differentiates Organization Theory research from Management Theory research. The latter ".. uses the perspective of a player and uses *in prevision* intervention-outcome logic: what intervention should a player use in the given context to realize the desired outcome." We have collected formulations into Table 1.

In our phenomenographic analysis we pay attention on various differences (object, problem owner, idea behind of solution) in the descriptions of research problem. From Table A we can find that the *object* in building project is not always the same, but Nunamaker et al. [5] and Walls et al. [1] are building an information system, March and Smith [6] and Hevner et al. [8] an IT artifact, Iivari [7] a meta-artifact and van Aken [9] as a management scientist does not tell the object of intervention. The publication

Table 1. Qualitative variations how the building problem could be formulated

Author(s)	The formulated building problem
Nunamaker et al. [5]	Could we build a system based on a certain concept and demonstrate usefulness of the concept by constructing the system?
Walls et al. [1]	Can we construct the system that solves the problem identified by the customer?
March and Smith [6]	Can we build an IT artifact to perform a specific task?
Iivari [7]	How can we develop a certain "meta-artifact" to support the development of IS artifacts?
Hevner et al. [8]	Can we construct an innovative IT artifact aimed at solving an important business problem?
van Aken [9]	What intervention should a player use in the given context to realize the desired outcome?

sequence of the articles selected shows that the perspective on research object is in the course of time narrowing from the whole information system to its part, IT artifact.

Walls et al. [1] clearly said that the customer is a *problem owner*, other researchers directly or indirectly said that the researcher is a problem owner. In the Walls et al.'s [1] case it may in the worst case lead to the situation where the customer stops the project before any concrete outcomes.

Nunamaker et al. [5] are only ones who inform their *idea*, concept, behind of solution. We think that other researchers except van Aken [9] will use the most advanced IT in their solutions, although they do not mention it. Van Aken [9] will utilize some relationship A $\rightarrow$ B of a certain theory in his intervention. In our field Davison et al. [13] used a similar relationship of a particular theory in their action research.

We can conclude that our phenomenographic analysis shows that there are a large variety of problem definitions in design research. It is possible to at least give *three different classifications* of problem definitions (categories). These classifications can be based on either research object or problem owner or an idea behind of solution. The phenomenographic analysis can be continued by searching combinations of two or three factors (object, owner, concept) but it does not shed much new light on research problem of design research.

Next we shall move outside of phenomeographic analysis and comment on the problem-solving paradigm by considering it graphically and developing a *framework* of a problem-solving situation in Fig. 1.

For design research we define: An organization stays now at a problematic state, called an initial state, and this organization likes to transform itself into a desired state by building a particular artifact. The described situation resembles March and Smith's [6] description: "Models represent situations as problem and solution statements. Methods are often used to translate from one model or representation to another in the course of solving a problem."

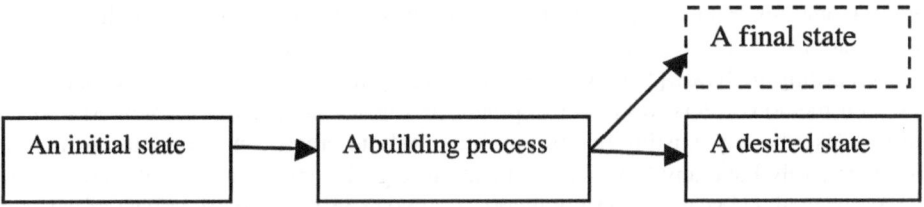

Fig. 1. A framework of a problem-solving situation in design research

To our mind, transition from the initial state to the desired state is unique and hopefully irreversible and this transition can be described. This description can be considered as a *descriptive method* ('we performed a building process in this way'). The Gregor's [10] taxonomy does not, however, have any type category for descriptive methods; it has type V category for prescriptive methods [11]. But a certain descriptive method can act as a starting point for developing a prescriptive method.

In Fig. 1 there is also a final state by which we like to demonstrate that in design project it will sometimes happen that designers will not exactly achieve the desired state but another state, called a final state. The latter can differ from the desired one because of some extra functionality or because of larger or less utility.

We emphasize that Fig. 1 can also be interpreted in such a way that at least the initial state is unknown and a researcher has some novel ideas to build a new artifact that did not exist beforehand. This can be based on new technology, new social or new information resources. We then have an *opportunity* problem: Which kind of a new artifact could we build by using either new technical, social or informational resources or their combination? Our idea is not totally novel because Iivari [3] has noted that ".. design science is also about potentiality. A new idea or artifact may provide totally new opportunities to improve practice long before practitioners recognize any problem."

We recommend that a problematic initial state and a desired state will be described by the tasks to be performed and resources needed in performing the tasks. A researcher can then consider all the resources, technical, social and informational resources and their new opportunities. The change method to be followed shows a road from the initial state to the desired state either by obeying consecutive phases or by stepwise moving from one state to the next state towards to the desired state.

4 Question B: Which Kind of Knowledge Does Design Research Produce?

In this section we shall collect different types of knowledge produced by design research. The main results are prescriptive knowledge but also conceptual and descriptive knowledge [14] as a side results are taken into account. We do not collect different knowledge types into table form because of much repetition created. We shall present our important addition at the end of this section. Design research produces instantiations too but we shall consider them in the next section.

According to Iivari [15], "Conceptual development as a category of constructive research methods refers to the development of various models and frameworks which do not describe any existing reality but rather help to create a new one, and which do not necessarily have any 'physical' realization (e.g., IS development methodologies)."

Walls et al. [1] state that design theory has two aspects. "The first aspect of a design theory deals with the design product and consists of meta-requirements, meta-design, kernel theories and testable design product hypotheses. The second aspect of a design theory deals with the design process consisting of design method, kernel theories and testable design process hypotheses. Information system development life cycle (SDLC) is a widely accepted informal information system design theory."

March and Smith [6] state that ".. design science products are of four types, constructs, models, methods, and instantiations. As in natural science, there is a need for a basic language of concepts (i.e., constructs) with which to characterize phenomena. These can be combined in higher order constructions, often termed models, used to describe tasks, situations, or artifacts. Design scientists also develop methods, ways of performing goal-directed activities." March and Smith continue that ".. it is important to determine why and how the artifact worked or did not work within its environment. The interaction of the artifact with its environment may lead to theorizing about the internal workings of the artifact itself or about the environment."

Hargadon and Sutton [16] describe various ways to store knowledge as follows: "It was evident that much of the knowledge of potential solutions resides in the minds of the individual designers as products they have seen or used before. Designers augment their individual memories and written materials by collecting, looking at, and talking about products or parts of products, which act as records of existing technologies. Designers stockpile old products and parts in their offices and hallways or hang them from the ceiling."

Lee [17] defines ".. the instrumental model of practice as including the following elements. A researcher formulates, tests, and validates a theory that specifies independent variables, dependent variables, and the relationships among them. In doing this, the researcher is careful to make sure that, first, the dependent variables represent the outcomes that the practitioner is interested in achieving and, second, the independent variables represent factors that not only indeed influence the outcomes but also can be manipulated or changed by the practitioner. A practitioner could then apply the theory by manipulating the independent variables in order to achieve the desired levels in the dependent variables."

Hevner et al. [8] repeat four types of products (constructs, models, methods, and instantiations) presented by [6]. Hevner et al. consider that ".. effective design-science research must provide clear contributions in the areas of design construction knowledge (i.e., foundations, system development methodologies, modeling formalisms, ontologies, problem and solution representations, design algorithms), and/or design evaluation knowledge (i.e., methodologies, new evaluation metrics)."

Van Aken [9] states that ".. a professional will make three designs: an *object-design*, the design of the intervention or of the artifact; a *realization-design*, i.e. the plan for the implementation of the intervention or for the actual building of the artifact; and a *process-design*, i.e. the professional's own plan for the problem solving cycle, or, put differently, the method to be used to design the solution to the problem". He continues that "Design-repertoires contain three types of design knowledge, according to the three types of designs discussed above. Within each of the three types of design knowledge, prescriptions are an important category. The prescription can be used as a *design exemplar*. A design exemplar is a general prescription which has to be translated to the specific problem at hand; in solving that problem, one has to design a specific variant of that design exemplar. The typical research product is the prescription discussed above, or the technological rule that is tested and grounded. According to van Aken [9] both successful and especially the less than successful applications, should be reported.

Iivari [3] uses [1, 17] to identify prescriptive design science knowledge both for design product (for the artifact: idea, concept, style; functionality, behavior; architecture, structure, and for design process: technological rules [12] and technical norms [18]). (In order to achieve A do {act1, act2, ..., actn}; If you want A and you believe that you are in a situation B, then you should do X; it is rational for you to do X; it is profitable for you to do X). Iivari [3] also specifically wish ".. to point out that it is not necessary for a kernel to be from some reference discipline external to IS. A kernel theory can be a theory specific to IS and generally that at the conceptual level the outcomes are new concepts and frameworks, at the descriptive level new theories and models."

In this section the citations above can be used as raw data for phenomenographic analysis and they show a chronologically increasing variety of research outcomes especially at the prescriptive level. There are, however, two large classes based on *design product* and *design process* (Walls et al. [1], Iivari [3] and van Aken [9]), and the latter even differentiates results into two classes (successful and less than successful).

In addition of phenomenographic analysis we found that Iivari [3] criticizes when Walls et al. [1] suggest that the information systems development life-cycle is a design theory. Iivari [3] is not aware of any kernel theory on which it is based. When the information systems development life-cycle consists of the following phases: requirements determination, design, construction, implementation, and operation, those phases are assumed to be consecutive. To our mind, also an *evolutionary approach*, sometimes called a state-transition approach, is possible and often used to improve an existing problematic system.

5   Question C: Which Kind of Innovations Will Design Research Produce?

In the previous section we analyzed different (abstract) knowledge types as outcomes of design research. Here we concentrate on different (concrete) innovations as outcomes of design research. They are considered as important results.

According to Nunamaker et al. [5] "The pivotal role of systems development in a framework of research is the result of the fact that the developed system serves both as a proof-of-concept for the fundamental research and provides an artifact that becomes the focus of expanded and continuing research."

Iivari [15] states that ".. technical development produces as its outputs 'physical' artifacts, the adjective 'physical' being interpreted here broadly to include executable software (e.g. CASE environments)".

According to Walls et al. [1] "A hypothesis that a certain method will result in an artifact which meets its goals can be verified by using that method to build the artifact and testing the artifact to see whether it satisfies its goals. Clearly, then, prototype construction is a major aspect of design theory research."

March and Smith [6] state that ".. constructs, models and methods can be instantiated in specific products, physical implementations. Progress is achieved when a technology is replaced by more effective one."

Iivari [7] likes to ".. emphasize more the nature of Information Systems as an applied, engineering-like discipline that develops various 'meta-artifacts' to support the development of IS artifacts."

According to Hevner et al. [8] "The result of design-science research in IS is, by definition, a purposeful IT artifact created to address an important organizational problem. Furthermore, artifacts constructed in design science research are rarely full-grown information systems that are used in practice. The instantiations produced may be in the form of intellectual or software tools aimed at improving the process of information system development. System development methodologies, design tools, and prototype systems (e.g., GDSS, expert systems) are examples of such artifacts."

Iivari [14] states that in his ".. view the primary interest of Information Systems lies in IT applications. I propose a typology for IT applications which provide an alternative categorization of services to that in [19]. The typology distinguishes seven archetypes of IT applications based on the function/role the application serves." The roles/functions are to automate, augment, mediate, informate, entertain, artisticize and accompany. In Iivari [3] there is the eighth archetype with role/function to fantasize.

Lee et al. [20] like to re-conceptualize artifact in IS design science ".. from just the 'IT artifact - to what we are calling the 'IS artifact'. We 'unpack' what has been called the 'IT artifact' into a separate 'information artifact' and 'technology artifact' that, together with a 'social artifact', interact to form the 'IS artifact'. An IS artifact is itself a system, in which the whole (the IS artifact) is greater than the sum of its parts (the IT artifact, the social artifact, and the information artifact), where the constituent parts are not separate, but interactive, as are any subsystems that from which a larger system emerges. Hence, our [Lee et al.] naming of it as an information system artifact or IS artifact".

In this section too the citations above can be used as raw data for phenomenographic analysis and we find two similar groups as in connection with Question A: March and Smith [6], Hevner et al. [8] and Iivari [3, 7, 14, 15 restricted to *IT artifacts* or meta-artifacts only. Nunamaker et al. [5], Walls et al. [1] and recently Lee et al. [20] emphasize an *information system* as a whole.

To our mind, it is interesting that Lee et al. [20] defined an IS artifact consisting of *technology, information and social artifacts,* and it nicely *corresponds to* our view that an information system is built of the *three types of resources* (technical, social and informational).

6   Question D: How Can We Specify a Goodness of Design Research?

In this section we shall first collect various ways to evaluate design research. Thereafter we shall present one correction.

Nunamaker et al. [5] state that ".. system development could be thought as a 'proof-by-demonstration'. The integrated research efforts can be identified by the stages through which they grow (concept – development – impact). Systems must be developed in order to test and measure the underlying concepts."

Walls et al. [1] emphasize both a design product and a design process as follows: "The design process is analogous to the scientific method in that a design, like a theory, is a set of hypotheses and ultimately can be proven only by construction of the artifact it describes. If it is to be a good theory, a design ·theory must subject to empirical refutation. An assertion that possession of a particular set of attributes will enable an artifact to meet its goals can be verified by building and testing the artifact. A hypothesis that a certain method will result in an artifact which meets its goals can be verified by using that method to build the artifact and testing the artifact to see whether it satisfies its goals."

March and Smith [6] state that ".. it [design science] is technology-oriented. Its products are assessed against criteria of value or utility – does it work? is it improvement? Design science consists of two basic activities, build and evaluate. Evaluation is the process of determining how well an artifact performs. Instantiations demonstrate the feasibility and effectiveness of the models and methods they contain. Evaluation refers to the development of criteria and the assessment of artifact performance against those criteria. Evaluation requires the development of metrics and the measurement of artifacts according to those metrics. Building the *first* of virtually any set of constructs, model, method, or instantiation is deemed to be research, provided the artifact has utility for an important task. The research contribution lies in the novelty of the artifact and in the persuasiveness of the claims that it is effective. Actual performance evaluation is not required at this stage. The significance of research that builds subsequent constructs, models, methods, and instantiations addressing the same task is judged based on 'significant improvement', e.g., more comprehensive, better performance." For evaluation of constructs, models, methods and instantiations March and Smith [6] present some universal criteria, respectively.

In the connection with discussion about the main research domain of the IS discipline Benbasat and Zmud [21] propose that ".. our focus should be on how to best design IT artifacts and IS systems to increase their compatibility, usefulness, and ease of use or on how to best manage and support IT or IT-enabled business initiatives."

Hevner et al. [8] propose that ".. prescriptive theories must be evaluated with respect to the utility provided for the class of problems addressed." According to their Guideline 3, "The utility, quality, and efficacy of a design artifact must be rigorously demonstrated via well-executed evaluation methods." They continue that ".. IT artifacts can be evaluated in terms of functionality, accuracy, performance, reliability, usability, fit with the organization, and other relevant quality attributes." They propose five evaluation methods (observational, analytical, experimental, testing and descriptive).

They stress on that ".. design-science research holds the potential for three types of research contributions based on the novelty, generality, and significance of the designed artifact." Hevner et al. [8] also state that ".. design-science research often simplifies a problem by explicitly representing only a subset of the relevant means, ends, and laws. Ends are represented using a *utility function*." To our mind [32], the utility function at the problematic initial state can be measured. The same utility function can be used for measuring the utility of the new instantiation at the desired state. We shall receive two values of the utility function before and after an innovation. If the latter is better than the former we have achieved progress.

According to van Aken [9] technological rules must be tested within the context of its intended use, and they must be grounded on scientific knowledge. "The utility of technological rules must be examined to the extent to which they fulfill the five key user-needs of practitioners (descriptive relevance, goal relevance, operational validity, non-obviousness and timeliness)".

Peffers et al. [22] developed the methodology of six steps: problem identification and motivation, definition of the objectives for a solution, design and development, demonstration, evaluation, and communication. They underline such criteria like the artifact's functionality with the solution objectives, budgets, results of satisfaction surveys, client feedback, or simulations etc.

According to Weber [23] "A theory has *emergent* attributes – attributes of the theory as a *whole* rather than attributes of its parts. Many such attributes exist, and researchers often differ in their views on the significance they ascribe to each of them. Nonetheless, some emergent attributes (importance, novelty, parsimony, level and falsifiability) have widespread acceptance among researchers as being significant when assessing the quality of a theory."

In this section the citations above can be used as raw data for phenomenographic analysis. We many times find a special emphasis of the *novelty* the outcomes of design research, and here design research resembles traditional research. But in design studies there are rarely new innovations, for example, Gregor and Hevner [24] did not find any new invention but many improvement innovations. The five typical criteria (*productivity, profitability, performance, efficiency and effectiveness*) were in many citations used in evaluation of design products for business applications (Tangen [25]). In addition, some criteria for design process too were proposed.

Among the articles read we found Iivari's [3] claim: "Evaluation as a DSR activity lies at the descriptive level. It studies how effective and efficient the artifacts are compared with existing artifacts." To our mind, Iivari might mean that measurement activities are similar as in descriptive studies. But we prefer such a view that when goals are directing build activities at the prescriptive level then also *evaluation activities* measuring satisfaction of goals *must be performed at the prescriptive level*.

7   Discussion

In this study based on some important articles on design research *we demonstrated a large variety* in definitions of research problem (Problem A), descriptions of knowledge produced (Problem B) and instantiations built (Problem C), and ways to evaluate results (Problem D). Phenomenography as a research method helped to pay attention to differences and encouraged to find some structures, often classifications. Especially in Question A it gave *three* different set of *classifications* for research problem in design research. The classifications based on either research *object* or *problem owner* or an *idea* behind of solution. Our *framework* of a problem-solving situation (Fig. 1) by which we can explain a common problem-solving situation can be in the future used to reduce a conceptual confusion in defining a research problem in design research, and also an opportunity alternative can be then taken into account for complementing a definition of a research problem.

Concerning knowledge produced (Problem B) and instantiations built (Problem C) a *variety* seems to be natural and it *will increase* in the course of advances in technology, social and informational innovations, and innovations can concern both design product and design process. Concerning Problem D improvement studies seem to play a central role in design research and hence some measurements are needed to test that improvement has achieved. The authors, however, did not ask from whose point of view improvement is considered. There can be different interested parties with *differing utility or goal functions*. For some cases there is Analytic Hierarchy Process (AHP) method [34] to take care those differing interests.

We also showed that the information systems development life-cycle with consecutive phases is not an only method for design research but also an *evolutionary* approach is possible and used. Our tentative guess is that our proposal to record a *descriptive method* in connection with a construction project of an information system or an IT artifact, and this descriptive method can act as a starting point when researchers want to develop a *prescriptive construction method* in design research. We like also to emphasize that evaluation of a certain information system or IT artifact will take place at the prescriptive level, not at the descriptive one.

A particular referee expressed a wish to compare phenomenography here and literature review as research methods. They both use secondary data as their starting point, but phenomenography differs from literature review in formulating categories (more abstract concepts) from original conceptions, and their relationships, possibly shown as structures.

We tried to collect all the best articles in design research from the high-ranked journals. But we must admit that our literature review is not exhaustive and there can be few excellent article to supplement our set of raw data. Hence, we recommend our colleagues to fulfill the results achieved here. Another limitation is based on the fact that the differences found in Problem A could show up in other problems (B, C and D) because conceptions on research problem, knowledge, innovation and evaluation of results are not totally independent. Fortunately, we considered phenomenographic results in the latter at the higher, more abstract levels than in connection with Problem A.

Acknowledgments. I very much thank Sal T. March, Alan R. Hevner, Allen S. Lee, Antti Arvela, Raimo Hälinen, Annikki Järvinen, Erkki Koponen and Mikko Ruohonen for their constructive comments on the earlier versions of this paper.

References

1. Walls, J.G., Widmeyer, G.R., El Sawy, O.A.: Building an information system design theory for vigilant EIS. Inf. Syst. Res. **1**, 36–59 (1992)
2. Lee, A.S.: MIS quarterly's editorial policies and practices. MIS Q. **25**(1), iii–vii (2001)
3. Iivari, J.: Twelve theses on design science research in information systems. In: Hevner, A.R., Chatterjee, S. (eds.) Design Research in Information Systems – Theory and Practice, pp. 43–62. Springer, Heidelberg (2010)
4. Marton, F., Booth, S.: Learning and Awareness. Lawrence Erlbaum, Mahwah (1997)
5. Nunamaker, J.F., Chen, M., Purdin, T.D.M.: Systems development in information systems research. J. Manag. Inf. Syst. **7**, 89–106 (1991)
6. March, S.T., Smith, G.F.: Design and natural science research on information technology. Decis. Support Syst. **15**, 251–266 (1995)
7. Iivari, J.: The IS core – VII: towards information systems as a science of meta-artifacts. Commun. Assoc. Inf. Syst. **12**, 568–581 (2003)
8. Hevner, A.R., March, S.T., Park, J., Ram, S.: Design science in information systems research. MIS Q. **28**, 75–105 (2004)
9. van Aken, J.E.: Management research based on the paradigm of the design sciences: the quest for field-tested and grounded technological rules. J. Manag. Stud. **41**, 219–246 (2004)
10. Gregor, S.: The nature of theory in information systems. MIS Q. **30**, 611–642 (2006)
11. Gregor, S., Jones, D.: The anatomy of a design theory. J. Assoc. Inf. Syst. **8**, 312–335 (2007)
12. Bunge, M.: Scientific Research II. The Search for Truth. Springer, Berlin (1967)
13. Davison, R.M., Martinsons, M.G., Ou, C.X.J.: The roles of theory in canonical action research. MIS Q. **36**, 763–786 (2012)
14. Iivari, J.: A paradigmatic analysis of information systems as a design science. Scand. J. Inf. Syst. **19**, 39–64 (2007)
15. Iivari, J.: A paradigmatic analysis of contemporary schools of IS development. Eur. J. Inf. Syst. **1**, 249–272 (1991)
16. Hargadon, A., Sutton, R.I.: Technology brokering and innovation in a product development firm. Adm. Sci. Q. **42**, 716–749 (1997)
17. Lee, A.S.: Rigor and relevance in MIS research: beyond the approach of positivism alone. MIS Q. **23**, 29–34 (1999)
18. Niiniluoto, I.: The aim and structure of applied research. Erkenntnis **38**, 1–21 (1993)
19. Lyytinen, K., Rose, G.M.: The disruptive nature of information technology innovations: the case of internet computing in systems development organizations. MIS Q. **27**, 557–595 (2003)
20. Lee, A.S., Thomas, M.A., Baskerville, R.L.: Going back to basics in design science: from the information technology artifact to the information systems artifact. Inf. Syst. J. **25**, 5–21 (2015)
21. Benbasat, I., Zmud, R.W.: The identity crisis within the IS discipline: defining and communicating the discipline's core properties. MIS Q. **27**, 183–194 (2003)
22. Peffers, K., Tuunanen, T., Rothenberger, M.A., Chatterjee, S.: A design science research methodology for information systems research. J. Manag. Inf. Syst. **24**, 45–77 (2007)
23. Weber, R.: Evaluating and developing theories in the information systems discipline. J. Assoc. Inf. Syst. **13**, 1–30 (2012)
24. Gregor, S., Hevner, A.: Positioning and presenting design science research for maximum impact. MIS Q. **37**, 337–355 (2013)
25. Tangen, S.: Demystifying productivity and performance. Int. J. Prod. Perform. Manag. **54**, 34–46 (2005)

26. Tesch, R.: Qualitative Research: Analysis Types and Software Tools. Falmer, New York (1990)
27. Kaapu, T.: Reaching the diversity of users' understandings: a methodological renewal. Acta Electronica Universitatis Tamperensis; 991. Tampereen yliopisto (2010). http://tampub.uta.fi/handle/10024/66645. ISBN: 978-951-44-8198-7
28. Järvinen, A.: Lääketieteen opiskelijoiden tieteellisiä ja ammatilllisia käsityksiä koskeva seurantatutkimus. (in Finnish) (A follow-up study on scientific and professional conceptions of Finnish medical students) Acta Univeristatis Tamperensis 197 Tampereen yliopisto (University of Tampere) (1985)
29. Bunge, M.: Scientific Research I. The Search for System. Springer, Berlin (1967)
30. Strauss, A., Corbin, J.: Basics of Qualitative Research - Grounded Theory Procedures and Techniques. Sage Publications, Newbury Park (1990)
31. Järvinen P. (ed.): IS Reviews 1991–2009 (2010). http://www.cs.uta.fi/reports/d-sarja/D-2010-6.pdf
32. Järvinen, P.: On research methods. Tampere, Finland, Opinpajan kirja (2012)
33. Jarvinen, P.: On reviewing of results in design research. In: ECIS 2007 Proceedings. Paper 72 (2007). http://aisel.aisnet.org/ecis2007/72/
34. Saaty, T.L., Vargas, L.G.: Models, Methods. Concepts & Applications of the Analytic Hierarchy Process. Springer, Heidelberg (2001)

Business Process
and Decision Management

Selecting the "Right" Notation for Business Process Modeling: Experiences from an Industrial Case

Jörn Wiebring[2] and Kurt Sandkuhl[1,3(✉)]

[1] The University of Rostock, Rostock, Germany
kurt.sandkuhl@uni-rostock.de
[2] Stadtwerke Rostock AG, Rostock, Germany
jorn.wiebring@uni-rostock.de
[3] ITMO University, St. Petersburg, Russia

Abstract. During the last 20 years, much research work has been spent on determining which notation is the "best" one for business process modelling in industrial practice. However, most of this work has been performed outside the actual application context, i.e. often in labs, academic environments or experimental settings. We aim at contributing to the field by presenting and discussing a case of selecting the notation for a complete organization. More concrete, the paper covers the process of making a decision which notation is the most appropriate one for a medium-sized organization from utility industries. The steps taken in this decision making process include the analysis of requirements originating from regulation in the domain, a survey among the future users of the notation, and the analysis and evaluation of organizational requirements. The main contributions of this paper are (1) a real-world example illustrating issues and challenges when deciding on the "right" process modeling notation including influences from the application domain, (2) a survey comparing the understandability of notations from the end user perspective and (3) lessons learned from the decision making process and the survey.

Keywords: Business process modelling · Experience report · Business process management · Process modelling notations

1 Introduction

During the last 20 years, business process management (BPM) has established itself as a key technique for systematically analyzing, improving and monitoring value creation and supportive processes in organizations. The effects attributed to BPM include optimization and continuous improvement of processes, improved control of efficiency and effectiveness, better alignment of organizational aims and IT-support, transparency of process structure and visualization of interdependencies between actors, processes, products and systems [27, 29]. Business process modelling is an important part of BPM and often its first phase. The aim of business process modeling is to capture existing processes in organization, improve them for future use and define them in an often normative way.

© Springer International Publishing Switzerland 2015
R. Matulevičius and M. Dumas (Eds.): BIR 2015, LNBIP 229, pp. 129–144, 2015.
DOI: 10.1007/978-3-319-21915-8_9

Much research work has been spent on determining which notation is the "best" one for business process modelling in industrial practice (see Sect. 2.2). However, most of this work has been performed outside the actual application context, i.e. often in labs, academic environments or experimental settings. We aim at contributing to the field by presenting and discussing a case of selecting the notation for a complete organization. More concrete, the paper covers the process of making a decision which notation is the most appropriate one for a medium-sized organization from utility industries. The steps taken in this decision making process include the analysis of requirements originating from regulation in the domain, a survey among the future users of the notation, and the analysis and evaluation of organizational requirements.

The main contributions of this paper are (1) a real-world example illustrating issues and challenges when deciding on the "right" process modeling notation including influences from the application domain, (2) a survey comparing the understandability of notations from the end user perspective and (3) lessons learned from the decision making process and the survey.

The remainder of this paper is structured as follows: Sect. 2 summarizes the background for this paper. Section 3 presents the industrial case which forms the frame for the research work. Section 4 gives an overview to the research approach and discusses the research questions investigated and motivating the survey. Section 5 introduces the design of the survey. Section 6 analyses the data collected during the survey and draws conclusions for the industrial case. Section 7 summarizes the paper and lessons learned.

2   Background

The background relevant for this work stems from three different areas briefly discussed in this section: business process modeling notations (Sect. 2.1), studies comparing these notations (Sect. 2.2) and BPM in utility industries (Sect. 2.3).

2.1   Notations for Business Process Modelling

Business process models can generally be represented in a variety of ways. Allweyer [3] proposed a classification distinguishing four types of representation techniques for process models: (1) Structured text descriptions using natural language are the simplest means of representation, and also highly flexible as there are no restrictions as to what terminology and formulations may be used. However, complex facts quickly become confusing with this approach, and the individuality of description shows the greatest variation between authors. (2) Tabular representations add a predefined (tabular) structure to natural language descriptions of business processes. However, there also are problems with using tabular representations to describe complex facts, as in the case of multi-nested structures or iterations on different levels. (3) Graphical representation without the use of a formal semantics is the third option. Models are represented using graphic elements, and how they are arranged or connected is meant to convey certain semantic meaning. These descriptions usually are easy to create, but leave room for misinterpretation since consistency in the use of symbols is not enforced by a formal notation. (4) Graphical representation with a more formal semantics use a predetermined language and notation to structure models. The language may contain both graphic and textual elements. The models can be checked to ensure that the language and notation are correct, which helps to avoid errors in the models.

In the remainder of this paper graphical representations are in focus, preferably with formal semantics. Aguilar-Savén [2] and Sandkuhl et al. [24] provide an overview and a description to graphical notations for business process modeling. When investigating the potentially suitable notations for the industrial case (Sect. 3) the following representations were considered:

- FlowCharts are a formalized graphic representation of a program logic sequence, work or manufacturing process, organization chart, or similar formalized structure [12]
- Unified Modelling Language: UML is a language for specifying, visualizing, constructing and documenting the artefacts of software systems. Within business modelling UML activity diagrams are frequently used for process modeling [5]
- Event-Process-Chains (EPC) are an approach to process modeling consisting of general notation rules, different functions and a set of views on single parts of an enterprise to model [25]
- Business Process Model and Notation (BPMN) is developed and maintained by the OMG as a standard for business process modeling based on a flowcharting technique similar to activity diagrams from UML [29, 30]
- Petri Net is a mathematical modeling language which initially was meant for the specification of distributed systems. Petri net can also be used for modeling business processes and work flows as place/transition nets [23]
- PICTURE is a domain-specific business process modeling language and method for public administrations [4]
- YAWL (Yet Another Workflow Language) is a language for business process and workflow modeling based on workflow patterns and an extension of the Petri net formalism [28]

2.2 Studies Comparing Notations for BPM

During the last 20 years, many researchers have been working on comparisons of different notations for business process modeling. In most of the cases, the comparisons were motivated by the quest for the "best" notation. There are at least as many ways to define what "best" means as there are ways to investigate or prove "bestness". Interpretations of "best" include

- the notation perceived as most understandable, useful or applicable by the users. Examples for work in this field include studies of graphical vs. textual notations [19], comparison of different notations [17], impact of secondary notation [26], and studies of user perception [14] and cognitive complexity [9]

- the notation which proved to fit best to the requirements of a specific application context. Contributions to this area come from quality frameworks like SEQUAL [13] and from application examples [10]
- the notation whose models produced the best results when evaluating them with defined criteria and metrics for these criteria. Examples include the definition of metrics [15] and influence factors for process models [16], and an overview to different measurement approaches [20]
- the notation which from an economic perspective leads to most cost savings or increase of efficiency. Contributions to this aspect come, e.g., from investigating the effects of structuredness [8], ways to measure effectiveness [11] and the effect of teaching a specific notation [22]

Ways to investigate "bestness" could include case studies, field studies, surveys, experiments in a lab environment or in the field, comparisons, and many more. On top of this variety, many works just focus on one or a few specific notations. If we would consider all existing notations, the number of potentially related works would grow even further.

2.3   BPM in Utility Industries

During the 1990s, when most of the national electricity and natural gas markets were still monopolized, the European Union decided to gradually open these markets to competition. In particular, the European Union decided to

- distinguish clearly between competitive parts of the industry (e.g. supply to customers) and non-competitive parts (e.g. operation of the networks);
- oblige the operators of the non-competitive parts of the industry (e.g. the networks and other infrastructure) to allow third parties to have access to the infrastructure;
- free up the supply side of the market (e.g. remove barriers preventing alternative suppliers from importing or producing energy);
- remove gradually any restrictions on customers from changing their supplier;
- introduce independent regulators to monitor the sector.

The above mentioned liberalization of the European energy market has led to substantial changes in market structures and processes. New market roles emerged from the political decision to separate competitive and non-competitive parts, like operation of energy supply networks, energy production and energy trade, to name just a few examples.

Companies in the energy and utility sector are facing a continuously changing business environment due to new regulations and bylaws from regulating authorities and due to competitors implementing innovative technical solutions. In this context, both the business processes and the systems supporting these processes need to be quickly adaptive. Examples for typical business functions are assets accounting, processing and examination of invoices (including revision-proof archiving of documents), automatic billing initiated by meter readings, meter data evaluation, maintenance management (disposition, workforce management and mobility), inventory management, and order management. Communication between the market roles and the services offered to end consumers are subject to regulations currently aiming at enforcing more dynamics on the market.

Furthermore, the regulation authorities in many European countries define high level process for the communication of different market roles in the energy sector. These processes not only define the activities to be performed but also the time frames for completing them and the roles involved. An example are the processes defined for the German market in [7], which define the "business processes for supplying customers with electricity", abbreviated "GPKE". Organizations active in the energy market are obliged by law to implement the defined processes, which includes electronic data exchange with other market roles and definition and documentation of internal processes. Based on this regulatory practice, the following requirements can be derived from GPKE that a process modeling language would have to meet:

- It must be possible to explicitly model roles and/or stakeholders participating in or related to processes
- The activities of a process and the information flow between in the processes have to be part of the model
- Relation between role and activity or process must be documentable
- It must be possible to represent the order of the processes
- Alternative and parallel processes or activities have to be expressible
- Events triggering the process must be presented
- The IT systems used in the processes or by the roles must be part of the model
- Annotations would be supportive for describing additional information

3 Industrial Case: Stadtwerke Rostock AG

The Stadtwerke Rostock AG, or SWR AG, is a regional supplier of electricity, gas, and heat in Rostock, the biggest city of the German federal state of Mecklenburg-Vorpommern. The distribution of electricity and gas and the service of respective grids are governed by the Stadtwerke Rostock Netzgesellschaft mbH, or SWR NG, a subsidiary of SWR AG, established due to German legal regulations on distribution and sales of energy. These legal regulations include instructions to document processes which are potentially able to discriminate competitors, e.g. by impeding market entrance. Therefore German Law released guidelines consisting of basic processes, which have to be implemented by every market partner. The basic processes are communicated from the regulating authority by publishing UML Sequence Diagrams. The way how to document the actual processes of the companies is not regulated but the companies are free to choose the notation.

In 2002, when the obligation to document processes was introduced by the regulating authority, SWR AG chose to document its processes using Flowcharts. The basic notation of Flowcharts was slightly altered in order to provide a method able to fulfill all legal and organizational requirements. As tool support to document the processes, MS Excel was chosen because the decentralized organizational structure of process documentation of the SWR AG required a lot of people to take part in the documentation of their respective processes.

Originally it was intended to not only document legally relevant processes, but to document all processes of the SWR AG and SWR NG, in order to analyze and improve them continuously. This goal was abandoned during the last years, due to problems which were caused by the chosen notation on the one hand, and the chosen tool and organizational paradigm on the other hand. These problems include:

- a mistakable notation, which is not precise enough for every set of facts,
- combined with a huge number of responsible persons with their own notion how to interpret the given notation,
- who are not always fully motivated for the task
- as it is time consuming due to problems with the tool or missing qualifications for process modeling.

As a consequence SWR AG is only using process models as legal documentation or to show processes to interns as part of their training on the job. Unfortunately process management of SWR AG ends here mostly despite the possibilities which would arise by using a more complete approach on process management. The models however are not used to analyze and improve processes as it was intended to.

4   Research Approach

The overall approach for deciding on the best notation for SWR AG consisted of several steps: the analysis of requirements originating from regulation in the domain (see Sect. 2.3), a survey among the future users of the notation (this section and Sect. 5), and the analysis and evaluation of organizational requirements (Sect. 6.2). Since the selection of an appropriate notation is a central topic for creating comprehensible and understandable process models, it represents a basis for selecting the best possible, companywide process management tool as well. But to find the most suitable notation for the industry case or any company, there are several questions that need answers.

There are two groups of questions needed for finding the best notation:

Group 1 focuses on the requirements towards the notation, in order to choose the applicable notations out of the plethora of existing notations. Requirements can exist because of legal reasons on one hand and because of company-specific reasons on the other hand. Therefore the research questions need to be:

Q1:   Which legal requirements exist for process models in the energy sector?
Q2:   Which requirements for process models exist in the industry case?

Group 2 includes the research questions specifically designed to deduce the most suitable notation out of the notations, which fulfill the requirements. Here, "most suitable" is regarded as a combination of the constructs "best understood" and "perceived most acceptable". In the most favorable case both constructs are fulfilled by one and the same notation. Therefore the research questions are:

Q3:   Which process notation is best understood by the employees of the industry case?

Q4:   Which process notation is perceived most acceptable by the employees of the industry case?

This makes a respective research method for each group necessary. Group 1 will be worked at using a qualitative research method, by analyzing legal guidelines and internal concepts of the industry case, such as the existing notation. Group 2 on the contrary is prone to using a quantitative research method, in this case a survey conducted under the employees of the industry case.

Using the criteria suggested by Bortz and Döring [6] it is possible to create several hypothesizes out of the existing research questions. The most interesting hypothesizes regarding business process modeling and their effects on the process management approach of the industry case are:

H1:   If the used notation is changed, future process models will be understood better

H2:   If the used notation is changed, future process models will be perceived more acceptable

The corresponding null hypothesis to these 2 hypothesizes would be:

H0:   The used notation has no impact on understanding and perception of process models

5   Survey Design and Data Collection

This section is about the relevant stages for obtaining the data to answer research questions and to verify or falsify hypothesizes: the identification of relevant notations (Sect. 5.1), the identification and design of the exemplary used process (Sect. 5.2) and the design of the survey (Sect. 5.3).

5.1   Relevant Notations for the Industrial Case

In order to determine the "right" notation for a company one step is to identify potentially relevant notations among the existing notations. For this purpose, criteria have to be established which originate from two sources:

As stated in Sect. 4 the first source of criteria is legal requirements, which result of the process guidelines accompanying legal regulations, such as the GPKE or the equivalent for gas delivery "GeLi Gas". These guidelines are focused on processes between market partners. Nevertheless requirements are valid for the documentation of internal processes as well. By analyzing these guidelines it is possible to derive the minimum of elements a notation has to offer in order to fit German law, which are mentioned in Sect. 2.3. Being legal regulations, these requirements are focused on functional aspects, such as roles (illustrated by the columns of the UML Sequence Diagrams), tasks (illustrated by the connection between columns or self-referring connections) and a definite order of these tasks, allowing for parallel or alternative execution (illustrated by numerical and alphabetical annotation of the tasks).

The second source of criteria is the company itself. Recent process documentation of the industry case reveals functional requirements the notation has to fulfill. Mostly these requirements are consistent with the requirements implied by regulations, since the internal notation of the industry case is based on the demand to fit to legal regulations. Nevertheless there are some additional, functional requirements as well, for example the necessity of including IT systems in the models. To identify non-functional requirements, which might be different from company to company, even within one industry sector, it is necessary to analyze further internal documents and concepts centered on process management. Interestingly a lot these non-functional requirements closely resemble the principles constructed by Moody [18]. For example, the demand for descriptive, graphic elements corresponds to the "Principle of Semantic Transparency". Furthermore, demanding non-redundant symbolic corresponds to the "Principle of Semiotic Clarity".

The identified criteria are shown on the left hand side of the matrix depicted in Fig. 1. This matrix also shows the notations evaluated and the score reached for each

		eEPC	UML	BPMN	Petri-Net	PICTURE	YAWL
Functional requirements	Roles can be expressed	XX	XX	XX	O	XX	O
	Message flow	X	XX	XX	X	XX	X
	Internal tasks*	XX	XX	XX	XX	XX	XX
	Explicit sequence of tasks*	XX	XX	XX	XX	XX	XX
	Alternative and parallel tasks	XX	XX	XX	X	X	XX
	Triggering events can be expressed	XX	XX	XX	X	X	X
	Connection to IT-systems	XX	X	X	O	X	O
	Annotations	O	XX	XX	O	X	O
Non-functional requirements	Few basic elements	XX	XX	XX	XX	O	X
	Illustrative visual language	XX	X	XX	X	XX	X
	Redundancy free basic elements	XX	XX	XX	XX	X	XX
	Assignment of tasks to roles	XX	XX	XX	O	X	O
	Understandable by non-technicians	XX	X	XX	O	XX	O
	Adjustable degree of abstraction	X	X	XX	X	XX	O
	Simple communication with market partners	XX	X	XX	O	X	O
		22	21	25	9	17	8

*= not relevant for evaluation since all notations gained the same result

Fig. 1. Evaluation of notations based on the criteria derived for the industrial case

notation and every criterion. The notations selected for evaluation were eEPC, UML Activity Diagrams, BPMN, Petri Nets, PICTURE and YAWL (see Sect. 2.3). The scores of the evaluation were inspired by a traffic light system and included "XX = notation fulfills requirement", "X = notation fulfills requirement partly" and "O = notation does not fulfill requirement". The evaluation of the notations was performed by a researcher notation by notation; the result of the evaluation checked by another researcher. The evaluation showed that eEPC, UML Activity Diagrams and BPMN fit best the given criteria for the industry case. Therefore they were subject of further investigating in the survey answering Q3 and Q4.

As stated in Sect. 2.1 Petri Nets and YAWL are most commonly used for modeling workflows, due to their strong, inherent logic. Therefore they are not unconditionally usable by all employees and end users. PICTURE however revealed some difficulties with modeling alternative and parallel sequences, hence this notation is not completely suited for the needs of the SWR AG either.

5.2 Design of the Sample Process

The first step to the design of the sample process is to decide on its subject. Since the cause of the survey is to find the "right" notation not only for experts, but for a major part of the employees of the industry case, it is vital to find a process which is applicable and understandable by every participant of the survey. Following e.g. Parsons and Cole [21], nullifying advantages (process-) experts may have over other participants is an important task in order to obtain valid results.

Using this thought, there are two questions to answer in order to find a good subject for the sample process. The first question is whether to choose an actually existing process, or a constructed process. Existing processes might be prone to expertise knowledge and therefore manipulating the results. The second question to answer is whether the process should have a background which is situated in the industry sector of the industry case, or be universally adaptable. Since e.g. administrative staff of a company is not fully involved in sector-specific tasks, this might be a source of expertise knowledge as well.

As a conclusion, the best way to assure that no expertise knowledge compromises the results of the survey and every participant solely follows the defined process to answer questions, is to choose a Sample Process which is either known to every participant or to none. An actually existing process was chosen which is potentially performed by every participant of the survey. Since there are some irregular practices when executing this process in praxis, the process defined and used in the survey is slightly abstracted. The chosen Sample Process is the process of reserving a conference room or another resource (e.g. car, beamer) via the groupware LOTUS Notes.

The next step is to transfer the Sample Process into the selected notations in order to create different notation-specific versions of the survey. To ensure equal conditions for every notation-specific version we not only made sure that every model consists of the same content matter but also that the secondary notation is adequate, e.g., the size of the textual parts has to be easily readable in all notations. Figure 2 shows the sample process in BPMN notation. Unfortunately the secondary notation for the eEPC-model

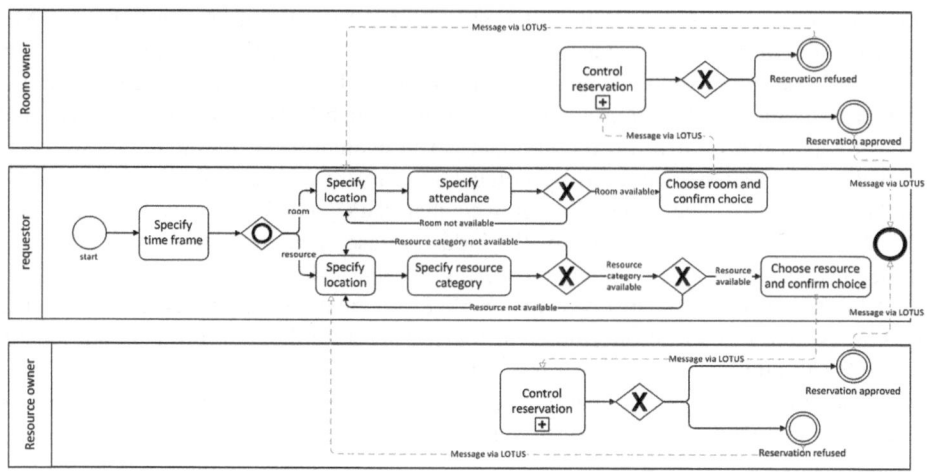

Fig. 2. Sample process used for the survey (BPMN notation)

is not as "attractive to the eye" as the other models, due to a discrepancy between syntactic rules and the aim to get every model on one A4-sized page each. Furthermore the so far used notation of the industry case uses two pages due to a graphic notation in combination with a tabular explanation of the tasks. This can't be changed, since this notation functions as a control group for the results of the survey.

5.3   Questionnaire and Data Collection

Generally speaking the questionnaire aims at measuring the impact of an independent variable, the process notation, on two dependent variables, understanding and perception. Therefore there will be four versions of the questionnaire, one for each notation (SWR AG Flow Diagram, eEPC, UML Activity Diagram, BPMN). The versions contain the same questions. Since there are two constructs for finding the "right" notation, understanding and perception, there have to be several types of questions in the questionnaire as well.

The construct of understanding is measured via questions about the content of the illustrated process. There are questions which aim at identifying and counting elements of the process, e.g. involved roles. Furthermore there are "yes or no"-questions aiming at identifying e.g. mutual exclusion of content. Most questions however are about following and interpreting the process flow correctly. Overall there are 17 content-related questions. For a correct answer one point is awarded to each question.

The construct of perception on the other hand is measured via five point Likert-scales for different aspects of the process model, e.g. the illustration of involved roles or their connection to respective tasks. This allows not only the deduction of average perception of the notation, but, together with two further questions about perceived strengths and weaknesses of the notation, assumptions about general problems with the respective notation as well.

For the realization of the questionnaire Google Forms were used, since it is for free as part of the Google Drive Suite and included all functionalities that were necessary. This included the illustration of several types of questions, the inclusion of pictures/models, relatively intuitive handling and most of all automatic capture of data collected via the survey and transformation in exportable formats like Excel. Furthermore it was possible to create links which to include in the e-mails sent to the participants.

Since the distribution of the questionnaire had to happen via the groupware LOTUS Notes there had to be a decision of whom to send the questionnaire to as well. The target group consisted of all employees who have constant access to LOTUS Notes and potentially work with the process documentation of the industry case. This excluded all operative technicians, e.g. electricians or warehouse staff. Technical white collar workers however were also a part of the survey. Altogether the questionnaire was sent to 349 potential participants.

To ensure that the survey is not compromised by expertise knowledge on notations the distribution of the questionnaire had to be randomized as much as possible. Within the limits of possibilities this was achieved by listing all participants alphabetically by their last name and assigning one of the four notations on a rotational basis. Following this concept every fifth participant in the list received the same version of the questionnaire.

6 Data Analysis and Interpretation

This section is about the obtained data and their interpretation (Sect. 6.1), and its value for the industrial case and general practice (Sect. 6.2).

All in all 113 of 349 potential participants of the survey actually took part. This means that roundabout 32,3 % of all potential participants answered, which we consider as a acceptable result. Furthermore all four versions of the survey were roughly answered by the same amount of participants. Flow Diagrams received 30 % of the participants, BPMN 25 %, UML 24 % and eEPC 21 %.

6.1 Results of the Survey

There is no definite "right" notation for the industrial case given by the defined criteria of understanding and perception, since different notations obtained the best results in the investigations of the respective constructs (see Table 1).

For the construct "understanding" results were obtained by assessing the responses of each participant and afterwards calculating the average score for each notation respectively. The UML Activity Diagram is ranked first, followed by the eEPC model, the SWR AG-Flow Diagram and the BPMN model in that order. Nevertheless the results for the averagely reached score are relatively close. In average participants of the UML-version of the survey scored 11,93 of 17 points, whereas participants of the BPMN-version scored 11,29 points. This result means, that the difference of the understanding between the notations ranked first and last is only 3,76 % for the

Table 1. Results of the survey

Notation	Average score understanding	Equals to percentage score	Variance in score understanding	Average perception	Variance in perception
Flow Diagram	11,32	66,58 %	4–16	2,14	1,0–3,8
BPMN	11,29	66,41 %	8–16	2,19	1,4– 3,6
UML	11,93	70,17 %	7–15	2,29	1,2–3,6
eEPC	11,50	67,64 %	7–15	2,70	1,4–5,0

industrial case. The currently used notation of Flow Diagrams is better understood than BPMN by only 0,17 % or 0,03 points, which is a negligible difference. BPMN-participants scored from 8 to 16 points, which is the best result regarding the variance of total scores of all notations. This could mean that a BPMN model can achieve a slightly broader understanding, even if just for participants who scored beneath average. Since the survey revealed that another notation than the SWR AG-Flow Diagram is ranked first, hypothesis H1 has to be considered as accepted.

For the construct "perception" the results are illustrated slightly different, since for obtaining the data scales were used which defined "1" as best and "5" as worst alternative of the ranking. The average perception of the notations is measured by averaging the perception of every participant and afterwards averaging all of this "perception-scores" for each notation respectively. The ranking of the construct "perception" is completely different from "understanding". The SWR AG-Flow Diagram is ranked first, followed by BPMN, UML Activity Diagram and eEPC in that order. Once again the results for each notation are relatively close, only the eEPC model was evaluated "much" worse than the other models. This is probably due to the already mentioned much more space-consuming secondary notation.

Interestingly the currently used notation and BPMN scored results with only minor differences, despite the fact that employees are used to working with the well-known Flow Diagrams. Nevertheless hypothesis H2 has to be rejected, since no notation is ranked higher than the currently used notation. In conclusion this means that the null hypothesis H0 has to be rejected, since an impact of the notation on process-understanding and perception of a model evidently exists.

Another interesting result is achieved by calculating the correlation of the two constructs (see Table 2). This was done using the software SPSS. All requirements for

Table 2. Correlation and significance

Notation	Correlation coefficient	2-sided significance	Significance via t-test
Flow Diagram	−0,209	0,235	0,024
BPMN	−0,488	0,008	0,051
UML	−0,264	0,183	0,432
eEPC	−0,341	0,103	0,294
		limit value $p = 0,01$	limit value $p = 0,05$

calculating the Pearson product-moment correlation coefficient, like interval-scaling and Normal distribution of the data, are fulfilled. All correlation coefficients are negative, which means that people who achieve a better result for the construct "understanding" will evaluate the "perception" of the model better as well and vice versa. The soundest correlation between the constructs exists for the notation BPMN (-0,488), followed by eEPC, UML Activity Diagram and SWR AG-Flow Diagram in that order. Interestingly only the result of BPMN is statistically significant, proven via a 2-sided significance test and a t-test for the equality of means. The results of the correlation for the other notations are statistically prone to be achieved at random, although it is possible to assume a significant correlation for the SWR AG-Flow Diagram, because of the result of the t-test.

6.2   Conclusions for the Industrial Case

Since none of the notations is ranked first for both constructs, understanding and perception, further evaluations are needed to identify the most suitable notation. One way to continue is to involve the key users of process models and let them evaluate the notations from the perspective of organizational requirements. A precondition for this is to decide which notations to include in this second investigation.

First notation to choose is the UML Activity Diagram, since it is ranked first for the construct "understanding" with a slight edge, but yet the biggest one considering all results. Flow Diagrams could be the second candidate for further investigation, since it is ranked first regarding the construct "perception". However, the future potential for this notation is not very promising. Years of using this notation revealed no advantage in understanding process models, quite on the contrary actually. Furthermore the difference in perception as compared to other notations is very small, although all other notations were supposedly mostly unknown to the participants of the survey.

Considering this, a second look at BPMN as a candidate notation might be justified. Here, the results of the calculation of the correlation coefficients are important. These calculations revealed that there is a high chance for improving process understanding when using the BPMN notation by improving its perception. The perception of BPMN is almost as good as the perception of the currently used notation Flow Charts, although BPMN is widely unknown by the employees of the industrial case. When the employees get used to BPMN the perception probably will improve and with this the understanding for process models using BPMN will also increase. Furthermore BPMN allows the creation of a "simple" and an "advanced" version of a process model by applying additional symbols, clarifying tasks and events. This corresponds to Moody's (2009) "Principle of Cognitive Fit" as well.

Thus, the evaluation by the key users focused on a comparison of an UML Activity Diagram and a BPMN model. Again, a real-world process from the industrial case was modeled in both notations and 10 questions were defined which the participants had to answer for both process models. These questions included the aspects control flow, model elements, perceived clarity of the structure and other aspects. 7 key users were invited to participate in the investigation, all of them either responsible for documenting processes in their organization units or members of the company-central modeling support team.

All participating key users identified BPMN as the preferred notation which we took as a clear vote for this notation. Due to this result and because of other advantages of BPMN, including simpler communication with market partners due to the widely spread use of the notation and potential use of future technologies like BPMN2BPEL-transformation, BPMN is considered the most future-oriented choice of the investigated notations, and therefore the "right" notation for the given industrial case.

7 Lessons Learned

One of the lessons learned is that the performed survey was both feasible and pertinent, although it has some limitations. From a technical set-up, we did not have any doubts that semantically similar process models could be developed in all selected notations and distributed as part of the survey. However, it was difficult to predict whether the participation in the survey would be sufficiently high and the reactions to the survey would be positive. Participation in the survey was voluntary, i.e. an invitation to participate in the survey in some companies might be considered a "hidden command" to do so but in the organizational culture of SWRAG this is a real voluntary activity. More than 30 % participated and judging from the replies the participants did not respond "quick and dirty" but answered the survey questions thoroughly. Also the informal reactions to the survey were positive. It was appreciated that the employees are involved in such a decision which will support the actual process of introducing the new notation.

The respondents were fairly evenly distributed on the departments. This indicates that neither the more technical nor the administrative qualification profiles were overrepresented. Thus, we expect the survey design to work for other utility companies, too. In order to verify this we would need to both perform the study in other companies and compare the qualification between the companies.

Regarding the survey results, we were surprised how close the results for the different notations were.

The work presented in this paper focuses on selecting a process modeling notation for a specific organization which already has a tradition of using a specific notation (flowcharts) but the need to switch to another one due to organizational demands.

The conclusion from our work is that other organizations can learn from the process of finding the appropriate notation, but probably not from the actual conclusion to use BPMN. The initial step, identification of requirements implied by bylaws and policies, proved to be required and useful. The process continued with investigating which notation would be best understood and accepted by the future users. This pre-selection of a notation is recommendable for organizations with an organizational culture including or putting an emphasis on participation of all stakeholders in decision processes. Since a notation will usually be applied on a 5–10 year timeframe, user participation with other organizational cultures since non-acceptance of a notation during a long time can be expensive. Inclusion of organizational requirements as a third step from our experience has to be considered as common practice for this kind of projects.

Acknowledgements. This work was partly financed by the German State of Mecklenburg – Western Pomerania with funds of the European Fund for Regional Development in the research project ECLORA. Furthermore, it was partially financially supported by Government of Russian Federation, Grant 074-U01.

References

1. Ahlemann, F.: Strategic Enterprise Architecture Management: Challenges, Best Practices, and Future Developments. Springer, Berlin (2012)
2. Aguilar-Savén, R.S.: Business process modelling: review and framework. Int. J. Prod. Econ. **90**(2), 129–149 (2004)
3. Allweyer, T.: BPMN 2.0: introduction to the standard for business process modeling. BoD–Books on Demand (2010)
4. Becker, J., Pfeiffer, D., Räckers, M.: Domain specific process modelling in public administrations – the PICTURE-approach. In: Wimmer, M.A., Scholl, J., Grönlund, Å. (eds.) EGOV. LNCS, vol. 4656, pp. 68–79. Springer, Heidelberg (2007)
5. Booch, G., Rumbaugh, J., Jacobson, I.: Unified Modeling Language (UML). Rational Software Corporation, Santa Clara (1998). Version, 1
6. Bortz, J., Döring, N.: Forschungsmethoden und Evaluation – Für Human- und Sozialwissenschaftler, 4th edn. Springer, Heidelberg (2006)
7. Bundesnetzagentur: Geschäftsprozesse zur Kundenbelieferung mit Elektrizität, GPKE. Konsolidierte Fassung ab 1 April 2012. https://www.bdew.de/internet.nsf/id/BBDE5740233A837FC1257830004D9AC0/$file/Konsolidierte_Lesefassung_GPKE.pdf Accessed 20 November 2014
8. Dumas, M., La Rosa, M., Mendling, J., Mäesalu, R., Reijers, H.A., Semenenko, N.: Understanding business process models: the costs and benefits of structuredness. In: Ralyté, J., Franch, X., Brinkkemper, S., Wrycza, S. (eds.) CAiSE 2012. LNCS, vol. 7328, pp. 31–46. Springer, Heidelberg (2012)
9. Figl, K., Laue, R.: Cognitive complexity in business process modeling. In: Mouratidis, H., Rolland, C. (eds.) CAiSE 2011. LNCS, vol. 6741, pp. 452–466. Springer, Heidelberg (2011)
10. Kalpic, B., Bernus, P.: Business process modelling in industry—the powerful tool in enterprise management. Comput. Ind. **47**(3), 299–318 (2002)
11. Khademhosseinieh, B., Seigerroth, U.: Towards evaluating efficiency of enterprise modeling methods. In: Skersys, T., Butleris, R., Butkiene, R. (eds.) ICIST 2012. CCIS, vol. 319, pp. 74–86. Springer, Heidelberg (2012)
12. Knuth, D.E.: Computer-drawn flowcharts. Commun. ACM **6**(9), 555–563 (1963)
13. Krogstie, J.: Model-Based Development and Evolution of Information Systems. A Quality Approach. Springer, London (2012)
14. Maes, A., Poels, G.: Evaluating quality of conceptual models based on user perceptions. In: Embley, D.W., Olivé, A., Ram, S. (eds.) ER 2006. LNCS, vol. 4215, pp. 54–67. Springer, Heidelberg (2006)
15. Melcher, J., Mendling, J., Reijers, H.A., Seese, D.: On measuring the understandability of process models. In: Rinderle-Ma, S., Sadiq, S., Leymann, F. (eds.) BPM 2009. LNBIP, vol. 43, pp. 465–476. Springer, Heidelberg (2010)

16. Mendling, J., Strembeck, M.: Influence factors of understanding business process models. In: Abramowicz, W., Fensel, D. (eds.) BIS 2008. LNBIP, vol. 7, pp. 142–153. Springer, Heidelberg (2008)
17. Mikula, S.: Qualität von Geschäftsprozessnotationen. Diploma-Thesis, Rostock University, September 2011
18. Moody, D.L.: The "Physics" of notations: towards a scientific basis for constructing visual notations in software engineering. IEEE Trans. Softw. Eng. 35(6), 756–779 (2009)
19. Ottensooser, A., Fekete, A., Reijers, H.A., Mendling, J., Menictas, C.: Making sense of business process descriptions: an experimental comparison of graphical and textual notations. J. Syst. Softw. 85(3), 596–606 (2012)
20. Overhage, S., Birkmeier, D.Q., Schlauderer, S.: Qualitätsmerkmale, -metriken und -messverfahren für Geschäftsprozessmodelle. WIRTSCHAFTSINFORMATIK 54(5), 217–235 (2012)
21. Parsons, J., Cole, L.: What do pictures mean? Guidelines for experimental evaluation of representation fidelity in diagrammatical conceptual modeling techniques. Data Knowl. Eng. 55, 327–342 (2005)
22. Recker, J., Dreiling, A.: Does it matter which process modelling language we teach or use? An experimental study on understanding process modelling languages without formal education. In: Proceedings of the Australasian Conference on Information Systems (ACIS), Australia, Toowoomba, 5th–7th December 2007
23. Reisig, W.: A Primer in Petri Net Design. Springer, Heidelberg (1992)
24. Sandkuhl, K., Stirna, J., Persson, A., Wißotzki, M.: Enterprise Modeling: Tackling Business Challenges with the 4EM Method. The Enterprise Engineering Series. Springer, Heidelberg (2014). ISBN 978-3662437247
25. Scheer, A.-W., Nüttgens, M.: ARIS Architecture and Reference Models for Business Process Management. Springer, Heidelberg (2000)
26. Schrepfer, M., Wolf, J., Mendling, J., Reijers, H.A.: The impact of secondary notation on process model understanding. In: Persson, A., Stirna, J. (eds.) PoEM 2009. LNBIP, vol. 39, pp. 161–175. Springer, Heidelberg (2009)
27. Smith, H., Fingar, P.: Business Process Management: The Third Wave, 1st edn. Meghan-Kiffer Press, Tampa (2003)
28. Van der Aalst, W.M., Ter Hofstede, A.H.: YAWL: yet another workflow language. Inform. Syst. 30(4), 245–275 (2005)
29. Weske, M.: Business Process Management – Concepts, Languages, Architectures, 2nd edn. Springer, Heidelberg (2012)
30. White, S.A.: Introduction to BPMN. IBM Cooperation 2 (2004)

Modeling and Animation of Crisis Management Process with Statecharts

Elena Kushnareva[✉], Irina Rychkova, and Bénédicte Le Grand

University Paris 1 Panthéon-Sorbonne, 12, Place de Panthéon, 75005 Paris, France
{irina.rychkova,benedicte.le-grand}@univ-paris1.fr,
elena.kushnareva@malix.univ-paris1.fr
http://www.univ-paris1.fr/

Abstract. Crisis management process has to comply with various norms and regulations; at the same time, it needs to constantly deal with uncertainty and adapt the process scenario to a current situation. These requirements make process design challenging: whereas conventional activity-oriented modeling formalisms ensure process control by design, they provide only limited support for run-time adaptability of a process scenario. State-oriented formalisms can overcome this deficiency and, thus, extend the process designers toolkit. In this paper, we consider the example of a flood management process implemented as a part of the COS Operation Center - a smart city solution developed by COS&HT company in Russia. We examine the existing (BPMN) specification of this process and propose an alternative way to specify the process based on statecharts formalism. We model, animate and test the process scenarios with Yakindu Statecharts tools.

Keywords: Statecharts · Process simulation · Process flexibility

1   Introduction

A natural or technological crisis can occur as a result of an unpredictable sequence of events, putting lives of people at risk. Crisis management process has to comply with various norms and regulations; at the same time, it needs to constantly deal with uncertainty and adapt the process scenario to a current situation.

Modern city administrations seek to automate crisis management, implementing it as a part of their process-aware information systems (PAIS). A PAIS is a software system that manages operational processes involving people and applications based on explicit process models [7].

PAIS design is mostly based on the activity-driven paradigm. According to this paradigm, a process is specified as an ordered set of activities that the system has to execute. This paradigm ensures that the crisis management process is compliant with its norms and regulations "by design". However, it supports only limited process flexibility in response to unforeseen situation at run-time. This is what we experience with the COS Operation Center (COSOC) - a smart city solution developed by the COS&HT company in Russia.

© Springer International Publishing Switzerland 2015
R. Matulevičius and M. Dumas (Eds.): BIR 2015, LNBIP 229, pp. 145–160, 2015.
DOI: 10.1007/978-3-319-21915-8_10

In this paper, we consider the example of a flood management process implemented as a part of COSOC. We examine the existing (BPMN) specification of this process and propose an alternative (state-oriented) specification of this process using the statecharts formalism [12].

The statecharts formalism allows a designer to focus on WHAT must be done (i.e., expected outputs or postconditions) instead of HOW it must be done (i.e., concrete activities and their ordering). As a result, the concrete activities that suit best a given situation can be selected or even invented by a process manager at run-time. We call this *deferred binding*.

Statecharts specifications are executable. In this work, we simulate the statecharts specification of the flood management process with YAKINDU SCT (http://statecharts.org/). We show how the instant animation of a process combined with deferred binding of activities improves the process understanding, enables interactive (re)design and testing of both mandatory and adaptable process scenarios and paves the road for automated recommendations.

Our findings can be summarised as follows:

- BPMN focuses on activities, their ordering and thus ensures *compliance by design*. The statecharts formalism, in contrast, focuses on the expected outcomes and allows for *deferred binding of activities* at run-time. We propose (and envisage for the future work) to combine these formalisms for crisis management process specification, ensuring at the same time the required degree of control and flexibility.
- YAKINDU SCT provides a simple yet powerful tool for animation of process scenarios. It can be used as a complement to more conventional process specification and analysis techniques. Developing a methodology for state-oriented and simulation-based process design and analysis needs to be addressed in the future.

The remainder of this paper is organized as follows. In Sect. 2, we discuss the related work. In Sect. 3, we introduce our running example - the flood management process on Oka River in Moscow Region, Russia. In Sect. 4, we provide a brief overview of the statecharts formalism. In Sects. 5 and 6, we show how the flood management process can be specified with statecharts and animated using Yakindu Statecharts Tools. In Sect. 7, we draw our conclusions and present the perspective of this work.

2   Related Work

Crisis management is widely addressed by researchers in management science: in [8,20] leading ideas on crisis management in a business environment are presented; in [6,16] the context, concepts and practice of risk and crisis management in the public sector are discussed; in [15], a multidisciplinary approach to crisis management is defined. These works are mostly targeted towards federal agencies, city administration, policy makers, practitioners and researchers in management and business administration. Up to our knowledge, only a few works discuss the challenges of crisis management or its supporting information systems. An example is [17], which highlights the importance of context-awareness in crisis management.

Crisis management process is an example of Case Management Process (CMP). Davenport [4] defines a case management process as a process that is not predefined or repeatable, but depends on evolving circumstances and decisions regarding a particular situation, i.e., a case.

Adaptive Case Management (ACM) is a paradigm developed by a group of practitioners [25]. The body of knowledge on ACM has been extensively developed by practitioners; the best solutions are regularly reported in the book series on WfMC Global Awards for Excellence in Case Management [26]. However, methodologies and formalisms for CMP modeling are rarely discussed.

According to ACM [25], CMP must be organized around *a collection of data artifacts* about the case; the tasks and their ordering shall be adapted at run time, according to the evolution of the case circumstances and case-related data [18].

We agree with the authors of [25] that the conventional, activity-oriented paradigm is very restrictive while specifying case management and crisis management processes in particular. Moreover, we claim that the capacity of PAIS to support process flexibility is inherent to the underlying process modeling paradigm [13].

Up to now, the activity-oriented paradigm remains the mainstream paradigm for PAIS design. Within the *activity-oriented paradigm*, a process is specified *imperatively*, as an ordered set of activities that the system has to carry out. Examples of activity-oriented formalisms include BPMN [14], YAWL [1], activity diagrams in UML [23].

To provide better support for process flexibility, activity-oriented formalisms are extended with *declarative* parts such as constraints or configurable elements [2,22]. Possibilities to add or modify the activities at run-time remain beyond the scope of these approaches.

Whereas the activity-oriented paradigm can be very efficient in specifying highly-regulated crisis management processes, it can hardly support the run-time flexibility and adaptability required while handling the critical situation since it encourages the *early binding* of activities (at design-time). On the other hand, *the product-oriented (or state-oriented) paradigm* focuses on scenario adaptation and supports the *deferred binding*: at design-time, the process scenario is specified with as a sequence of events; the concrete activities that will produce these events can be selected or even invented at run-time. Examples of product-oriented modeling formalisms include state machines in UML [23], generic state-transition systems or state machines, such as FSM [9] or statecharts by D. Harel [10] created for the specification and analysis of complex discrete-event systems.

Several research groups report on approaches to design and specify case management processes based on the product-oriented paradigm: in [19] an approach that combines product- and activity-oriented paradigms is presented. The case handling paradigm is presented in [3]. Other formalisms extend product-oriented paradigm with the notions of goal and context [21, 24]. These formalisms support automated recommendations and user guidance, providing that for each goal all the situations (states) in which this goal is achievable are known. However, such formalisms focus on high-level system specifications and rarely support process analysis and simulation.

To conclude, we consider that combining an activity-oriented formalism with a state-oriented formalism can provide a process designer with a set of tools to (1) ensure the compliance and control over process execution and (2) better support the run-time process adaptability.

3   Activity-Oriented Model and Process Control

3.1   Flood Management Process in COS Operation Center

The COS operation center (COSOC) is a cross-domain information system developed by COS&HT in Russia. In this paper, we discuss the example of a *flood management process*, supported by COSOC.

Floods on the Oka River in the Moscow region are seasonal events caused by an increase in the flow of the river, provoked by intensive snow melting during the spring months. Floods on Oka also represent substantial risks for the critical infrastructure facilities situated in the area: a railway bridge, a pontoon road bridge, an electric power plant, industrial storage facilities, etc.

The flood emergency is triggered when the water level in the Oka River rises above 10 cm. Table 1 provides a brief description of the major phases of the flood. The flood crisis terminates when the water level gets back to normal, the response operations are terminated and the post-crisis reconstructions begin.

The goal of the flood management process in COSOC is to dispatch the assignments for operation procedures according to the crisis development and in agreement with the Emergency Management Guidelines [5] defined by the Ministry for Emergency Situations (MES). The selected procedures are carried out by MES, police taskforce, fire brigades, etc. The execution of the flood management process is monitored and controlled by the COSOC process manager.

The underlying processes in COSOC (including flood management process) are specified with BPMN - an activity-oriented modeling formalism. Figure 1 illustrates the (simplified) model of the flood management process implemented in COSOC.

3.2   Modeling Flood Management Process with BPMN

Following the flood scenario in Table 1, the BPMN model identifies its major phases and specifies the operation procedures accordingly. The list of events processed by COSOC is presented in Fig. 2-a.

The decision-making logic is modeled with a complex gateway G4 in the BPMN diagram. Here, various operation procedures can be (inclusively) selected.

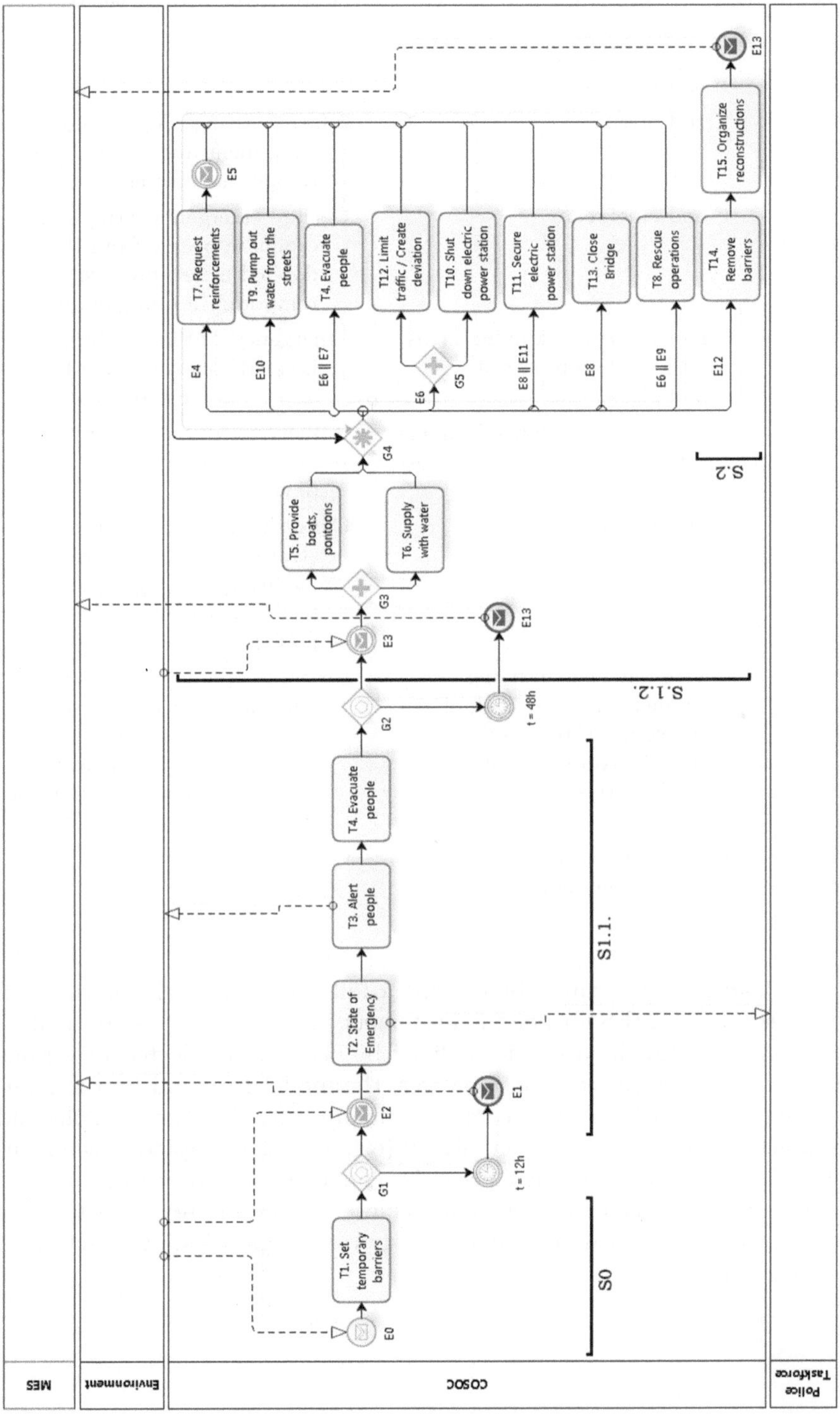

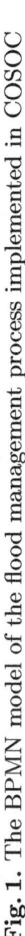

Fig. 1. The BPMN model of the flood management process implemented in COSOC

Table 1. Flood Scenario Driven by the changing water level in the Oka River

Water level rise	Threats / Expected consequences	Response
>10 cm	Flood alert	Inform citizens, deploy the equipment and set up temporary barriers
>10 cm and keeps rising	Flood emergency	Declare emergency situation, evacuate people from the flooded zones; prepare temporary accommodation
> 25 cm	Minor damages in living areas; risk of disrupted water supply	Emergency water supply; patrol flooded zones, provide boats and reinforce water barriers
>40 cm	Risk of severe damage in living areas	Rescue operations; secure bridges and organize deviations
>45 cm	Disrupted road traffic	Close the pontoon bridge; secure strategic infrastructure facilities (industrial storages, factories, electric power plant, etc.)
> 60 cm	Severe damages in living and industrial areas; Risk of presence of toxic substances in the river; Disrupted electricity supply	Rescuing operations; chemical and biological control of water; evacuation of industrial storage facilities; temporal accommodation for citizens
> 75 cm	Disrupted railway communication	Close the railway bridge

The provided model ensures (by design) a full compliance with norms and regulations defined by MES for flood management process. It also supports flexible scenario execution: the activities defined by G4 can be selected in various combinations, repeated or skipped. However, the model is bound by the number and kind of activities. When complex (unforeseen) situations unfold and predefined activities cannot be accomplished (e.g., due to disrupted telecommunication, lack of resources etc.) new activities cannot be added at run-time.

Run-time adaptability of the process scenario can be improved with state-oriented specifications that do not require early (at design) binding of activities to a process scenario.

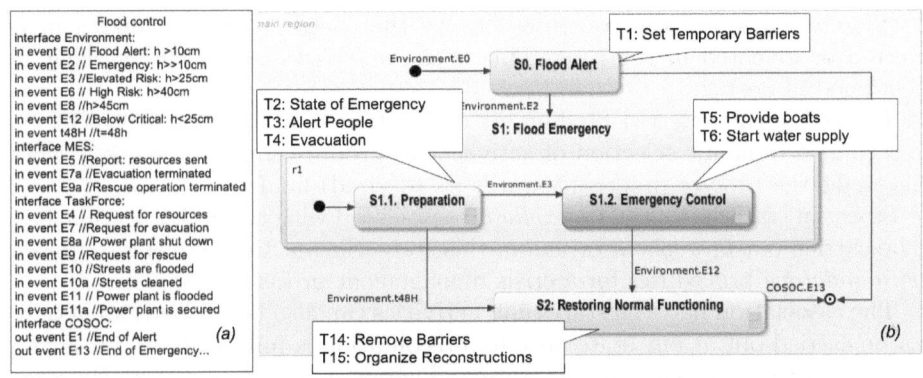

Fig. 2. High-level specification of the flood management process

4   State-Oriented Model and Process Adaptability

4.1   Statecharts

The statecharts formalism specifies a hierarchical state machine (HSM) that extends classical finite state machine (FSM)[9] by providing:

(i) depth - the possibility to model states at multiple hierarchical levels, with the notion of abstraction/refinement between levels;
(ii) orthogonality - the possibility to model concurrent or independent submachines within one state machine;
(iii) broadcast communication - the possibility to synchronize multiple concurrent submachines via events.

A state $s \in S$ in statechart represents a state of the system at a given time.

A state s consists of a (possibly empty) *hierarchy* of substates, representing (possibly concurrent) state machines. These substates provide the details about their parent state (or superstate).

The *active configuration* of a state s is the set of substates of s that are activated at the current moment.

Events that occur in the environment or result from some activity execution trigger *state transitions* in statecharts. The *triggering event e[c]* (interpreted as *e occurs and c holds*) of a transition t is an event that must occur in order for t to take place. Here $e \in E$ is the event that triggers the transition; $c \in C$ is a condition that prevents the transition from being taken unless it is true when e occurs; all these parameters are optional.

Some state-oriented approaches (e.g., Petri Net) explicitly associate a state transition with the execution of some activity: they consider a triggering event as an outcome of some *concrete activity* that is defined at design time. With statecharts, we do not specify the activities and focus uniquely on the expected outcomes (triggering events). We consider that the same outcome can be achieved in different ways and the concrete activity that needs to be executed can be selected or invented in run-time. This is the *deferred activity binding* that we mentioned in Sect. 2.

Thanks to the deferred binding, at design-time, the process enactment can be seen as a dynamic selection of activities to produce some outcomes (events) that make the process progress towards its (desired) final state.

States in statecharts can be *explicitly* associated with the activities that have to be carried out *throughout* or *within* this state. Such activities would represent the *mandatory* procedures for a crisis management process.

The association between states and activities can also be *implicit*: an activity can be carried out at any state once its precondition is fulfilled (i.e., if it is "not forbidden for performance at this state"). Therefore, any state of statechart can be associated with a (possibly empty) set of mandatory activities and a (possibly empty) set of optional activities.

In case of unforeseen situations (i.e., when a mandatory activity cannot result in a desired outcome and an expected triggering event does not occur) - the process manager can select an activity from the list of optional activities in order to compensate/resolve the situation and to eventually produce the desired triggering event.

Activities with their preconditions and postconditions can be modeled in a separate model called activity chart [11]. The list of optional activities can be maintained and extended dynamically at run time. New activities can be added to the activity chart by the process manager without affecting the statechart. The activity specification is out of scope for statecharts models and will not be further considered in this paper.

5   Modeling Flood Management Process with Statecharts

5.1   High Level Specification

We start the statecharts specification defining three main states for the flood management process: S0: Flood Alert, S1: Flood Emergency and S2: Restoring Normal Functioning. S1 is refined in two (exclusive) substates: S1.1.: Preparation and S1.2.: Emergency Control. S1.1 is the state where preparations of the city facing the flood are carried out according to the MES regulations in place. S1.2 is triggered when the water level in Oka River rises above 25 cm (E3 in the list of Flood control events). The black circle indicates that S1.1 is entered by default once S1 is entered (Fig. 2-b). With this high-level specification, we provide a correspondence with the original BPMN specification (the states are indicated in Fig. 1).

In the statecharts notation states are depicted by rectangular boxes with rounded corners. The substate-superstate relation is depicted by boxes encapsulation.

5.2 Introducing Concurrent Areas

We model four different domains of flood management from our example as four concurrent substates of the S1.2 Emergency Control: Living Area, Transport, Electric Power Plant (EPP) and Resources. Concurrent substates are depicted by regions within an AND-superstate separated by dashed lines.

When entering S1.2., the process simultaneously enters the (default) state in each corresponding concurrent substate. Black circles with an outgoing arrow indicate default states.

Living Area sub-machine defines three states: Elevated_Risk, High_Risk and Unsecured. The transitions between these states describe how a flood will progress and will be managed: Elevated_Risk is entered when the water level h rises above 25 cm (E3). The events received from Police Taskforce (e.g., requests for evacuation, rescue operations etc.) or from the environment (further rise of water level) trigger the High_Risk state. The events E7a, E9a, E10a trigger the transition back to the safer state Elevated Risk. These events result from the execution of some operation procedures (e.g., evacuation, rescue, pumping the water out of the streets or others). The state Unsecured is triggered when the event E4 indicating the lack of resources during execution of an operation procedure occurs.

Along those lines Electric_Power_Plant and Transport concurrent substates define the submachines that show how the corresponding infrastructure objects are managed during the flood. According to the regulations, the power plant must be Shut Down when the water level rises above 40 cm (E6). If the water keeps rising there is a risk that this facility will be flooded. Here the Unsecured state is triggered. The Normal_Functioning is maintained for the Transport area; when the water h rises above 40 cm only Limited Traffic is supported; when the water level h exceeds 45 cm threshold the pontoon bridge has to be closed (Bridge Closed).

In our example, each state of the statechart can be associated with the list of mandatory and optional activities that must/can be carried out upon entering, upon exiting and while in this state. With the state-oriented paradigm, the objective of the flood management process can be reformulated as follows: the process participants (i.e., MES and Police Taskforce) should respond to the events that occur in the environment (e.g., rise of water, weather changes, etc.) by executing the operation procedures and producing the outcomes in order to maintain the secure functioning of the city in specified domains.

6 Simulation with Yakindo Statecharts Tools

We have designed the process specification described previously with the YAKINDU SCT modeler. The YAKINDU simulation environment allows us to instantiate the statecharts specification and to simulate the underlying process.

Fig. 4 illustrates an execution of a flood management process modeled in Fig. 3. The process starts when the water level in Oka River rises above 10 cm (see the event E0 in Table 1) and enters the state S0_Flood_Alert. The event

E2 triggers the state S1_Flood_Emergency and enters its default (exclusive) sub-state S1_1 Preparation (Fig. 3).

When the water level rises above 25 cm - the S1_2_Emergency_Control state is entered.

Figure 4-a illustrates an active configuration of the statecharts upon the realisation of a sequence of events: $E0 \rightarrow E2 \rightarrow E3 \rightarrow E7$. When the event E7 (Request for evacuation) occurs, it triggers a transition to the High_Risk state of the Living Area region. In response, the process manager assigns the tasks for evacuation.

According to our scenario "played" in YAKINDU, the water level rises above 40 cm (E6) and then above 45 cm (E8). These events trigger the corresponding configurations (the latter is shown in Fig. 4-b). In response to the threat, specific tasks for securing the power plant (e.g., Pumping water, Evacuating equipment) are assigned by the process manager. One (or several) of such actions produces a desired event E11a (Power plant is secured), which triggers a transition from Unsecured to Shut_Down state in our statechart (Fig. 4-c).

As the process continues, some of the crisis handling activities (e.g., evacuation) produce the E4 (lack of resources) event (Fig. 4-d). If it occurs repeatedly, E4 triggers the Federal_Alert state (Fig. 4-e). The triggering event in our model specifies that this state is activated if the E4 event occurs while the Unsecured state of the Living Area or the Power_Plant_Unsecured state is active.

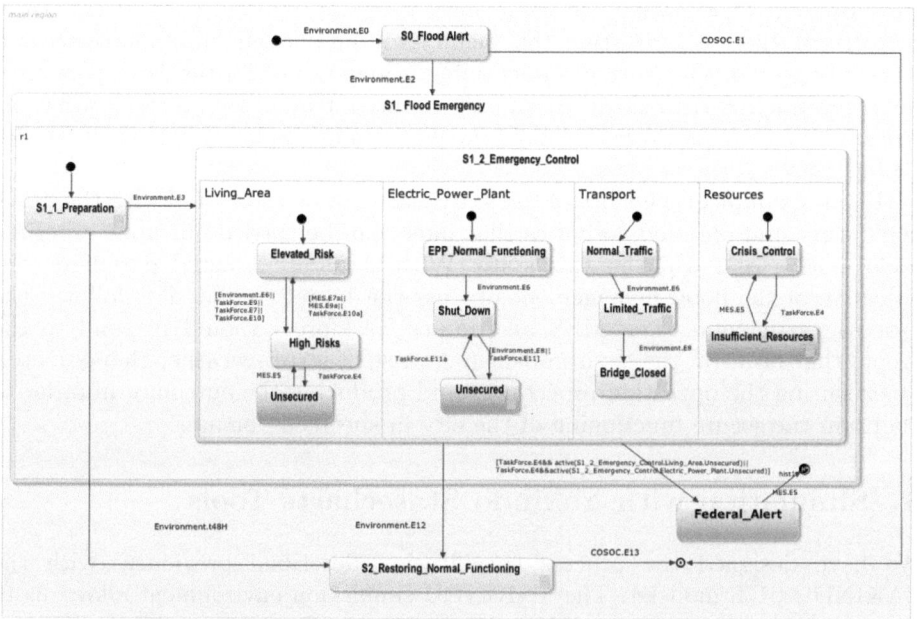

Fig. 3. Explicit resource management

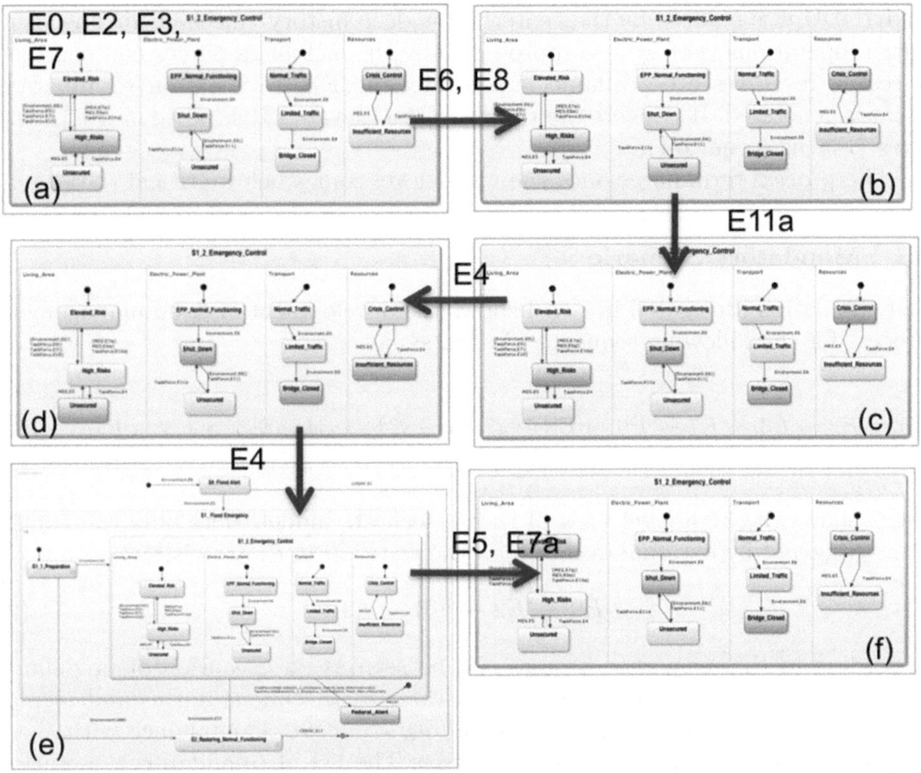

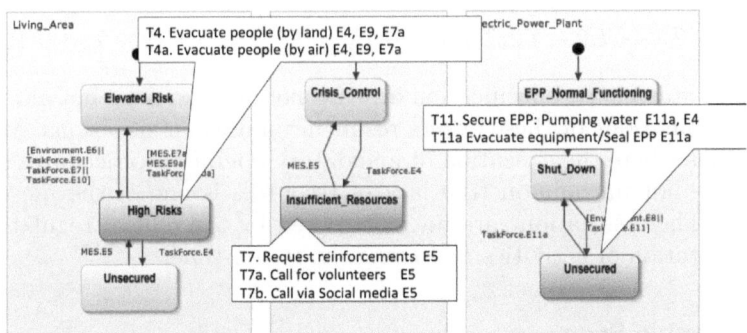

Fig. 4. Simulation of the flood management process with YAKINDU SCT

Fig. 5. Adaptive scenarios

This models "an interruption" - a situation of high priority that requires the involvement of military forces or other reserves in order to protect citizens.

When the required resources are available (E5) - the system returns back to the configuration where this interruption occurred - in statecharts and in

YAKINDU it is realised by the "entering by deep history" mechanism The evacuation operations that were compromised by the lack of resources can continue once the resources are available. Eventually the E7a (evacuation terminated) event is generated. It triggers the return to the Elevated_Risk state in the Living Area (Fig. fig:scenario-f).

The process terminates once the water level comes below critical (E12).

6.1   Mandatory Scenario

Our simulation illustrated in Fig. 4 shows the development of flood management process for the following sequence of events:

$$E0 \rightarrow E2 \rightarrow E3 \rightarrow E7 \rightarrow E6 \rightarrow E8 \rightarrow E11a \rightarrow E4 \rightarrow E4 \rightarrow E5 \rightarrow E5 \rightarrow E7a \rightarrow E12 \tag{1}$$

Fig. 2 shows the high level view of the statecharts model. Here only the transitions triggered by external events (i.e., the water level h) are visible:

$$E0 \rightarrow E2 \rightarrow E3 \rightarrow E12 \tag{2}$$

According to this view, the process can be seen as an execution of predefined operation procedures in response to the water raise. Official norms and regulations are usually focused on such *mandatory scenarios*. Compliance with them is essential for crisis management processes. The list of (mandatory) operation procedures can be specified for each state, similarly to the BPMN specification. These procedures can be carried out on *entering*, on *exiting*, *throughout* or *within* a state. The resulting mandatory process scenario can be represented as follows:

$$E0 - T1 \rightarrow E2 - T2, T3, T4 \rightarrow E3 - T5, T6 \rightarrow E12 - T14, T15 \tag{3}$$

The detailed statecharts specification involves not only external but also internal events. Combinations of these events result in unforeseen situations. Moreover, the situations where the execution of mandatory operation procedures are compromised are not uncommon (the lack of resources is one of the most typical situations). These situations are not considered by the official regulations and require adaptation of activities and scenarios at run-time.

6.2   Adaptable Scenario

The process can be seen as an execution of mandatory procedures defined by MES and other (optional, adapted) activities justified by a concrete situation. We refer to this process scenario as *adaptable scenario*.

The goal of the process can be seen as "to maintain a safe state". This means that at run-time, if the process enters some "unsafe state", the process manager will select or propose activities in order to generate an event that shall trigger the transition back to the "safe state". In case of "selection", the process manager will select among the activities enabled (i.e., with valid precondition) in the Activity chart associated with the process. If the process manager decides to propose a new activity that better suits the situation - she will add the activity into the activity chart by specifying its precondition and its expected outcome. Activity charts remain out of scope for this work.

In Fig. 5 we show the alternative activities that can be carried out at a given state in order to "produce" a desired event that would trigger a transition to a "safe" state. For example, in High_Risk state of a Living_Area submachine, we define two alternative ways to execute the evacuation of people from the flooded areas: by land or by air (when the former is not possible). Both activities, in case of successful termination, can produce the event E7a (evacuation successfully terminated) and thus trigger a transition to Elevated_Risk state.

There is more then a single *adaptable process scenario* that can be realised within the same sequence of events:

$$a) \rightarrow E7{-}T4 \rightarrow E7a \rightarrow ... \ b) \rightarrow E7{-}T4, T4a \rightarrow E7a \rightarrow ... \ c) \rightarrow E7{-}T4, T4a, T4 \rightarrow E7a \rightarrow ... \tag{4}$$

A more interesting case can be seen for the Resource management area: besides a predefined activity Request Reinforcement that consists in contacting the MES, the process manager defines two other activities that (based on her experience) lead to the same outcome (E5). During the process execution, the alternative activities can be carried out in combination or iteratively until the desired effect is obtained and the transition to Crisis_Control is triggered. The corresponding process scenarios that can be realised can look as follows:

$$a) \rightarrow E4 - T7 \rightarrow E5 \rightarrow ... b) \rightarrow E4 - T7, T7, T7a \rightarrow E5 \rightarrow ... c) \rightarrow E7 - T7b, T7a \rightarrow E5 \rightarrow ... \tag{5}$$

Note that some of the activities may not even be known at design (e.g., T7b - Call for reinforcements via social media).

7   Conclusion and Perspectives

In this paper, we reported on our experience of modeling crisis management process with the statecharts formalism [12]. We also presented the results of the simulations conducted with YAKINDU SCT. Whereas conventional activity-oriented modeling formalisms ensure process control by design, they provide only limited support for run-time adaptability of a process scenario. The formalism of statecharts can overcome this deficiency and, thus, extend the designers toolkit. In particular, it provides capabilities for animated design and paves the road for automated recommendations. In our future work, we are going to further explore these capabilities. Below, we present some of these perspectives.

7.1   Combining Activity-Oriented and State-Oriented Paradigms for Improving Process Flexibility

Business Process Model and Notation (BPMN) is a defacto standard for business process modeling and simulation. Various modeling environments (e.g. Bizagi,

Aris, Signavio etc.) support modeling, simulation and validation of the resulting process models. These and similar tools focus on designing the *activities* and combining these activities into *scenarios*. While the ordering of activities (control flow) can be configured at run-time, the number and kind of activities have to be predefined at design-time. For knowledge-intensive processes such as crisis management, activities are also a subject of run-time adaptation. Such adaptation is not supported by activity-oriented paradigm and its corresponding formalisms.

Following the state-oriented paradigm, a process designer does not need to design activities, but only their desired results. As for BPMN, the numbers of states and state transitions in statecharts are explicitly specified at design time. Activities, however, are not associated with state transitions and do not need to be explicitly defined by the model. They can be linked or even defined on fly.

In response to unforeseen situations, the process manager can select from available activities. Thanks to deferred binding, she can also define a new activity better adapted for a situation.

Combining activity-oriented and state-oriented formalisms, we aim to improve the process flexibility. With BPMN, we can specify the "obligatory" part of the process and validate the compliance with norms and regulations. With statecharts, we can focus on the adaptive part. The activities prescribed by BPMN can be explicitly linked to statecharts states, whereas the other (optional) list of activities can be maintained on fly by a process manager, providing greater flexibility of a process.

7.2   Exploring Animated Design

Statechart formalism and YAKINDU SCT enable an animated design process for crisis management. The simple yet powerful visual formalism of statecharts allows a process designer to focus on the situations (states) and to reason in terms of "safe" - "unsafe" states, setting up the objectives of the process (i.e., "to maintain the safe state").

Desired case handling outcomes (events) are designed independently from the activities that actually produce these outcomes. As a result, a process is simulated with a sequence of (desired/undesired/external/internal) events whereas a decision about a concrete activities can be made reflecting a concrete situation (an active configuration, a history of previously triggered active configurations, a history of events occured etc.).

Developing a design framework where different process scenarios (desired or undesired events) can be played and analysed is our objective. Such framework can help the domain experts to improve the process and possibly to find some situations that they have never considered before and be prepared to handle them.

7.3   From Management to Recommendations

From the system perspective, the state-oriented paradigm creates a recommendation system where the process manager plays the leading role in scenario definition. Unforeseen situations are handled within the system enabling a seamless improvement of the process.

We aim at analyzing situations together with the identification of a desired target state in order to generate recommendations.

References

1. van der Aalst, W., Ter Hofstede, A.H.: Yawl: yet another workflow language. Inf. Syst. **30**(4), 245–275 (2005)
2. van der Aalst, W., Pesic, M., Schonenberg, H.: Declarative workflows: balancing between flexibility and support. Comput. Sci.-Res. Dev. **23**(2), 99–113 (2009)
3. van der Aalst, W., Weske, M., Grünbauer, D.: Case handling: a new paradigm for business process support. Data Knowl. Eng. **53**(2), 129–162 (2005)
4. Davenport, T.: Thinking for a Living: How to Get Better Performances and Results from Knowledge Workers. Harvard Business Press, Boston (2005)
5. The ministry of the Russian Federation for civil defense, emergencies and elimination of consequences of natural disasters: Emergency management guidelines (2013). http://www.mchs.gov.ru/
6. Drennan, L., McConnell, A.: Risk and Crisis Management in the Public Sector (Routledge Masters in Public Management). Routledge, Abingdon, New Edition (2007)
7. Dumas, M., van der Aalst, W.M., Ter Hofstede, A.H.: Process-aware Information Systems: Bridging People and Software Through Process Technology. Wiley, New York (2005)
8. Fink, S.: Crisis management: Planning for the Inevitable. American Management Association, Reed Business Information, Inc, New York (1986)
9. Gill, A.: Introduction to the Theory of Finite-State Machines. McGraw-Hill, New York (1962). http://opac.inria.fr/record=b1082931
10. Harel, D.: Statecharts: a visual formalism for complex systems. Sci. comput. Program. **8**(3), 231–274 (1987)
11. Harel, D., Pnueli, A.: On the Development of Reactive Systems. Springer, Heidelberg (1985)
12. Harel, D., Politi, M.: Modeling Reactive Systems with Statecharts: The STATE-MATE Approach. McGraw-Hill, Inc., New York (1998)
13. Kushnareva, E., Rychkova, I., Le Grand, B.: Modeling business processes for automated crisis management support: lessons learned. In: IEEE 9th International Conference on Research Challenges in Information Science (RCIS) (2015)
14. OMG: Business process model and notation (2011). http://www.omg.org/spec
15. Pearson, C., Clair, J.: Reframing crisis management. Acad. Manage. Rev. **23**(1), 59–76 (1998)
16. Penuel, K., Statler, M., Hagen, R.: Encyclopedia of Crisis Management. SAGE Publications, Inc., Thousand Oaks (2013)
17. Ploesser, K.: A Design Theory for Context-Aware Information Systems. Nova Publishers, Hauppauge (2012). http://eprints.qut.edu.au/60865/
18. Pucher, M.: The elements of adaptive case management. In: Swenson, K. (ed.) Mastering the Unpredictable, pp. 89–134. Meghan-Kiffer Press, Tampa (2010)
19. Reijers, H.A., Limam, S., Van Der Aalst, W.: Product-based workflow design. J. Manage. Inf. Syst. **20**(1), 229–262 (2003)

20. Review, H.B.: Crisis Management: Mastering the skills to prevent disasters. Harvard Business Essentials (2004)
21. Rolland, C., Souveyet, C., Moreno, M.: An approach for defining ways-of-working. Inf. Syst. **20**(4), 337–359 (1995)
22. Rosemann, M., van der Aalst, W.: A configurable reference modelling language. Inf. Syst. **32**(1), 1–23 (2007)
23. Rumbaugh, J., Jacobson, I., Booch, G.: Unified Modeling Language Reference Manual, 2nd edn. Pearson Higher Education, London (2004)
24. Soffer, P., Yehezkel, T.: A state-based context-aware declarative process model. In: Halpin, T., Nurcan, S., Krogstie, J., Soffer, P., Proper, E., Schmidt, R., Bider, I. (eds.) BPMDS 2011 and EMMSAD 2011. LNBIP, vol. 81, pp. 148–162. Springer, Heidelberg (2011)
25. Swenson, K.: Mastering The Unpredictable: How Adaptive Case Management Will Revolutionize The Way That Knowledge Workers Get Things Do. Meghan-Kiffer Press, Tampa (2010)
26. Swenson, K., Palmer, N., Manuel, A., Carlsen, S.: Empowering Knowledge Workers. BPM and Workflow Handbook Series. Future Strategies Inc, Mississauga (2013)

Change Point Detection and Dealing with Gradual and Multi-order Dynamics in Process Mining

J. Martjushev[1,2], R.P. Jagadeesh Chandra Bose[2]([✉]),
and Wil M.P. van der Aalst[2]

[1] University of Tartu, Tartu, Estonia
[2] Eindhoven University of Technology, Eindhoven, The Netherlands
{martjushev,jcbose}@gmail.com, w.m.p.v.d.aalst@tue.nl

Abstract. In recent years process mining techniques have matured. Provided that the process is stable and enough example traces have been recorded in the event log, it is possible to discover a high-quality process model that can be used for performance analysis, compliance checking, and prediction. Unfortunately, most processes are not in steady-state and process discovery techniques have problems uncovering "second-order dynamics" (i.e., the process itself changes while being analyzed). This paper describes an approach to discover a variety of *concept drifts* in processes. Unlike earlier approaches, we can discover *gradual drifts* and *multi-order dynamics* (e.g., recurring seasonal effects mixed with the effects of an economic crisis). We use a novel adaptive windowing approach to robustly localize changes (gradual or sudden). Our extensive evaluation (based on objective criteria) shows that the new approach is able to efficiently uncover a broad range of drifts in processes.

1 Introduction

In today's dynamic marketplace, organizations are expected to be flexible and quickly adapt to changing circumstances so as to reduce costs and to improve performance. New legislations such as the WABO act [10] and the Sarbanes-Oxley Act [15], extreme variations in supply and demand, seasonal effects, natural calamities and disasters, deadline escalations [2], etc., force organizations to change their processes. Processes may change suddenly or gradually. The drift may be periodic (e.g., due to seasonal influences) or one-of-a-kind (e.g., the effects of new legislation). For process management it is crucial to discover and understand such *concept drifts* in processes.

Processes executed in today's world are often supported and controlled by information systems, which record events in the form of *event logs*. Process mining aims to *discover, monitor* and *improve* real-life processes by extracting knowledge from event logs [1]. Although most business processes change over time, contemporary process mining techniques cannot capture such "second-order dynamics" and analyze these processes as if they are in *steady-state*. However, *detecting and understanding concept drifts is of imminent importance for organizations*.

© Springer International Publishing Switzerland 2015
R. Matulevičius and M. Dumas (Eds.): BIR 2015, LNBIP 229, pp. 161–178, 2015.
DOI: 10.1007/978-3-319-21915-8_11

Although the topic of concept drift is well-studied in various branches of the data mining and machine learning community [3,12,16,21], it has only been recently introduced in the context of process mining [4]. Contemporary concept drift approaches focus on changes in relatively simple structures (e.g., data values and frequencies). Process models are complex artifacts describing behavior involving concurrency, choices, loops, cancelation, etc. Traditional approaches cannot be used to discover the "process of process change". There are three main topics when dealing with concept drifts in process mining [4]:

– *Change (point) detection:* the first and most fundamental problem is to detect that a process change has taken place. If so, the next step is to identify the time periods at which changes have taken place.
– *Change localization and characterization:* once a point of change has been identified, the next step is to characterize the nature of change, and identify the region(s) of change (localization) in a process.
– *Change process discovery:* unraveling the evolution of a process, i.e., the discovery of the change process describing the "second-order" dynamics.

In this paper, we build on the approach in [4] and present novel techniques for detecting process changes and the points at which they changed by analyzing event logs. More specifically, (i) we present an approach to *automatically identify the points (time periods) of change,* (ii) we propose a technique for *change detection using adaptive windows,* (iii) we characterize the notions of *gradual drifts* and *multi-order dynamics* and propose techniques for detecting them, and (iv) we propose an *objective* evaluation framework for change detection. The proposed techniques have been implemented as the Concept Drift plug-in in ProM.[1] The approach was evaluated using a variety of synthetic and real-life event logs.

The remainder of this paper is organized as follows. Section 2 provides the background on change detection techniques based on hypothesis tests. Section 3 presents an approach for automatically identifying change points. An adaptive windowing technique for change detection is presented in Sect. 4. Section 5 characterizes the notions of gradual and multi-order changes and presents techniques for detecting them. Section 6 proposes an approach for evaluating change detection techniques objectively. Section 7 presents and discusses experimental results. Related work is presented in Sect. 8. Finally, Sect. 9 concludes the paper.

2   Background

In this section, we present a brief overview of the change detection technique presented in [4] upon which the concepts presented in this paper are based.

Processes can change with respect to the three main process perspectives, viz., control-flow, data, and resource. Such changes are perceived to induce a drift in the concept (process behavior), e.g., in the way which activities are executed *when, how,* and by *whom.* One can consider an event log $\mathcal{L}$ as a time

---

[1] See www.processmining.org for more information and to download ProM.

series of traces (traces ordered based on the timestamp of the first event). The basic premise in handling concept drifts is that *the characteristics of the traces before the change point differ from the characteristics of the traces after the change point.* The problem of change (point) detection is then to identify the points in time when the process has changed, if any. Change point detection involves two primary steps: (i) capturing the characteristics of the traces, and (ii) identifying when these characteristics change.

The control-flow perspective of a process characterizes the relationships between activities. Dependencies between activities in an event log can be captured and expressed using the *follows* (or *precedes*) relationship, also referred to as *causal footprints*. Bose et al. [4] proposed four features characterizing the control-flow dependencies between activities. These features are shown to be effective in detecting process changes. An event log can be transformed into a data set $\mathcal{D}$, which can be considered as a time series (as depicted in Fig. 1), by these features. Change detection is done by considering a series of successive populations[2] of feature values (of some population size w, see Fig. 1) and investigating if there is a significant difference between two successive populations. The premise is that differences are expected to be perceived at change points provided appropriate characteristics of the change are captured as features. The difference between populations is assessed using *statistical hypothesis testing* [18]. Hypothesis tests yield a significance value (the so-called *p-value*), whose range is between 0 and 1, assessing the validity of the null-hypothesis, which typically states that the two populations come from the same distribution. A plot of p-values corresponding to the trace indices captured by populations is inspected to see if significant differences (and thereby process changes) exist. *The p-values are plotted against the indices at the end of the left populations.* Figure 2 depicts a representative *p*-value plot. Process changes stand out as *troughs* in the p-value plot. This approach is effective in detecting sudden drifts as shown in [4,5].

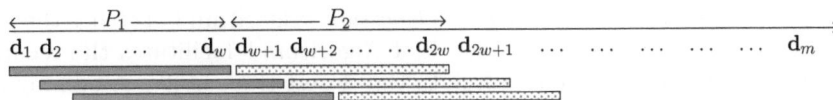

Fig. 1. Basic idea of detecting drifts using hypothesis tests. The data set of feature values is considered as a time series for hypothesis tests. P_1 and P_2 are two populations of size w.

Techniques for dealing with concept drift can be broadly classified into *online* and *offline* depending on whether or not the presence of changes or the occurrence of drifts needs to be uncovered in real-time. In this paper, we focus on offline drift detection. However, our techniques can easily be adapted to the online setting.

---

[2] A moving window is used to generate the series of populations.

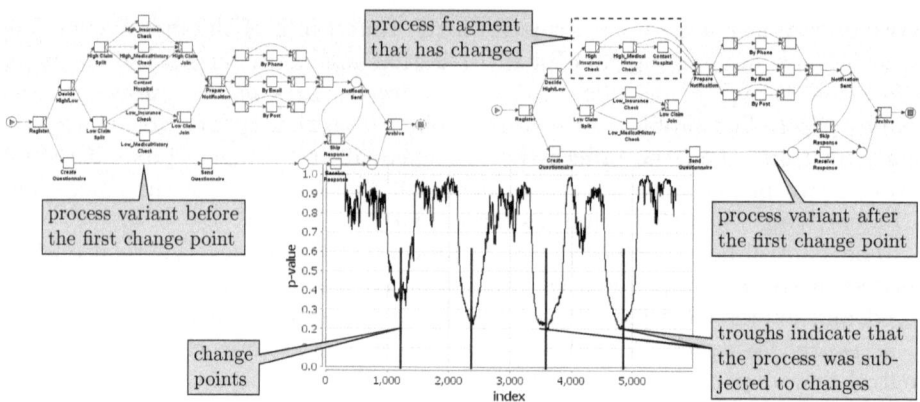

Fig. 2. A plot of *p*-values of the hypothesis tests. X-axis represents the trace index and Y-axis represents the *p*-value. Troughs in the plot signify process changes. Process variants before and after a change point can be inspected to identify the fragments that have been changed.

3   Change Point Detection

Process changes manifested in an event log are detected by inspecting the p-value plot of the hypothesis tests over feature values captured for the traces [4].[3] This suffers from the limitation that change and change point detection both need to be done manually by visual inspection. In this section, we present *an automated approach for detecting the points of change*. The basic idea is to first choose an a priori threshold for p-value, $\hat{p}$, to detect the presence of changes. If the significance value (i.e., p-value) of the hypothesis test for two populations P_1 and P_2 is less than $\hat{p}$, we report that there is a change in the process. Having detected that the process has changed, we further explore the two populations to identify the *closest point* of change using a *recursive bisection*. Algorithm 1 sketches the basic idea while Fig. 3 illustrates this. Step 5 of Algorithm 1 facilitates the recursive exploration of the change point search to the closest trace index. Assuming that the p-value is minimum corresponding to the two populations on the right hand side and is less than the threshold $\hat{p}$ (Step 4, Algorithm 1), Fig. 3(b) depicts the recursive search for change point within the right population.

Once a change point has been detected, analysis proceeds as before using a sliding window starting from the first index after the end of the right population. Compared to [4], the location of the change point can be determined more precisely.

---

[3] The presence of troughs in the p-value plot indicates that the process was subjected to changes.

Algorithm 1. Change Point Detection

1: Let P_1 and P_2 be the two populations where we have detected a change (i.e., its hypothesis test's p-value $< \hat{p}$).

2: Split the two populations P_1 and P_2 into halves, P_{11} and P_{12} for P_1 and P_{21} and P_{22} for P_2.

3: Apply a hypothesis test on the left (P_{11} and P_{12}), center (P_{12} and P_{21}), and right (P_{21} and P_{22}) population pairs as illustrated in Fig. 3(a). Let p_{left}, p_{center}, and p_{right} be their respective p-values.

4: Let $p_{min} = \min\{p_{left}, p_{center}, p_{right}\}$. Let P^1_{min} and P^2_{min} be the corresponding populations of p_{min}.

5: If $p_{min} < \hat{p}$, set $P_1 = P^1_{min}$ and $P_2 = P^2_{min}$, goto Step 1, else return the index/time point corresponding to the trace at end of P_1 as the change point.

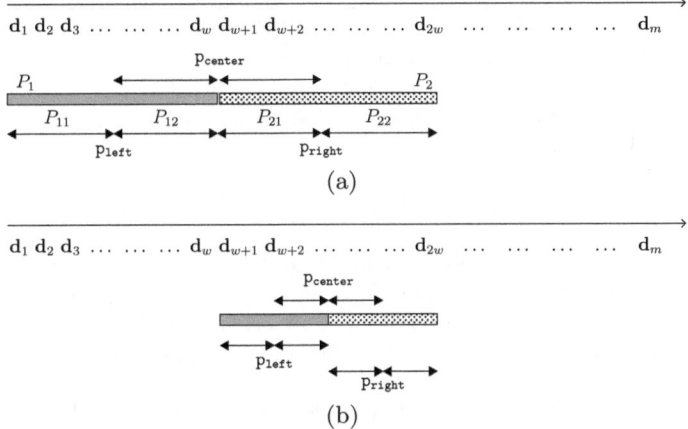

Fig. 3. Basic idea of our recursive bisection approach to detect and localize change points. (a) change point search by considering the left, center, and right sub-populations (b) recursive search for change point in the right population.

4   Adaptive Windowing Approach for Change Detection

The statistical hypothesis test analysis for change detection discussed above uses a *fixed* population size. The goodness of the results depends on the population size, which is largely dependent on the application and the focus of analysis. Typically, one sees a lot of noise in the p-value plot for small populations and the plot tends to be smooth as the population size increases. This can be attributed to the fact that as the population size increases (i.e., as we consider more cases), the variability in the nature of cases reduces and attains a stability. A small population size might result in false positives, i.e., detecting concept drifts that do not exist, while a large population size might result in false negatives, i.e., drifts remain undetected. In order to address this issue, we propose the use of *adaptive windows* where in the population sizes are automatically adapted based on the characteristics of the data stream. We adapt the ADWIN technique [3], an approach for online change detection using an adaptive size sliding detection window. Algorithm 2 presents the adaptive window approach for change detection. The basic idea is to use minimum and maximum size limits for populations and extend the population sizes until a change has been detected or the populations reach the maximum size limit. If the maximum size is reached, we discard the historically old data (i.e., the left most population) and proceed with the hypothesis tests with recent data. When a change has been detected, we identify the change point and proceed with hypothesis tests using two new smaller populations (of minimum size) with the new left population starting at the first index after the old right population and the new right population starting at the first index after the new left population (Steps 5–6, Algorithm 2).

Algorithm 2. Change Detection Using Adaptive Windows

Require: a minimum population size $w_{\min}$, a maximum population size $w_{\max}$, p-value threshold $\hat{p}$, a step size k, and a data stream of values $\mathcal{D}$

1: Let P_{left} and P_{right} be two populations of size $w_{\min}$ with P_{right} starting at the first index after the end of P_{left}.

2: **repeat**

3:     Apply a hypothesis test over P_{left} and P_{right}. Let p be its p-value.

4:     **if** $p < \hat{p}$ **then**

5:         Identify the change point within P_{left} and P_{right} using Algorithm 1.

6:         Create two new populations P'_{left} and P'_{right} of size $w_{\min}$ with P'_{left} starting at the first index after the end of P_{right} and P'_{right} starting at the first index after the end of P'_{left}. Set $P_{\text{left}} = P'_{\text{left}}$ and $P_{\text{right}} = P'_{\text{right}}$.

7:     **else**

8:         Extend the left and right populations by a step size k. Reassign the right population to start at the first index after the end of the extended left population P_{left}.

9:         **if** the size of the population $\geq w_{\max}$ **then** discard the left population P_{left}. Split the right population P_{right} into two halves and use them as the left and right populations.

10:         **end if**

11:     **end if**

12: **until** the end of P_{right} doesn't reach the end of $\mathcal{D}$

As mentioned earlier, the p-values are plotted against the indices at the end of the left populations. When a change has been detected or when the populations reach a maximum size, we create new populations. This creates a gap between the indices at the end of the old and new left populations. To have a continuous p-value plot, we connect the p-values at the old and new indices (corresponding to the old and new left populations) by a straight line.

5   Dealing with Gradual Drifts and Multi-order Dynamics

In this section, we characterize the notions of *gradual* and *multi-order changes* and present techniques for detecting such changes.

5.1   Gradual Drifts

In gradual drifts, one concept fades gradually while the other takes over. This phenomenon of gradual change can be modeled in many ways by means of functions that describe how things grow or decay as time passes. For example, the change can be linear between two sources as illustrated in Fig. 4. In the figure, initially until t_1, only the process variant M_1 is in operation, i.e., all cases emanate from M_1 until t_1. The gradual change between process variants M_1 and M_2 happen *linearly* between t_1 and t_2, i.e., the cases from M_1 and M_2 constantly decrease and increase respectively. The degree of decrease/increase is characterized by the *slope* as illustrated in Fig. 4(a)–(c). Subsequently, from t_2, all cases emanate only from M_2. As another example, one can notice an *exponential rate of increase/decrease* of cases from two processes as illustrated in Fig. 5. Here, the degree of change between t_1 and t_2 is characterized by the function $e^{-\lambda t}$ for M_1. The probability of a case emanating from M_2 at any instant of time between t_1 and t_2 is modeled as $1 - p_{M_1}$ where p_{M_1} is the probability of a case being from M_1.

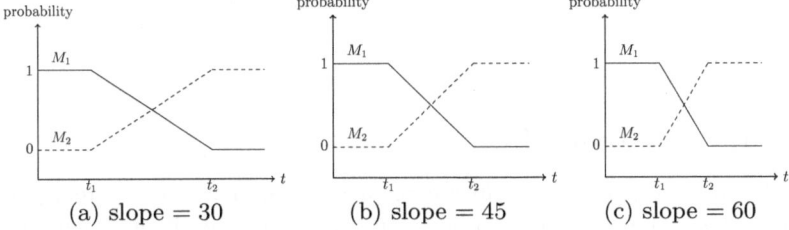

Fig. 4. Different variants of linear gradual drift between t_1 and t_2 for processes M_1 and M_2. The rate of change is characterized by the slope.

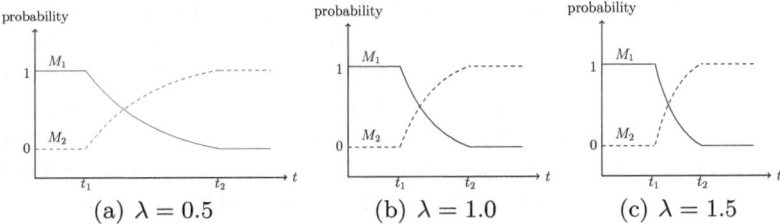

Fig. 5. Different variants of exponential gradual drift between t_1 and t_2 characterized by the function $e^{-\lambda t}$ for M_1.

Analyzing event logs for concept drifts under gradual changes can be done using hypothesis tests on features characterizing the process execution behavior. However, since the transition between two processes M_1 and M_2 is gradual/smooth, the p-values tend to be higher compared to sudden drifts if the conventional sliding window approach is considered. Furthermore, if detected, the troughs tend to be wider, in proportion to the duration for which the gradual change is operational. Therefore, to detect gradual drifts, we advocate the use of *non-continuous populations* as illustrated in Fig. 6. The intuition behind this is that the *gap* between populations makes it easier to pick up differences even when instances from both processes co-exist. Provided a proper choice of the gap is made, at the onset of gradual change, the populations P_1 and P_2 capture instances only from M_1 and M_2 respectively; a hypothesis test on these two populations should yield a significantly lower p-value, thus facilitating the detection of a change.

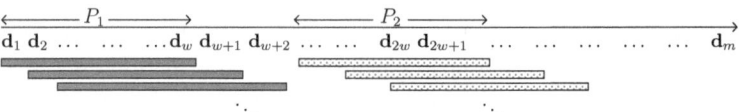

Fig. 6. General idea of gradual drift detection using hypothesis tests on non-continuous populations: P_1 and P_2 are deliberately separated by a gap.

5.2   Multi-order Dynamics

In this section, we extend the notion of process changes to also include *multi-order dynamics* where process changes can happen at multiple levels of (time) granularity, e.g., weekly and yearly recurring drifts may be mixed with drifts due to economic developments. For example, suppose an organization induces a process change from M_1 to M_2 after 24 weeks. Furthermore, let us assume that there are two variants of process M_1, viz., M_{11} and M_{12}, and two variants of process M_2, viz., M_{21} and M_{22}, which the organization recurringly changes every six weeks within/after the first 24 weeks respectively.[4] Figure 7 illustrates this phenomenon. Each time unit in the figure corresponds to six weeks. We can see that process changes happen at two-levels in this example. One change induced every six weeks and another change happening at 24 weeks (time unit 4 in the figure) between M_1 and M_2. When dealing with concept drifts, one has to take into consideration the presence of such multi-order dynamics. The framework for change detection using hypothesis tests can still be used for detecting multi-order changes. However, *instead of considering populations based on a fixed volume of traces/cases, we should consider populations at different time scales.* Populations comprising cases within shorter-time periods are to be used for detecting *micro-level* changes while larger time periods are to be chosen for *macro-level* changes. For example, using populations comprising of cases in a time period up to six

---

[4] To simplify discussion, the duration for which a process variant is active is kept uniform. However, in reality, processes can be deployed for varying durations and can be changed at varying intervals.

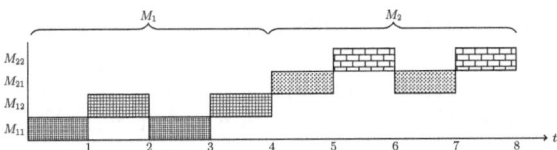

Fig. 7. Illustration of multi-order changes involving four process variants: micro-level drifts (e.g., the alternation of M_{11} and M_{12}) operate at a different time scale than the macro-level drift from M_1 to M_2.

weeks, we would be able to detect the seven *micro-level* change points in Fig. 7. Instead, if we choose the populations to comprise of cases from a time period between 12 weeks and 24 weeks, we would be able to detect the single *macro-level* change between M_1 and M_2 at time unit 4 in Fig. 7.

6 Objective Evaluation of Change Detection Techniques

The automatic detection of change points proposed in Sect. 3 provides an *objective evaluation mechanism* for change detection techniques. We adopt classic metrics in data mining such as the number of true positives (TP), false positives (FP) and false negatives (FN), and derived metrics from these, viz., precision, recall, and *F1*-score as objective measures. In order to define these metrics, we use a lag period l surrounding a detected or actual change point. The interpretation of these metrics (see Fig. 8) is as follows:

- *TP:* a change point is detected at $\hat{t}$ and there is an actual change within $\hat{t} \pm l$
- *FP:* a change point is detected at $\hat{t}$ but there is no actual change within $\hat{t} \pm l$
- *FN:* an actual change happened at $\hat{t}$ but no change has been detected within $\hat{t} \pm l$

Precision measures the fraction of detected changes that are correct while *recall* measures the fraction of actual changes that have been detected. In other words, *precision* $= TP/(TP + FP)$ and *recall* $= TP/(TP + FN)$. A measure that combines both precision and recall is the *F1-score*, defined as the harmonic mean between precision and recall, i.e., *F1-score* $= 2.precision.recall/(precision + recall)$. *Techniques that are able to detect changes with a high precision and recall (both close to 1.0) are preferred over others.*

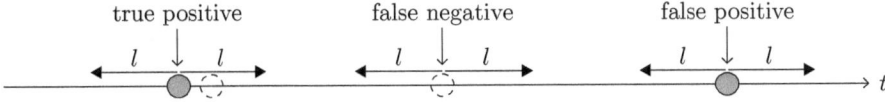

Fig. 8. Objective evaluation of change detection techniques. The solid circle and the dashed circle indicate a detected change and an actual change respectively.

7   Experiments and Discussion

The various concepts presented in this paper have been implemented in the Concept Drift plug-in in ProM. In this section, we discuss the results of applying these concepts for change (point) detection on several logs.

7.1   Sudden Drifts

We use the synthetic insurance claim event log [4] to assess the goodness of the change and change point detection techniques proposed in this paper. This event log contains 6000 traces and 58783 events distributed over 15 activities and incorporates a sudden drift phenomenon over five process variants. The event log contains 1200 traces from each process variant with the change points induced at 1200, 2400, 3600, and 4800. The approach presented in [4] was shown to detect the presence of all the four changes. However, the change points had to be detected manually. We have applied the adaptive windowing approach using the Kolmogorov-Smirnov test (KS-test) [18] over the data stream obtained on the J-measure feature [4] for each activity pair. Figure 9 depicts the average p-value plot of the KS-test on all activity pairs using a minimum population size of 100, maximum population size of 500, step size of 20 and a p-value threshold of 0.4. The red dots in the plot indicate the *automatically* detected change points using the approach presented in Sect. 3. The change points are detected at indices 1207, 2415, 3598, and 4793. Using a lag window of 20 traces, we have the following metrics (TP = 4, FP = 0, FN = 0, precision = 1.0, and recall = 1.0), i.e., we are able to detect all changes within 20 traces of the actual change points, which is quite promising.

7.2   Multi-order Dynamics

In order to conduct a controlled experiment involving multi-order changes, we have modeled a process exhibiting drifts at different time scales using

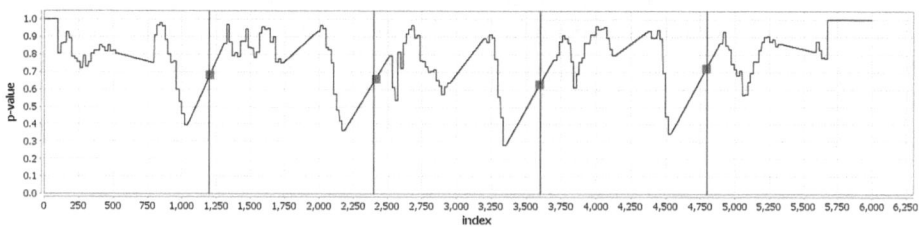

Fig. 9. Average p-value (over all activity pairs) using the adaptive windowing technique for KS-test on the J-measure estimated for each trace. The red dots indicate the *automatically* detected change points. The X-axis represents the trace index and Y-axis represents the p-value of the test. The solid vertical lines indicate the actual change points (Color figure online).

CPN tools [8]. We considered four process variants pertaining to the insurance claim example and generated an event log exhibiting multi-order changes as illustrated in Fig. 7. Two of the process model variants recurred alternatively every 6 weeks within the first 24 weeks while the other two process variants recurred alternatively every 6 weeks in the next 24 weeks. In practice, the arrival rate of cases can be different at different time periods. However, for simplicity and ease of discussion, we have modeled instances to arrive at a constant rate over the entire period. Furthermore, instances were modeled to arrive only during working hours and on week days at the rate of approximately 3 instances per hour. The event log contains 5647 cases and 57530 events distributed over 15 activities. There are 7 micro-level drift points induced at indices 629, 1346, 2038, 2802, 3444, 4156, and 4845 in this event log and one macro-level drift at index 2802.

As mentioned earlier, one needs to look at populations in terms of varying time periods rather than the number of traces when dealing with multi-order changes. Micro-level and macro-level drifts can be detected by considering populations comprising of cases defined over shorter and longer time periods respectively. Since the micro-level drifts are induced every 6 weeks, to detect these changes, we need to consider populations that do not exceed 6 weeks. Figure 10(a) depicts the average p-value of the KS-test on the J-measure over all activity pairs using a minimum population size of 3 days, maximum population size of 6 weeks, step size of 1 day, and a p-value threshold of 0.4. We can see that we are able to detect all the 7 drifts. Also, we are able to automatically detect the exact change points. Figure 10(b) depicts the average p-value of the KS-test on the J-measure over all activity pairs using a minimum population size of 12 weeks, maximum population size of 24 weeks, step size of 3 days and a p-value threshold of 0.2. We can see that by choosing a longer time period, we are able to detect the lone macro-level drift. The drift point is automatically detected at 2802 (the actual drift point is also 2802), which is accurate.

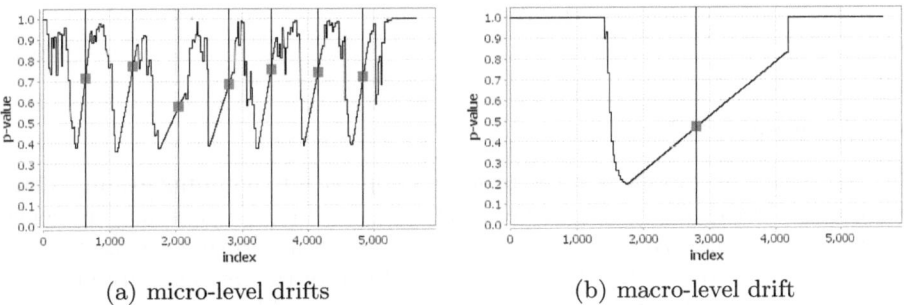

(a) micro-level drifts   (b) macro-level drift

Fig. 10. Detection of multi-order changes. Average p-value (over all activity pairs) using the adaptive windowing technique for KS-test on the J-measure estimated for each trace. The red dots indicate the automatically detected change points. Both micro-level drifts (left) and macro-level drifts (right) are detected using appropriate time scales. The solid vertical lines indicate the actual change points (Color figure online).

It is imperative to note that the adaptive windowing approach and the change point detection technique are both sensitive to the p-value threshold. Figure 11 depicts the objective metrics for the micro-level drift detection using a lag period of 2 days (50 traces) for different p-value thresholds. We can see that a choice of low p-value thresholds results in high false negatives (low recall) while a choice of high p-value thresholds results in high false positives (low precision). The $F1$-score increases with increasing p-value thresholds (due to increasing true positives) up to a certain point and deteriorates with further increase of p-value threshold (due to increasing false positives). The absolute p-values of the hypothesis tests are in turn dependent on the degree of change. We notice high p-values in scenarios where the process changes are minimal and concentrated over (affecting) only a few activities in the process. In such cases, the p-values will be less only for those features that involve the activities affected by the change. The high p-values overall is due to the effect of aggregation (average) that we do over all activity pairs. In other words, the absolute p-values are inversely proportional to the extent of change and the number of activities affected by the change.

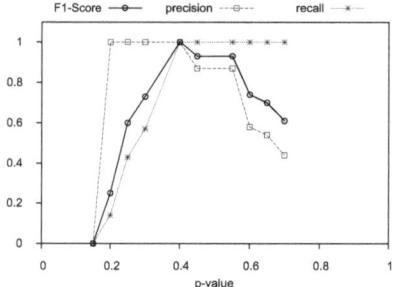

Fig. 11. Influence of p-value threshold on change detection.

7.3   Gradual Drifts

We now assess the goodness of the proposed approach in handling gradual drifts. We consider both the scenarios where the change is linear as well as exponential between two sources. Again CPN tools is used to create drifting processes allowing for a controlled experiment. We have used two of the process variants of the insurance claim example [4] and generated event logs with linear and exponential graduality. We first discuss the results on linear graduality. We considered an event log containing 2000 traces and 19346 events distributed over 15 activities. The linear drift was induced between the traces 1100 and 1200. Figure 12(a) depicts the average p-value obtained using adaptive windowing technique for the KS-test on the J-measure over all activity pairs using a minimum population size of 200, maximum population size of 300, step size of 10, gap size of 100, and a p-value threshold of 0.35. The drifts are detected at 1128 and 1229 (the actual drifts are at 1100 and 1200). Using a gap size of 50 (with the rest of the configuration remaining the same), the drifts are detected at 1158 and 1199. We can also see that for gradual changes, the width of the troughs are wider. We now consider an example of exponential gradual drift. We considered an event log containing 2000 traces and 19183 events distributed over 15 activities. An exponential drift was introduced between 900 and 1200 traces with a decay rate of $\lambda = 0.005$ for the first process variant. Figure 12(b) depicts the average p-value obtained using adaptive windowing technique for the KS-test on the J-measure over all activity pairs using a minimum population size of 200, maximum population size of 300, step size of 10, gap size of 300, and a p-value threshold of 0.35. The drifts are detected at 907 and 1198 (the actual drifts are at 900 and 1200). Using a gap size of 100 (with the rest of the configuration remaining the same), the drifts are detected at 907 and 998. By choosing an appropriate gap size, we are able to detect the change points very close to the actual change points.

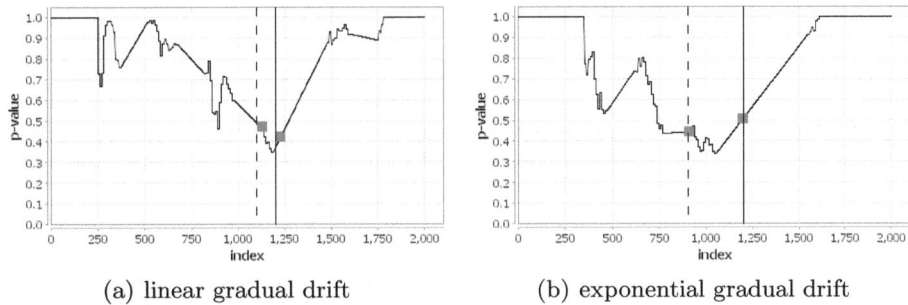

(a) linear gradual drift   (b) exponential gradual drift

Fig. 12. Detection of gradual changes using non-continuous populations. The red dots indicate the detected start/end of gradual change. The dashed and solid vertical lines indicate the start and end respectively of the actual gradual change (Color figure online).

7.4 Case Study

We have applied the concepts presented in this paper on several real-life event logs. In this section, we discuss the results of one such experiment of analyzing drifts from the all-in-one-permit handling process of a large Dutch municipality. Since October 1, 2010, the All-in-one Permit for Physical Aspects (omgevingsvergunning) has come into force through the WABO act [10]. This entails an overarching procedure for granting permission for projects like the construction, alteration or use of a house or building, etc. Now, the municipalities have one permit, one procedure and one set of submittal requirements, followed by one legal remedies procedure and enforcement by one authority. We considered an event log containing 184 cases and 4391 events distributed over 38 event classes (activities). The cases arrived between 19 Oct 2010 and 29 Dec 2011. We have applied the adaptive windowing approach with minimum and maximum population sizes of 10 and 30 respectively and a p-value threshold of 0.3 on the J-measure feature over all activity pairs. Figure 13 depicts the resulting drift plot along with the drift points. We see that there are three change points pertaining to traces at indices 50, 113, and 157. We have partitioned the event log into four parts, $\mathcal{L}_0$ comprising of cases from 1 to 49, $\mathcal{L}_1$ comprising of cases from 50 to 112, $\mathcal{L}_2$ comprising of cases from 113 to 156, and $\mathcal{L}_3$ comprising of cases from 157 to 184. We mined process models from these four event logs and analyzed for the changes that transpired between them.

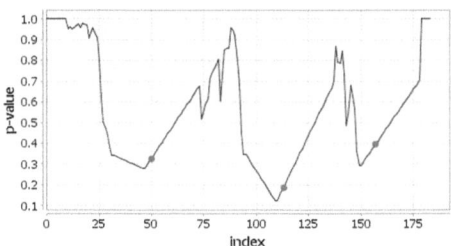

Fig. 13. Average p-value (over all activity pairs) using the adaptive windowing technique for KS-test on the J-measure estimated for each trace. The red dots indicate the detected change points (Color figure online).

The basic process comprises of four high-level steps: (i) registration and acknowledgements, (ii) procedural check 1, (iii) procedural check 2, and (iv) final assessment and decision. The changes primarily correspond to the procedural check steps. There is a change w.r.t two activities viz., suspend the time limit and Procedure change 2 || Activities regular procedure 2 between the two model variants corresponding to logs $\mathcal{L}_0$ and $\mathcal{L}_1$. In the variant mined using $\mathcal{L}_0$, these activities are executed in only 6 and 7 cases respectively out of the 49 cases whereas in the latter these are executed for each and every case. In this variant corresponding to log $\mathcal{L}_2$, the organization introduced some new activities pertaining to shipments and licence exemptions. Furthermore, the activities Waw permit aspect 1 and Waw permit aspect 2 are being phased out. This is noticed in the fact that these activities are executed in only 14 of the 43 cases whereas in its previous variant these activities are executed for each and every case. The process variant corresponding to $\mathcal{L}_3$ differs from $\mathcal{L}_2$ in the fact that these two activities are completely phased out.

7.5   Time Complexity Analysis

The change detection technique using hypothesis tests on a data stream of feature values proposed in [4] uses a sliding window that moves by one unit to generate successive populations. The number of hypothesis tests to be performed overall is directly proportional to the number of cases in an event log. Furthermore, this has to be repeated for different data streams, one for each feature (e.g., the J-measure on the follows relation over all activity pairs). For logs with many cases and/or large number of activities, this tends to be computationally expensive. One can improve this by progressing the sliding window by k units rather than one (for some $k \geq 2 \in \mathbb{N}$).[5] Figure 14(a) depicts the average computational time along with the 95 % confidence intervals over five independent runs for the insurance claim log (considering the J-measure over all activity pairs) for a fixed population size and different step sizes. We can see that time complexity reduces k-fold for a step size of k. This novel idea allows us to speed up concept drift analysis significantly with only a minor loss in terms of accuracy.

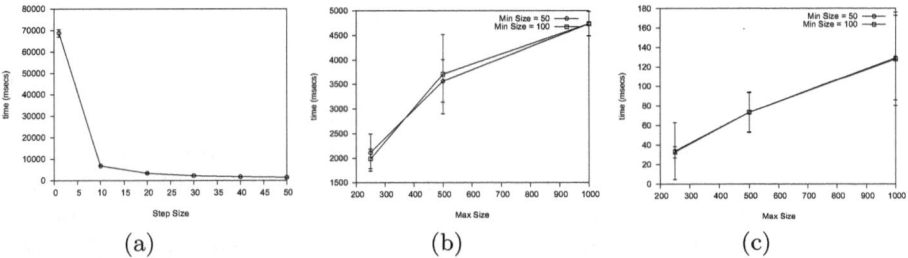

(a)   (b)   (c)

Fig. 14. The influence of step size and population sizes on the computational time for change detection and change point search. (a) Influence of step size (b) Influence of min/max size for change detection (ADWIN) (c) Influence of min/max size for drift point search (ADWIN)

The computational complexity of the adaptive windowing technique depends on the min/max population size thresholds since the time for each hypothesis test is dependent on the size of the population. Figure 14(b) and (c) depict the average computational time along with the 95 % confidence intervals over five independent runs for the insurance claim log (considering the J-measure over all activity pairs) on a fixed step size. We can see that the complexity only depends on the maximum population size: doubling the minimum population size has hardly any effect whereas the change detection and localization times depend linearly on the maximum population size.

8   Related Work

Process flexibility has been one of the "hotspots" in BPM/WFM research during the last two decades, e.g., collections of typical change patterns [11,19], extensive taxonomies of various flexibility approaches and mechanisms [14,17], and

---

[5] This is incorporated in the adaptive windowing technique (the step size parameter) presented in this paper.

classifications of process changes [13] have been provided. Despite the many publications on flexibility, most process mining techniques assume a process to be in steady state. A notable exception is the approach by Günther et al. [7], which attempts at using process mining to provide an aggregated overview of all changes that have happened so far. However, this approach assumes that change logs are available, i.e., modifications of the workflow model are recorded. At this point in time very few information systems provide such change logs.

This paper builds on [4] where the concept drift problem in process mining was analyzed for the first time. Since [4], several other techniques have been developed for dealing with concept drifts in process mining [6,9,20]. Carmona and Gavaldà [6] have proposed an online technique for detecting process changes. They first create an abstract representation of the process in the form of polyhedra using the prefixes of some initial traces in the event log. Subsequent traces are sampled and assessed whether they lie within the polyhedra or not. If a sample lies within the polyhedra, it is considered to be from the same process. If significant number of samples lie outside the polyhedra, a process change is said to be detected. Although Carmona and Gavaldà [6] use the adaptive windowing technique like us, their technique differs from our approach in several ways: (i) their approach constructs an abstract representation of a process unlike ours where we consider features characterizing the traces, (ii) their approach is applicable only for change detection whereas our framework is applicable for both change (point) detection and change localization (for change localization, refer to [5]), and (iii) their approach handles only sudden drifts whereas we present techniques for dealing with sudden, gradual, and multi-order dynamics. Furthermore, the tool support provided by the authors does not detect change points and does not work on logs with multiple process changes, i.e., it doesn't detect the presence/absence of multiple changes and doesn't report when (the trace index) process changes have happened. The tool just reports that a change exists and terminates (if changes exist) and does not terminate if no changes exist. In contrast, our plug-in can handle multiple process changes and can detect both the presence of and the points of change in addition to being able to assist in change localization.

Weber et al. [20] attempt at detecting concept changes by comparing models mined from event logs using a sliding window with a representative ground truth model. They use a probabilistic deterministic finite automata (PDFA) as a representation for a process and use statistical tests for detecting if the mined distribution, or its PDFA representation, has changed significantly from the ground truth. One of the challenges with this approach is the number of samples (traces) required to mine a good representative model that can be compared with the ground truth model. In contrast, our approach relies on characteristic differences in the features defined over traces for change detection.

To our best knowledge, we are the first to address the notion of *gradual* and *multi-order* changes in process mining.

9   Conclusions and Future Work

Although most business processes change over time, contemporary process mining techniques tend to analyze these processes as if they are in steady-state. For process management it is crucial to discover and understand such concept drifts in processes. In this paper, we proposed an adaptive windowing technique for change detection and a novel means of detecting change points automatically. Furthermore, we characterized the notions of gradual and multi-order changes and proposed techniques for detecting such changes. Our initial results show that the proposed techniques are very promising, i.e., we are able to detect changes accurately. In this paper, we have considered process changes only from a control-flow perspective. In the future, we would like to extend this to also include data/resource perspective changes. Furthermore, we would like to evaluate our approach using additional real-life case studies where concept drift is analyzed at runtime thereby providing users immediate diagnostics regarding recent changes.

Acknowledgments. J. Martjushev is grateful to Archimedes Foundation and the Ministry of Education and Research for funding his research through the national scholarship program, Kristjan Jaak.

References

1. van der Aalst, W.M.P.: Process Mining: Discovery Conformance and Enhancement of Business Processes. Springer, New York (2011)
2. van der Aalst, W.M.P., Rosemann, M., Dumas, M.: Deadline-based escalation in process-aware information systems. Decis. Support Syst. **43**(2), 492–511 (2011)
3. Bifet, A., Gavaldà, R.: Learning from time-changing data with adaptive windowing. In: Proceedings of the SIAM Data Mining Conference, pp. 443–448 (2007)
4. Bose, R.P.J.C., van der Aalst, W.M.P., Žliobaitė, I., Pechenizkiy, M.: Handling concept drift in process mining. In: Mouratidis, H., Rolland, C. (eds.) CAiSE 2011. LNCS, vol. 6741, pp. 391–405. Springer, Heidelberg (2011)
5. Bose, R.P.J.C.: Process Mining in the Large: Preprocessing, Discovery, and Diagnostics. Ph.D. thesis, Eindhoven University of Technology (2012)
6. Carmona, J., Gavaldà, R.: Online techniques for dealing with concept drift in process mining. In: Hollmén, J., Klawonn, F., Tucker, A. (eds.) IDA 2012. LNCS, vol. 7619, pp. 90–102. Springer, Heidelberg (2012)
7. Günther, C.W., Rinderle-Ma, S., Reichert, M., van der Aalst, W.M.P.: Using process mining to learn from process changes in evolutionary systems. Int. J. Bus. Process Integr. Manag. **3**(1), 61–78 (2008)
8. Jensen, K., Kristensen, L.: Coloured Petri Nets: Modelling and Validation of Concurrent Systems. Springer, Heidelberg (2009)
9. Luengo, D., Sepúlveda, M.: Applying clustering in process mining to find different versions of a business process that changes over time. In: Daniel, F., Barkaoui, K., Dustdar, S. (eds.) BPM Workshops 2011, Part I. LNBIP, vol. 99, pp. 153–158. Springer, Heidelberg (2012)
10. Ministerie van Infrastructuur en Milieu: All-in-one Permit for Physical Aspects: (Omgevingsvergunning) in a Nutshell (2010)

11. Mulyar, N.: Patterns for Process-Aware Information Systems: An Approach Based on Colored Petri Nets. Ph.D. thesis, Eindhoven University of Technology (2009)
12. Pechenizkiy, M., Bakker, J., Žliobaitė, I., Ivannikov, A., Kärkkäinen, T.: Online mass flow prediction in CFB boilers with explicit detection of sudden concept drift. SIGKDD Explor. **11**(2), 109–116 (2009)
13. Ploesser, K., Recker, J.C., Rosemann, M.: Towards a classification and lifecycle of business process change. In: BPMDS, vol. 8 (2008)
14. Regev, G., Soffer, P., Schmidt, R.: Taxonomy of flexibility in business processes. In: Business Process Modeling, Development, and Support (2006)
15. Sarbanes, P., Oxley, G., et. al.: Sarbanes-Oxley Act of 2002 (2002)
16. Schlimmer, J., Granger, R.: Beyond incremental processing: tracking concept drift. In: Proceedings of the Fifth National Conference on Artificial Intelligence, vol. 1, pp. 502–507 (1986)
17. Schonenberg, H., Mans, R., Russell, N., Mulyar, N., van der Aalst, W.M.P.: Process flexibility: a survey of contemporary approaches. In: Dietz, J.L.G., Albani, A., Barjis, J. (eds.) Advances in Enterprise Engineering I. LNBIP, vol. 10, pp. 16–30. Springer, Heidelberg (2008)
18. Sheskin, D.: Handbook of Parametric and Nonparametric Statistical Procedures. Chapman & Hall/CRC, Boca Raton (2004)
19. Weber, B., Rinderle, S., Reichert, M.: Change patterns and change support features in process-aware information systems. In: Krogstie, J., Opdahl, A.L., Sindre, G. (eds.) CAiSE 2007 and WES 2007. LNCS, vol. 4495, pp. 574–588. Springer, Heidelberg (2007)
20. Weber, P., Bordbar, B., Tino, P.: Real-time detection of process change using process mining. In: Imperial College Computing Student Workshop, Department of Computing Technical Report, vol. DTR11-9, pp. 108–114 (2011)
21. Widmer, G., Kubat, M.: Learning in the presence of concept drift and hidden contexts. Mach. Learn. **23**(1), 69–101 (1996)

Quick Decide — A Tool to Aid the Analytic Hierarchy Process for Group Decisions

Igor Kovbasiuk[1], Welf Löwe[2], Morgan Ericsson[2], and Anna Wingkvist[2(✉)]

[1] Softwerk, Växjö, Sweden
igor.kovbasiuk@softwerk.se
[2] Department of Computer Science, Linnaeus University, Växjö, Sweden
{welf.lowe,morgan.ericsson,anna.wingkvist}@lnu.se

Abstract. To take simple decisions comes naturally and does not require additional considerations but when there are multiple alternatives and criteria to be considered, a decision-making technique is required. The most studied and developed technique is the Analytic Hierarchy Process (AHP). We focus on the practical implementation of AHP and study the set of features that are necessary when the process involves several experts together with a set of non-functional requirements, such as portability and usability. Since no existing tool satisfy all our requirements, we design and implement a new AHP tool called Quick Decide. We perform a user experiment to evaluate our tool, and find that it fulfils all our requirements. To support our usability requirements, we extend AHP with an external consistency check, which measures the distance between expert opinions to avoid results that are mathematically correct but provide no semantic value (e.g., two opposite extreme opinions).

Keywords: Analytic Hierarchy Process · Group decision making · User experiment · Application

1 Introduction

Everything we do is the result of taking a decision. However, when the decision process involves many alternatives or a goal that is complex and consists of many criteria, it can be very difficult. It is almost impossible to make a decision and still keep all the criteria in mind. We have observed this multiple times, when we rely on the Goal-Question-Metric approach [1] to elicit quality models, where tens of questions and metrics, respectively, need to be weighed by importance (e.g., Wingkvist et al. [2]).

The number of alternatives and criteria are what makes the process so complex, so if we are able to reduce these numbers, the process should become easier. For example, if we could compare alternatives pairwise with respect to a criterion, we would only need to focus on three things. The problem now becomes to combine the pairwise judgments and synthesize the total priorities.

The Analytic Hierarchy Process (AHP) is an effective decision-making approach that is based on this idea. A decision is decomposed into a hierarchy of

© Springer International Publishing Switzerland 2015
R. Matulevičius and M. Dumas (Eds.): BIR 2015, LNBIP 229, pp. 179–193, 2015.
DOI: 10.1007/978-3-319-21915-8_12

easily comprehendible sub-problems that each can be analyzed independently. Thus a complex decision-making problem is simplified into many small comparison tasks. The AHP is flexible, straightforward, and provides a rational and consistent way for decision-making [3,4].

The calculations to synthesize the priorities and check the consistency of the judgments can quickly become complex, so while it is possible to use AHP without tool support, it quickly becomes tedious. We have used the process manually to elicit quality models on several occasions, and while the results were satisfactory, the overhead was significant; the sessions had to be guided by an AHP expert and it often took until the next meeting to get the final result. Another problem with a manual process is that it scales poorly with the number of people involved in the decision.

Based on the issues we experienced with manual use of AHP, we first investigated potential tools that could aid the process. We found neither of these sufficient for our needs, so we designed and implemented our own tool named *Quick Decide* using a design science approach [5]. Quick Decide is designed for the web and mobile devices, and can be found at http://qtools.se:8080/QuickDecide. We perform an experiment to test the usability of our tool and to determine how well it fulfils the requirements.

2   The Analytic Hierarchy Process

In AHP, a decision is decomposed according to the following four steps [4]:

1. Define the problem and gather information related to it.
2. Structure the decision hierarchy from the top with the goal of the decision, then the objectives from a broad perspective (criteria with subsequent dependent sub-criteria) to the lowest level, which usually is a set of alternatives.
3. Construct a set of pairwise comparison matrices. Each element in the upper level is used to compare the elements in the level immediately below with respect to it. Thus, there are two types of comparisons: children criteria with respect to the parent criterion (branch criteria) and alternatives with respect to bottom level criteria (leaf criteria).
4. For each element, use the priorities obtained from the comparisons to weight the priorities in the level immediately below. Then for each element in the level below add its weighted values and obtain its overall or global priority.

AHP is a hierarchical process, and the information related to the decision forms a *decision tree*. The root of the tree is the *goal* that represent the main problem that is analyzed in the decision. When the tree is constructed, the goal is decomposed into *criteria* that are easy to comprehend and that can be analyzed independently. Each of these criteria can be decomposed into *sub-criteria*, and so on. The leaves are considered *alternatives*. Figure 1 shows the structure of a decision tree with a goal, criteria, sub-criteria, and alternatives. To generalize the structure, we refer to the alternatives as *leaf criteria* and the goal and all internal criteria (e.g., criteria, subcriteria, subsubcriteria, etc.) as *branch criteria*.

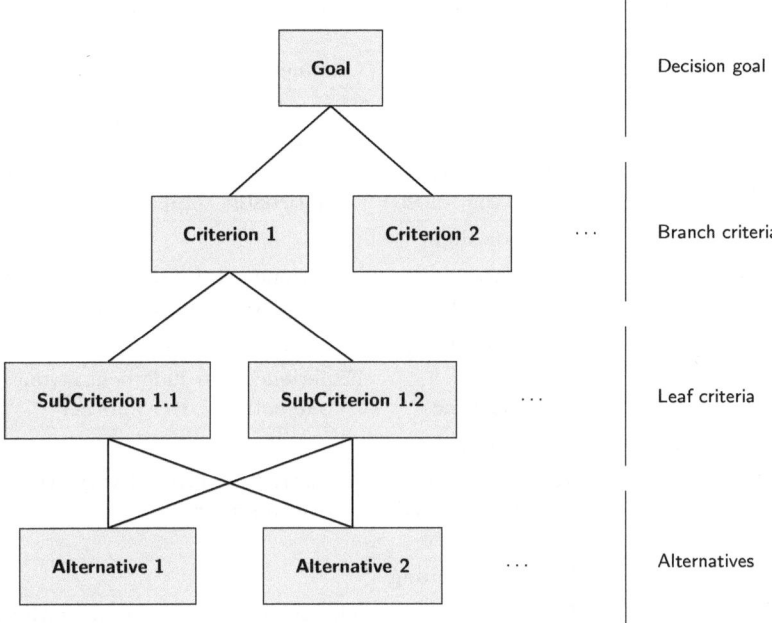

Fig. 1. Decision tree example

We refer to a tree with branch and leaf criteria as a *criteria tree*. Note that the only difference between a decision tree and a criteria tree is the terminology used.

When we elicit quality models, we start from a single goal *Quality* and decompose it into a hierarchy of factors (questions in GQM) that affect quality and metrics. The goal and the factors are branch criteria, and the metrics are leaf criteria. The decision problem is to determine how much of an impact each of these factors and metrics have on the overall quality with respect to their parent. The goal Quality is divided into the branch criteria Quality-for-owner and Quality-for-customer. Quality-for-customer is in turn divided into the branch criteria Easy-to-understand, Easy-to-use, and Easy-to-find, and so on. The leaf criteria are metrics such as Topic-heading-is-relevant or Paragraph-is-readable (both are used to answer Clarity, which is part of Easy-to-understand).

A decision problem has one or more *owners* that define the tree. The tree is used by several *experts* that compare and judge the criteria. According to the AHP, experts determine *weights* by *pairwise comparison* of the criteria with respect to a parent criterion (or goal). The weights are set according to the fundamental scale of absolute numbers (cf. Table 1). This scale indicates how much more important one element is compared to another with respect to comparison basis, against which they are compared. We refer to each of the criteria in a pairwise comparison as *comparates*, and the parent criterion as the *comparison*

Table 1. The fundamental scale of absolute numbers [4]

Intensity of importance	Definition	Comment
1	Equal importance	Two activities contribute equally to the objective
1.1–1.9	If the activities are very close	Such small numbers will not be too noticeable compared to other weights
2	Weak or slight	
3	Moderate importance	Experience and judgment slightly favor one activity over another
4	Moderate plus	
5	Strong importance	Experience and judgment strongly favor one activity over another
6	Strong plus	
7	Very strong or demonstrated importance	An activity is favored very strongly over another
8	Very, very strong	
9	Extreme importance	The evidence favoring one activity over another is of the highest possible order

basis. We differ between a pairwise comparison that involves branch criteria, *branch comparison* and one that involves leaf criteria, *leaf comparison.*

In the quality model example, we want to determine how much impact a factor or a metric has on the overall quality with respect to a parent factor or the goal. For example, we compare Topic-heading-is-relevant with Paragraph-is-readable with respect to their importance to determine Clarity. Topic-heading-is-relevant is a comparate and Clarity is the comparison basis. Since we consider Topic-heading-is-relevant a leaf, we perform leaf comparison. One of the experts involved when we designed the actual quality model determined that Topic-heading-is-relevant was 3 compared to Paragraph-is-readable, which according to the scale suggests moderate importance, i.e., that the experts experience and judgment slightly favored Topic-heading-is-relevant to determine Clarity.

In addition, AHP incorporates a useful technique to check the (internal) *consistency* of the expert's evaluations, i.e., that the state of weights is proper enough to allow for further AHP processing. *Internal inconsistency* ensures that the judgments of an expert are mutually concordant to reduce bias in the decision-making process. It is defined by notion of the *consistency index*, which is calculated based on a principal eigenvalue of a comparison matrix. This index is compared with the same index obtained as an average over a large number of reciprocal matrices of the same order whose entries are random. If the ratio of the consistency index compared to that from random matrices is significantly smaller (10 % or less), we accept comparison matrix. Otherwise, we attempt to improve consistency [4].

In our quality model example, one expert stated that Topic-heading-is-relevant is 3 if Paragraph-is-readable is 1 with respect to Clarity. Assume that another expert makes the opposite claim, i.e., that Paragraph-is-readable is 3 if Topic-heading-is-relevant is 1 with respect to clarity. The average result of their opinions is 1, which even if it mathematically correct is not semantically valuable. To avoid these situations, we introduce an *external consistency* check to ensure that experts' opinions agree enough to get meaningful resulting priorities. The external consistency check is done by ensuring that opinions of experts differ within a defined distance between each other. We use a distance of 3. For example, judgments {*1–2, 1–4, 1–5*}, {*1–1, 1–2, 1–3*}, {*2–1, 1–2, 1–1*} are considered consistent while judgments {*1–2, 1–4, 1–6*} are considered inconsistent because of the outlier *1–6*. In judgments {*3–1, 1–2, 1–3*}, *3–1* is an outlier and in {*3–1, 1–2, 1–3*} both *3–1* and *1–3* are outliers. If the external consistency check fails, the tool informs the decision problem owner about the situation, so he or she can follow up with the respective experts.

After both consistency checks are done, the consolidated results are calculated. These results include *prioritized* criteria tree and *ranking of alternatives*. In the quality model example, we use weights in the interval [0,1]. Based on the decision problem, we determined that Quality-for-owner is 0.8 of Quality (the goal), and that Easy-to-understand, Easy-to-use, and Easy-to-find have priorities 0.182, 0.545, and 0.273 with respect to Quality-for-owner.

3   Quick Decide — an AHP Tool

The main goal of Quick Decide is to consolidate opinions of multiple experts that participate in a decision-making activity. According to the AHP a decision is created and its goal is specified at the beginning of the decision-making process. Criteria and alternatives are then added. Experts participate in the decision by performing pairwise comparisons. These two activities, adding criteria or alternatives and performing pairwise comparisons should be possible to perform in parallel. After all comparisons are performed the results, priorities of criteria and alternatives, are calculated.

Working with complex decision involving large criteria tree and several alternatives can be difficult to handle for a person not familiar with AHP. Hence, a tool should be user-friendly and simple to use. Users should clearly understand which comparisons that are left to be performed by them. In the case of inconsistent judgments, the error messages should be clear, so it is obvious what to change in order to make judgments consistent. Furthermore, when checking the results, users should understand the result and see their contribution to it. The tool should also be fast and easy to use during the decision-making activity. Mobile devices, such as smart phones, tablets, and low-power notebooks (e.g., Chromebooks) are often used during meetings. Since we want experts to be able to use our tool in parallel, we consider it critical to support these platforms.

3.1   Refinement into Requirements

Based on the AHP decision-making process and our context, we derive the following required features:

F1. Decision creation, goal specification.
F2. Decision tree development: add, remove, modify alternative; add, remove, modify criterion.
F3. Multiple experts can perform pairwise comparisons: comparing alternatives with respect to leaf criterion (leaf comparison); comparing criteria with respect to parent branch criterion (branch comparison).
F4. Describe the contribution of each user into the final result.
F5. Work without alternatives, developing and prioritizing criteria tree.
F6. Consolidation of different experts opinions on the results stage: automated consolidated results calculation and owner controlling the consolidation process.
F7. External consistency check before final results calculation to improve accuracy and transparency of the results.

Users should be able to perform features F2, F3 in parallel; a decision owner can add new criteria or alternatives to the decision while experts perform pairwise comparisons on existing parts of the decision tree.

We also define the following usability [6] requirements:

U1. (F4) final result should be clear and users should see their contribution to it;
U2. (F2, F5) application should not force users to add alternatives and allow prioritization of standalone criteria tree;
U3. (F5) users should clearly see which comparisons are left to be performed by them in the decision;
U4. (F3, F5, F6, F7) error message about inconsistent judgments should be clear and help the user make corresponding changes;
U5. (F6, F7) decision owner should be able to have vision and control of experts' opinions consolidation process.

The tool should be free to use, and portable to both mobile devices and personal computers. We refer to these requirements as the free and portability [7] requirements, respectively.

3.2   Evaluation of Existing Tools

The evaluation of existing AHP tools is performed with respect to the required features, as well as the portability and free requirements. Since neither of the existing tools fulfil all our requirements, we do not evaluate how well the existing tools conform to our usability requirements.

MakeItRational (http://makeitrational.com/) is the best solution of the analyzed tools and the most expensive. It is available on desktop and as a web app, but the web app requires Microsoft Silverlight, so it cannot be used on (all) mobile devices. MakeItRational provides almost all required features, though consolidation of experts' opinions is done manually ("if you cannot agree, use the average value"). It provides sufficient statistics to analyze the results.

Transparent Choice (http://transparentchoice.com/) is web-accessible but has less functionality compared to MakeItRational. No error message is provided when weights are inconsistent. No consolidation of experts' opinions is available, they are regarded separately.

Super Decision (http://www.superdecisions.com/) is only installable as a desktop application. It is more academic-oriented than the previous two. It provides fewer features and is free.

Table 2 provides a detailed evaluation of existing solutions. Neither of these provide the required functionality, i.e., criteria tree prioritization without alternatives, automated consolidation of different experts opinions with external consistency check.

Table 2. Evaluation of existing AHP tools

	Features							Portability	Free
	F1	F2	F3	F4	F5	F6	F7		
MakeItRational	✓	✓	✓	✓					
Transparent Choice	✓	✓	✓					✓	
Super Decision	✓	✓							✓

3.3 Architecture

Since neither of the existing tools provided all required features we determined that a new application needs to be developed. Since portability is an important requirement, we decided that a web-based application (web app) is the best solution. With modern web standards, a web app can easily be adapted to mobile devices (e.g., screen sizes, touch, etc.). A web app also reduces development cost and do not require installation on client devices. We use the Google Web Toolkit (GWT) and Google App Engine to develop and deploy the Quick Decide.

The front end is designed using the Model-View-Presenter (MVP) GUI design/architecture pattern [8]. This pattern is engineered to facilitate automated unit testing and improve separation of concerns in the presentation logic. The pattern components are:

- A model that defines the data to be displayed or otherwise acted upon in the User Interface (UI);
- A view that displays data (the model) and routes user commands (events) to the presenter to act upon that data;

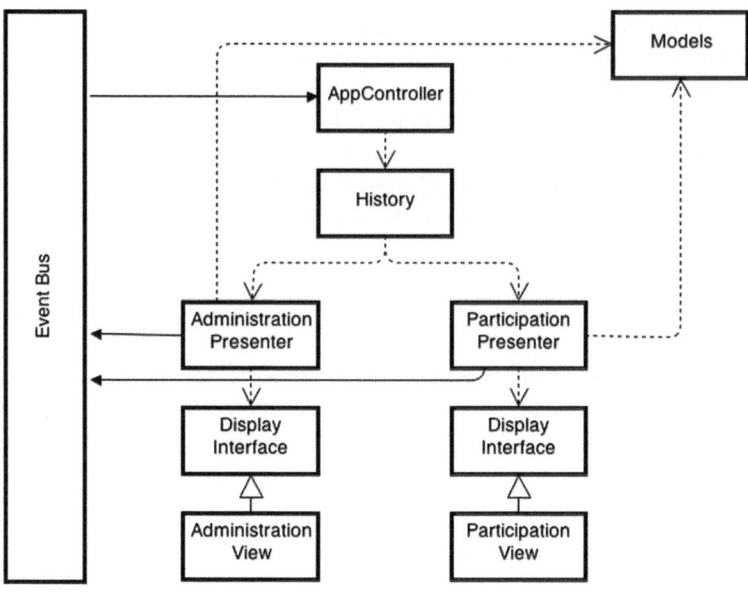

Fig. 2. MVP pattern in Quick Decide

— A presenter that acts upon the model and the view. It retrieves data from
repositories (the model), and formats it for display in the view. It contains UI
business logic for the view front end.

An advantages of the MVP pattern is that views are loosely coupled to
the model. The presenter is responsible for binding the model to the view and
handling user events. Since portability is an important requirement, separation
of view and presenter is useful to provide different views for mobile and PC
users while still reusing the same presenter. Moreover, decoupled views allow us
to develop and enhance these independent of the presenter and the model, which
improves usability.

Figure 2 shows the implementation of MVP in Quick Decide. The model
represents the business objects of our domain; Decision, Alternative, Criteri-
aTreeNode, Person, Expert, Comparison, and ExpertOpinion.

A view contains all of the UI components that make up the application. These
components are tables, labels, buttons, text-boxes, etc. Views are responsible
for the layout of the UI components and have no notion of the model. A view
implements the display interface of the corresponding presenter. The switching
between views is tied to the history management within the presentation layer.

A presenter contains all of the logic for the application, view transition and
data interactions with server Remote Procedure Calls (RPC). To handle logic
that is not specific to any presenter and instead resides at the application layer,
we introduce the AppController component. It contains the history management
and view transition logic. Any view transition is directly tied to the history
management.

Application events (such as changing view, RPC result, etc.) are transmitted via an Event Bus. Presenters add handlers for user events (button click, list item selection) that transform these into application events, which are sent to the Event Bus. Handlers to events from the Event Bus are added in AppController.

3.4   User Interface Design

The usability requirements are set to help reduce the complexity of AHP and decision-making processes in general. The screenshots are based on the example

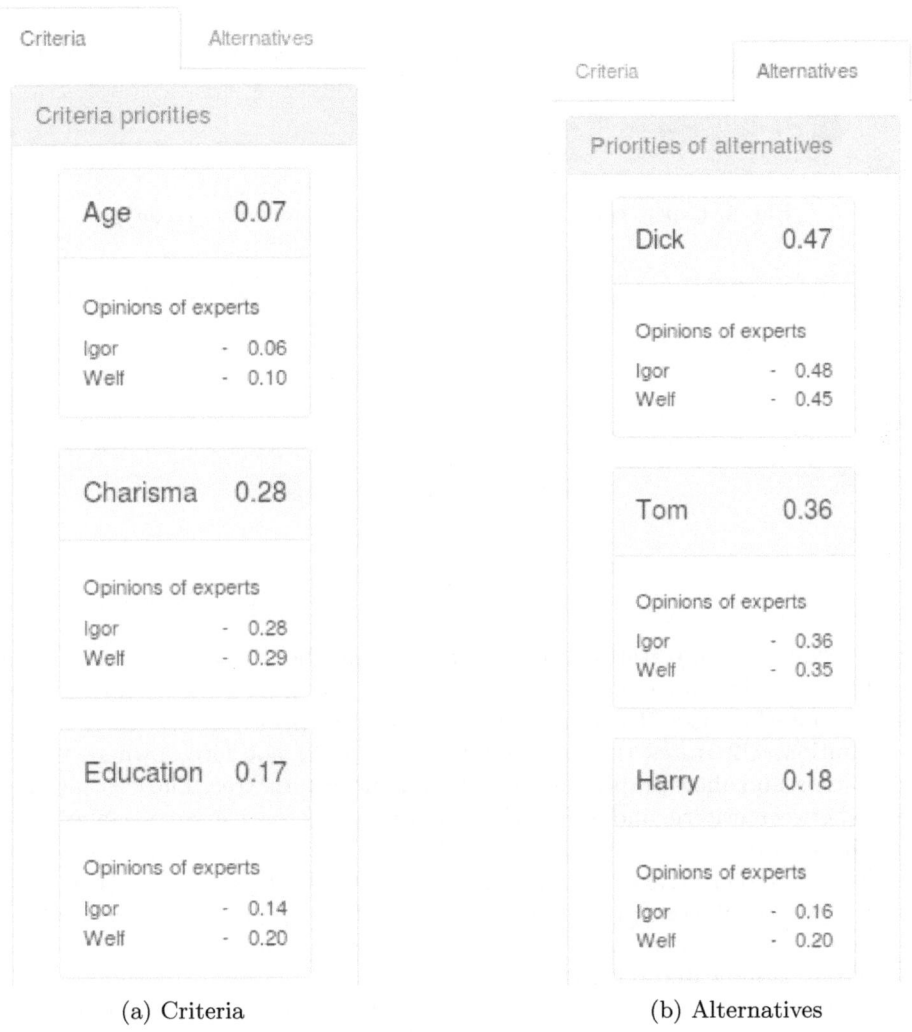

(a) Criteria   (b) Alternatives

Fig. 3. Multiple experts results

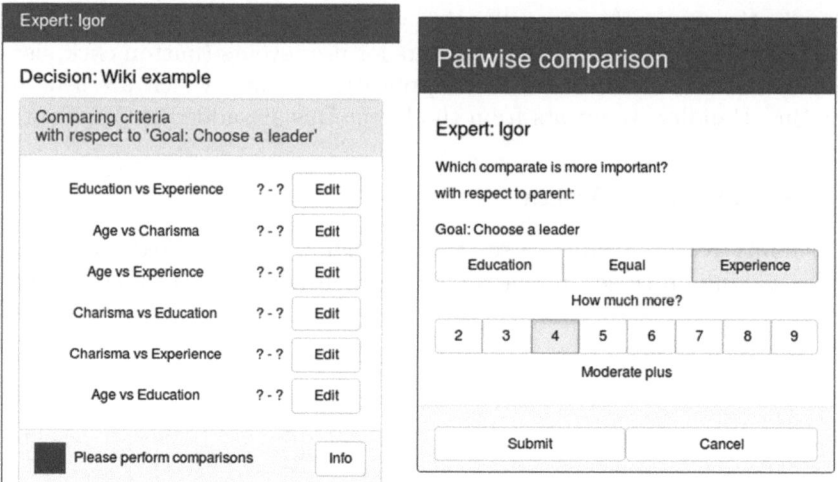

Fig. 4. Expert comparison (left), pairwise comparison (right)

Fig. 5. States of comparison

from Wikipedia[1]. U1 states that the final result should be clear and that it should be possible for experts to view their contribution to it. Figure 3 shows the user interface used to communicate the overall priorities and each experts contribution. U2 states that the application should not force owners to add alternatives and allow prioritization of standalone criteria tree. The user interface differs between criteria and alternatives, and if no alternatives are specified, that tab will be empty.

Users should clearly see which comparisons are left in the decision (U3). Each expert observes all comparisons to be performed in expert comparison view (cf. Fig. 4). On this page, comparisons are grouped by comparison basis and state of each group is indicated (cf. Fig. 5).

The error message about inconsistent judgments should be clear and help the user to make corresponding changes (U4). When comparisons are inconsistent, it is indicated with the corresponding color of the comparison group (cf. Fig. 5).

---

[1] http://en.wikipedia.org/wiki/Analytic_hierarchy_process_-_leader_example.

If an expert clicks on the info button, he or she receives suggestions on what comparisons to change in order to get a consistent result.

Decision owner should be able to have vision and control of experts' opinions consolidation process (U5). Vision and control over consolidation process are implemented in Comparisons tab of owner decision page. Vision implies an overview of each expert opinion on each comparison. Control implies an external consistency check, which assists with finding outliers and disagreements in opinions. The distance for the external consistency check is manually specified so the owner can control the precision.

4   Evaluation

The usability requirement is evaluated with a user experiment where we observe usability indicators [9], such as number of questions and time to finish the task, and comparing these with the manual process. The purpose of the experiment is to analyze the process of experts participating in criteria tree prioritization, both manual and with the tool (designed application) to compare manual and automated criteria prioritization. We want to evaluate usability from the point of view of someone participating in a decision-making problem (an expert). Since we only consider usability for experts that use the tool to make a decision and not for administrators that use the tool to set up a decision, we only evaluate features F4 (describe the contribution of each user) and F5 (criteria tree prioritization), and rely on the usability requirements U1–U4.

We designed the experiment to determine whether our hypothesis: if the tool-enabled criteria tree prioritization is user-friendlier, and if it can be accepted (or rejected). We used subjects that have no prior knowledge or experience of AHP. The subjects (students) were given a decision-problem and perform pairwise comparison of criteria with respect to their parent and calculate the priorities (dependent variable). The subjects were randomly assigned to the manual or tool group. Each group (3 students) should produce a prioritized criteria tree and description of each user contribution to the result (derived using AHP) (independent variable). We record the time it took for each group to finish, the number of questions asked during the decision problem, and any user feedback on the decision problem (independent variables). We expected the experiment to take 20–30 min for the manual group and 5–10 min for the group that used Quick Decide.

The experiment started with a short introduction to AHP, the decision criteria tree example and the task to be done. The decision problem (cf. Fig. 6) focused on whether someone should pursue a doctorate or go work in industry. The group that used the manual process performed the task with the help of a predefined spreadsheet (offered as part of the experiment). The group that used Quick Decided finished the task in 12 min, compared to 15 min for the group that used the manual process. This suggests that there might be faster to use the tool, however the features that we focus on in the experiment are not very time-consuming, so the time gained might be more significant in a more elaborated real-world scenario. There was a significant different in the number of

Fig. 6. The decision problem given to the experiment participants

questions asked and problems encountered during the task. The group that used the manual process stated that the scale is rather big and confusing. During comparisons they had to go back to the scale, to see what scale numbers mean. As a result, they could not focus on comparisons. When they calculated the priorities they asked how to combine together weights; since there were three experts in the group they had to use cubic root for calculations. In the end they had some disagreements over final results. Users with very low or very high initial opinions were not satisfied with the final result since it was significantly different from their initial opinions. This process is automated in Quick Decide, and users see the final results and each expert contribution to it. It is almost the same as in a spreadsheet program, so the tool does not make much difference here. It makes a difference during the external consistency check that finds disagreement before the result calculation. However, this was not the focus of this experiment.

The group that used Quick Decide did not have any additional questions during the process, but also had some disagreements over final results. In the tool, text corresponding to each scale number is displayed, and consolidated weights calculation is automated. Consequently, these questions did not rise during working with the tool. Thus, in comparison with semi-manual work with a spreadsheet, the number of question is reduced while performing task with the tool.

Both groups provided some general feedback on AHP. They thought numbers in the scale can be misleading. They correspond to different text descriptions like "slightly favored" and "strongly favored" (cf. Table 1). At the same time, the user can understand these as multipliers, e.g., 5 means five times as important or 500 %, which is incorrect. This issue can be solved by spending more time on explaining the scale. As an alternative solution, numbers can be eliminated from the comparison stage. Only corresponding text could be presented to the users. This approach would be especially suitable for inexperienced users. Some users were dissatisfied with the Quick Decide user interface, for example some buttons were too small and text labels were unaligned.

5   Related Work

There is a long history of computer software to support Multiple Criteria Decision Making (MCDM). One early example implemented the Vector Maximal Decomposition Programming method to support the decision maker through a series of ordinal comparisons [10]. The first software implementation of AHP, Expert Choice, was developed in 1983 [11]. During the 90s, spreadsheet software, e.g., Microsoft Excel and Visual Basic made it easier to implement MCDM [11]. The first web-based MCDM applications also appeared, e.g., WWW-NIMBUS [12]. There is now a wide range of MCDM tools available [13], including the AHP tools discussed in Sect. 3.2.

One early use of AHP in software engineering was the cost-value approach to requirement prioritisation [14,15]. There are several studies that use AHP to assess software quality, e.g., Koscianski and Candido Bracarense Costa [16], and Tsourakis and Estrella [17]. The effort by Kanellopoulos et al. [18] to weight metrics in quality models using AHP is very similar to the approach we use, but we customize the models for different system owners, and hence, require a more flexible AHP tool.

6   Conclusion and Future Work

We rely on AHP, for example, when we elicit quality models from domain experts and we found the process time consuming and confusing. The aim of this study was to improve use of AHP with a tool that asks users to prioritize alternatives and criteria, and perform all the necessary computations to present the final priorities done by the group. Given the context we expect the tool to be useful in, we require that it can be used with minimal set-up and available on multiple devices, including smartphones and tables.

An initial study shows that none of the existing tools that we were able to find matched all of our requirements, so we decided to develop our own tool, Quick Decide and evaluate it in a user experiment. The experiment compares the tool with the manual process. We find that the tool improved the time it took to complete a decision problem and reduced the number of misunderstandings and problems encountered during the process. For example, common issues for the group that did not use the tool was to understand how to combine priorities and remember how the scale works. Both groups found the scale confusing, but the group with the tool had a constant reminder of how the numbers should be interpreted. There was no significant difference in time (12 min with the tool and 15 min without), but we consider this due to the nature of the decision problem in the experiment. A more elaborated real-world problem might result in a larger time gain for the tool, given the increased number of computations to, for example, check external consistency.

Based on the comments and questions from the participants in the experiment, as well as the time difference, we conclude that our tool Quick Decide is easier and faster to use compared to manual AHP.

The usability experiment is just an initial study, and more extensive one should be performed to improve application assessment. We have already replaced the manual process and spreadsheets with Quick Decide, so we also collect user input and feedback from any decision problems we run, as well as our own experience. Based on the user experiment, we identified several possible improvements to the tool that should be included in future versions. For example, the tool should not only provide a message showing which comparison group is inconsistent, but also suggest which comparisons should by changed and how, in order to get consistent results. We also need to consider how priorities are used. Sometimes priorities are already defined in external application or documents. Then it is a good idea to allow the user to set priorities manually instead of forcing them to perform comparisons. Given the confusion about how the scales work, we should perhaps only show the text description and not the scale number during comparison. This can be easier to understand and to work with for an inexperienced user.

Acknowledgment. The authors want to thank the reviewers for their insights to improve the paper.

References

1. Basili, V.R., Caldiera, G., Rombach, H.D.: The goal question metric approach. In: Marciniak, J.J. (ed.) Encyclopedia of Software Engineering, vol. 1, pp. 528–532. Wiley, New York (1994)
2. Wingkvist, A., Ericsson, M., Löwe, W., Lincke, R.: A metrics-based approach to technical documentation quality. In: Proceedings of the 7th International Conference on the Quality of Information and Communications Technology, pp. 476–481 (2010)
3. Saaty, T.L.: How to make a decision: the analytic hierarchy process. Eur. J. Oper. Res. **48**(1), 9–26 (1990)
4. Saaty, T.L.: Decision making with the analytic hierarchy process. Int. J. Serv. Sci. **1**, 83–98 (2008)
5. Hevner, A.R., March, S.T., Park, J., Ram, S.: Design science in information systems research. MIS Q. **28**(1), 75–105 (2004)
6. Nielsen, J.: Usability Engineering. Morgan Kaufmann Publishers Inc., San Francisco, CA, USA (1993)
7. Mooney, J.D.: Bringing portability to the software process. Technical report TR 97–1, Department of Statistics and Computer Science, West Virginia University, USA (1997)
8. Potel, M.: MVP: Model-View-Presenter the Taligent programming model for C++ and Java. Taligent Inc (1996)
9. Dumas, J.S., Redish, J.C.: A Practical Guide to Usability Testing, 1st edn. Intellect Books, Exeter, UK (1999)
10. Dyer, J.S.: A time-sharing computer program for the solution of the multiple criteria problem. Manage. Sci. **19**(12), 1379–1383 (1973)
11. Murat, K., Koksalan, M., Wallenius, J., Zionts, S., et al.: Multiple Criteria Decision Making: From Early History to the 21st Century. World Scientific, Singapore (2011)

12. Miettinen, K., Mäkelä, M.M.: Interactive multiobjective optimization system WWW-NIMBUS on the Internet. Comput. Oper. Res. **27**(7), 709–723 (2000)
13. French, S., Xu, D.L.: Comparison study of multi-attribute decision analytic software. J. Multi-Criteria Decis. Anal. **13**(2–3), 65–80 (2005)
14. Karlsson, J., Olsson, S., Ryan, K.: Improved practical support for large-scale requirements prioritising. Requirements Eng. **2**(1), 51–60 (1997)
15. Karlsson, J., Ryan, K.: A cost-value approach for prioritizing requirements. IEEE Softw. **14**(5), 67–74 (1997)
16. Koscianski, A., Costa, J.C.B.: Combining analytical hierarchical analysis with ISO/IEC 9126 for a complete quality evaluation framework. In: Proceedings of the 4th International Symposium and Forum on Software Engineering Standards. IEEE, pp. 218–226 (1999)
17. Tsourakis, N., Estrella, P.: Evaluating the quality of mobile medical speech translators based on ISO/IEC 9126 series: definition, weighted quality model and metrics. Int. J. Reliable Qual. E-Healthc. (IJRQEH) **2**(2), 1–20 (2013)
18. Kanellopoulos, Y., Antonellis, P., Antoniou, D., Makris, C., Theodoridis, E., Tjortjis, C., Tsirakis, N.: Code quality evaluation methodology using the ISO/IEC 9126 standard. Int. J. Softw. Eng. Appl. **1**(2), 17–36 (2010). http://arXiv.org/abs/1007.5117

Business Information Systems Development

The Most Prominent Software Development Concepts Cited in IT Professionals' Blogs

Deniss Ojastu[✉], Tarmo Robal, and Ahto Kalja

Department of Computer Engineering,
Tallinn University of Technology, Tallinn, Estonia
{deniss.ojastu,tarmo.robal,ahto.kalja}@ttu.ee

Abstract. Current paper attempts to identify and categorise the most prominent software development concepts at present time. To achieve that, we employed the method of text mining on weblogs written by software development practitioners. Large volume of text extracted from the most popular professional blogs provided basis for frequency analysis of relevant concepts. These concepts were then categorised using a recognised ontology of software development. The results of this study can be used for updating an existing software development ontology, for constructing checklists to be used by both technical specialists and inexperienced clients prior to starting a software project and, finally, for constructing relevant courses and trainings for non-technical clients.

Keywords: Software development concepts · Client-vendor relationship in software development · Text mining · Term-frequency analysis

1 Introduction

With information technology being ubiquitous in today's world and any modern industry being more and more dependent on software, the question of a general IT literacy is becoming of a higher relevance. Thus, the most prominent political and business leaders stood behind the nation-wide initiatives promoting basic programming skills such as "Year of Code" [1] and "Hour of Code" [2] both in USA and the United Kingdom [3] in 2012–2014. People ranging from former U.S. President Bill Clinton to Facebook creator Mark Zuckerberg to physicist, cosmologist, and author Stephen Hawking have expressed the belief that basic software computer programming is an essential skill in today's world [4]. One can find similar initiatives across the world, both public- and private-ran, ranging from so-called hackathons to coding schools to IT literacy courses (not to be confused with computer usage courses).

The question of a general IT literacy becomes especially relevant in software development situations where software is ordered by non-specialists. There are numerous studies confirming that close involvement of customers during development phase positively contributes to outcome of software projects [5–8].

However, Martin et al. [9] point out well that programmers and customers do not always speak quite the same language, even when they both speak English (or any other language), and that it is easy for a customer to become baffled by a programmer. Non-specialists are simply not trained to be customers of software development and

© Springer International Publishing Switzerland 2015
R. Matulevičius and M. Dumas (Eds.): BIR 2015, LNBIP 229, pp. 197–212, 2015.
DOI: 10.1007/978-3-319-21915-8_13

therefore cannot effectively set requirements, prioritise among various alternatives and evaluate the interim outcomes of the process until it is too late. Dorn [10] cites an example from a programming course experiment where non-technical students mixed up Java with JavaScript and therefore failed to deliver what was required.

Similar mistakes, when done by non-technical clients in the world of large software development projects, can cause misunderstandings which can become rather costly. Cerpa and Verner [11] found in their analysis of 70 failed development projects that one of the factors which contributed to a project failure most was "Customer/Users had unrealistic expectations". Authors defined a failed software project to be the one which took much longer to complete and cost significantly more than planned. Nelson [12] and Hoda et al. [13] also confirm that poor requirements definition and lack of user involvement in software development process are among the primary reasons for major failures in software projects.

However, it is not practical nor realistic that non-technical clients (clients here and further defined as business or governmental officials ordering software from external vendors or software developers from their own organisations) would know the domain of software engineering as extensively as the specialists themselves. As one participant of a similar earlier study [14] outlined: *"This is work of a software developer that things get done and there is no need to teach to everyone how software development goes. After all, in a visit to a doctor, the doctor does not assume that the patient knows all the terms in Latin."*

Hence, we see it as important to define an extent for (and reasonable limits to) the optimal knowledge of software development on behalf of non-technical clients. One natural source of identifying and measuring relative importance of various concepts within the domain of software development are the practitioners of the domain itself. For scalability of data we undertook text mining of the most prominent weblogs written in English from around the world which focus on various elements of software development and are written by (former) software developers themselves. By using word term frequency analysis and clustering the relevant word terms according to a recognised ontology within software engineering, we were able to construct the set of most prominent software development concepts.

We intend to use this set of prominent software development concepts in two major ways in our future studies. First, we intend to construct domain ontology for customer profiling and comparison to the competences which can be relevant for a specific project. Second, the result of our study can be used as an input to (yet not the only basis for) the courses and programmes within both formal and non-formal education in software development basics for non-technical clients.

2   Related Works

2.1   Establishing Common Working Ground Between Development Team and Customers

To overcome misunderstandings between software developers and their customers, and increase efficiency of software projects, several researchers suggest establishing common semantical ground in multidisciplinary software development situations. Thus, Shim et al. [8] propose that the system users and developers can establish a collegial working environment and both assume responsibility for developed features. Participants of the projects where such methodology was applied reported that development teams could better reach predefined goals of effectiveness and efficiency. The main benefit, as indicated by the projects' participants, was improvement of the access to mutual expertise.

Majchrzak et al. [6] suggest a strategy in which project participants continuously verbally expand on a concept, domain, or knowledge that is new to them. It is supposed to facilitate client learning which, in turn, should lead to enhanced understanding of technology, organisational and work environment in which the system will operate. The study by Majchrzak et al. [6] of 17 homogenous IS design projects shows that teams using more collaborative environment have engendered more client learning and achieved better IS design phase outcomes.

Similarly, Tena et al. [15] found in their experiments that not using the same terminology has led to several problems in multidisciplinary web development projects. As one example, when designing an e-commerce website, web designers with a computer background distinguished terms 'navigate' (following a planned course, leading to the use of menus or action buttons) and 'browse' (looking around without seeking anything in particular, leading to the use of search fields or tables). However, graphic web designers and even usability experts used both 'navigate' and 'browse' without distinction. That led to problems, such as when referring to "use an element to browse around the products" the graphic designers proposed a layout to render an action menu, while the web developer thought of it as a search bar. As a solution, authors suggest establishing shared vocabulary which collects common tasks related to the user interaction with web systems.

2.2 Text Mining as a Tool for Constructing a Domain Vocabulary

One way to construct common domain vocabulary is to apply text mining techniques on a large volume of text related to a domain. Thus, Lenin Babu et al. [16] constructed an ontology for software architecture by generating a vocabulary that includes the terms in this domain. This was done by parsing the Wikipedia pages. Similarly, Liping and Lidong [17] applied text mining on scientific publications in computer and information science in order to construct shared vocabulary for the domain of IT security. Tena et al. [15] extracted and classified terms and definitions related to user interaction design patterns from common interaction design pattern libraries such as Yahoo Patterns, Designing Interfaces, Quince Patterns, and RIA Patterns. As a result, they have created a list of common web user tasks with definitions and explanations which they later validated against the panel of experts.

Text mining can also be used for enriching already existing domain vocabularies and ontologies. Speretta and Gauch [18] evaluated semantic relatedness of different words by extracting the terms from the relevant sample Web pages – and thereby could suggest making improvements in an existing domain ontology. Faatz and Steinmetz [19] substantially enriched topically related ontologies by mining the large corpus of newspapers and Web pages through Google queries.

Social media as a combined expression of people's opinions is one specific data source for constructing and improving domain vocabularies. Plangprasopchok and Lerman [20] constructed so-called "folksonomies" by analysing vast amount of metadata people used on Flickr when uploading their photos. The authors then compared their results with some existing ontologies – and made suggestions on how to incorporate the structured statistics on the content generated by large amount of Web users into a domain ontology. Barua et al. [21] analysed common discussion topics and spotted trends found in a programming question and answer website Stack Overflow. Lambiotte et al. [22] analysed more than 68 000 blog feeds for extracting common topics of interest in various times.

Thus, in line with previous research, we treat the large volume of semi-structured text on the Web as one viable source for constructing a common domain vocabulary.

3   Research Problem

As could be seen, previous research on interaction between software developers and their customers found that it is useful to have (a) active involvement on behalf of software customers and (b) shared semantical framework to avoid misunderstandings. In our study, we intend to supply previous research with actual data on what basic technical terminology knowledge would be beneficial for clients with little or no previous exposure to software development to have.

To be precise, shared semantical framework in such software projects consists of two sides. On one hand, there is an industry domain in which software is being created (e.g. medicine, logistics, building construction etc.) and which the software development team might be incompetent in. On the other hand, there is a domain of software engineering which the clients ordering software might be incompetent in. Current study (along with intended future studies) focuses on the second side of a potential shared semantical ground, namely the general domain of software development (see Fig. 1).

As such, the primary research question of this study is: what are the most prominent concepts and definitions from the domain of software development that non-technical clients could know? While in previous exploratory study we surveyed the software development team members, we now intend to look for the answer by applying text mining techniques on domain opinion leaders' weblogs.

4   Research Method

4.1   Expert Blogs as a Data Source

We decided to use blogs written by software development specialists as a data source for this study. As such, we treat these blogs as a proxy for software engineering specialists' perspective. Instead of asking the specialists direct questions, we analyse massive amount of text written by them and extract data relevant for us.

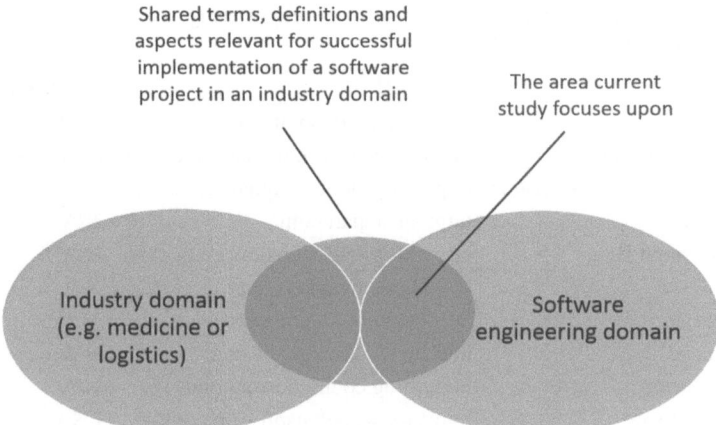

Fig. 1. Focus area of current paper.

In order to identify potential relevant blogs, we first made several search queries on Google search engine, such as "the most influential blogs in software development", "popular blogs in software development", "top software development blogs". We found several listings of relevant blogs where we copied the names and URLs from. These listings were both constructed by Internet user community (such as http://www.quora.com) as well as by categorisation according to quantitative criteria (such as http://www.alexa.com). As a result, we got a list of 206 blogs in English which focus upon various aspects of software engineering. It needs to be said that although the major topic of all of these blogs is related to software engineering, on manual inspection several blog posts were only party or not at all related to software development (but instead to technology investment or even politics). However, we did not do any filtering based on that, since such blogs posts were rather exceptions.

Agarwal et al. [23] defined and looked for the most influential blogs and bloggers in their study. The influence of blogs was measured, above others, by the measure of referral to it by other blogs. Amount of site visits and inlinks to a particular Web site are also the cornerstones of algorithm measuring the influence of individual websites by such Web resources as Google PageRank and Alexa Global rank. We used combination of these two resources for evaluating the measure of influence of a particular blog – and thus select the most influential blogs within software development written worldwide in English (that is, the blogs written by specialists which have high number of readers as well as referrals in the other Web resources).

After adjusting Alexa Global Rank to the same score scale as Google PageRank (scale of 0 to 10) we found the average of these two and defined an arbitrary threshold for blog popularity (equalling 3, 5). Every blog above this threshold was included in our source selection. As a result, 132 blogs were included in our study. Table 1 presents top 10 most popular blogs among them to exemplify our source selection.

We included a blog country parameter whenever the location of a blogger was explicitly stated at the blog. As expected, quite many blogs originated from the countries where English was a native language: USA (58 instances), Canada

Table 1. Top 10 most popular blogs on software engineering according to combination of Google PageRank and Alexa Global rank

Blog name	Blog URL	Country of origin
SitePoint	http://www.sitepoint.com/	Australia
Smashing Magazine	http://www.smashingmagazine.com/	Germany
Signal vs. Noise by Basecamp	http://blogcabin.37signals.com/	USA
A List Apart	http://alistapart.com/	N/A
StackExchange Blog	http://blog.stackoverflow.com/	N/A
Tuts+	http://code.tutsplus.com/	N/A
Script&Style	http://davidwalsh.name/s/	N/A
WebAppers	http://www.webappers.com/	N/A
Coding Horror	http://blog.codinghorror.com/	N/A
Joel on Software	http://www.joelonsoftware.com/	USA

(8 instances), the United Kingdom (4 instances). In addition, there were 1-2 instances each from Belarus, France, Germany, India, Israel, the Netherlands, Slovenia, and Switzerland (all other blogs did not explicitly state the blogger location).

RSS feeds from these selected blogs were extracted and downloaded at a specific point of time (first days of the calendar year 2015) to have similar temporal reference for all of them. The amount of items included in a RSS feed is custom-defined by a blog author. In order to avoid over-representation of postings from some of the blogs (which displayed, for instance, 200 or 300 latest postings in a RSS feed as compared to 5–7 in some other blogs), we limited the number of postings included in RSS feeds that have more than 50 items with only 10 latest posts. Limitation of 10 was inherent in the web-based open-source full-text RSS feed converters http://feedenlarger.com/ and http://www.wmutils.com/fulltextrss/ that we used in order to make sure we got full text of blog posts (instead of snippets). In total, 1 829 blog posts were extracted. The vast majority of them were written during the year 2014, while in some lower-activity blogs the latest blog posts included items written in 2013 or even in 2012.

4.2   Applying Text Mining on Selected Weblogs

Text mining, according to Miner [24], fundamentally addresses the issue of how to process large amount of text data to extract meaningful and useful information. Essentially, text mining "turns text into numbers" [24]. In our study, we were particularly interested in the term frequency analysis as one branch of text mining field. That is, the concepts which have more frequent representation across and within the blogs, are considered more important.

We chose to use the open-source software RapidMiner to perform out data manipulation: it has both many relevant pre-defined operators as well as rather user-friendly graphical user interface [24]. First, we had to perform preprocessing of text which means converting unstructured text into the structured vector-space model [24]:

1. Choosing the scope of the text to be processed: we chose only headlines and the body text of the blogs postings.
2. Removing irrelevant common document parts: we removed all words which are part of HTML like <head>, <body> etc.
3. Normalising cases: converting text into all lower case.
4. Normalising spelling: unifying misspellings and other spelling variations into a single token (for example, words "colour" and "color").
5. Tokenising: breaking text into discrete items called tokens (first, on the level of words and then on the level of sentences).
6. Removing stopwords: removing common words which do not have semantic significance for our paper (e.g. "the", "no", "such", "why" etc.).
7. Filtering tokens by length: we excluded any words shorter than 3 characters and longer than 25 characters in order to avoid "noise".
8. Stemming: removing prefixes and suffixes to normalize words; for example, run, running, and runs would all be stemmed to run.

Next, we generated n-Grams of tokens (with *n* value of 3): grouping separate tokens (words) into a series of words and thereby constructing phrases consisting of maximum three words as opposed to single words only.

The process described above is called creating a vector and it allows to quantify and structure tokens according to quantitative value such as term frequency. Its visualisation is presented in Fig. 2. Defining values for different steps such as filtering tokens by length or stemming was found through testing several alternatives and checking the outcome so that no seemingly relevant results are lost.

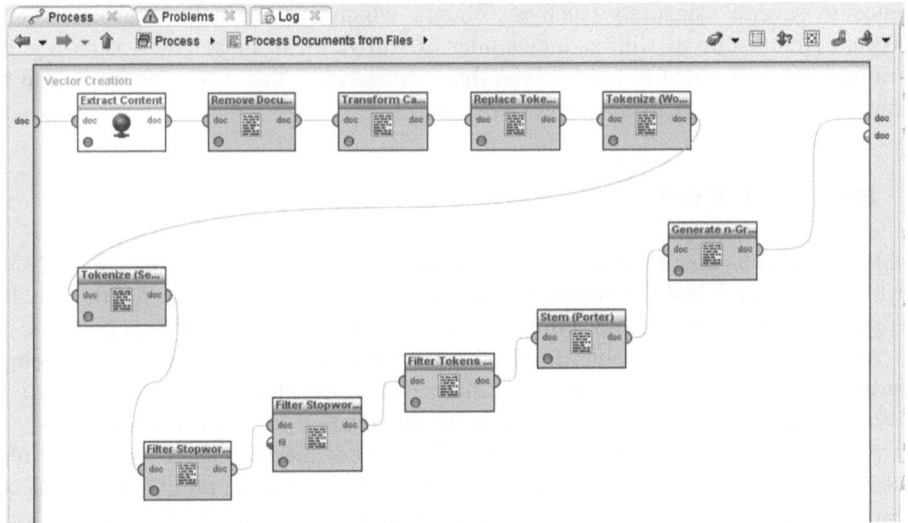

Fig. 2. Scheme of preprocessing text and creating a vector of text data for further analysis (screenshot from RapidMiner)

As a result, we got the list of 68 779 regular attributes (unique words or combinations of words). Since it is a vast amount of data, we had to set some arbitrary limits for the regular attributes to be analysed and categorised further. Only those regular attributes were taken into further consideration that both (1) were present in at least 10 out of 132 blogs and (2) were mentioned at least 25 times across these blogs (the particular number for arbitrary criteria were motivated by the need to capture significant amount of data, yet not be overwhelmed with its subsequent processing).

We then manually went through this list, removed all frequent words and combinations of words which did not obviously specifically relate to the field of software development (such as "show", "eliminate", "consider", "nearly", "previous", "score" etc.). In addition, we removed the words with ambiguous meaning which can both relate to software development as well as have some common generic meaning (for example, "get": "get" as a type of call to database as opposed to "get" in general meaning; "source": "source" of data for an information system as opposed to "source" in any other meaning). After excluding all such words, we got 456 regular attributes matching our set criteria.

At last, we manually classified the filtered list of the most prominent regular attributes according to the internationally respected "Guide to the Software Engineering Body of Knowledge SWEBOK" [25]. SWEBOK has been developed and created by many individuals and continuously reviewed during its 20-year history as an authoritative definition of the software engineering profession. It presents 15 general categories of the domain of software development (the whole list can be seen in Table 2).

The decision to classify a certain word or a combination of words was made by searching for it in SWEBOK (setting it as a search parameter across SWEBOK guide document) – and then including it in the category where it was (mostly) present. If there has been ambiguity about it, we decided it collegially. In some cases one word could be related to several categories (such as 'client', which can mean both an element in software architecture as well as a customer of software). In those cases, such regular attributes were allocated to two or even three categories – that is, certain terms can be found multiple times across several categories.

5   Results of Study

Table 2 presents distribution of 456 concepts related to the domain of software development which had the highest frequency across the analysed blogs. One can also see some of the most frequent terms within each category for illustration purpose.

As can be seen from Table 2, all 15 categories of the domain of software engineering are represented. Thus, it shows that software development practitioners cover all various aspects of the domain in their communication to wider audience.

At the same time, as illustrated in Fig. 3, some of the categories were more represented than the others. Concepts related to the category of computing foundations are clearly prevalent. It shows that terms and definitions belonging to the area of computing foundations are ubiquitous in everyday language of software specialists. That provides us with an interesting, albeit not that surprising input for non-technical clients of software engineering: the path towards understanding dynamics of software development starts through knowing the very basics of the domain. It is important to

Table 2. Distribution of the most frequent terms according to SWEBOK's 15 categories of the domain of software engineering.

A category within software engineering	No. of different high-frequency terms	No. of high-frequency terms being mentioned	Examples of some high-frequent terms within a category
Computing foundations	185	48428	'code', 'data', 'developer', 'web', 'system', 'html', 'program', 'object', 'website', 'server', 'response', 'client', 'execute', 'log', 'message', 'error', 'database' etc.
Software design	61	15681	'design', 'app', 'applic', 'software', 'input', 'field', 'command', 'plugin', 'framework', 'interfac', 'secur', 'button', 'layout' etc.
Software engineering economics	49	11484	'product', 'business', 'company', 'client', 'market', 'goal', 'money', 'pay', 'startup', 'price', 'enterprise', 'consume' etc.
Software construction	25	5411	'api', 'script', 'integrat', 'standard', 'platform', 'environ', 'commit', 'fetch', 'gui' etc.
Software engineering management	22	6315	'project', 'manage', 'iterat', 'deliv', 'measur', 'hire', 'progress', 'risk', 'employees', 'vendor, 'backlog', 'project management' etc.
Mathematical foundations	19	6802	'function', 'string', 'path', 'parent', 'loop', 'variable', 'algorithm', 'condition' etc.
Software testing	17	3579	'test', 'tester', 'unit test', 'test case', 'write test', 'tdd', 'run test', 'test driven' etc.
Software maintenance	16	3872	'version', 'update', 'install', 'maintain', 'licens', 'upgrad', 'migration', 'scheduler', 'devop' etc.
Software construction	25	5411	'api', 'script', 'integrat', 'standard', 'platform', 'environ', 'commit', 'fetch', 'gui' etc.

(Continued)

Table 2. (*Continued*)

A category within software engineering	No. of different high-frequency terms	No. of high-frequency terms being mentioned	Examples of some high-frequent terms within a category
Software engineering management	22	6315	'project', 'manage', 'iterat', 'deliv', 'measur', 'hire', 'progress', 'risk', 'employees', 'vendor, 'backlog', 'project management' etc.
Software requirements	13	5576	'requirements', 'feature', 'input', 'documentation', 'specification', 'analysi', 'scenario', 'use case' etc.
Software engineering professional practice	12	2971	'team', 'skill', 'career', 'team member', 'iso', 'copyright', 'hacker', 'team work' etc.
Software engineering models and methods	11	1707	'agile', 'sprint', 'scrum', 'product owner', 'lean', 'agile development', 'kanban' etc.
Software configuration management	10	3964	'releas', 'configur', 'libraries', 'live', 'deliv', 'deploi' etc.
Software engineering process	9	922	'deploy', 'merge', 'web design', 'workshop', 'write code', 'development process' etc.
Software quality	7	1098	'bug', 'quality', 'inject', 'inspect', 'defect', 'working software', 'fix bug'
Engineering foundations	4	1524	'event', 'paramet', 'cause', 'attribute'

stress that the category of "computing foundations" does not only include programming aspects – but covers basics of information technology as a whole (see Table 2 for some examples).

Software design is another category of terms and definitions which has been often represented across the blogs of software practitioners. Many concepts within this category relate to web design. Thus, it might be important for non-technical clients to be aware of various elements of system design and web design specifically – in order to make sure that software vendors and their clients mean the same things when they discuss the prospective piece of software.

Interestingly, software engineering economics and software engineering management were also among quite prominent categories in the IT blogs we analysed. It shows that business and management aspects of software engineering play an important role

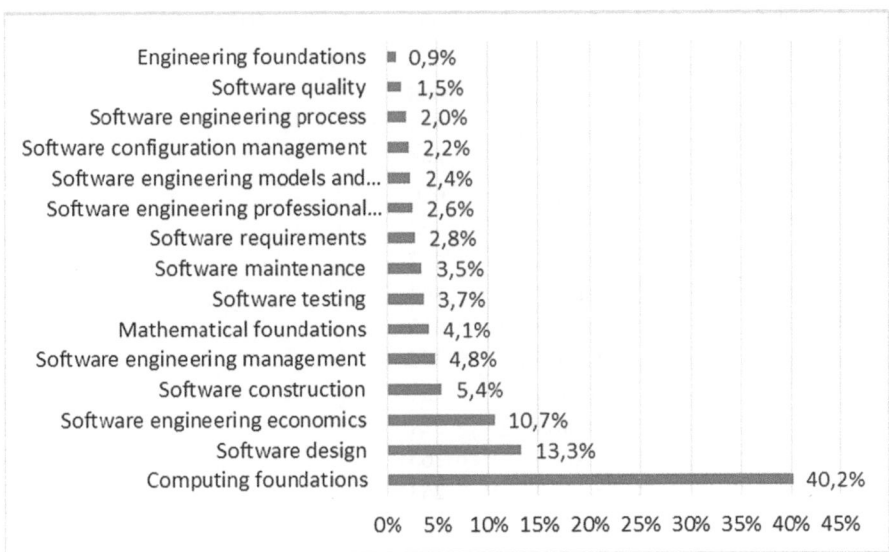

Fig. 3. Distribution of high-frequent IT-related terms and definitions across software engineering categories taken from SWEBOK

for those software specialists who have achieved the status of the opinion leaders. As for non-technical clients, these two areas are precisely those where they could potentially show their strong sides – thus, it may be beneficial for them to understand the aspects relating to software economics and software process management in particular.

Another interesting aspect worth noting are concrete IT companies, technologies, programming languages and frameworks that have been mentioned most across the most popular blogs in the industry (see Table 3). We consider it as an additional input for non-technical clients to be aware of – it is probably beneficial to know what these terms mean, what they relate to and what role they play in software engineering.

6 Discussion

Current study on the IT-related concepts across the most popular blogs within software engineering in English worldwide allowed us constructing the most frequently present words and combination of words within a domain. We could see from the results that, above all, it might be good for non-technical clients to know the basics of computing foundations. Overall, non-technical clients could get to know various aspects from different areas of software engineering: from setting software requirements to testing, to configuration and maintenance.

Although some of the concepts related to mathematical foundations and engineering foundations were also frequently present, we assume that they are not that important for non-technical clients to know since they relate to details of how programming is done.

Table 3. The most frequent companies, brands and technologies mentioned in analysed blogs

Term	Term frequency
google	1006
twitter	715
github	695
php	680
java	493
json	472
git	443
wordpress	415
facebook	366
microsoft	351
android	324
ios	265
rubi	263
apache	246
chrome	211
python	196
linux	193
iphone	168
mongodb	166
jquery	159
mysql	159
mac	145
netflix	139
amazon	135
scala	114
azure	109
visual_studio	108
oracle	104
firefox	100

As of process of conducting the study, the note of caution is that the most time-consuming part of it is the data preparation and after-processing. That is in particular related to filtering data on the most frequent IT-related concepts: there is namely a lot of manual work to be done in order to select the relevant data.

6.1 Implications for Theory and Practice

We see several ways of applying the results of this study. First, our intention for the future work is to construct the ontology based on the list of frequent terms and definitions. The objective of such ontology is to map the overall domain of software engineering and create a structured knowledge out of it. It is namely common to use data mining for constructing or updating the domain ontologies (see for example [16, 18, 19]).

One potential practical implication of such ontology is creating a graphical user interface where both technical specialists and non-technical clients could specify, based on pre-defined options, the areas of required /possessed knowledge. That is, technical specialists could specify what knowledge they would expect or at least find useful for their clients to have. At the same time, non-technical clients could specify what knowledge they already have and feel comfortable with. That allows both of these groups to identify "white spots" in their shared knowledge map prior to start of software project – and possibly to help to improve their communication from day one.

Another potential implication of this study is using the resulting list of most prominent software engineering concepts for constructing and evaluating courses and trainings on basics of software development for non-software specialists. Thus, this list can be used for validating already existing academic or vocational courses: which of the terms and definitions are present in curriculum and which of them are absent.

Third way of expanding the results of this study is to establish a temporal perspective – and apply the same methodology on most popular professional IT blogs after a certain period (e.g. in one or two years). It would allow to follow the rise and fall in software development domain trends.

6.2   Limitations

This study has several inevitable limitations that are important to outline.

First, choosing professional blogs as information input for non-technical clients can be argued against, since many of these texts are specifically aimed at software developers, and thus can have too much technical information of no importance for the non-developers. On the other hand, we are precisely interested in getting an insight into everyday language of software specialists – and subsequent studies can then focus on testing this insight for a benefit of non-technical clients.

Second, it shall be recognised that our data holds a certain time-stamp and may lose significance after certain time, since the domain of software development is constantly changing. A subsequent replication of the same methodology on older/newer weblog postings would probably allow differentiating between lasting concepts and passing trends.

Third, during source identification, we had to rely on Google queries and several constructed lists we found on the Web to pre-select the blogs as a source material. It cannot guarantee that we have covered indeed all the most important blogs from the domain. As of source selection, we relied on combination of algorithms from Google PageRank and Alexa Global rank, so we can at least be more certain that the blogs selected for the study are indeed among the most popular ones across the world.

Later, we had to do an arbitrary decision on setting the minimum criteria that combination of those two ranking mechanisms shall exceed (we selected 132 out of 206 blogs which exceeded that criteria). Setting this particular arbitrary minimum criterion was guided by objective to reasonably reduce the amount of sources to be processed.

Another major arbitrary decision had to be made when pre-processing data: we had to manually exclude a lot of terms and definitions which we either did not see as fitting into domain of software engineering or as clearly overlapping with some wide-spread semantic meanings from other domains. While doing that, we tried to follow the best practices of pre-processing data for data mining (guided by Miner [24] and other authors).

Data categorisation was the last major stage when arbitrary decisions had to be made. We had to manually process constructed list of frequent terms and definitions and categorise it according to software engineering ontology SWEBOK [25] by searching for them in SWEBOK document guide. In several instances, it was not obvious how to categorise a specific term. In these cases we either placed it several times into multiple categories or decided to exclude it for better objectivity.

All in all, abovementioned methodological shortcomings may have influenced the final outcome of the study. At the same time, since we deal with large amount of data and are interested in larger trends, the precise numbers of occurrences of particular software development terms are of lesser importance from the holistic point of view.

7   Conclusions

In our study, we made pre-selection of blogs from the domain of software engineering and ran the ranking algorithm by combing two major website ranking tools. Resulting list of the most popular blogs originated from various countries and were written in English. We then extracted all the text from the RSS feeds of respective blogs and applied pre-processing and text mining methods on these volumes of text.

The result was the set of the most frequent terms and definitions related to the domain of software development. At last, we categorised this resulting set using the wide-spread software engineering ontology SWEBOK. Correspondingly, among 456 terms included in this set, the large number of them belonged to the category of computing fundamentals, while categories of software design and software engineering economics were also often represented.

The categorised set of relevant IT concepts provides a basis for constructing or updating an existing domain ontology as well evaluating or constructing trainings and courses within the domain. All in all, the results of this study can assist in bridging the gap between knowledge of technical specialists and their non-technical clients. In our future studies we intend to build upon these results and create actual tools that can be used in practice for evaluating and improving the gaps in knowledge on behalf of non-technical clients.

Acknowledgements. This research was partially supported by the European Union through the European Regional Development Fund (ERDF).

References

1. Year of Code. http://www.yearofcode.org
2. Hour of Code. http://code.org
3. The UK Hour of Code. http://uk.code.org/
4. Shein, E.: Should everybody learn to code? Commun. ACM **57**(2), 16–18 (2014)
5. Butler, T., Fitzgerald, B.: A case study of user participation in the information systems development process. In: Kumar, K., DeGross J.I. (eds.) Proceedings of the 18th International Conference on Information Systems, pp. 411–426. Association for Information Systems, Atlanta, GA (1997)
6. Majchrzak, A., Beath, C.M., Lim, R.A., Chin, W.W.: Managing client dialogues during information systems design to facilitate client learning. MIS Q. **29**(4), 653–672 (2005)
7. Takats, A., Brewer, N.: Improving communication between customers and developers. In: Proceedings of the Agile Development Conference, pp. 243–252. IEEE Computer Society, Washington, DC (2005)
8. Shim, J.T., Sheu, T.S., Chen, H.-G., Jiang, J.J., Klein, G.: Coproduction in successful software development projects. Inf. Softw. Technol. **52**(10), 1062–1068 (2010)
9. Martin, A., Noble, J., Biddle, R.: Programmers are from Mars, Customers are from Venus: A practical guide for customers on XP Projects. In: Proceedings of the 2006 Conference on Pattern Languages of Programs, pp. 1–9. ACM, New York (2006)
10. Dorn, B.: Reaching learners beyond our hallowed halls. Commun. ACM **54**(5), 28–30 (2011)
11. Cerpa, N., Verner, J.M.: Why did your project fail? Commun. ACM **52**(12), 130–134 (2009)
12. Nelson, R.R.: IT project management: infamous failures, classic mistakes, and best practices. MIS Q. Executive **6**(2), 67–78 (2007)
13. Hoda, R., Noble, J., Marshall, S.: The impact of inadequate customer collaboration on self-organizing agile teams. Inf. Softw. Technol. **53**(5), 521–534 (2010)
14. Ojastu, D., Robal, T., Kalja, A.: Expectations of software development practitioners for non-technical clients. In: Databases and Information Systems VIII: Selected Papers from the Eleventh International Baltic Conference, Baltic DB&IS 2014, pp. 317–330. IOS Press, Amsterdam (2014)
15. Tena, S., David D., Paloma D., Ignacio A.: Bridging the communication gap: a user task vocabulary for multidisciplinary web development team. In: Proceedings of the 13th International Conference on Interaccion Persona-Ordenador. ACM, New York (2010)
16. Lenin Babu, T., Seetha Ramaiah, M., Prabhakar, T.V., Rambabu, D.: ArchVoc – towards an ontology for software architecture. In: 2nd Workshop on Sharing and Reusing Architectural Knowledge - Architecture, Rationale, and Design Intent. ACM, New York (2007)
17. Liping, Q., Lidong, W.: A study on IT-security vocabulary for domain document classification. In: 7th International Conference on Computational Intelligence and Security, pp. 521–525 (2011)
18. Speretta, M, Gauch, S.: Using text mining to enrich the vocabulary of domain ontologies. In: ACM International Conference on Web Intelligence and Intelligent Agent Technology, pp. 549–552 (2008)
19. Faatz, A., Steinmetz, R.: Ontology enrichment with texts from the WWW. In: Proceedings of the 1st Semantic Web Mining Conference at the ECML (2002)
20. Plangprasopchok, A., Lerman, K.: Constructing folksonomies from user-specified relations on flickr. In: Proceedings of the 18th International Conference on World Wide Web, pp. 781–790 (2009)

21. Barua, A., Thomas, S.W., Hassan, A.E.: What are developers talking about? An analysis of topics and trends in stack overflow. Empirical Softw. Eng. **19**(3), 619–654 (2014)
22. Lambiotte, R., Ausloos, M., Thelwall, M.: Word statistics in blogs and RSS feeds: towards empirical universal evidence. J. Informetrics **1**(4), 277–286 (2007)
23. Agarwal, N., Liu, H., Tang, L., Yu, P.S.: Identifying the influential bloggers in a community. In: Proceedings of the International Conference on Web Search and Web Data Mining, pp. 207–218. ACM, New York (2008)
24. Miner, G.: Practical Text Mining and Statistical Analysis for Non-structured Text Data Applications. Academic Press, Oxford (2012)
25. Bourque, P., Fairley, R.: SWEBOK 3.0: Guide to the Software Engineering Body of Knowledge. http://www.computer.org/portal/web/swebok (2014). IEEE Computer Society Press

Towards a Consumer Preference-Based Taxonomy for Information Systems Development

Eric-Oluf Svee[✉] and Jelena Zdravkovic

Department of Computer and Systems Sciences, Stockholm University,
Box 7003, 16407 Kista, Sweden
{eric-sve,jelenaz}@dsv.su.se

Abstract. A fundamental problem in many disciplines is the classification of objects within a domain of interest. This struggle is willingly undertaken to accrue the benefits of a shared vocabulary, with the concomitant reduction in complexity allowing for easier study of complex domains. Taxonomies are one such type of controlled vocabulary, and their development within information systems has moved from the *ad hoc* towards more standardized methods. However, the consumer preferences that catalyze and drive the development of many such systems have been little explored within information science research. This study presents a solution for this deficiency: a taxonomy structure of consumer preferences, based on extendible concepts derived from economic theory, marketing and psychology, and developed extending a known/generic taxonomy development method. A use case from the higher education domain— a platform for online education—has been used to demonstrate the efficacy of the proposed solution.

Keywords: Value · Consumer value · Consumer preferences · Requirements engineering

1 Introduction

Historically, after the first information systems were developed for specific hardware, the software industry shifted to standardization—providing products that satisfy the needs of most users. This has led to a situation, in which users miss desired functionality, or they are provided with, or pay for, functionality they do not need. Broad, general-purpose software is often complex, slow, and more prone to errors [1].

To be successful in the current environment, information system developers must create value with products tailored for their users, and while also derive investigating and capturing the values of those same users to provide best-fit, or entirely, new features [8].

Additionally, while the impact of quantitative values on information systems is both readily seen and acknowledged within software engineering, qualitative values of users have been researched to a much lesser degree, in particular *consumer values*. Several attempts to address this deficiency these values within the development space have been made; however, none have had an explicit consumer focus.

© Springer International Publishing Switzerland 2015
R. Matulevičius and M. Dumas (Eds.): BIR 2015, LNBIP 229, pp. 213–227, 2015.
DOI: 10.1007/978-3-319-21915-8_14

This is a glaring failure because the values of an individual have a direct effect on their behavior as a consumer. Furthermore, it is well-established that such values play a role in the acceptance of an information system. Kluckhohn's [9] definition of values—that they are *a conception explicit or implicit, distinctive or an individual or characteristic of a group, of the desirable which influences the selection from available modes, and means of action*, has been adopted by many studies on values in the context of software development.

The classification and organization of such concepts play an important role in both information science research and management by helping investigators and practitioners understand and analyze complex domains. Miller and Roth [13] emphasize that one such classification schema, *taxonomy*, is useful in discussion, research, and pedagogy.

In our view, taxonomies possess more than simply descriptive purposes. In addition to description, faceted concepts ("nodes") identified through theoretical as well as empirical studies of consumer preferences can serve as: (a) an information source about a quality portfolio for information system development, (b) an aid to relate a personal perception or a preference of consumer about an information system (such as "aesthetics" or "trust" for example) to an appropriate taxonomy facet which is linked with a requirements model (such as a goal-, or a feature-model), or (c) a navigation mechanism to identify a desired level of support for a certain preference, such as "simplicity", or for some its underlying facet such as "basic functionality".

In our previous work [23], we have proposed to elicit requirements for lines of information systems by using a using Consumer Preference Meta-Model as a starting point (§2). The central aspects of CPMM concern possible segmentation of users (i.e. consumers), as well as several known user value frameworks—such as Holbrook's [4] from the marketing discipline, and Schwartz classification [21] from psychology. Being conceptualized as a generic model, CPMM was meant to be extendible to include other relevant user value frameworks.

In this study, the goal has been to propose a *taxonomy structure* for a systematic classification and relation of consumer preferences, and its inclusion in CPMM to constitute a model capable to capture any kind of preference entailed.

This is realized in our study by presenting a method for the creation of such a taxonomy, as well as guidelines for how it could be utilized within information systems development. The described use case—a platform for online education—demonstrates the efficacy of the solution by presenting the mapping of the taxonomy facets to system features to be developed.

The paper is structured accordingly: Sect. 2 provides background about a method for taxonomy development, consumer values of users, and modeling consumer preferences. Section 3 describes the method used to develop the primary contribution of this research: a consumer values taxonomy, along with a method for utilizing and evolving it. Section 4 demonstrates the theoretical results from Sect. 3 within an application domain to generate a feature model. Section 5 concludes the study and provides a look towards future work.

2 Background

In this section brief overviews of the topics and the results related to the research of this paper are presented.

2.1 Taxonomies

Whereas some classification schemes are purely based on conceptual distinctions [10], others are empirically derived [2]. The first are generally referred to as typologies, the latter are usually called taxonomies [19]. In brand management research, different approaches for classifying brands exist. For instance, [17] propose a brand typology based on involvement and a motivational dimension. They distinguish between low involvement (e.g. paper towels) and high involvement (e.g. life insurance). When referring to the motivational dimension, they distinguish between 'think' (e.g. car battery) and 'feel' (e.g. perfume). Another brand typology is based on brand aspects (physical, textual, meaning, experience) that can be open or closed.

An assumption in the extant literature is that such 'holistic patterns of multiple variables' [5] provide more insights into the differences between objects than atomic variables. They represent typical configurations of variables (here: consumers' individual brand personality patterns) that differ from other typical configurations, usually along the dimensions of a framework developed in conceptual research or in a theory (here: the dimensions of the brand personality construct as described by Aaker [1]). Hence, taxonomies are of descriptive value to researchers.

2.1.1 Development Method for Taxonomies Within Information Systems

Nickerson [14] presents a method for developing taxonomies within information systems, contained within which are two distinct conceptual paths: empirical-to-conceptual and conceptual-to-empirical.

Defining Meta-characteristic. A meta-characteristic is specified at the beginning of the taxonomy development process and it will serve as the basis for the choice of characteristics in the taxonomy. Each characteristic should be a logical consequence of the meta-characteristic and the choice of the meta-characteristic should be based on the purpose of the taxonomy.

Refinement of Meta-characteristic. After selecting the meta-characteristic, it is necessary to refine it, as one of the key uses for taxonomies is for topic delineation and demarcation. This process is based on the purpose of the taxonomy and in turn based on the users and their expected use of the taxonomy.

Assign Ending Condition. Next, the conditions that end the taxonomy process need to be determined. Note that there are both objective and subjective ending conditions: a fundamental objective ending condition is that the taxonomy must consist of dimensions each with mutually exclusive and collectively exhaustive characteristics, whereas a subjective ending conditions are, at a minimum, concision, robustness, comprehensiveness, extendibility, and explanatory [14].

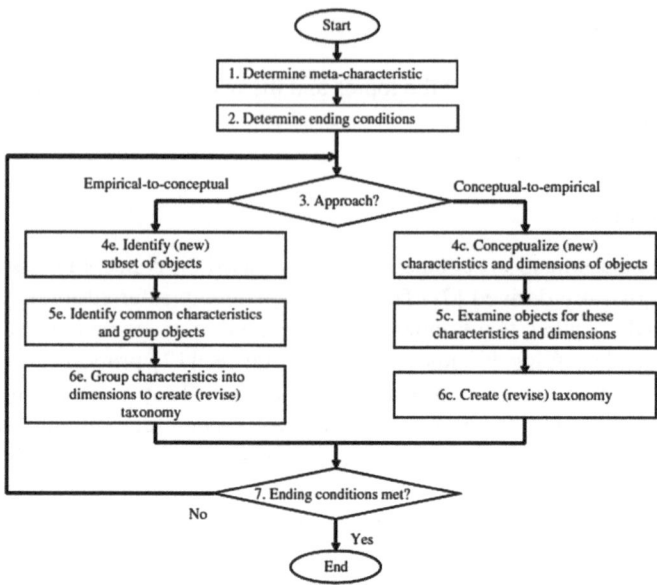

Fig. 1. Taxonomy development method [14]

Decision on Approach. After these steps the researcher can begin with either an empirical approach or a conceptual approach. The choice of which approach to use depends on the availability of data about objects under study and the knowledge of the researcher about the domain of interest. Nickerson provides two alternatives: empirical-to-conceptual or conceptual-to-empirical [14] as seen in Fig. 1.

In the empirical-to-conceptual approach, the researcher identifies a subset of objects that they wish to classify. These objects are likely to be the ones with which the researcher is most familiar or that are most easily accessible, possibly through a review of the literature. The subset could be a random sample, a systematic sample, a convenience sample, or some other type of sample. Next, the researcher identifies common characteristics of these objects. The characteristics must be logical consequences of the meta-characteristic.

In the conceptual-to-empirical approach, the researcher begins by conceptualizing the dimensions of the taxonomy without examining actual objects. This process is based on the researcher's notions about how objects are similar and how they are dissimilar. Since this is a deductive process, little guidance can be given other than to say that the researcher uses their knowledge of existing foundations, experience, and judgment to deduce what they think will be relevant dimensions.

The result of this process is an initial taxonomy based on a conceptual-to-empirical approach. At the end of either of these steps, the researcher asks if the ending conditions have been met with the current version of the taxonomy. Both objective and subjective conditions must be checked. Since this is the first iteration, it is likely that none of the objective conditions will be met so the process is repeated. In subsequent iterations the objective conditions must be evaluated and if not met, the process is repeated. If the objective conditions have been met, then the subjective conditions need to be examined. In repeating the method, the researcher must again decide which approach to use. Since new objects may have been identified or new domain knowledge may have been obtained in the previous iteration, the researcher can use the previous heuristics anew to decide which approach to apply in the next iteration. Iterations of the design process may add new dimensions and existing dimensions may be eliminated.

2.2 Values

At the highest level, value is viewed as the relative status of a thing, or the esteem in which it is held, according to its real or supposed worth, usefulness, or importance [15]. Value is also the perception of a need-satisfying capability in an object.

Holbrook's Typology of Consumer Value [21] refines the value concept towards consumer preferences, focusing on those held by individuals during a value exchange, referring to them as consumer values, and classifying them into a Typology of Consumer Values. According to Holbrook, a consumer value is "an interactive, relativistic preference experience"; interactive entails an interaction between some subject and an object, relativistic refers to consumer values being comparative, preferential refers to consumer values embodying the outcome of an evaluative judgment, and experience refers to consumer values not residing in the product/service acquired but in the consumption experience. Three consumer value dimensions are the basis for his typology: Extrinsic/Intrinsic, Self-oriented/Other-oriented, and Active/Reactive.

2.3 Consumer Preference Meta Model (CPMM)

Our conceptualization of consumer preferences [23] included three perspectives – business modeling, addressing the core concepts related to the exchange of a Value Object of concern, such as a line of software products; consumer modeling, where peoples' preferences about the product line are modeled according to existing theories; and segment modeling, which is designed to enable profiling of the consumer.

Consumer is a role representing a group of people in the consideration for the evaluation of the value object, based on individual preferences. Any of the value frameworks can be taken into consideration, and can categorize its values as a measure; these can be quantitative and/or qualitative; these are seen as driving consumers' desires to participate in the exchange process, i.e. as Consumer Driver, which should be satisfied through a consumption experience of the Value Object. Quantitative Measure is used for storing the numerical rankings or importance of the values as perceived by consumers, for an individual or a group of persons, while Qualitative Measure represent captured examples of perceived values. Additionally, different value frameworks could be used integrated to combine their values or measures, and for that the Mapping association class is used. A Segment encompasses the information characterizing a subclass of consumer, further distinguishing it from demographics and context of use properties. A Segment is used to refine the Measures to elicit a variety of subclasses of consumers. Demographics encompass consumer characteristics, such as age, ethnicity, education, and similar. Context of Use reflects an individual's context, where the main

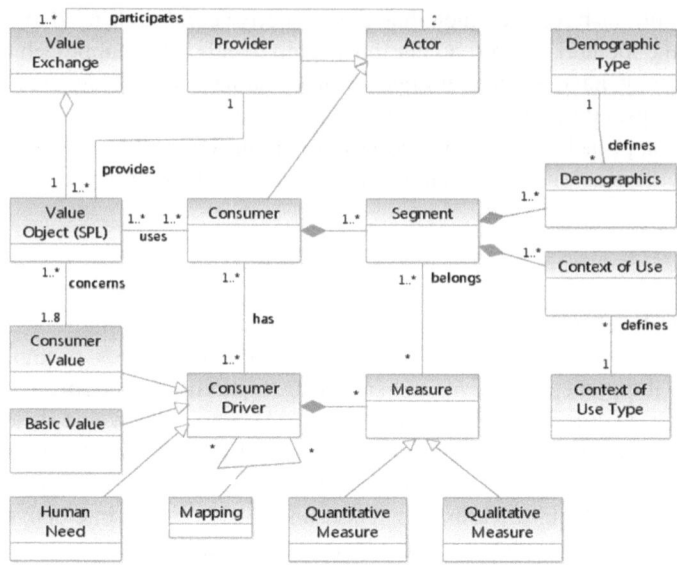

Fig. 2. Consumer preference meta-model (CPMM) from [23]

attributes for context of use are location, where the consumer will use a value object and environment, and which objects, devices, services, and regulations and under which weather conditions the value object will be used.

In this study's proposal of a taxonomy of consumer values, we aim to further improve CPMM and its use to become able to map and process a wider range of perceived values of consumers than mandated by the three value frameworks from Fig. 2; that is to be able to use the taxonomy as a unique point of linking between perceived values of consumers and the taxonomy facets, further transformed to the features of a system to be developed.

3   Method and Application

To construct the Consumer Value Taxonomy, the base method of Nickerson introduced in Sect. 2.1 is utilized. It presents a generic approach for taxonomy development and applied it within information systems [14]. Our approach also introduces concepts from anthropology and retail marketing, providing the benefits of obtaining a base taxonomy that is designed for use within information systems, while including a hybrid concept base for obtaining a rich extend of value-centric nodes.

3.1   Initial Taxonomy Scoping and Definition of Meta-characteristic

The Consumer Preference Meta-model (CPMM) from Sect. 2.3 provides both the theoretical foundations for consumer-aware information systems development.

During the first iteration of taxonomy scoping, the class *Perceived Value* replaces *Consumer Driver*. *Perceived Value* is a more agnostic term than CPMM's native *Consumer Driver*, and thus allows for multiple types of values to be used during initial taxonomy scoping.

According to Sanchez [18] the major features of perceived value are that the concept implies an interaction between a subject (a consumer or customer) and an object (a product); that value is relative by virtue of its comparative, personal, and situational nature; and that value is preferential, perceptual, and cognitive-affective in nature.

To conclude, an instantiation of CPMM using the class *Perceived Value* in place of *Consumer Driver* captures the present *Context of Use* to be described by the taxonomy. These function as the initial meta-characteristic, as per [14].

3.2 Refining Meta-characteristic

To refine *Extendibility*, a study was undertaken that had two parts built to mirror each of Nickerson's recommended approaches: Empirical-to-Conceptual and Conceptual-to-Empirical. To demonstrate its efficacy for use within information systems development, it was necessary to have a focus for the taxonomy. The area of online education was chosen because of the many challenges faced when creating courseware that will be appealing to diverse student audiences. Many argue that for online systems to be successful in attracting students' attention and encouraging learning, one of the crucial factors is to develop such systems to support both intrinsic and extrinsic motivations/values of students [7, 11, 12].

Through a better understanding of the preferences that consumers have in this area, it should be possible to build a consumer preference taxonomy through the use of Nickerson's approach. Accordingly, an empirical case study was conducted in two parts:

1. Interviews were conducted on a smaller representative sample (N = 24) to elicit preferences regarding an online education system (value object), in the scope of consumer preferences, and fulfilling their qualitative measures.
2. An implementation of Schwartz's Value Theory—the European Social Survey (ESS)—was administered to a representative sample of students (N = 224) who applied for master's programs at Swedish universities in the fall of 2011 [3].

The results were used to create a value profile for college-age students who intended to study at Swedish universities at master's level.

Using the taxonomy it was possible to trace the qualitative measures acquired during the interview process to a known value framework [4]. The established mapping between the frameworks of Holbrook and Schwartz [22] made it possible to weight the importance of the qualitative measures elicited in the individual interviews according to the survey results. These results were used to refine the taxonomy, whose terms were then used to develop feature models based on the weighting.

3.3   Extendibility

In the presented taxonomy, the subjective ending condition *Extensibility* has been used to allow for continuous refinement and development. According to Nickerson, whether a taxonomy is extensible can be answered using the question "Can a new dimension or a new characteristic of an existing dimension be easily added?" [14].

3.4   Decision on Approach

3.4.1   Qualitative Date Capture (Conceptual-to-Empirical)

The first part of the study involved profiling consumer preferences through individual interviews, wherein students were asked to describe their preferences for an online education system. This process adheres to the Conceptual-to-Empirical path detailed by [14]. The interviews included individuals from both the Domestic and International segments, and were analyzed using Conversational Analysis. Table 1 presents several examples.

Table 1. Examples of qualitative measures obtained during the interview process

Question	Examples of qualitative measures	
	Domestic	International
5	-Quick	-Quality
	-Few seconds (response time)	-Low price
	-Update latest information	-Optimal
	-Chat with the teacher	-Money
	-Fixed time for help	-Value
8	-Passionate teacher	-Like
	-Topic	-Interested in course
	-Listen	-Exercises
	-Lecture	-Good
	-Lots of information	-Helping
	-Get update	-Understand

These qualitative measures can be traced from the lower nodes in the taxonomy to terms related to specific value frameworks, in this case Holbrook's Value Typology [4]. This is accomplished by matching the qualitative measure with the most complete level within the taxonomy possible. For example, working from the top downward, one would know the methods that were used to discover the quality term (using the value framework within its branch of the taxonomy) and then continue refining the taxonomy until the ending condition has been met.

Alternatively, working from the bottom of the taxonomy upward, the qualitative measure is matched against the lowest node possible. This matching relies on the expertise of the taxonomist: a term must be a unique node, but certain terms could be potentially matched to different frameworks.

In the current case example, the values are matched to Holbrook's Value Typology [4]. Differences between the two populations can be seen in their understanding of the values *Hedonism* and *Benevolence*. Not only is Hedonism prioritized differently (the domestic students consider it to be their most important value, whereas for international students it ranks sixth) the means they use to express it are quite different. Domestic students derive hedonic pleasure from having the latest information available quickly, along with easy access to an instructor when questions arise. International students however are focused on experiences optimized for economics and efficiency.

Benevolence is ranked in nearly the converse of Hedonism: it is ranked first for international students and fifth by the domestic cohort. For domestic students, many of the same concepts as Hedonism apply: passionate teachers who are able to convey information quickly and interestingly. International students focus instead on interesting courses supported by both helpful, understanding instructors and a large number of exercises to develop competence.

To summarize, the qualitative/conceptual study collected the preferences of a student population as qualitative measures and using a bottom-up approach matched the measures to the lowest node in the taxonomy possible. The taxonomist's expertise was replied upon to place the term within the correct value framework. This matching allowed us to see what value framework within the taxonomy was most appropriate for the qualitative measure, further allowing accessing the methods available within it.

3.4.2   Quantitative Value Capture (Empirical-to-Conceptual)

This survey was an implementation of the European Social Survey [3]. An implementation of the Portrait Values Questionnaire (PVQ) of Schwartz, the European Social Survey (ESS) [3] includes 20 items, most from the PVQ with several revised to encompass additional ideas in order to better cover the content of the ten original values found in the SVT, was used in this study.

Schwartz developed the Portrait Values Questionnaire (PVQ) [20] as a simplified means to measure the basic values [21] that his Value Theory (SVT) contains. PVQ focuses on a universally applicable method for capturing and describing values across cultures and it has been applied in numerous places, including business strategy development support [CITE].

The ESS includes 20 short verbal portraits of different people, and for each portrait, respondents are asked to compare a person portrayed in each question by answering, "How much like you is this person?" A 6-point scale is used to capture possible answers with 1 being the strongest and 6 being the weakest. Each portrait then describes a person's goals, aspirations, or wishes that point implicitly to the importance of a single basic value [20].

3.4.3   Study Structure

The Swedish Agency for Higher Education Services (*Verket för högskoleservice*, http://www.vhs.se) coordinates the admission process for all higher education courses and programs, evaluates foreign upper secondary school qualifications, and administers the supporting systems throughout Sweden.

Data for research purposes is available from the Agency for a small processing fee, and the authors contracted to receive a simple random sample of applicants (R = 270 for each of 12 different populations).

The primary part of the survey consisted of the 20 questions that constitute the ESS which, via statements tailored to each participant's gender, capture basic values. A small set of questions for capturing information on demographics, and context of use, such as participant's gender, cultural origin, devices used for connecting to the Internet, and others, was appended to the ESS.

Twelve specific population profiles were requested from VHS, as detailed in [23]. Additionally, applicants had the opportunity to elect whether to receive information from third parties, and therefore the lists received included only those persons who had agreed to receive information from third parties. This significantly impacted population groups. The queries were randomized by VHS within the available cohort.

3.4.4   Data Analysis

The survey's results are presented along a single segment/demographics variable, namely "Nationality," within which "Domestic" indicates students with Swedish nationality and "International" indicates all those with other citizenships. Table 2 summarizes the results of the ESS for both the population segments, displaying the preference of the two student (consumers) populations.

Table 2. ESS implementation results

Rank	Domestic	International*	Δ
1	Hedonism	Benevolence +4	−0.577
2	Self-determination	Universalism +2	0.262
3	Stimulation	Self-determination −1	0.054
4	Universalism	Stimulation −1	0.441
5	Benevolence	Achievement +1	0.795
6	Achievement	Hedonism −5	0.138
7	Power	Security +2	−1.046
8	Tradition	Conformity +2	0.492
9	Security	Tradition −1	0.746
10	Conformity	Power −3	0.946

*# indicates relative position of value compared to Domestic population

These composite value profiles from the 224 participants (97 men, 127 women) are ranked on a scale of 1–6, with weights closer to 1 indicate a strong personal identification with the value, and those approaching 6 indicate a lack thereof.

In this case example, the taxonomy was used to express high-level intentions of stakeholders, which were then transformed into feature models describing high-level requirements for the product-specific architectures. Feature modeling [1, 6] was used to derive system requirements for a line of similar information system solutions. Such feature models describe high-level requirements for solution-specific architectures.

Suppose in the case study that an international student says that the system should support online exams; first we could trace up the nodes and levels of the taxonomy from its lower levels to discover which abstract values this reflects, and then, according to the importance given to a value by Schwartz's questionnaire (e.g., "Ethics"), decide if and how we could implement online exams. This is then documented in a feature model

Alternatively, the business stakeholder says to "Develop features based on Power", we look to/find the concrete domain specific proposals/qualities in the taxonomy (such as "choose your seat on exam") and then build such features. We would rely on the feature models, developed from the taxonomy, to see how to best implement such a system that supports the key values of importance to users. Similarly a government agency could have a higher-level policy goal/directive that is then implemented via feature models.

Such weighting for the importance of values could be provided by a custom survey, by Schwartz as seen in the example, or via another value framework such as Serv-QUAL [16]. Recall that the agnosticism of the taxonomy development process detailed in Sect. 3 allows for flexibility in choice of value framework.

4   Results

The steps detailed in Sect. 3 produced the Consumer Values Taxonomy (CVT), as seen in Fig. 3.

The CVT began with a generic instantiation of the CPMM, in which Perceived Value was used as the meta-characteristic. Once populated this instantiation saw Perceived Value replaced by Consumer Values of Holbrook, further refining the meta-characteristic. The updated version of CPMM includes the CVT in place of the value frameworks seen in Fig. 1, where a version of CVT with Holbrook's Value Typology is used.

Next an ending condition of Extendibility was selected to reinforce the iterative nature of the taxonomy development within this area. Selecting the conceptual-to-empirical

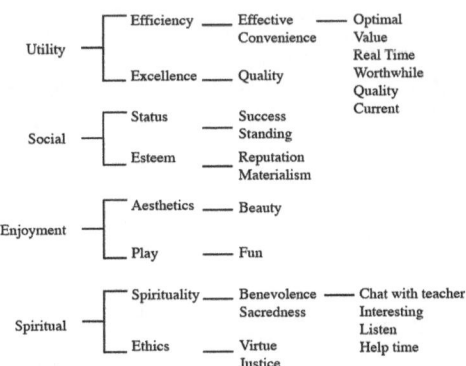

Fig. 3. Consumer values taxonomy, based on Holbrook's typology of consumer values

approach allowed for the use of Holbrook's Typology of Values to be used for the lower nodes of the taxonomy.

To further refine the results toward a feature model, the bottom-up approach in the taxonomy made established mapping between the two value frameworks of Holbrook and Schwartz [22]. This relationship made it possible to weight those Holbrook's consumer values that were verbally expressed in the individual interviews as qualitative measures by utilizing the survey results.

4.1   Feature Model Derived from Case Study

In this step, the information captured in CPMM is used to create feature models describing high-level requirements for the product-specific architectures. Feature modeling is a theory where features are used as the basis for analyzing and representing commonality and variability of systems in a solution domain [6].

The feature model seen in Fig. 4 is based only on the two with the widest divergence in the study: Hedonism and Benevolence. The choice of these values was motivated by the desire to show that even highly divergent values could be utilized within the taxonomy to develop feature models appropriate to a specific population, while also allowing for common features to be teased out.

Transforming the obtained feature models to the system requirements artifacts modeled with Use Cases involves the following activities:

- For common features across the feature models, Use Cases are elicited from a common feature by creating a corresponding Use Case Diagram and further documenting the interactions for each Use Case. The stakeholders involved in the elicitation of the use cases could be domain experts, and/or the representatives from the consumer segments. For instance in Fig. 4, "Video Archive of Lectures" will be

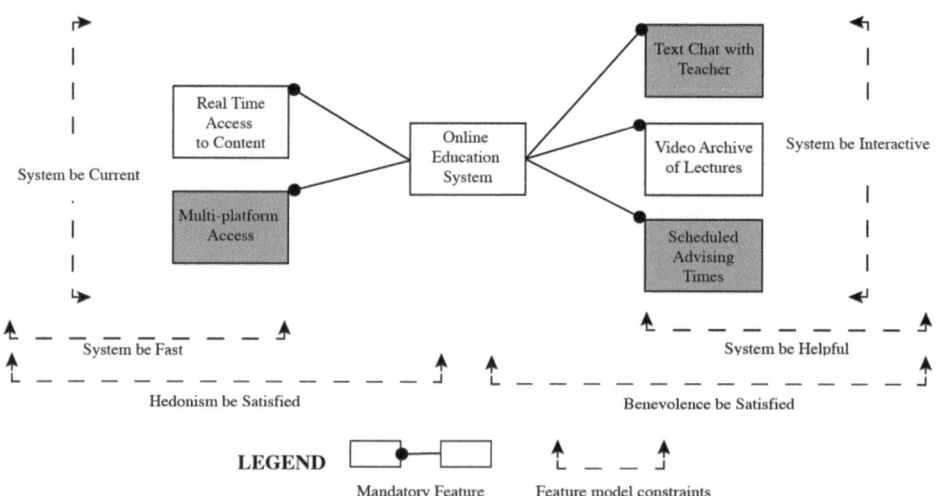

Fig. 4. Feature model for domestic students. Shaded features are for this population

used to derive the Use Cases to, for instance, *Choose a verification method, Perform the verification*, and *Present the outcome*.

* For those features specific to one or more product, configurations are transformed to Use Cases similar to the previous alternative. However, apart from the domain experts, the consumer stakeholders are chosen from the segments requiring the features. The obtained requirements artifacts represent variability in the line, and must be labeled accordingly, i.e. to complement the core and common function-alities for the products containing those features. An example of a feature specific to a product is "Scheduled Advising Times" in Fig. 4.

In addition to the above guidelines, it is needed to decide how the alternative and conflicting preferences will be handled in the process, such as when they are elicited during goal modeling. Both behaviors may be found in a single segment, and can either be resolved based on the organizational preferences in the goal models themselves, or upon feature modeling, i.e. when documenting Use Cases for development.

Apart from the qualitative measures of consumer values used to elicit the intentions and the features for different product configurations, the quantitative measures of Basic Values enable setting the rankings on the qualitative ones to use them as prioritizations in the development of products. To repeat, Schwartz's theory defines values as desirable, trans-situational goals, varying in importance, which serve as guiding prin-ciples in peoples' lives. The ranking of these values via the PVQ is an important aspect of how they can be utilized within this method for the prioritization of system features discovered during requirements elicitation.

To summarize, the qualitative/conceptual study collected the preferences of a student population as qualitative measures and, using established mapping between the two value frameworks [22], it was possible to utilize the survey results to weight those Holbrook's consumer values that were verbally expressed in the individual interviews.

5 Conclusions and Future Work

Numerous benefits accrue by engaging users through a targeted understanding of the values that they hold important, a priori to system development and use. As a con-trolled vocabulary within a specific domain, a taxonomy of consumer values would provide a basis for a number of possible uses and innovations. For example, such a taxonomy would act as a quality portfolio for information system development, pos-sibly forestalling common user acceptance testing such as heuristic evaluation, instead relying on the deeper, more powerful motivations held by end-users—motivations such as ethics, or playfulness that are not currently captured through common software development processes—to guide the work.

Additionally, consumer preference taxonomy would aid in understanding the per-sonal perceptions or preferences of consumers about an information system (such as "aesthetics" or "trust" for example) to an appropriate taxonomy facet that linked with a requirements model (such as a goal-, or a feature-model). It would also be a navigation mechanism to identify a desired level of support for a certain preference, such as "simplicity", or for some its underlying facet such as "basic functionality".

In this study, we have proposed a *taxonomy structure* as a base for a systematic classification and relation of consumer preferences, and its inclusion in CPMM to constitute a model capable to capture any kind of preference entailed.

This base structure was developed using a known method for taxonomy creation within information systems (Nickerson) and was further refined towards domain/system specific facets that capture both quantitative/empirical and qualitative/conceptual values through the use of known method for working with consumer preferences (CPMM).

The case example demonstrates the possibility to create an upper structure of a consumer values taxonomy resulting in a taxonomy for a domain of interest. This taxonomy was used to create feature models for representing requirements for information systems that support the values of the end users.

Regarding future work, we are currently working with a large text corpus sourced from social media to gauge the efficacy of this approach on an enterprise level. The goal is to leverage such a taxonomy to develop a classifier for use within Natural Language Processing. Scaling the current method for an enormous amount of data will require significant planning and testing. Additionally research has been initiated to propose patterns for more efficient application of the taxonomy, by providing reusable system models corresponding to distinct taxonomy facets.

References

1. Aaker, J.L.: Dimensions of brand personality. J. Mark. Res. **34**(3), 347–356 (1997)
2. Cannon, J.P., Perreault, W.D.: Buyer–seller relationships in business markets. J. Mark. Res. **36**(4), 439–460 (1999)
3. European Social Survey (ESS): Data, Round 6. http://www.europeansocialsurvey.org/data/download.html?r=6. Accessed 25 Jan 2015
4. Holbrook, M.B. (ed.): Consumer Value: A Framework for Analysis and Research. Psychology Press, London (1999)
5. Homburg, C., Workman, J.P., Jensen, O.: A configurational perspective on key account management. J. Mark. **66**(2), 38–60 (2002)
6. Kang, K., et al.: Feature-oriented Domain Analysis (FODA) Feasibility Study. Software Engineering Institute, Technical Report, CMU/SEI-90-TR-021 (1990)
7. Keller, J., Suzuki, K.: Learner motivation and e-learning design: a multi-nationally validated process. J. Educ. Media **29**(3), 229–239 (2004)
8. Kim, W.C., Mauborgne, R.A.: Blue ocean strategy: from theory to practice. Calif. Manag. Rev. **47**(3), 105–121 (2005)
9. Kluckhohn, C.: Values and value-orientations in the theory of action: an exploration in definition and classification. In: Parsons, T., Shils, E. (eds.) Toward a General Theory of Action, pp. 388–433. Harvard University Press, Cambridge (1951)
10. Krapfel, R.E., Salmond, D.J., Spekman, R.E.: A strategic approach to managing buyer–seller relationships. Eur. J. Mark. **25**(9), 22–37 (1991)
11. Martens, R., Gulikers, J., Bastiaens, T.: The impact of intrinsic motivation on e-learning in authentic computer tasks. J. Comp. Assist. Learn. **20**(5), 368–376 (2004)
12. McCombs, B., Vakili, D.: A learner-centered framework for e-learning. Teachers Coll. Rec. **107**(8), 1582–1600 (2005)

13. Miller, J., Roth, A.: A taxonomy of manufacturing strategies. Manage. Sci. **40**(3), 285–304 (1994)
14. Nickerson, R.C., Varshney, U., Muntermann, J.: A method for taxonomy development and its application in information systems. Eur. J. Inf. Syst. **22**(3), 336–359 (2013)
15. Oxford English Dictionary: The Compact Edition. Oxford University Press, Oxford (1971)
16. Parasuraman, A., Zeithaml, V.A., Berry, L.L.: Servqual. J. Retail. **64**(1), 12–40 (1988)
17. Rossiter, J.R., Percy, L., Donovan, R.J.: A better advertising planning grid. J. Advert. Res. **31**(5), 11–21 (1991)
18. Sánchez-Fernández, R., Iniesta-Bonillo, M.Á.: The concept of perceived value: a systematic review of the research. Market. Theory **7**(4), 427–451 (2007)
19. Sanchez, J.C.: The long and thorny way to an organizational taxonomy. Organ. Stud. **14**(1), 73–92 (1993)
20. Schwartz, S.H., Melech, G., Lehmann, A., Burgess, S., Harris, M., Owens, V.: Extending the cross-cultural validity of the theory of basic human values with a different method of measurement. J. Cross Cult. Psychol. **32**(5), 519–542 (2001)
21. Schwartz, S.H., Tamayo, A., Porto, J.B.: Basic human values: their content and structure across countries. Valores E Comportamento Nas Organizações (Values Behav. Organ.) **1**, 21–55 (2005)
22. Svee, E.-O., Zdravkovic, J., Giannoulis, C.: Consumer value-aware enterprise architecture. In: Cusumano, M.A., Iyer, B., Venkatraman, N. (eds.) ICSOB 2012. LNBIP, vol. 114, pp. 55–69. Springer, Heidelberg (2012)
23. Zdravkovic, J., Svee, E.-O., Giannoulis, C.: Capturing consumer preferences as requirements for software product lines. J. Requirements Eng. **20**(1), 71–90 (2013). doi:10.1007/s00766-013-0187-2

Code Transformation Pattern Alignments and Induction for ERP Legacy Systems Migration

Algirdas Laukaitis[✉]

Vilnius Gediminas Technical University, Sauletekio al. 11,
LT-10223 Vilnius-40, Lithuania
algirdas.laukaitis@vgtu.lt

Abstract. In this paper, we present a system that helps us to analyze legacy system reports and to transform these reports using Report Definition Language (RDL) language. The system is semi-automatic, and transforms legacy system reports using programming language specific patterns. Innovations that help us to solve the problem of semi-automatic report generation include a method of legacy system source code analysis, a semi-automatic source code pattern induction algorithm and the use of natural language processing to refine automatically generated report. The system that we suggest has been tested using different types of reports. This helped us determine the set of patterns required for a particular type of legacy system.

Keywords: Automatic report transformation · Source code alignment · Code pattern induction · Knowledge representation

1 Introduction

An automatic business report transformation and generation can be analyzed from the perspective of general question of automatic source code transformation. Usually, the automatic source code transformation is done by using code transformation patterns that are created manually. But, the development of code transformation patterns can be difficult task. This can explain why we find that most of business software upgrade projects are done by directly rewriting legacy system code.

Nevertheless, there are cases when we have a number of completed business system upgrade projects. Then, we can try to use a machine learning approach in order to induce code transformation patterns. In this paper, we provide a comprehensive research report on our efforts to develop semi-automatic report transformation tool that induces transformation patterns from completed software upgrade project code base.

There are many Commercial Off-The-Shelf (COTS) report development products that allow programmers to generate report [21], but there is no product that helps automatically transform business report code from one programming

© Springer International Publishing Switzerland 2015
R. Matulevičius and M. Dumas (Eds.): BIR 2015, LNBIP 229, pp. 228–240, 2015.
DOI: 10.1007/978-3-319-21915-8_15

language to another. Thus, we suggest the architecture and algorithms of the system that automatically transforms legacy systems report. The main innovation that we suggest is the proposal to use machine learning algorithms in order to induce report transformation patterns from completed legacy systems upgrade source code repositories. We test our method and the system by transforming reports for Microsoft Dynamics products family [5,18].

The rest of the paper is organized as follows. Section 2 presents some background and related works in the context of report source code analysis and transformation. Section 3 presents the architecture of our system. Section 4 describes the general process and algorithm of source code alignment. We suggest the use of a source code pattern model to integrate the respective knowledge sources into an overall source code alignment algorithm. This algorithm can be seen as a generalization of the commonly accepted the longest common subsequence (LCS) problem for source code alignment.

In Sect. 5, we describe the source code pattern induction method and algorithm. Here, the term source code pattern relates to a consecutive sequence of aligned and abstracted source code statements. Our approach to learning a source code pattern works in three stages. In the first stage, we compute an alignment between report statements, and in the second stage, we abstract the aligned pairs of the source code segment. In the third stage, we use generalized version of these patterns and refine them manually in order to cover all positive cases of completed reports upgrade projects.

In Sect. 6, we describe the various elements of the new report source code generation model. The keystone of the source code generation model is the source code pattern feature function and source code constraint satisfaction function. Additionally, we require that a generation of a new source code be composed from a set of code patterns that covers the old and the new report versions. Finally, Sect. 7 presents some conclusions and future work.

2   Background and Related Work

Developing the report transformation system is a very complex task because it requires a huge code pattern base to transform many types of possible reports. Additionally, the report transformation system must support many software engineering tasks, such as program understanding, code quality analysis, code verification, automatic code pattern induction, code generation. In order to describe these software engineering tasks and define the background of our problem, this section introduces several basic elements of the suggested report transformation method from user perspective. We introduce these elements with the use of use-case diagram of our system which is shown in Fig. 1. The following list provides a short description of some of these use-cases.

1. **Programming as Pattern Evolution.** Traditionally, a programmer handles business system upgrade process by manual inspection of the system source code. He edits, compiles, and tests source code by using some integrated development environment (IDE). In our system we suggest to manage

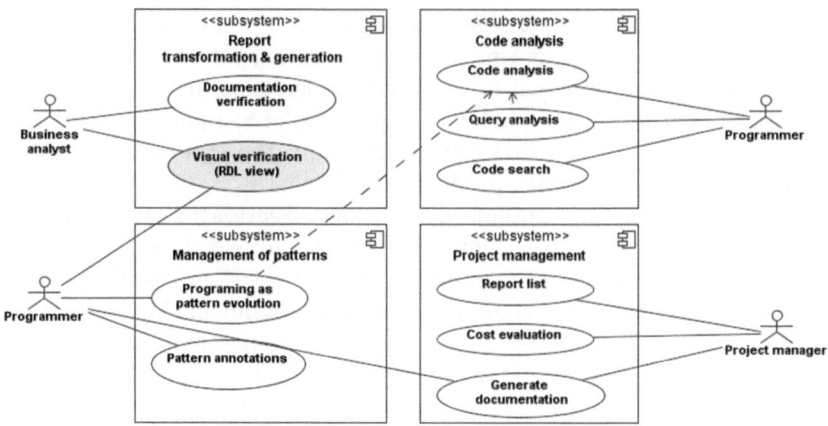

Fig. 1. Use case diagram of the report generation tool.

source code transformation pattern base as an alternative to direct source code editing. All source code transformations must be made by code transformation patterns and the programmer can change only these transformation patterns.

2. **Code Analysis.** First, we need to analyze report source code and only then, we start to transform it to the RDL language description. The analysis of source code is based on several forms of code presentation. We use abstract syntax tree (AST) and dependency graphs as the main forms of source code presentation.

3. **Code Search.** Code search is used to find similar fragments of report source code.

4. **Query Analysis.** All reports that we are transforming are based on some set of queries from a database. Our system allows to extract these queries and re-optimize them for further processing.

5. **Documentation Verification.** We use the method based on formal concept analysis (FCA) for the report documentation verification. The details on the method can be found in [13,14].

6. **Generate Documentation.** Our system generates documentation on all transformations that were used to generate report from legacy system. Documentation generation is based on a set of patterns that are written by report transformation expert.

7. **Pattern Annotations.** We mentioned above that report source code transformation is based on the set of transformation patterns. Our system allows for report transformation expert to annotate each fragment of report source code with the pattern from our pattern database.

As we can see from these functional requirements, there is a number of research papers that are related to our method. Theoretical aspects of language learning can be found in [1,6]. From these works, we know that given enough data we can use greedy approach to learn code transformation models. We use noisy channel model [2, 4] to align two versions of report source code when there is several possible alignments. Such approach has been proposed in [11, 12] for ERP system upgrade. We adopted it for the report transformation system in our research project.

There is a large body of work on software merging systems that influenced our approach on report source code analysis (see [16, 17] for review). Many available software merge tools like Unix *diff* or *diff3* are based on textual merge techniques [8, 9] without consideration of software syntax and semantics. We take basic structure of their algorithm and then we add source code semantics and syntax components into suggested dynamic programming framework. Several methods that consider syntax in software merging can be found in [3], and methods for semantic merge can be found in [7]. All these methods rely on a specific programming language.

The source code clone detection is yet another area of research that has made a contribution to our better understanding of the report system source code alignment and analysis [20]. The source code clone detection systems search for copied (with or without any modification) source code fragments. Various clone detection techniques are very similar to the methods used to solve the general problem of a source code search [15, 19]. These techniques can be used for the report upgrade problem to compare the two code segments that are semantically identical but syntactically different.

3 Architecture of the System

As we already mentioned, the main idea behind our approach to the source code transformation is to use machine learning components that learn code transformation patterns from completed legacy systems modernization projects. Thus, in this section we present the architecture of an automatic report generation system and we describe components that are related to the machine learning and to the source code representation. In Fig. 2, we can see a basic set of these components.

We can see from this figure that we decided to use transducer induction and relational learning as the main machine learning components. Induced source code patterns that transform original report source code to the set of new reports are stored in RDL object repository, which is based on SQL Server.

The following list provides more details about main components that we use to induce source code transformation patterns.

1. **RDL Learning.** It is package of several components that tries to induce transformation patterns. Transducer induction component is responsible for induction of transformation pattern that is based on AST report source code representation. Relational statistical model component implement statistical modeling approach for source code pattern induction. We use stochastic optimization approach when our source code base contains cases with conflicts between transformation patterns.

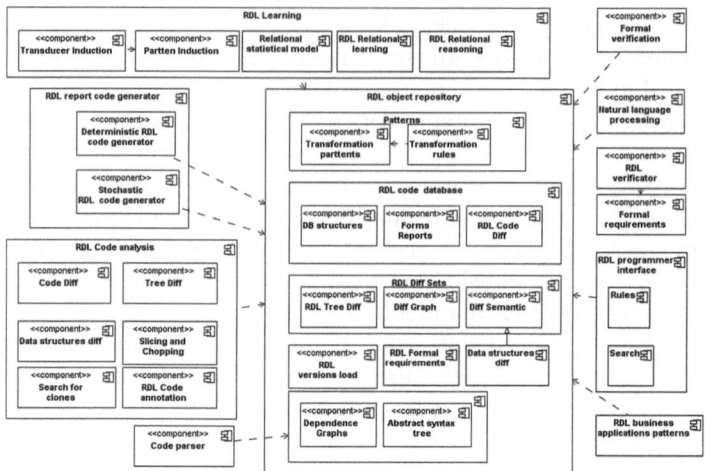

Fig. 2. Architecture of RDL report generation tool.

2. **RDL Report Code Generator.** RDL code report generator component is responsible for generating report in RDL language. It generates several versions of report and sorts them based on the metric that measures similarity between original and generated report.

3. **RDL Code Analysis.** The component is responsible for representation of the original legacy system report as well as for the report which is described in RDL language.

4. **Natural Language Processing.** We use natural language processing component for two tasks. First we use it for processing request from the user to modify generated report. Additionally, we use it for generating natural language descriptions as part of documentation about report transformation.

5. **RDL Programmer Interface.** Automatically generated report must be reviewed by transformation expert. Additionally, all induced report transformation patterns are verified by the same transformation expert. RDL programmer interface component is responsible for supporting interface between the report generating system and report transformation expert.

6. **RDL Business Applications Patterns.** Report transformation patterns are used to transform components of legacy system report. RDL business applications patterns are patterns that generate business report based on abstract semantic concepts.

7. **Formal Verification.** We use formal verification component as part of verification of generated report.

4   Alignment of the Source Code

In this section, we present general report source code alignment process and source code alignment algorithms that we use to align legacy system report source code with manually transformed RDL source code. Our approach to the source code alignment utilizes the observation that code segments from different versions of the same report, by their nature, have a high degree of structural similarity. Figure 3 shows the main steps of the report source code alignment component. In the following, we give a description for each of the steps.

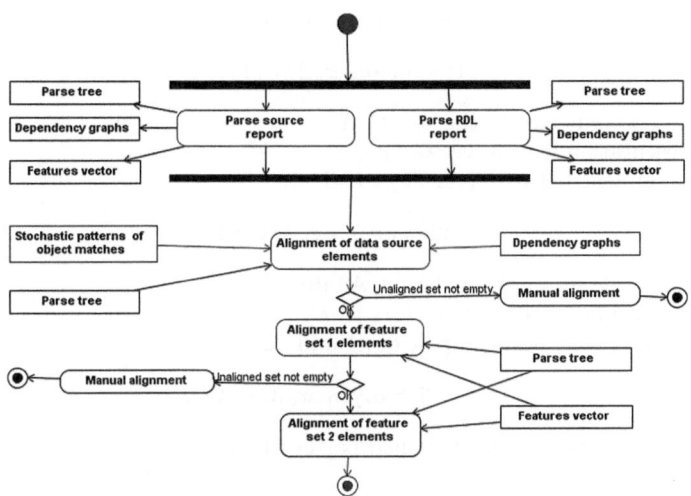

Fig. 3. Process of reports source code alignment.

1. **Parse Source Code.** We parse legacy system report as well as semantically equivalent report written in RDL language. The result is a set of dependency graphs and AST for the report. Additionally we create a set of feature vectors for each element of the report.
2. **Alignment of Data Source Elements.** At first, we try to align only database queries from both reports. If all elements of the report queries have been aligned then we proceed to the next stage of alignment. Otherwise, we require that alignments must be reviewed by programmer.
3. **Alignment of Feature Set 1 Elements.** We split all elements of the report features into two sets. The first set represents elements that must be fully aligned.
4. **Alignment of Feature Set 2 Elements.** But we don't require manual alignment from the set of report features that does not influence report semantic. Such set can be page margins, background color etc.

Essentially we can see that we align the source code in several stages. Each stage of the alignment uses the same algorithm that we present below.

Algorithm 1. Alignment of report source code units

1: We start by loading and parsing two semantically equivalent reports.
2: **for** Each report **do**
3:    **for** Each AST node **do**
4:       Get database feature vector f.
5:    **end for**
6: **end for**
7: Find alignments between pairs of reports features vectors $f1,f2$.

$$A1 = argmax_a MV(f1, f2)$$

8: **for** Each code unit pair in the set $A1$ **do**
9:    Get presentation feature vectors $p1,p2$.
10:    Find alignment between pair of $p1$ and $p2$.

$$A2 = argmax_a MV(p1, p2)$$

11:    **for** Each code unit pair in the set $A2$ **do**
12:       Get presentation feature vectors $k1,k2$.
13:       Find alignment between pair of $k1$ and $k2$.

$$A3 = argmax_a MV(k1, k2)$$

14:       Search pattern base for matched pattern list.
15:    **end for**
16: **end for**

We can see that the main point of the algorithm is the dynamic programming value function $MV(\cdot, \cdot)$. In order to define the match value of two program segments we use expression $MV(OV1_i(1, b), OV2_j(1, c))$ that is similar to expression used by [10].

$$MV(OV1_i(1, b), OV2_j(1, c)) =$$

$$\max \begin{cases} MV(OV1_i(1, b-1), OV2_j(1, c-1), CP_h) + MV(OV1_i(b, b), OV2_j(c, c)) \\ +MVP(OV1_i(b, b), OV2_j(c, c)) \\ \\ MV(OV1_i(1, b-1), OV2_j(1, c-1), CP_h) + MV2(OV1_i(b), OV2_j(c)) \\ +MVP(OV1_i(b), OV2_j(c)) \\ \\ MV(OV1_i(1, b), OV2_j(1, c-1), CP_h) + MVP(NULL, OV2_j(c)) \\ \\ MV(OV1_i(1, b-1), OV2_j(1, c), CP_h) + MVP(OV1_i(b, b), NULL) \end{cases}$$

,

where MVP is the value function used by this dynamic programming algorithm to focus on the best fit between two code fragments by matching source code pattern. We must note that an intuitive interpretation of this approach is to choose the code segment that provides maximum information for the next stage of report generation process i.e. the report source code generation. The MVP value function is the key factor in producing the final source code alignment when dynamic programming is used. We define it as follows (MVP is based on following feature functions):

$$MVP(OV1_i(b,b), OV2_j(c,c)) = \sum_{k}^{N} w_k \cdot h_k(OV1_i(b,b), OV2_j(c,c))$$

$$+ \sum_{m}^{L} c_m \cdot f_m(OV1_i(b,b), OV2_j(c,c)),$$

where $h_k(\cdot, \cdot)$ is feature function of the code match segment and $f_m(\cdot, \cdot)$ is feature function of the match between code segments and code patterns. w_k and c_m are weight coefficients.

The MV2 function is defined as follows:

$$MV2(OV1_i(b), OV2_j(c)) = MV(OV1_i(b,b), OV2_j(c,c))$$
$$+ \ln(MV3(OV1_i(b), OV2_j(c)) + 1),$$

where MV3 returns the number of exact-match statements below b and c with shuffle invariant (it simply change order if program statements not influence each other slices)

Partial matching between source code segment and code pattern may happen because some feature functions are not sensitive to source code statement names. Next, we give a description of all feature functions that we used to match source code segment and code pattern. It is important to note that final alignment score is computed by summing separate statement scores.

We identify several sets of features that are used as a signature to match arbitrary pieces of source code. There are many source code features that can be considered to characterize a node of AST. We used the following seven features:

1. Exact match. Pattern is just a code segment from completed report upgrade project.
2. LCS match of functions.
3. LCS match of database references.
4. LCS in control flow graph.
5. LCS in number of data elements set.
6. LCS in read operations of the statements.
7. LCS in global incoming dataflow.

5   Pattern Induction

We have seen in the previous section that a software engineer responsible for the business report transformation must accomplish two major tasks: try to find segments of code that are semantically important and then to transform these segments to the new version of the report. We stated that in order to accomplish these task automatically, we need high quality source code patterns with broad base of report source code cases. The main problem is that the report transformation engineers do not have time or skills to develop a good source code pattern base.

Thus, the report transformation tool should try to induce source code patterns from the previously completed reports transformation projects. But our theoretical analysis and empirical study has shown that such induction is impossible with 100 % accuracy. Even after we generated the new version of the report, further analysis is required to identify potential errors in the source code. By bearing this in mind, we provide an overall summary and analysis of the basic pattern induction algorithm that we developed during this project.

Algorithm 2. Induction of report code transformation pattern

1: $PatternList = new\ List()$.
2: **for** Each aligned , matched segment pair of report source code **do**
3:     Get set of AST nodes. $CodeSegment = AST.getNode()$
4:     **for** Each pair of AST nodes **do**
5:         Remove operator.
6:         Put $CodeSegment$ to $PatternList$.
7:         CALL UpdateList($PatternList$).
8:     **end for**
9: **end for**
10: **for** each $CodeSegment \in PatternList$ **do**
11:     CALL InduceTreeTransducer($CodeSegment$)
12:     CALL UpdateTransducerProbabilities($CodeSegment$)
13: **end for**
14: **Procedure** UpdateList(List $PatternList$)
15: **for** Each generalization and specialization operator **do**
16:     Get new transformed code pattern.
17:     Find number of positive and negative matches of particular segment.
18:     **if** $Negative\ examples\ number \geqslant threshold$ **then**
19:         Return.
20:     **else**
21:         Put new code segment to $PatternList$.
22:         CALL UpdateList($PatternList$).
23:     **end if**
24: **end for**

The whole idea of our approach for pattern induction is that we suggest to take evolutionary path in modifying life cycle of reports transformation project. We suggest to use our source code alignment algorithm and then to try to induce patterns of source code by removing some nodes from abstract syntax tree or replacing them by some class label. Then these patterns must be verified by experienced programmer against the source code base of all completed report upgrade projects.

The Algorithm 2 of pattern induction unites known learning techniques of tree transducer and incorporates mechanism to deal with issues specific to the report source code learning. Additionally, it provides a way for the semi-automatic refinement of the AST transducer with only a few interactions with the report upgrade expert. It is important to note that the associated problems with source code pattern induction include: (1) the choice of the source code AST abstraction and transformation, (2) the choice of the source code AST nodes features, (3) the measure of similarity between code and pattern, (4) the selection of a fragment in the code to be compared with the code pattern. We can see that all these problems are addressed in the Algorithm 2 and it has two stages. In first stage we select unmatched segments of code and make series of transformations and substitutions to build a set of pattern candidates. At the second stage we sort candidate pattern set and present them for an expert verification. Additionally, in this approach, we add feature vectors of statement in order to match different source code fragments. Moreover, the implementation of the source code alignment algorithm is more robust once structural details of the code have been abstracted and represented as sequence of entities.

6   Report Transformation Process

Only when we have sufficient source code transformation pattern base we can start automatic source code transformation process. In this section we present a novel process and algorithm that helps to generate new report from old one and which requires little intervention from programmer. In the Fig. 4 we present the basic steps of this process.

We shortly describe each step in this process.

1. Load Old Report code. The process is responsible for old report source code parsing and building dependency graph.
2. Extract database components. Most of business report semantic is described by database queries. We extract these queries from report source code and we build sequential queries call graph.
3. Extract other data structure components. Such components like database procedures of functions we process separately from database queries.
4. Select database unit. We select database query, function etc.
5. For each database unit we look for the source code pattern in the patterns repository.
6. Generate RDL database unit. We generate database queries in RDL language if we find adequate transformation pattern.
7. Generate RDL report representation unit. We generate new report representation elements after new report queries where generated from the set of patterns.

The main idea behind general process of report generation is that we split generating process into two parts. The first part of the process is concerned with database queries and the second part of process is concerned with report

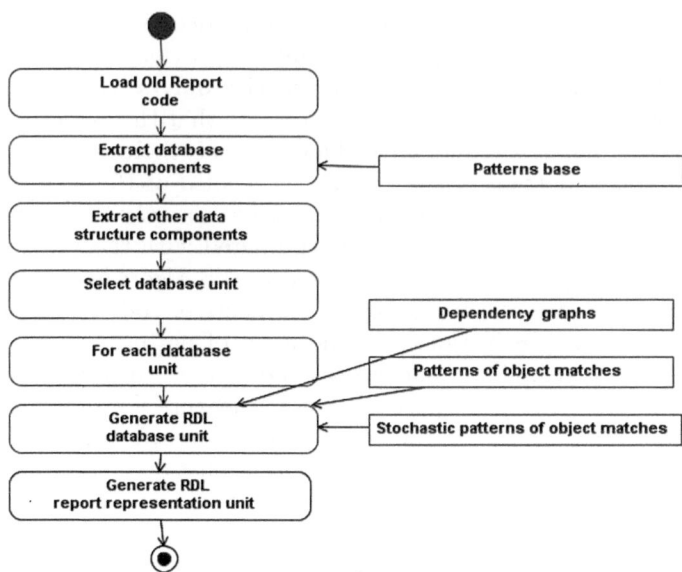

Fig. 4. Process of reports generation.

Algorithm 3. New report generation

1: $NewReport \Leftarrow''$ {initially we set NewReport program code to empty strings}
2: Generate database components.
3: Generate other data structure components.
4: Calculate old report feature vector.
5: Search for the patterns set.
6: **for** Each pattern i such that $1 \leqslant i \leqslant number\_of\_code\_patterns$ **do**
7:     Insert database queries.
8:     Insert representation elements.
9:     **if** $NewReport_i passverification$ **then**
10:        $NewReport_i$ put into set of candidates
11:    **else**
12:        **for** Each empty AST node **do**
13:            remove node
14:            **if** $NewReport_i passverification$ **then**
15:                $NewReport_i$ put into set of candidates
16:            **end if**
17:        **end for**
18:    **end if**
19: **end for**
20: Formal verification of generated ERP system code.
21: Report about transformation.

---

representation elements. We generate the final report by using decision patterns that are checked and modified by professional programmer. Such approach allows us to achieve more robust results and better quality of final report system code.

7   Conclusion

We presented general framework that enables us to transform business reports using semi-automatic approach. Presented framework focuses on RDL language but we think that some ideas in this framework can be applied to other languages as well. The framework presented in this paper can increase the quality of source code and decrees time of upgrade project. But in order to achieve this, developers must invest their time to build pattern base that is used to align and transform source code from one report definition language to another.

This paper is the first attempt to use machine learning, artificial intelligence and online learning in order to develop source code transformation patterns. Additionally, we think that we were able to suggest a general method for using machine learning approach for information systems engineering. The basic idea behind this method is that machine learning is used to detect and sort code patterns and then domain experts refines some of the patterns for the final use to generate new version of information system.

Our preliminary theoretical analysis shows that it is impossible to have fully automated solution of this upgrade process unless we put more constrains on pattern language. Nevertheless, it is possible to solve significant amount of conflicts with the framework suggested in this paper. Additionally, we can note that the quality of generated source code can be increased by constantly updating knowledge base from the new projects.

References

1. Angluin, D., Smith, C.H.: Inductive inference: theory and methods. ACM Comput. Surv. **15**(3), 237–269 (1983)
2. Baum, L.E.: An inequality and associated maximization technique in statistical estimation of probabilistic functions of a Markov process. Inequalities **3**, 1–8 (1972)
3. Buffenbarger, J.: Syntactic software merging. In: Estublier, J. (ed.) ICSE-WS 1993/1995 and SCM 1993/1995. LNCS, vol. 1005, pp. 153–172. Springer, Heidelberg (1995)
4. Dempster, A.E., Laird, N.M., Rubin, D.B.: Maximum likelihood from incomplete data via the EM algorithm. J. Roy. Stat. Soc. **39**(B), 1–38 (1977)
5. Ehrenberg M.: Microsoft Dynamics AX 2012. A New Generation in ERP (2011)
6. Gold, E.M.: Language identification in the limit. Inf. Control **10**(5), 447–474 (1967)
7. Horwitz, S., Prins, J., Reps, T.: Integrating noninterfering versions of programs. ACM Trans. Program. Lang. Syst. **11**(3), 345–387 (1989)
8. Hunt J.W., McIlroy M.D.: An algorithm for diferential file comparison. Computer Science Technical report 41, Bell Laboratories (1975)
9. Hunt, J.W., Szymanski, T.G.: A fast algorithm for computing longest common subsequences. Commun. ACM **20**(5), 350–353 (1977)

10. Kontogiannis, K.A., DeMori, R., Merlo, E., Galler, M., Bernstein, M.: Pattern matching for clone and concept detection. In: Wills, L., Newcomb, P. (eds.) Reverse Engineering, pp. 77–108. Kluwer Academic Publishers, Norwell (1996)
11. Laukaitis, A.: Automation of merging in ERP revision control. In: Skersys, T., Butleris, R., Butkiene, R. (eds.) ICIST 2012. CCIS, vol. 319, pp. 1–14. Springer, Heidelberg (2012)
12. Laukaitis, A.: Automation of upgrade process for enterprise resource planning systems. In: Skersys, T., Butleris, R., Butkiene, R. (eds.) ICIST 2013. CCIS, vol. 403, pp. 70–81. Springer, Heidelberg (2013)
13. Laukaitis, R., Laukaitis, A.: Natural language processing and the conceptual model self-organizing map. In: Kedad, Z., Lammari, N., Métais, E., Meziane, F., Rezgui, Y. (eds.) NLDB 2007. LNCS, vol. 4592, pp. 193–203. Springer, Heidelberg (2007)
14. Laukaitis A., Vasilecas O.: Formal concept analysis and information systems modeling. In: Proceedings of the 2007 International Conference on Computer Systems and Technologies, CompSysTech 2007, vol. 45, pp. 93–104 (2007)
15. McMillan C., Hariri N., Poshyvanyk D., Cleland-Huang J., Mobasher B.: Recommending source code for use in rapid software prototypes. In: 34th International Conference on Software Engineering (ICSE), pp. 848–858 (2012)
16. Mens T.: A formal foundation for object-oriented software evolution. Ph.D. thesis, Vrije Universiteit Brussel - Faculty of Science - Departement of Computer Science - Programming Technology Lab, August 1999
17. Mens, T.: A state-of-the-art survey on software merging. IEEE Trans. Softw. Eng. **28**(5), 449–462 (2002)
18. Microsoft Corporation. Microsoft Dynamics NAV (2012)
19. Paul, S., Prakash, A.: A framework for source code search using program patterns. IEEE Trans. Softw. Eng. **6**(20), 463–475 (1994)
20. Roy C.K., Cordy J.R.: A survey on software clone detection research. Technical report. Queens University at Kingston (2007)
21. Vaucouleur, S.: Code query by example. Enterp. IS **5**(1), 99–123 (2011)

Passive Condition Pre-enforcement
for Rights Exporting

Wenhui Lu, Jyrki Nummenmaa$^{(\boxtimes)}$, and Zheying Zhang

School of Information Sciences, University of Tampere, 33014 Tampere, Finland
{wenhui.lu,jyrki.nummenmaa,zheying.zhang}@uta.fi

Abstract. Condition pre-enforcement is one of the known methods for rights adaptation. Related to the integration of the rights exporting process, we identify issues introduced by condition pre-enforcement and potential risks of granting unexpected rights when exporting rights back and forth. We propose a solution to these problems in a form of a new algorithm called Passive Condition Pre-enforcement (PCP), and discuss the impact of PCP to the existing process of rights exporting.

Keywords: Digital rights management · Rights exporting · DRM interoperability · Condition pre-enforcement

1 Introduction

According to the shipment statistics published by RIAA, digital formats comprised 68 % of total revenue of US music industry in 2014 [6]. Digital Rights Management (DRM) [7] is to protect digital content from piracy and improve the business opportunities. DRM here refers to a system to protect high value digital assets and to control their distribution and usage. Examples of such systems include Windows Media DRM [8], and Open Mobile Alliance (OMA) DRM version 2 [9].

Carlisle and Navin [10] observed that different DRM systems have in fact locked-in consumers to proprietary technologies of respective companies in the digital music market (and accompanying digital players). Interoperability between different systems is needed to deal with distinctions among DRM systems and to export rights from one system to another.

Koenen et al. in 2004 [13] proposed three approaches to interoperability in DRM systems, i.e. full format interoperability, connected interoperability, and configuration-driven interoperability. Full format interoperability is based on the idea of a universal standard, which does not seem to be a likely development [11]. Connected and configuration-driven approaches can be supported by DRM interoperability. Schmidt et al. [14] introduced the concept of intermediated DRM and listed four general tasks for the intermediary DRM, i.e. Content and rights reformatting, data management, condition evaluation, and dynamical state evaluation. Based on their work, we characterized rights exporting further [5]; enriched the concept of rights adaptation [4]; introduced our rights model to better illustrate the problem domain; and proposed a decomposition method to potentially improve the rights exporting performance [2, 3].

© Springer International Publishing Switzerland 2015
R. Matulevičius and M. Dumas (Eds.): BIR 2015, LNBIP 229, pp. 241–254, 2015.
DOI: 10.1007/978-3-319-21915-8_16

In addition, Serrão et al. [19] studied interoperability using intelligent brokerage mechanisms, while the Coral Consortium [12] tried to standardize DRM interoperability, however, without addressing rights adaptation [1]. The Digital Media Project group proposed their interoperable DRM standard in 2007 [15]. Doncel et al. [16] studied the potential of MPEG Extensible Middleware to serve DRM interoperability in the MPEG-21 standard. The Marlin developer community [17] is attempting to provide truly interoperable and open digital content sharing platform, but the outcome is still not known. Jamkhedkar et al. [18] proposed a framework for usage management enabling interoperability.

Although DRM exists primarily as a way of controlling how consumers access purchased content to ensure that they pay for what they get, DRM is not just a controlling technology. A fair DRM ecosystem should enable sharing while respecting the conditions and requirements that rights holders have associated with their content. The above mentioned research results have proposed general technology frameworks and approaches to DRM interoperability. In addition to a framework, a refined process leveraged with techniques and algorithms to support the decision making in the rights exporting is needed for the ecosystem of distributing digital content. We have studied such techniques and algorithms from the perspective of rights decomposition and adaptation for interoperability [2–5] into the decision making process of rights exporting. In particular, our line of research is language-independent, i.e. it is not dependent of the language that is used to manage the digital rights. In this paper, we analyze the potential problems when rights are exported back and forth, and propose a new integrated process to improve exporting result and reduce risks of violating the principles of rights exporting [5]. With the integrated process, we discuss how to improve the overall process with identified issues.

The remainder of the paper is organized as follows. In Sect. 2, we give an introduction to the main concepts in rights exporting. In Sect. 3, we analyze issues related with previous work in the area, and in Sect. 4 we propose the use of Passive Condition Pre-enforcement (PCP) to solve these issues. In Sect. 5, we discuss the impacts of PCP on rights exporting, and on Sect. 6 possible optimization. Section 7 concludes the paper.

2 Rights Exporting

Following our previous work [5], which in turn is based on the work of Safavi-Naini et al. [1], we define the rights exporting as a task to provide the usage rights from a domestic DRM system to a target DRM system. We define rights exporting in the procedure GenericExport. Notably GenericExport does not give implementation details, so it can be refined into different implementations.

```
GenericExport
```

   Input: A set of rights instances $(R_1(A), R_2(A), ...R_n(A))$ to
   be exported from DRM system A to DRM system B.
   Output: A set of exported rights instances
   $(R_1\check{}(B), R_2\check{}(B), ...R_n\check{}(B))$ on B, and a set of remaining
   rights instances $(R_1\check{}(A), R_2\check{}(A), ...R_n\check{}(A))$ on A after
   exporting.
     Condition:
   if IsExportable(A, B)==true, then{
       for each R_x (x=1,2,...n) {
               Export$(R_x(A), B)\Rightarrow R_x\check{}(B) + R_x\check{}(A)$ }}
       else {
       $R_x\check{}(B) = \emptyset$; $R_x\check{}(A) = R_x$}

The definition of *GenericExport* allows to discuss export modes (i.e. copy or move) and directions, as well as results [5] but it does not address how to achieve a trustworthy output $R_x(A)$ and $R_{x'}(B)$ from the algorithm *Export($R_x(A)$, B)*. To apply *GenericExport* for concrete rights instances, it is necessary, of course, to analyze the exportability of rights from the domestic system to the target system.

In the most simplified scenario, the algorithm *Export($R_x(A)$, B)* just needs to decide whether $R_x(A)$ can be exported to the target system B in the format of $R_x(B)$, which can be defined as *Decide($R_x(A)$, B)*. As decision making is the core of the algorithm *Export ($R_x(A)$, B)*, we take the algorithm as a tool to describe the process of decision making for rights exporting. The decision needs to be made according to a set of criteria such as the availability of the right, the permission types, the condition types, the linkage, and the internal structure of right on a target system [4]. Based on the defined criteria, the algorithm of decision making can be achieved. We define the output of the decision making, i.e. the decision $D(R_x(A), B)$, to be either "accepted" (D_a) or "rejected" (D_r), as explained below.

- "Accepted" means that the $R_x(A)$ can be expressed and governed by the target system B as $R_x(B)$. That is to say, if $D(R_x(A), B)$ is D_a, $R_{x''}$ equals to R_x, and $R_{x'}$ equals to either $\emptyset$ in the move mode or R_x in the copy mode.
- "Rejected" means that $R_x(A)$ cannot be properly expressed or governed by B. That is to say, if $D(R_x(A), B)$ is D_r, $R_{x''}$ equals to $\emptyset$ and $R_{x'}$ equals to R_x.

As the value of $R_{x'}$ depends on the mode of rights exporting, we define the mode of rights exporting for $R_x(A)$ as $M(R_x(A), B)$, and the move mode as M_m and the copy mode as M_c. The mode of rights exporting shall be agreed between systems A and B according to the desired behavior defined by the business model, which for us makes it an external decision that is only included as a parameter in the algorithms.

We further integrated [20] the process of rights exporting with rights decomposition [2, 3] and rights adaptation [1, 4]. As a result, *GenericExport($R_x(A)$, B)* can be refined as the algorithm below.

```
int Export(R_x(A),B){ int ret=0; // default value to zero
    Decide(R_x(A), B)⇒D(R_x(A),B);
    If D(R_x(A),B)==D_a, then{
        If M(R_x(A),B)== M_m ,then{
            R_x``(B)=R_x; R_x`=∅;}
        else {
            R_x``(B)=R_x; R_x`(A)=R_x; }}
    else {
        If IsDecomposable(R_x(A)), then {
            Decompose(R_x(A))⇒{i∈n:R_xdi(A)}
            for i∈n { ret +=1;
                Export (R_dai(A),B) ⇒ R_xdi``(B)+ R_xdi`(A);
                R_x``(B) += R_xdi``; R_x`(A)+=R_xdi`;}
            if (ret==n) then {ret=1;R_x``(B) =∅;
R_x`(A)=R_x;}
            else{ret=0;}}
        else if IsAdaptable(R_x(A),B)==true, then{
            Adapt(R_x(A),B)⇒ R_xa(A)
            ret=Export (R_xa(A),B) ⇒R_xa`(A)+R_xa``(B)
            if (ret==0) then{R_x``(B) += R_xa``;
R_x`(A)+=R_xa`;}
            else {R_x``(B) =∅; R_x`(A)=R_x;}}
        else {ret =1;R_x``(B) =∅; R_x`(A)=R_x;}}
    return ret;}
```

And *Export* can be illustrated as Fig. 1.

We have concluded that the principle of trustworthy rights exporting [5] is to maximize the amount of rights to be exported and to prevent generating extra rights.

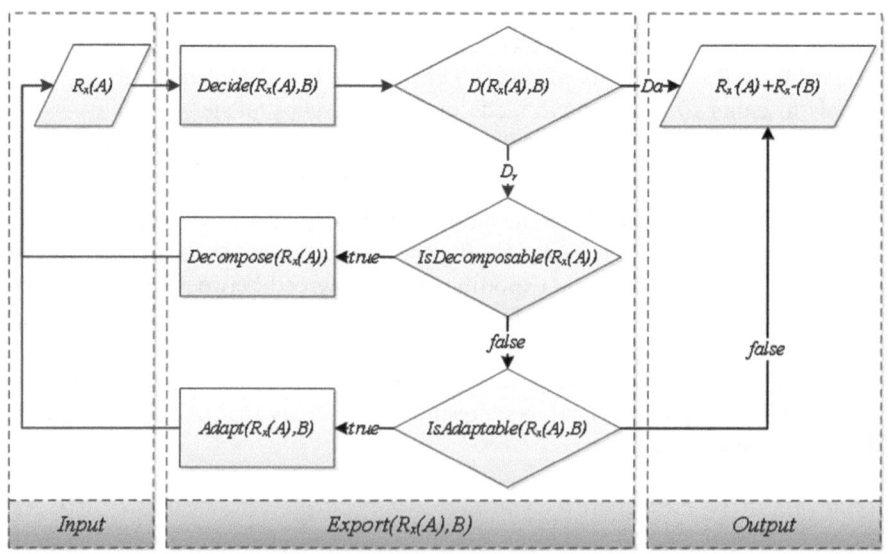

Fig. 1. The flow diagram of *Export()*.

- In the copy mode: $R_{x''} \rightarrow R_x$ where $\emptyset \subset R_{x''} \subseteq R_x$; and $R_{x'} == R_x$.
- In the move mode: $R_{x''} \rightarrow R_x$ where $\emptyset \subset R_{x''} \subseteq R_x$; and $R_{x'} \rightarrow \emptyset$ where $\emptyset \subseteq R_{x'} \subset R_x$; and $R_{x'} \cup R_{x''} \subseteq R_x$.

The notation R_x represents a unified and system-agnostic definition of specific rights while the notation $R_x(A)$ represents a rights instance governed by system A. $R_x(A) = R_x$ means the rights instance $R_x(A)$ grants an end user with rights defined by R_x on system A.

To elaborate on the needs of decision making in rights exporting and its integrated process, we use the following example throughout the paper. We assume that an end user named Jack has a few music files protected by Windows Media DRM (WMDRM) v10 [8] on his PC. Jack wants to use those music files on his mobile phone which uses a DRM system based on OMA DRM v2 [9]. Therefore Jack needs to export both the content and the rights from one DRM system to another. The rights on his PC are expressed based on the rights expression language (REL) used in WMDRM, which includes a first-level root license (RL) that covers all music files with a specific expiration date X (ExpirationDate) as the condition defined by the DRM system, two second-level root licenses, i.e. RL-A and RL-B, defined by two companies A and B from which Jack purchased those music files, and four leaf licenses, i.e. LL-1, LL-2, LL-3, and LL-4, defined for each music file, as illustrated in Fig. 2. Company A defines a second-level license RL-A to play a music file (Play) and to burn a file into a CD as a part of playlist (PlaylistBurn), and requires to disable all rights if clock is reset to an earlier time (DisableOnClockRollback). Company A also defines a leaf license LL-1 for file #1 to play and burn the file into CD without any conditions. Company B defines a second-level license RL-B to burn a file into a CD with a maximum count of Y times (PlaylistBurnTrackCount) and to play a media file for Z times (PlayCount).

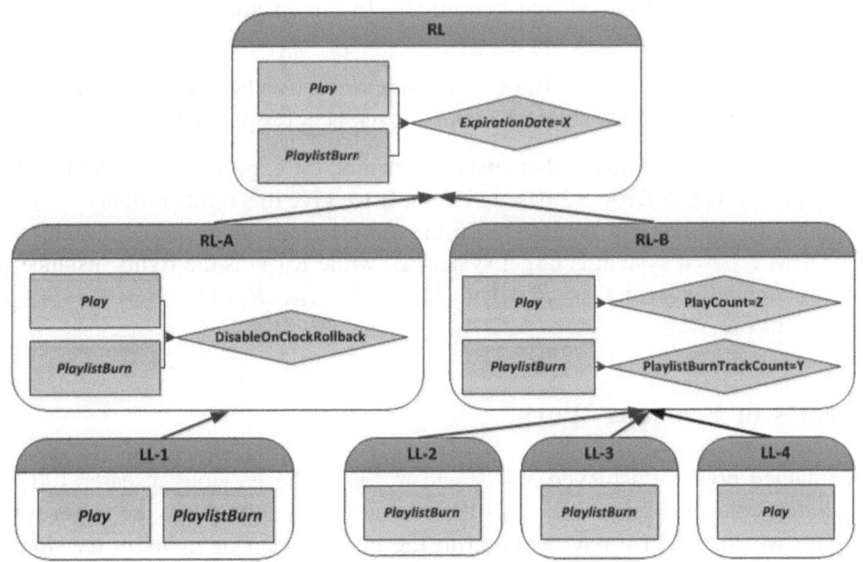

Fig. 2. Example WMDRM rights to be exported

Company B also defines three leaf licenses, i.e. LL-2 and LL-3, which grant file #2 and #3 the rights to burn without any condition, and LL-4 which grants file #4 the rights to play without any condition. As WMDRM 10 does not officially support the copy mode [8], the exporting mode is the move mode.

The rights on the WMDRM based system can be expressed in the REL-agnostic rights model we introduced previously [2, 3], as illustrated in Fig. 3.

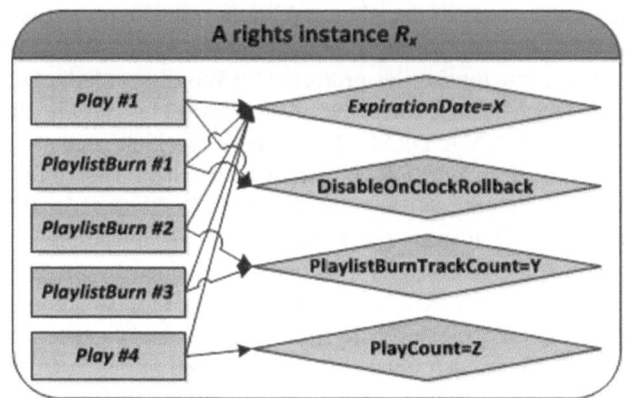

Fig. 3. Example rights illustrated by rights model

In order to determine if a rights instance is exportable to OMA DRM 2, we need to check all the criteria of rights exporting [4], i.e. types of permissions, types of conditions, types of linkages, multiple conditions, shared conditions, capacity of multiple conditions, and capacity of shared conditions. In our example the following causes failures in passing the criteria.

- The permission type PlaylistBurn is not supported by OMA DRM v2; and
- The condition type to DisableOnClockRollback is not supported by OMA DRM v2.

Therefore, currently the rights instance cannot be exported from WMDRM 10 based system to OMA DRM v2 based system. If we give this rights instance as input to algorithm *Export*, then the WMDRM 10 based system is the domestic system A and OMA DRM 2 based system is target system B, while $R_x(A)$ is the rights instance. The result of rights exporting is $R_{x''}(B) = R_{xd1} + R_{xd2ad1}$; $R_{x'}(A) = R_{xd3} + R_{xd2ad2}$, as illustrated in Fig. 4.

3   Issues in Previous Work

We explained how we achieved $R_{x'}(B)$ and $R_{x}(A)$ in the previous research [20]. The research has concentrated on the rights that are moved or copied into the target system. However, we should also pay attention to the management of rights in the domestic system. In our previous work, the pre-enforced condition was not put back for those

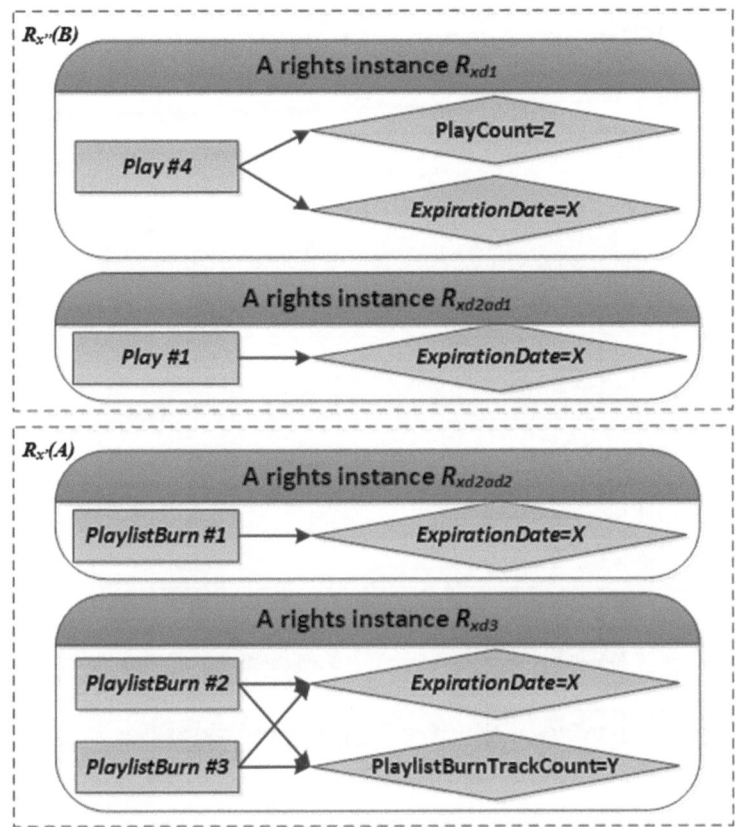

Fig. 4. Example rights after rights exporting [20]

rights instance staying on the domestic system after rights exporting. As illustrated in Fig. 4, the pre-enforced condition is not added back to $R_x(A)$. In our example, *DisableOnClockRollback* was originally applied to both permission *PlaylistBurn #1* and *Play #1*. *Play #1* got exported to system B after pre-enforcement and *PlaylistBurn #1* stayed at system A. Therefore permission *PlaylistBurn #1* should link back to condition *DisableOnClockRollback*. The corrected result of rights exporting should be presented as illustrated in Fig. 5.

Moreover, the condition pre-enforcement was not fully discussed in earlier research [1–5, 20] which could potentially lead to breach of the principle of rights exporting [5]. Consider our previous example, where we try to export $R_{x''}(B)$ from system B back to system A. There, *DisableOnClockRollback* is going to be missing compared with the original conditions linked to permission *Play #1*. In particular, it means that when we consider exporting rights from A to B and back to A, the rights become less restrictive. This is against the principle of rights exporting [5]. In the following sections, we will study how to improve the proposed rights exporting method by performing condition pre-enforcement in the context of rights exporting.

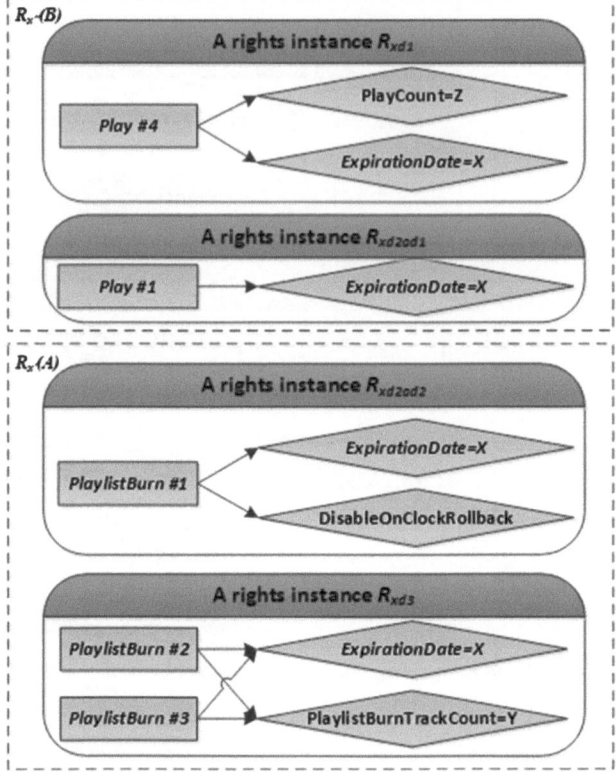

Fig. 5. Example rights after rights exporting (corrected)

4 Passive Condition Pre-enforcement

Safavi-Naini et al. [1] introduced the idea of pre-enforcement for constraints that cannot be checked or satisfied by the target system. We adapted the concept into our rights model [4] and formulated a Boolean attribute *isPre-enforcable* to indicate if the condition can be pre-enforced. However, we did not provide sufficient information on the situation in which condition pre-enforcement can be performed and how to perform the condition pre-enforcement.

Condition pre-enforcement is a method to satisfy the condition before rights exporting in order to remove the linkage from instances of permission which are linked to the condition. For example, Jack has a right instance to chat via a piece of software on his PC after he registers on a website. In this case, the registration is the condition instance. Now Jack wants to export the right to his mobile phone. However, the system on his phone does not support the registration to this website. Therefore, Jack has to first register on the website on his PC before the system on his PC can allow the instance of right to be exported to his phone. Once the condition instance is enforced, it becomes true from then onwards, and has no impact on the validity checking for the instance of rights. In such a scenario, the condition is pre-enforced by performing a specific action on the domestic system before right exporting. We define it as Active Condition Pre-enforcement (ACP).

In addition, condition pre-enforcement can be also achieved passively by rights exporting, depending on the characteristic of the target system. In the example presented in the introduction chapter, *DisableOnClockRollback* can be pre-enforced as OMA DRM v2 supports secure clock implementation, which pre-enforces the condition. In such a case, the condition *DisableOnClockRollback* will always be satisfied once the rights are exported to the target system. If certain type of condition can be automatically satisfied after rights exporting, then we define it as Passive Condition Pre-enforcement (PCP). In the ACP case, the domestic system performs the pre-enforcement without further input from the target system; while in the PCP case, the domestic system needs input from the target system to decide whether PCP can be achieved. PCP does not require any explicit action on the domestic system in order to achieve the same results as ACP. Therefore PCP should be the preferred approach compared with ACP. As the issues we presented only occur with PCP, we will focus on PCP and leave ACP for further research.

To further generalize PCP, we introduce a set of properties to represent the characteristic of the target system B: $C_{SSC}(B)\{C_{SSC1}(B), C_{SSC2}(B), C_{SSC3}(B)...\}$. Those properties should be a System Stateless Condition (SSC), and are not modifiable. An example of such a condition is whether or not a secure clock is deployed on the current system. Moreover, those types of conditions might not be verified on the DRM system in question but should be verified by some other DRM system(s). For example, *DisableOnClockRollback* is a condition type that can be verified by WMDRM 10 but not by OMA DRM 2. As OMA DRM2 demands secure clock implementation, systems based on OMA DRM 2 should have an associated instance of $Cssc_x(B)$ that has the type of *DisableOnClockRollback* and the value of the condition should be true as a static value. There might be an SSC that can be verified on the target system but is not verified. For example, a DRM based ticket system could grant all types of access within one year and after one year the system will be obsolete as the certificate used on the system will expire in one year. In such a case, the DRM system has an SSC with the condition type expiration time. Still the system is capable to handle other rights with expiration time based condition to be exported from other systems to itself. So an SSC does not necessarily imply that the system does not support such condition types.

Even if the target system has an SSC that matches the condition type of the condition the domestic system wants to export, it does not automatically mean that the condition can be pre-enforced. For example, a target system has an SSC that is an expiration dated 2020. If the domestic system is to check whether a condition with expiration date on 2014 can be pre-enforced, the *isPre-enforcable* attribute of that condition should be set to false; otherwise we violate the principle of rights exporting [5] by exporting less restrictive rights to the target system. Moreover, there might be multiple SSCs with the same condition type. As all SSCs are stateless and are applied to the DRM system, the relationship between SSCs is an intersection relationship when determining whether PCP can be performed. It means that as long as the intersection of all SSCs from the target system is no less restrictive than the condition to be pre-enforced, the PCP can be performed. For those SSCs with different condition types than the type of condition in question, they cannot influence whether the intersection of

SSCs can be no less restrictive than the condition in questions or not. For example, an SSC with count based type cannot influence the determination of PCP with time based type. Therefore, only the intersection of SSCs with the same condition type is compared with the condition in question.

To sum up, we formalize PCP as an algorithm as follows.

```
Algorithm Passive Condition Pre-enforcement:

Input: A condition instance Cx(A) to be applied for PCP
check on DRM system A before exporting to DRM system B,
and A set of PCP condition instances from DRM system B:
CSSC(B){CSSC1(B), CSSC2(B), CSSC3(B)…CSSCn(B)}
   Output: Cx.isPre-enforcable
   I = U;
For CSSCi(B) ∈CSSC(B){
       If (CSSCi(B).type== Cx(A).type){
           I=I CSSCi(B) ;}}
If (I ⊆ Cx(A)){
   Cx.isPre-enforcable = true ;}
Else {
   Cx.isPre-enforcable = false ;}
```

5   Passive Condition Pre-enforcement Impacts on Rights Exporting

As one of the methods for rights adaptation, the PCP can be used to remove the condition with an unsupported type, or to simplify the structure of a rights instance as it reduces the linkage between the condition instance and any of its linked permission instances. As a part of condition pre-enforcement, it is regarded as the second preferred method for rights adaptation among other adaptation methods [4].

The result of PCP is adapted instances of rights. If those adapted instances can be exported, then the instances shall be expressed and mandated by the target system. In the example illustrated in Fig. 5, R_{xd2ad1} is exported to system B as the condition *DisableOnClockRollback* is removed due to PCP. However, if the user decides to move R_{xd2ad1} from system B back to system A, then after exporting back to A the instance does not have *DisableOnClockRollback* condition attached, like the original rights instance had before exporting R_{xd2ad1} from A to B. Therefore, by performing rights exporting from A to B and back to A, we achieve less restricted rights, which violates the principle of rights exporting [5]. This is because that SSCs describe what have been restricted by default by the DRM system. Potentially different system enforces different set of SSCs. If this is not handled in the rights exporting, it could cause exporting less restrictive rights to another system. This seems to be a common issues even without the context of PCP. We simply the identified issue when generalizing PCP. For example, system A could implement maximum year number to be 999 while the other system B could implement maximum year number to be 9999. Porting rights with time condition e.g. "valid from 2013" from A to B would actually grant user much longer period than it does originally on A. Such an issue needs to be addressed as part of SSCs.

In order to prevent the breach in rights exporting, we need to apply SSCs of the domestic system to all rights instances to be exported before making final decision on whether each instance can be exported to a target system or not, which can be defined as *AddSSC($R_x(A)$, B)*.

The SSCs are system level conditions that apply to all rights to be exported. If one of SSCs on domestic system cannot be expressed or mandated by the target system, then we shall not try to export any rights between the two systems. Therefore, before making decision on individual rights exporting, we shall verify if it is even feasible to perform rights exporting between the two systems. We have defined a statement *IsExportable(A, B)* as a part of the Export task [5]. The feasibility check for SSCs from the domestic system to the target system shall contribute to the value of *IsExportable(A, B)*. If some of the SSCs cannot be supported by the target system, i.e. $C_{SSCi}(A).type \notin$ *B.supportedConditionType* [4], then *IsExportable(A, B)* shall return false; otherwise, it depends on other aspects of the two systems to determine the value of *IsExportable(A, B)*. Other aspects could be for example, business decision on interoperability between two systems. We leave those aspects to future research.

SSCs could be conditions that the system does not support itself. If a target system has an SSC that cannot be supported by the domestic system, it is theoretically possible that the domestic has the same SSC itself. In such a case, we shall not set *IsExportable (A, B)* to be false yet as both system have the same SSC even though neither of the system supports such a condition. For example, both DRM systems are OMA DRM 2 based and they both support secure clock implementation. Therefore, they both have *DisableOnClockRollback* condition as one of the SSCs even though they don't support such a condition. In such a situation, we know that both systems share the identical SSC. When exporting rights between them the restrictiveness of the rights shall not change given the impact of the specific SSC. Therefore, the system should ignore such an SSC when checking *IsExportable(A, B)*.

To sum up, the feasibility check of rights exporting can be formalized as an algorithm below.

```
Input:, A set of PCP condition instances from domestic
DRM system A: CSSC(A){CSSC1(A), CSSC2(A), CSSC3(A)...CSSCn(A)}
and A set of PCP condition instances from DRM system B:
CSSC(B){CSSC1(B), CSSC2(B), CSSC3(B)...CSSCn(B)}
   Output: IsExportable(A, B)
   IsExportable(A, B)=true;
   For CSSCi(A) ∈CSSC(A){
       If (CSSCi(A).type ∉ B.supportedConditionType){
           Boolean hasSameSSC = false;
           For CSSCj(B) ∈CSSC(B){
                If (CSSCj(B)== CSSCi(A)){
                    hasSameSSC=true;
                    break;}}
           If (!hasSameSSC){
                IsExportable(A, B)=false;
                Return ;}}}
```

Once *IsExportable(A, B)* is checked and it is feasible to perform rights exporting, then all exported rights shall apply for all condition instances in $C_{SSC}(A)$. If an identical

SSC exists in both $C_{SSC}(A)$ and $C_{SSC}(B)$, then there is no need to apply such a condition to the rights to be exported as it does not have impacts on the restrictiveness of the rights after exporting. As all SSCs are stateless conditions, condition division [4] can be applied to each permission in the rights to be exported. Therefore, we can simply add duplicated SSC instances and link them to each permission instance to be exported.

6   Optimization and Discussion

IsExportable should ensure all SSCs to be added are supported by the target system. However, because of adding conditions, the internal structure of rights instances become more complex than before. It increases the effort of rights exporting in general. Therefore, we shall try to minimize the amount of SSCs to be applied.

Conditions in $C_{SSC}(B)$ are applied to all rights on system B. If any conditions in $C_{SSC}(A)$ share the same condition type with some conditions in $C_{SSC}(B)$ and are less restrictive than the intersection of those on system B, then those SSCs on A do not need to be added to rights to be exported since those conditions in $C_{SSC}(B)$ enforce more restrictive rights. So, PCP shall be applied to $C_{SSC}(A)$ before applying them to rights to be exported.

In order to minimize $C_{SSC}(A)$, we shall not only apply PCP to $C_{SSC}(A)$, but also other adaptation methods that could reduce the amount of condition instances, such as Condition Merge [4]. If some SSCs share the same condition type, merging them into one instance to represent the intersection of all those SSCs would be the recommended approach to further optimize the performance of rights exporting. For example, for time based condition, like an instance before 2015 and another instance with time interval between 2010 and 2016. Then the interval can be represented as between 2010 and 2015. However, some of the SSCs cannot be supported by the domestic system and those SSCs cannot be optimized at all.

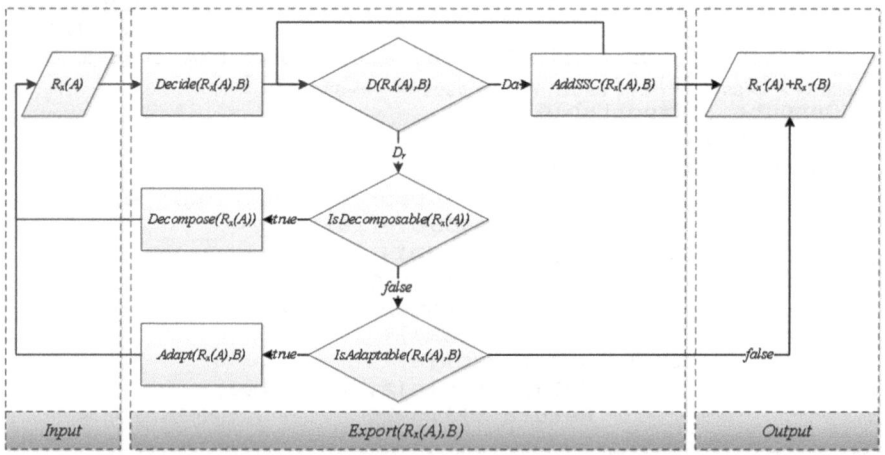

Fig. 6. *Export()* with *AddSSC($R_x(A)$, B)* integrated

As $C_{SSC}(A)$ are applied to those rights to be exported to B, there is no need to add them to those rights going to stay on A. Therefore, it is not recommended to apply them at the beginning phase of rights exporting. Moreover, rights decomposition could lead to fine grained granularity of a rights instance. Applying $C_{SSC}(A)$ only to those rights instances that have received accepted decision seems an optimal approach. As *IsExportable* ensures that all $C_{SSC}(A)$ are supported by B, we just simply need to make sure if the increased complexity on the internal structure of the rights could change the decision or not. If the decision is reject, then we can put the rights instances back to iterations of the rights exporting process with the tag to indicate that $C_{SSC}(A)$ is already applied to the rights instance. By using the tag, we ensure the process will not apply $C_{SSC}(A)$ to the rights instance and its output instances from later iterations. The optimized and integrated process can be illustrated in Fig. 6.

7   Conclusions

Previously, we proposed an integrated process for rights exporting [20]. In this work, we identified issues that require further elaboration and resolution. They are all related to the condition pre-enforcement we demonstrated in the case study of previous research. As a solution, we introduced the concept of PCP. During the integration of PCP to rights exporting process, we examined the impact of the integration and identified potential risks of violating the rights exporting principles [5]. Then, we provided a solution to eliminate such risks. Furthermore, we pointed out places where optimization could be applied in order to minimize the performance overhead introduce by the PCP integration, and we proposed our recommendation on optimization.

The key contributions of the paper, first of all, is to generalize a new approach for performing condition pre-enforcement by utilizing the characteristics of DRM systems. PCP as a method for rights adaptation is a brand new approach that potentially removes dependencies from unsupported conditions. Secondly, the integration of PCP disclosed the fact that rights exporting back and forth could potentially violate the rights exporting principle if system characteristics between two systems are not taken into consideration in rights exporting. We not only identified the potential issues but also provided a solution to address them. Moreover, we integrated the solution into our established process for rights exporting, which helps other researchers to continue work on this topic without losing the big picture of the problem domain.

References

1. Safavi-Naini, R., Sheppard, N.P., Uehara, P.: Import/Export in digital rights management. In: Proceedings 4th ACM Workshop on Digital Rights Management, pp. 99–110 (2004)
2. Lu, W., Zhang, Z., Nummenmaa, J.: A generic data model with a decomposition operation for DRM interoperability. In: Proceedings IEEE International Conference Wireless Communications, Networking and Information Security (WCNIS), pp. 630–634 (2010)
3. Lu, W., Zhang, Z., Nummenmaa, J.: Rights decomposition for DRM interoperability. Int. J. Wireless Commun. Netw. 2(2), 630–634 (2010)

4. Lu, W., Zhang, Z., Nummenmaa, J.: Deploying adaptation in rights exporting. In: 8th IEEE International Workshop on Digital Rights Management Impact on Consumer Communications, pp. 522–526 (2012)
5. Lu, W., Zhang, Z., Nummenmaa, J.: Characterizing trustworthy digital rights exporting. In: Aseeva, N., Babkin, E., Kozyrev, O. (eds.) BIR 2012. LNBIP, vol. 128, pp. 85–95. Springer, Heidelberg (2012)
6. RIAA: News and Notes on 2014 RIAA music industry shipment and revenue statistics. http://riaa.com/media/D1F4E3E8-D3E0-FCEE-BB55-FD8B35BC8785.pdf (2014). Accessed 11 April 2015
7. Liu, Q., Safavi-Naini, R., Sheppard, N.P.: Digital rights management for content distribution. In: Proceedings Australasian Information Security Workshop Conference on ACSW Frontiers, vol. 21, pp. 49–58 (2003)
8. Microsoft WMDRM: Digital rights management features. https://msdn.microsoft.com/en-us/library/windows/desktop/dd757031%28v=vs.85%29.aspx. Accessed 11 April 2015
9. OMA DRM v2, OMA: Digital Rights Management V2.2. http://technical.openmobilealliance.org/Technical/technical-information/release-program/current-releases/drm-v2-2 19 April 2011. Accessed 11 Apr 2015
10. Carlisle, G., Navin, C.: Issues and challenges in securing interoperability of DRM systems in the digital music market. Inter. Rev. Law Comput. Technol. **20**(3), 271–285 (2006)
11. Heileman, G.L., Jamkhedar, P.A.: DRM interoperability analysis from the perspective of a layered framework. In: Proceedings 5th ACM workshop on digital rights management, Architectures, pp. 17–26 (2005)
12. Coral consortium: CORAL consortium is dissolved. https://eric-diehl.com/coral-consortium-is-dissolved/ 3 Jan 2013. Accessed 11 April 2015
13. Koenen, R.H., Lacy, J., MacKay, M., Mitchell, S.: The long march to interoperable digital rights management. Proc. IEEE **92**, 883–897 (2004)
14. Schmidt, A.U., Tafreschi, O., Wolf, R.: Interoperability challenges for DRM systems. In: Proceedings IFIP/GI Workshop on Virtual Goods, Ilmenau, Germany (2004)
15. Chen, X., Huang, T.: Interoperability issues in DRM and DMP solutions. In: IEEE on Multimedia and Expo, pp. 907–910 (2007)
16. Doncel, V.R., Delgado, J., Chiariglione, F., Preda, M., Timmerer, C.: Interoperable digital rights management based on the MPEG extensible middleware. Multimedia Tools Appl. **53**(1), 303–318 (2010)
17. Marlin: Marlin architecture overview. http://www.marlin-community.com (2006). Accessed 11 April 2015
18. Jamkhedkar, P.A., Heileman, G.L., Lamb, C.C.: An interoperable usage management framework. In: Proceedings of the Tenth Annual ACM Workshop on Digital Rights Management (2010)
19. Serrão, C., Rodriguez, E., Delgado, J.: Approaching the rights management interoperability problem using intelligent brokerage mechanisms. Comput. Commun. **34**(2), 129–139 (2011)
20. Lu, W., Zhang, Z., Nummenmaa, J.: Decision-making in rights exporting: the integrated process. In: Proceedings of the 5th International Conference on Management of Emergent Digital EcoSystems (MEDES), pp. 219–226 (2013)

Research in Progress

A Business Process Based Method
for Capability Modelling

Hasan Koç[1(✉)] and Kurt Sandkuhl[1,2]

[1] University of Rostock, Albert-Einstein-Straße 22, 18059 Rostock, Germany
[2] ITMO University, St. Petersburg, Russia
{hasan.koc,kurt.sandkuhl}@uni-rostock.de

Abstract. Enterprises are confronted with rapidly changing situations in regulations, globalization, time-to-market pressures and advances in the technology. Management and design of the capabilities is emerging into an important
field to tackle these challenges. On the contrary, our findings from a systematic
literature analysis reveal the lack of contributions in methodological support for
developing capabilities. In this respect we introduce a business process based
method for capability design, which is a part of a lately proposed capability
driven development (CDD) approach. The main contributions of this paper are
(i) a component wise structured capability modelling method based on business
processes of an enterprise and (ii) a demonstration of the method application in a
use case from the utilities industry.

Keywords: Capability modelling · Business context · Method engineering ·
BPM · Capability design · Capability driven development

1 Introduction

The organizations are confronted with a turbulent environment due to rapid changes in
regulations, globalization, time-to-market pressures as well as the advances in the
technology. For a sustainable competitive advantage the enterprises need to adjust their
offerings to the dynamically changing circumstances [5]. To tackle these challenges
and to offer flexible and agile business services the management and design of capabilities is emerging into an important field. In this context the Capability Driven
Development (CDD) approach is proposed within the EU-FP7 project "Capability as a
Service" (CaaS) that envisions the customization of the services on the basis of the
capabilities and adjustment delivery according to the current context [8].

A capability is defined in CDD as the ability and capacity that enable an enterprise
to achieve a business goal in a certain context [8]. Thus, a capability is related to
specific business services, a defined application context for these business services and
goals of the enterprise to be reached. Our investigation of methods and approaches on
capability design has shown that proposed solutions usually neglect the context surrounding the capability delivery (see Sect. 2). The main contributions of this paper to
this field are (i) a component wise structured capability modelling method based on
business processes of an enterprise and (ii) a demonstration of the method application
in a use case from the utilities industry. The method constitutes the core of CDD

© Springer International Publishing Switzerland 2015
R. Matulevičius and M. Dumas (Eds.): BIR 2015, LNBIP 229, pp. 257–264, 2015.
DOI: 10.1007/978-3-319-21915-8_17

approach and consists of a number of method components supporting different aspects of the capability modelling.

The paper is structured as follows: Sect. 2 summarizes the state of the art in the capability design methods and discusses the findings shortly. Section 3 describes the use case followed by our modular approach to methodology engineering and presents the method components as well as the application of the capability design method. Finally Sect. 4 discusses the reflections, draws conclusions and addresses future developments.

2   State of the Art in Methods of Capability Modelling

We conducted a systematic literature review by following the guidelines from Kitchenham [1] to reveal the state of the art in capability modelling methods. First we formulated our research questions, namely (i) which methods are proposed to design capabilities and (ii) which research areas are being investigated in capability design methods. In the second step we identified A+, A and B Journals based on the rankings from [2, 3]. Moreover we populated the list of journals with A and B ranked conferences from [4]. As a result a total of 112 journals and 18 conferences were analysed. We searched for the papers which included the term {capability} in abstract and one of the following terms {method, modeling, modelling, proc*, design, step, practice} in keyword. The paper selection step was executed by abstract reading followed by a full-text reading. Out of 380 publications 17 journal articles and 7 conference papers were found to be relevant. After the full-text reading 7 publications remained, which were further analysed for data collection.

The main findings that motivate the business process based method introduced in this paper are as follows: The capability design and development methods (i) propose steps and procedures to design capabilities, which cannot be integrated to or developed by analysing the existing enterprise models, (ii) focus on low level capabilities decoupled from enterprise goals and (iii) do not provide support to tackle the contextual changes in the capability delivery.

3   A Method for Designing Capabilities

3.1   Use Case Definition

SIV.AG is an independent software vendor for the utilities industry in regulated and non-regulated markets, with particular focus on Germany. The company owns a business service provider (BSP) that performs a complete business process for a business function outside of an organization. The BSP as such provides services for the customers running kVASy®, SIV´s industry specific ERP platform. The BSP deals with intercompany business processes between partners in the utility market that requires exchange of messages about energy consumption. The messages have to be validated against a set of syntactic and semantic rules, which are subject to change by regulatory bodies. If an exception occurs in validating or processing the message, the BSP acts as a clearing centre involving the manual interaction of a human agent, which causes extra costs on the side of the utility as well as operational efforts, such as the arrangement of BSP's human resources schedule. This is a contractually specified performance of business tasks by SIV Services on behalf of one or more SIV customers. Currently clearing policies do not support *dynamic routing behaviour*, i.e. to decide whether or not the individual case should be routed from customer to the BSP. The decision is based on run-time data such as the backlog size of the customer, the type of service supported and the type of the exception, which essentially need to be captured as a context model. The use case is depicted simply in Fig. 1 (numbers refer to variations in the use case, see the 3rd method component).

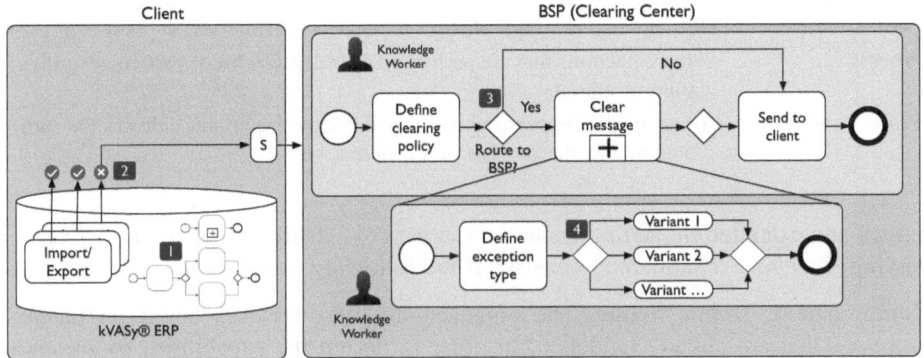

Fig. 1. SIV use case and variations

3.2   A Business Processes Method for Capability Design

Capability design is the systematic process of developing organizational capabilities that can be configured according to their application context. The CDD applies modular approach to methodology engineering by dividing the methodology into several method components. In doing so the method user could focus on those parts of the method that are needed and select the components relevant for a specific tasks "on demand" from a repository.

The way methods and method components are applied within CDD is an extension of the method conceptualization proposed by Goldkuhl et al. [6]. In a broader perspective a method component consists of concepts, activities and a notation. The concepts specify which aspects of reality are important and what should be captured in a model. The activities describe in concrete terms how to identify the relevant concepts in a method component and the notation specifies how the result of the procedure should be documented. The method components share the common conceptual basis and are based on the CDD meta-model [8]. An excerpt of the important concepts is described in Table 1.

Existing enterprise models, e.g. goals models, business process models, concepts models and patterns can be used as input when modelling the capabilities. We propose a method which takes the starting point of the capability design as a process underlying a business service under consideration. The business process should at the end be

Table 1. Concepts used in designing capabilities [8]

Concept	Explanation
Capability	The ability and capacity that enable an enterprise to achieve a business goal in a certain context
KPI	Measurable properties that can be seen as targets for achievement of goals
Context set	Describes the set of context elements that are relevant for design and delivery of a specific capability
Context element range	Specifies boundaries of permitted values for a specific context element and for a specific context set
Context element	Any information characterising the situation of an entity [10]
Goal	Desired state of affairs that needs to be attained
Process	Series of actions that are performed in order to achieve particular result to support a goal
Process variant	A part of the process, which uses the same input and delivers the same outcome as the process in a different way

refined and extended by adding context awareness to establish a capability delivery in varying situations. The method consists of the following components:

Component 1. Define Scope. The organisation offers services based on business processes that are already modelled. In order to design the capabilities by means of business processes the capability designer first selects the service and sets the scope of the capability design. The selection can depend on various factors, such as optimizing the services with high process costs or managing services that frequently change and hence require the adjustment of business processes. Then the abstraction level is determined, at which the processes supporting the business service to be improved are identified.

In line with the use case defined in Sect. 3.1 the scope of the capability delivery is set to increase the throughput of energy consumption data messages (MSCONS) and to increase the rate of automation. After consultation with domain experts and business service managers, the "exception clearing in market communication" service is selected, which should deliver "dynamic BSP support" as a capability. This capability envisions offering context-dependent support in exchange of messages where faulty processes must be cleared.

Component 2. Develop or Update Enterprise Models. This method component analyses in the first activity the enterprise models to make sure that selected business process models are up-to-date and applies changes if required. Moreover, the capability should be aligned with the goals that an enterprise aims to achieve. To check if business goals are satisfied during the capability delivery, KPIs are used to measure the achievement of goals. The second activity analyses and updates the goal models as well as KPIs, if any exist. If no goals model is available, then they can be developed based on the guidelines proposed in [9]. Since an alignment of goals is required on the business service level, method user should rather model the capability related goals and not the enterprise objectives on a general basis. The last activity relates goals, business process models, KPIs and capabilities, which is used as input in the next method component. This method component uses BPMN 2.0 and 4EM Notation [9] to represent the important concepts such as goals, processes and KPIs.

During the method application in the use case we observed that business process models that are required by the capability were up-to-date. In contrast there was no *goals model* available in SIV.AG, thus the model had to be developed from the scratch [12]. Here the involvement of the domain experts and product owners to modelling sessions was required.

Component 3. Context Modelling. A capability is defined by specific business services, a defined application context for these business services and goals of the enterprise to be reached. In this component the capability designer models the context of the capability delivery, i.e. the potential application context where the offering is supposed to be deployed. For this purpose the designer executes three activities subsequently, "find variations, capture context element" and "design context".

Find Variations. Identifies the variability in the business process models and focuses on their possible variations. By further specifying variability in the following activity, the method user aims to develop a context element. This activity requires business process models, goals model, KPIs and a defined capability as an input. The output produced is a business process model including the process variants and variation points. The method user is supported with following guidelines on what constitutes a process variant and how to distinguish variability from standard decisions:

- Different than a decision point, a process variant is always relevant for capability delivery. For each decision point the method user evaluates the condition expression at that point and determines how the decision is met, i.e. data-based, event-based or context-based.
- Context-based resolution of the decision point indicates that the subsequent task should be modelled as a process variant; otherwise the point is represented with a standard gateway.
- Data-based and event-based resolution uses process variables as an input.
- A process variable is produced during the activities of a given process. On the other hand a context element or context-based data is an external influence on the process itself, which should not exist as a process instance or data in the system.
- A context element can act as a filter and determine which variables have to be gathered from process instances.

For the use case at hand the variations in the business process models are analysed in the first activity. The service area of BSP has to implement potential variations of the clients' way to perform business. One variation is the need to adjust the standard software systems for the organizations in question, which implements the core processes. The second cause of variation is the configuration for the country of use, i.e. the implementation of the actual regulations and bylaws. The third variation is related to the resource use for implementing the actual business process for the customer, i.e. the provision of technical and organizational capacities. Last but not least, the fourth variation is the application of the solution that remedies the faulty message, which is carried out by the knowledge worker at BSP. In this case the outsourcing business services need to be dynamically routed; i.e. it should be resolved at run-time whether the individual case should be handled by the BSP. This decision is based on run-time data such as the backlog size of the customer, the type of service supported and the type of the exception, which essentially need to be captured as a context model. For the case at hand we decided to analyse the last variation. All four variation types are shown in Fig. 1.

Capture Context Element. Elaborates the concept of context by studying the change factors and capturing them as "context element candidates". In line with the definition of context in CDD (see Table 1), we assume that characterizing information as such can stem from the factors of change, since they mainly cause variations in the business processes. Thus a substantial analysis of process models is required to capture a context element. We propose the following guidelines for this activity:

- To be classified as a context element, the change factor must be measurable, i.e. its value must be retrieved from an information system.
- Context element is an external influence on the process, which should not exist as a process instance or data in BPM.
- Context elements are decisive for the resolution of variation points.

In SIV use case we investigated the factors influencing the routing decision. Alongside with the schedule of the knowledge workers in BSP, we determined that the clearing policy between the client and SIV establishes the main factor for resolving this variation point. A clearing policy typically includes specifications about the message types, message versions, application references and critical backlog. Each time a knowledge worker has to reach a routing decision, (s)he compares the actual values of these parameters with the values from the clearing policy. As such, they are external to the processes and the values produced during the process execution cannot be known a priori. Consequently we specified these parameters as context elements, which are decisive for capability delivery (see Table 2).

Table 2. A simplified view of SIV context model

Factor	Context element	Context element range	Measurable property
Clearing policy between SIV and client	Message type	MSCONS	UNH.S009
	Application reference	VL, TL, EM	UNB.S005
	Critical backlog	Exceeded	Backlog size

Design Context. Links the capability under study to the contextual influences by creating a "container" (a context set), including the permitted ranges of the context elements for capability delivery (context element ranges) and what attributes to measure to enable reasoning about the context elements (measurable properties). Finally, the properties of the context elements relevant to capability design (context indicators) are identified.

For the sake of brevity, we only select the context elements in SIV case that are related to contractual agreement. In Design Context activity, we defined the attributes to be measured in order to provide values of context elements (measurable properties) as well as the boundaries of permitted values for the context elements (context element ranges). After the expert evaluation we gathered the context element ranges defined for a customer in a context set, which should dynamically support routing decisions. The context elements have a common degree of similarity in each of the clients. We thus benefited from defining context elements only once and updating the ranges of the elements when modelling the context of a different client. A tabular view of context set of the use case is shown in Table 2. It should be emphasized that currently a tool for capability modelling is in development, which allows for the modelling of the context in line with the notation proposed in [7] and meta-model introduced in [8].

4   Conclusion and Outlook

This paper proposed a method for modelling capabilities based on business processes of an enterprise. Starting point for our work on the one side was a systematic literature analysis in this subject area and on the other side the included CDD approach and industrial use case of the CaaS project.

The business process-based method was developed component-based and illustrated by applying it in one use case. The application of Goldkuhl's method conceptualization [6] was perceived as very useful. We started with making the perspective explicit, i.e. that a "business process" is the starting point on "capability" as a main focus of attention. Based on the CaaS meta-model we designed an initial set of method components and activities which all included what concepts had to be considered, what procedure to take and how to document it. Experiences gathered during the method engineering are detailed in an earlier work [7].

Obviously, the precondition for using the business processes based method is that the processes have been identified and documented. In this context, two questions arise as (i) whether or not domain experts have to be involved and (ii) whether the quality of a process description is high enough. Concerning the first question, our perception is that the key to a good capability model is a thorough understanding of the business process model and the underlying general business logic. Either the modeller has this understanding – which in most modelling projects might not be the case - or a domain expert has to be involved. Thus, our recommendation would be to include a domain expert in the capability modelling team. For the latter question high quality does not only address the completeness and accuracy of the process description but also an adequate level of granularity and richness in description. If the process description is not sufficiently detailed or only covers the "happy flow" without exceptions or deviations, the identified variation points and aspects might be incomplete. The "richness" aspect addresses the fact that even if there is a high level of detail in the process description, it still is required to identify the information, event or decision in the process causing the variation.

To sum up, the method is expected to be useful for enterprise with clearly defined business process, which need to have variations and are supported by highly automated execution environments. If these requirements cannot be fulfilled, then the organisation should consider applying goals-based or concepts-based capability development methods as described in [11]. The business process-based method as such needs further elaboration and application in more industrial use cases in order to collect experiences and contribute to maturity. Finally future work intends to report on the generalizability of the approach including the threats to validity and scalability.

Acknowledgments. This work has been performed as part of the EU-FP7 funded project no: 611351 CaaS – Capability as a Service in Digital Enterprises.

References

1. Kitchenham, B.: Procedures for performing systematic reviews. Keele University Technical report TR/SE-0401. July 2004. ISSN:1353-7776
2. Schrader, U., Hennig-Thurau, T.: VHB-JOURQUAL2: method, results, and implications of the German academic association for business research's journal ranking. BuR Bus. Res. **2** (2), 180–204 (2009). URN: urn:nbn:de:0009-20-21663
3. Peffers, K., Ya, T.: Identifying and evaluating the universe of outlets for information systems research: ranking the journals. J. Inf. Technol. Theory Appl. (JITTA) **5**(1), Article 6, 63–84 (2003)
4. WI-Association: WI-Orientierungslisten. WIRTSCHAFTSINFORMATIK 50, 155–163 (2008)
5. Teece, D., Pisano, G., Shuen, A.: Dynamic capabilities and strategic management. Strat. Manage. J. **18**, 509–533 (1997)
6. Goldkuhl, G., Lind, M., Seigerroth, U.: Method integration: the need for a learning perspective. IEE Proc. Softw. **145**(4), 113–118 (1998). (Special issue on information system methodologies)
7. Sandkuhl, K., Koç, H.: Component-based method development: an experience report. In: Frank, U., Loucopoulos, P., Pastor, Ó., Petrounias, I. (eds.) PoEM 2014. LNBIP, vol. 197, pp. 164–178. Springer, Heidelberg (2014)
8. Bērziša, S., Bravos, G., Gonzalez Cardona, T., Czubayko, U., España, S., Grabis, J., Henkel, M., Jokste, L., Kampars, J., Koç, H., Kuhr, J.-C., Llorca, C., Loucopoulos, P., Juanes Pascual, R., Pastor, O., Sandkuhl, K., Simic, H., Stirna, J., Zdravkovic, J.: Capability driven development: an approach to designing digital enterprises. Bus. Inf. Syst. Eng. (BISE) **15**(1), 15–25 (2015). doi:10.1007/s12599-014-0362-0
9. Sankuhl, K., Stirna, J., Persson, A., Wißotzki, M.: Enterprise Modeling: Tackling Business Challenges with the 4EM Method. The Enterprise Engineering Series. Springer, Heidelberg (2014). ISBN 978-3662437247
10. Dey, A.K.: Understanding and using context. Pers. Ubiquit. Comput. **5**, 4–7 (2001)
11. España, S., Grabis, J., Henkel, M., Koç, H., Sandkuhl, K., Stirna, J., Zdravkovic, J.: Strategies for capability modelling: analysis based on initial experiences. In: Persson, A., Stirna, J. (eds.) CAiSE 2015 Workshops. LNBIP, vol. 215, pp. 40–52. Springer, Heidelberg (2015)
12. Zdravkovic, J., Stirna, J., Kuhr, J.-C., Koç, H.: Requirements engineering for capability driven development. In: Frank, U., Loucopoulos, P., Pastor, Ó., Petrounias, I. (eds.) PoEM 2014. LNBIP, vol. 197, pp. 193–207. Springer, Heidelberg (2014)

Modeling for Viability

Marite Kirikova[(✉)]

Department of Artificial Intelligence and Systems Design,
Riga Technical University, Riga, Latvia
marite.kirikova@rtu.lv

Abstract. One of the attractive features of enterprises is their viability. However, it is not easy to measure and control values of attributes that could indicate
the level of enterprise viability. Moreover, an enterprise usually is a system of
systems that has to function as an ecosystem both from functional and from
structural viewpoints. One of the means for modeling for viability is St. Beer's
Viable Systems Model. However, this model ecosystemically considers viability
only from the functional perspective. In reality the organizations still have their
structural units that strive for their own viability even they do not directly
resemble the functions prescribed by the Viable Systems Model. The paper
suggests to not neglect this striving for viability and proposes a novel approach
for modeling structural units to move towards a possibility to estimate their
viability in the enterprise.

Keywords: Viable systems model · Business process architecture · Enterprise
architecture · Systems of systems

1 Introduction

In the 21st century information systems have to support a high variety of enterprise
activities, since the enterprises must be inventive, humanistic, cognitive,
community-oriented, liquid, agile, sensing, global, and sustainable [1]. Due to and
increasing variety in enterprise environments, they are forced to transform or engineer
themselves continuously [2] in order to obtain and maintain their relative viability.

The means for modeling an enterprise form the point of view of viability is a Viable
Systems Model (VSM) that has been reported as one of the alternatives of highly
competitive enterprise models [3–5]. The VSM is rooted in ideas of cybernetics and
comprises five mutually related systems at a number of fractal levels [5]. As defined
originally, this model considers the enterprise from the point of functions to be performed and does not directly address the structural units. Thus, what is important is that
all functions prescribed by VSM are in place, but it is not so important who actually
performs them. This looks very attractive from the point of organizational flexibility: to
the changes in external environment, an enterprise answers by changing its functions
(and processes) and appropriately restructuring its internal organizational architecture.
However, structural changes in organizations not always bring expected good results
[6]. One of the reasons is resistance to the changes by structural units not wanting to
lose their organizational identity.

© Springer International Publishing Switzerland 2015
R. Matulevičius and M. Dumas (Eds.): BIR 2015, LNBIP 229, pp. 265–272, 2015.
DOI: 10.1007/978-3-319-21915-8_18

This research in progress paper proposes to use and extend possibilities of current enterprise architecture modeling methods for looking at the enterprise as an eco-system of relatively autonomous structural units, each of which is represented by the architecture elements corresponding to the VSM, i.e. the enterprise is considered as a system of systems [7]. When there is a need for change, the possibility and cost for keeping the identity of structural unit versus losing it could be calculated in terms of time and money.

The paper is structured as follows. In Sect. 2 VSM is shortly explained and compared to the Business Process Classification Framework (PCF) provided by American Productivity and Quality Center [8]. The brief description of related work is presented in this section, too. In Sect. 3 the proposed approach is described and in Sect. 4 brief conclusions are provided.

2 Related Work

Viability is a capacity of a system to maintain a separate existence over time and to do it despite ongoing changes in the environment (even if these changes have not been foreseen) [5]. This feature of enterprises was studied in depth by S. Beer, the founder of VSM. Since then the VSM has been applied in organizational sciences [3–5]; industrial control systems [9]; autonomic systems design [10]; reliability engineering [11]; and other areas.

The VSM is illustrated in Fig. 1 (on the left). It reflects 5 interrelated function systems (System 1 to System 5), each of which has a unique role in the model (System 1 is operating system; other four systems are managerial ones). Each subsystem (ONE

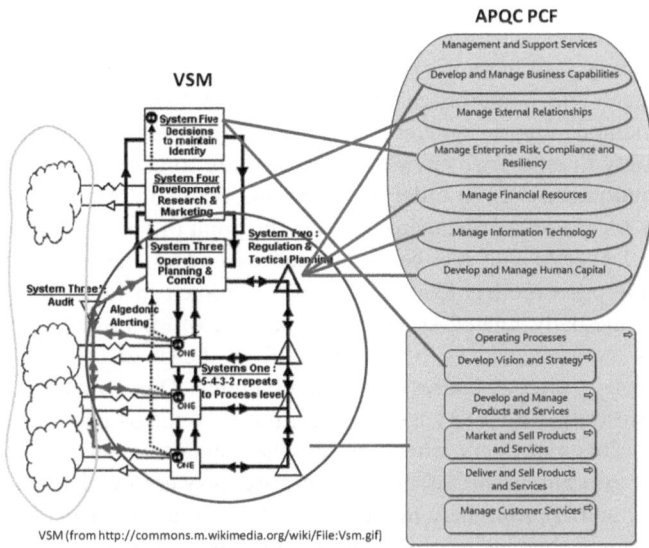

Fig. 1. VSM adopted and elements of PCF adapted from [8]

in Fig. 1) in the operating system can be a viable system itself, i.e., at a smaller scale of representation, it can have similar, composed of five function systems, structure. In general, the functions of the Systems 1–5 can be performed by arbitrary actors (human actors, cross-departmental teams, software agents, etc.) In VSM besides System 1 there are also the following systems: Regulations and Tactical Planning System 2 that ensures smooth cooperation of relatively independent parts (business processes) of the operating system; Operations and Planning Control System 3 that cares for optimal work and auditing (System 3*) of System 1; Development, Research and Marketing System 4; and Organizational Identity Management System 5 that ensures balance between intensions of System 4 and goals of the rest of the whole super system of five Systems.

In Fig. 1 in comparison to VSM the structure of one of the versions of American Productivity and Quality Center's Process Classification Framework (PCF) is presented [8]. This is just to illustrate that the structuring of processes differ considerably in VSM and PCF. The processes of VSM are very clearly organized around the operating processes that serve different segments of external environment. However, in PCF these segments are not emphasized as a first class citizen. While on a deeper level the mapping of process elements might be possible, still the main emphasis in both frameworks differ.

Looking from the point of view of organizational functionality, each operational unit in the model could be presented by the set of PCF operating processes presented in Fig. 1; and the functions could be performed by particular performers regardless to which organizational structure unit they belong to. Thus, the main purpose to achieve viability would be fulfilled from the point of view of VSM. In reality companies have their historically introduced structural units which might be not aware of their role (or the role of their employees) in the viability of the enterprise. However, these structural units have a purpose to save their identities regardless of changes in the environment or the enterprise. This wish to preserve the identity is backed-up by well established knowledge distribution inside a unit that gives an opportunity to do activities fast fully utilizing not only explicit but also tacit knowledge of the unit.

Viability in enterprise modeling is not largely researched. The most of work is devoted to viable enterprise architectures from the point of view of enterprise architecture management [9]. Some issues relevant to viability analysis, such as monitoring of environment are discussed in [10]. In [11] four properties for enterprise analysis using ArchiMate are proposed, namely application usage, system availability, service response time, and data accuracy. VSM based principles for enterprise architecture development are presented in [12]. A philosophical discussion on relationship between an enterprise, enterprise architecture, and environment are given in [13].

While there is a number of enterprise modeling approaches available, e.g. [14], so far none of them clearly deals with aspects important from the point of view of VSM, such as correspondence between the number of functional sub-units and internal and external customers, internal ability to change the number of functional units, correspondence of knowledge distribution and information resources to functions; and environment dependent capacity to change knowledge and information. In the next section we will discuss one possible approach for using enterprise architecture model elements for reasoning about impact of intended changes on the viability of the enterprise. The approach takes into consideration variability of internal and external customers of the enterprise and the level of effort in knowledge and information transfer in case of changes of functional and organizational structures.

3   Using Enterprise Architecture Elements for Reasoning About Viability

In discussing the proposed approach we will take a system of systems [7] (or eco-systems) perspective. The enterprise will be considered as a system of systems, where each system is a subunit of an enterprise. We will apply VSM to each subunit of an enterprise (Fig. 2). As it was earlier described in the paper, this is not the ordinary way to look at the viability of the enterprise, because the enterprise's functionality rather than organizational structure are relevant from the point of view of viability. Here the structural units are considered due to natural striving of a structural units to keep their identity as viable parts of the enterprise. The approach presented below aims at providing tools for reasoning about the benefit of this strive to the enterprise.

Each organizational unit has processes that support internal or external "customers" (Fig. 3). Thus it has particular performers (human beings, software programs, devices) behind these processes. These performers are the main constituents, which in an integrated manner may yield the viable identity of the structural unit. Any changes in the enterprise have impact on the processes of one or more structural units. Changes in the processes may cause changes in the supporting resources that is one of the most sensitive issues in an organizational change management [15, 16].

To describe the proposed approach let us consider an university as an enterprise. One of its structural units is project management department. Suppose some funding institution has issued a new call for projects that has requirements considerably different to compare to all other projects handled at the university. This is an issue when a new process could be established in the project management department to handle new

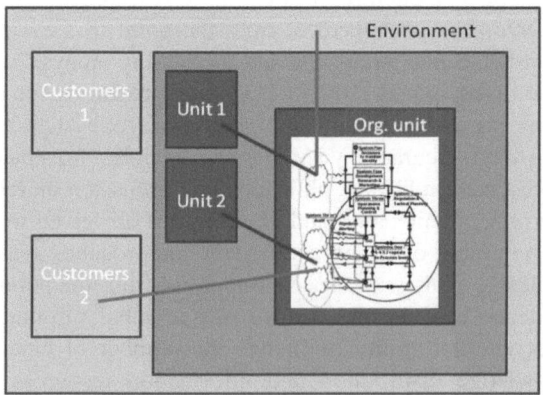

Fig. 2. Each organizational unit as a viable system

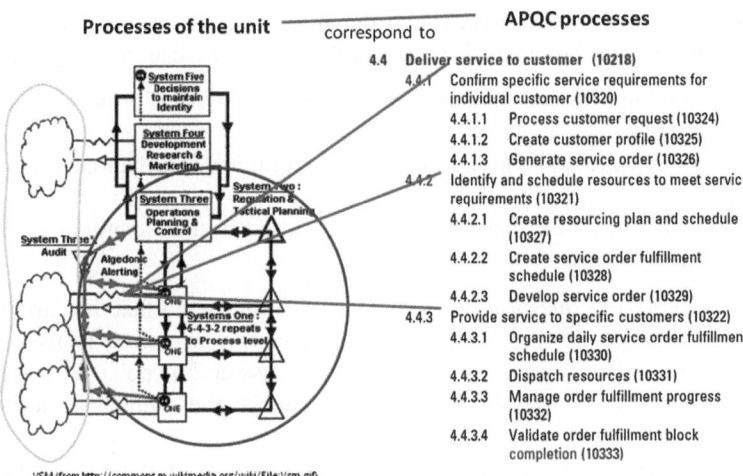

Fig. 3. Processes for delivering value to other structural units or the environment of the enterprise

type projects. However, there is a question how the introduction of the new process will impact (1) viability of the structural unit and (2) viability of the university as a whole.

To analyze this, first of all it is necessary to understand what resources are needed to perform the process. Enterprise architecture pattern showing three different types of resources (human, software and technical ones) can be used [17] (see Fig. 4). On the basis of this pattern it is possible to analyze correspondence between the number of functional subunits and the number of internal and external customers; internal ability to change the number of functional subunits; the correspondence between functions and knowledge distribution and information; and environment dependent capacity to change knowledge and information.

Correspondence between the number of functional subunits and internal and external customers. This issue concerns ability of structural unit to establish new process for new internal or external needs. In the abovementioned example it is an

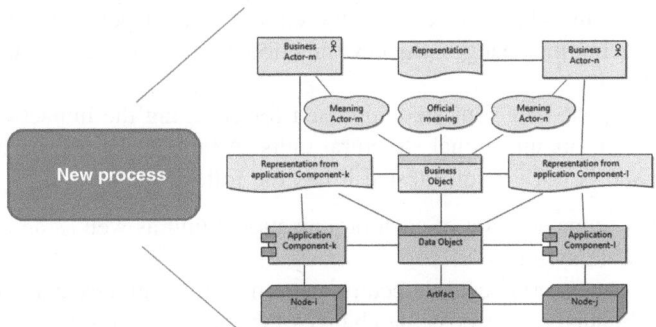

Fig. 4. Enterprise architecture pattern for performing new process

ability to establish the new process for the new type of projects. To answer this question each layer in the enterprise architecture archetype can be analyzed [17]:

- Are there human resources that can embrace the new type of project in their current daily activities?
- Are there software applications that can be configured to handle a new type of projects?
- Do technical devices can handle extra load caused by new configurations of software and new incoming information?

If the answers to all questions is "yes", it can be concluded that the current number of functional subunits of the project department is corresponding to the number of external and internal customers. In case any of the answers in "no" then it is necessary to discuss the ability of the structural unit to change the number of its functional subunits.

Internal ability to change the number of functional subunits depends on possibilities to change either human knowledge and/or the number of participants, software applications, and/or infrastructure. These changes will require financial and time resources. Estimation of the availability of resources with respect to each needed change is necessary to evaluate the ability to change the number of functional sub-units. To answer this question, it is necessary to analyze *correspondence of knowledge distribution and information resources to functions* taking into consideration intended functional changes and the differences in this distribution to compare to the previous situation. Here not only the costs of introduction of new knowledge and software applications matters, but also time taken off from previous activities has to be taken into consideration in case of new knowledge acquisition by existing employees. If the structural unit is able to change the number of its functional subunits from financial point of view and it has sufficient time resources, the issues where the unit depends on other organizational units have to be considered. We will denote these issues as *environment dependent* ones regardless if it is internal environment of the unit or external environment of the enterprise the unit belongs to.

Environment dependent capacity to change knowledge and information depends on possibilities outside the unit to provide needed knowledge (availability of educational courses, availability of human resources (in case new employees are to be assigned for new processes), availability of programmers for application development or technical staff for infrastructure changes). Only if the environment dependent capacity is sufficient for introducing the changes, the new functional structure can be introduced in the organizational unit.

Thus, we propose here four step approach for checking the impact of changes on the viability of the organizational structural units. Although the approach itself seems pretty simple and is not yet fully tested it has the following strength:

- It is based on consideration of each organizational unit as well as an enterprise as a whole as viable system.
- It is based on enterprise architecture pattern, which guides and helps to keep consistent the analysis of possible changes through all four steps.

- It gives an opportunity to discover problems with respect to the changes so that in the most of cases the decision making in one step of the approach is accompanied with acquisition of new knowledge, which can be used in the next step(s) of the approach.

The development of the approach is still in its initial phase. It is intended to back up the approach with appropriate enterprise model management or enterprise architecture management tools that help to apply the approach in a way that all knowledge about the enterprise in the given situation is utilized in the most effective way.

4   Conclusions

While viability of enterprises is an important issue in organizational change management and a viable systems model is available, it is still not possible to apply it in a seamless way because it does not take into consideration internal strive for identity of different structural units of enterprises.

The paper proposes the approach for viability analysis in the situation of intended changes that gives an opportunity to see whether an enterprise unit is able to continue to be viable after the changes. The approach consists of the following four steps:

(1) Analyze the correspondence between the number of functional sub-units to internal and external customers
(2) Evaluate the internal ability to change the number of functional units
(3) Analyze the correspondence between knowledge distribution and information resources and functions
(4) Check the environment dependent capacity to change knowledge and information.

The approach is based on the use of concepts of VSM (especially the relationship between functional units (processes) in the organizational unit and their internal or external customers) and the enterprise architecture pattern, which represents human, software and technical aspects of the enterprise.

The development of enterprise model management or enterprise architecture management tools supporting the proposed approach is a matter of further research.

Acknowledgment. The research reflected in this paper is partly supported by the grant of Latvian Council of Science.

References

1. Missikoff, M., Charabilidis, Y., Gongcalves, R., Popplewell, K. (eds.): FInES Research Roadmap 2025: Final Document (Version 3.0). European Communities (2012). http://cordis. europa.eu/fp7/ict/enet/documents/fines-research-roadmap-v30_en.pdf
2. Abraham, R., Tribolet, J., Winter, R.: Transformation of multi-level systems – theoretical grounding and consequences for enterprise architecture management. In: Proper, H.A., Aveiro, D., Gaaloul, K. (eds.) EEWC 2013. LNBIP, vol. 146, pp. 73–87. Springer, Heidelberg (2013)

3. Hoverstadt, P.: The Fractal Organization: Creating Sustainable Organizations with the Viable Systems Model. Wiley, Chichester (2008)
4. Espejo, R., Reyes, A.: Organizational Systems. Managing Complexity with the Viable System Model. Springer, Berlin (2011)
5. Perez, R.J.: Design and Diagnosis for Sustainable Organization. Springer, Berlin (2012)
6. Sturdy, G.R.: Business Process Reengineering: Strategies for Occupational Health and Safety. Cambridge press, Cambridge (2010)
7. Bilal, M., Daclin, N., Chapurlat, V.: Collaborative networked organizations as system of systems: a model-based engineering approach. In: Camarinha-Matos, L.M., Afsarmanesh, H. (eds.) Collaborative Systems for Smart Networked Environments. IFIP AICT, vol. 434, pp. 227–234. Springer, Heidelberg (2014)
8. PCF: Process classification framework (2012). http://www.apqc.org/process-classification-framework
9. Buckl, S., Matthes, F., Schweda, C.M.: Viable system perspective on enterprise architecture management. In: Proceedings of the 2009 IEEE International Conference on Systems, Man and Cybernetics, pp. 1483–1488. IEEE (2009)
10. Proper, H.A.: Enterprise architecture: informed steering of enterprises in motion. In: Hammoudi, S., Cordeiro, J., Maciaszek, L.A., Filipe, J. (eds.) ICEIS 2013. LNBIP, vol. 190, pp. 16–34. Springer, Heidelberg (2014)
11. Närman, M., Buschle, M., Ekstedt, M.: An enterprise architecture framework for multi-attribute information systems analysis. Softw. Syst. Model. **13**(3), 1085–1116 (2014)
12. Zadeh, M.E., Lewis, E., Millar, G., Yinan Yang, Thorne, C.: The use of viable system model to develop guidelines for generating enterprise architecture principles. In: Proceedings of the 2014 IEEE International Conference on Systems, Man and Cybernetics (SMC), pp. 1020–1026. IEEE (2014)
13. Kandjani, H., Bernus, P.: The enterprise architecture body of knowledge as an evolving discipline. Kluwer Academic Publishers (1998). https://www.academia.edu/3862307/The_Enterprise_Architecture_Body_of_Knowledge_as_an_Evolving_Discipline
14. Sandkuhl, K., Stirna, J., Persson, A., Wißotzki, M.: Enterprise Modeling: Tackling Business Challenges with the 4EM Method. Springer, Heildelberg (2014)
15. Henkel, M., Bider, I., Perjons, E.: Capability-based business model transformation. In: Iliadis, L., Papazoglou, M., Pohl, K. (eds.) CAiSE Workshops 2014. LNBIP, vol. 178, pp. 88–99. Springer, Heidelberg (2014)
16. Beer, S.: Diagnosing the Systems for Organizations. Wiley, Chichester (1985)
17. Kirikova, M., Pudane, M.: Viable systems model based information flows. In: Catania, B., Cerquitelli, T., Chiusano, S., Guerrini, G., Kämpf, M., Kemper, A., Novikov, B., Palpanas, T., Pokorny, J., Vakali, A. (eds.) New Trends in Databases and Information Systems. AISC, vol. 241, pp. 97–104. Springer, Heidelberg (2014)

Towards Graphical Query Notation
for Semantic Databases

Kārlis Čerāns$^{(\boxtimes)}$, Jūlija Ovčiņņikova, and Mārtiņš Zviedris

Institute of Mathematics and Computer Science, University of Latvia,
Raina Blvd. 29, Riga 1459, Latvia
{karlis.cerans, julija.ovcinnikova,
martins.zviedris}@lumii.lv

Abstract. We describe a notation and a tool for schema-enabled visual/diagrammatic creation of SPARQL queries over RDF databases. The notation and the tool support both the standard basic query pattern comprising a main query class and possibly linked condition classes and means for aggregate query definition and placing conditions over aggregates including also aggregation of aggregate results. We discuss the applicability of the tool for ad-hoc query formulation in practical use cases.

Keywords: Visual query creation · SPARQL · RDF databases · Semantic technologies

1 Introduction

The semantic technologies built around the RDF [1, 2], OWL [3] and SPARQL [4] standards are the basis for the Semantic Web [5] and Linked Data [6], as well as they may well be used in enterprise-level use cases. The semantic technologies offer much higher-level view on data than do the classic relational databases (RDB) with their corresponding SQL query language thus enabling more direct involvement of various domain experts in data set definition, exploration and analysis.

The availability of the data in the semantic information landscape is ensured mainly via mappings into RDF/OWL from original data sets in various formats, notably the relational databases, where exists a W3C mapping standard R2RML [7], as well as numerous mapping formalisms (see e.g. Virtuoso RDF Views [8], D2RQ [9], ontop [10] and RDB2OWL [11]). The RDF data stores such as Virtuoso [8] and Stardog [12] provide native RDF data storage possibility.

The classical approach to data access in relational databases involves creating user interface applications for common operations over the data and then asking programmers to create on-demand SQL queries in the case of non-standard information requests. A similar approach can be followed also in the case of RDF databases and SPARQL queries, however, this approach will not respond to the expectation for the direct domain expert involvement in the data access. Therefore a number of approaches such as ViziQuer [13, 14] and Optique VQS [15] for visual/diagrammatic creation of SPARQL queries have emerged. The practical experience with the ViziQuer tool with the medical domain experts have confirmed the importance of the visual query creation

© Springer International Publishing Switzerland 2015
R. Matulevičius and M. Dumas (Eds.): BIR 2015, LNBIP 229, pp. 273–281, 2015.
DOI: 10.1007/978-3-319-21915-8_19

concept, however, it has also confirmed a further need in support of aggregate query generation that is a very typical custom query kind over the data. The problem addressed in this paper is presenting a visual query notation and tool for aggregate query definition and translation into SPARQL.

We base the work on the availability of the aggregate queries in SPARQL version 1.1. [4]. The task of visual/diagrammatic query creation is quite challenging since the diagrammatic notations for aggregates in the queries is not common even for query creating systems also in the much widely established area of RDB/SQL databases.

In the rest of the paper we introduce first the basic visual query notation, including already the simplest patterns for aggregate query construction, followed by direct grouping and subquery constructs usable for more involved query generation. The practical use aspects of the approach is discussed in the final section of the paper. The illustrations in the paper are given on a mini-University example, however they can be carried over directly to more practical use cases, including the medical domain.

2   Basic Query Notation

This section outlines the basic visual query SPARQL notation, including specification of class information, attribute selection, conditions and links, similar to [13, 14], as well as new simple aggregate attribute definition. The visual/diagrammatic query generation is based on the data schema definition as OWL ontology or RDF Schema; for the construction illustration we shall use the following mini-University ontology, presented in Fig. 1 in graphical OWLGrEd[1] ontology editor notation [16].

Figure 2 illustrates two basic visual queries and their corresponding SPARQL queries. The first query selects all student names, student ID and student card ID. The second query selects all successful completed registrations (mark >= 4) for large courses (at least 6 credit points) and displays mark, student name and course name.[2] Each query contains a single main query class (shown as orange round rectangle) as well as possibly a number of condition classes (shown as violet rectangles), linked to the query class via links corresponding to the object properties between the classes in the ontology (chains of condition classes and links from condition classes to the main class are allowed, as well). Each of the class boxes in the query represents an instance resource belonging to the class. The class attributes (shown in white letters) define instance properties (attributes) that are to be included in the query output. The conditions (shown in pink/dark) restrict the rows to be returned by the query.

The queries in Fig. 2 contain just the attribute values, not the URIs of the involved instance resources. The inclusion of the instance URI in the query output can be specified either with <<select>> stereotype for the class, or by including the class instance name (e.g. R for *Registration*) into the attribute list for the class.

---

[1] The ontology editor can be downloaded from http://owlgred.lumii.lv/.

[2] The prefix ont: in the examples stands for http://lumii.lv/ontologies/UnivExample.owl#. that is the URI for the mini-University ontology itself.

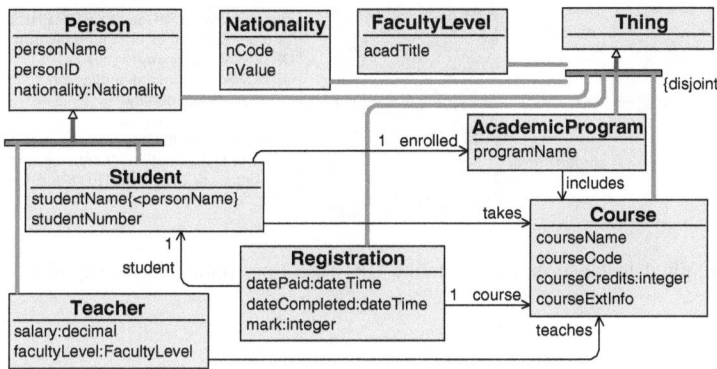

Fig. 1. Example: a mini-University ontology in the OWLGrEd notation

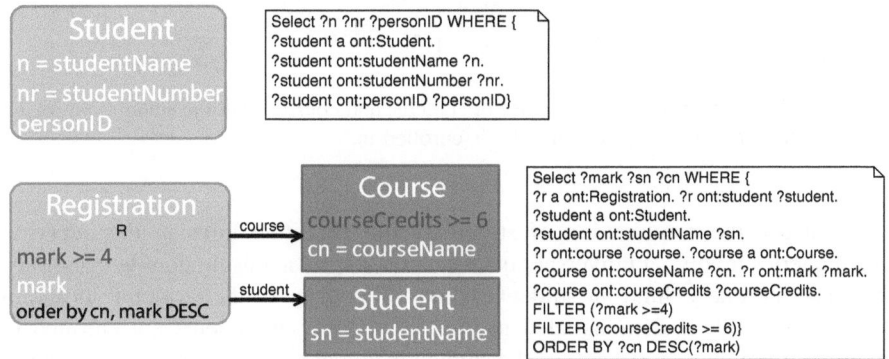

Fig. 2. Basic query examples

Figure 3 shows the optional attribute (marked by the keyword OPTIONAL) and optional link notation (as the blue dashed line) as well as a negation link (marked in red and the stereotype {not}). The whole query fragments placed behind the optional or negation links (from the viewpoint of the main query class) are in optional or negation group. If a negation link connects class instances that are already connected, as in Fig. 4 example, it is to be interpreted as a condition asserting non-existence of the respective link, after the query structure has been created from the other "structural" links. We use the {condition} stereotype on the link to mark its condition semantics; this stereotype can be used also on affirmative/positive edges, asserting the existence of the respective link (the optional link with the {condition} mark makes a void requirement on the query contents). The non-condition loops including negation or optional links are not allowed. There is a requirement for the entire diagram to be connected via non-condition links; if the query logics would require several non-connected components, they are to be connected with un-labelled strict or optional links marking the query structure.

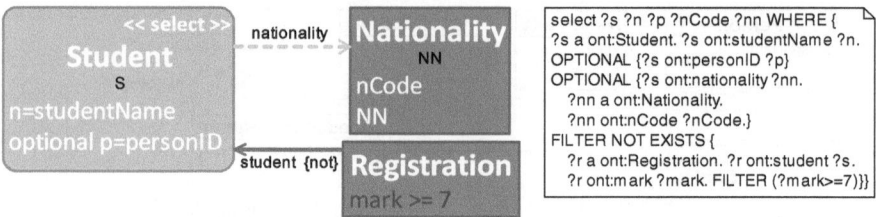

Fig. 3. Explicit instance names, instance URI selection; optional and negation links

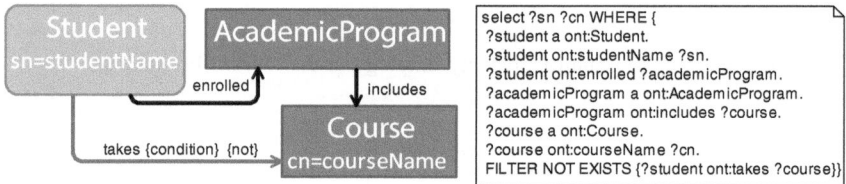

Fig. 4. Negated condition link: select names of students and courses with the student not taking a course included in academic program (s)he is enrolled in.

One can use the combination of structural and condition links in the query to formulate queries involving universal quantification, expressed using double negations. For instance, the query "find all students taking all courses of the academic program they are enrolled in", is demonstrated in Fig. 5 via "find all students not enrolled in academic program including a course the student is not taking". A corresponding query with the structural semantics of both negation links would not be allowed due to the loop with two structural negations emerging.

The basic query notation allows for simple aggregate query introduction in the case, if the grouping set for all aggregate function applications coincides with the set of all selected non-aggregate attributes in the query. An aggregate attribute is introduced as an expression where the aggregate function (count, sum, avg, min, max, group_concat) is applied to the attribute name; the aggregation over the instance URI is possible also via the <<count>> or <<count distinct>> stereotype for the class.

The SPARQL query for such a simple aggregated query is generated in two steps: first, for every class instance with aggregate attributes a SPARQL-subquery is generated involving the aggregated attributes from this class instance and the grouping set of all non-aggregated attributes in the query; then all subqueries are joined together into a single SPARQL query (cf. examples in Figs. 6 and 7).

Figure 6 contains two examples, where, first, a student name is selected together with the corresponding count of taken courses and sum of credits within those, restricting the result rows to those having course credit sum at least 9. The conditions in the query classes are evaluated before aggregate applications, therefore the row filter depending on the aggregate value is defined in the *having*-compartment of the class

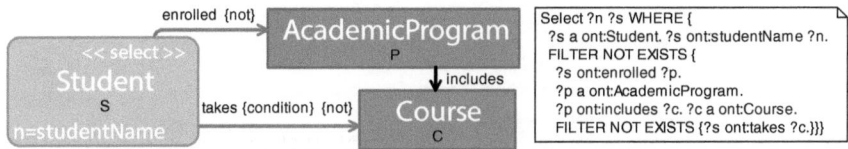

Fig. 5. Double negation: structural and condition negations determine the query structure.

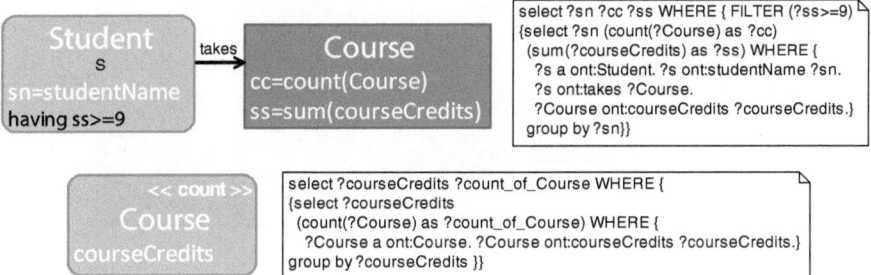

Fig. 6. Simple aggregation: basic examples

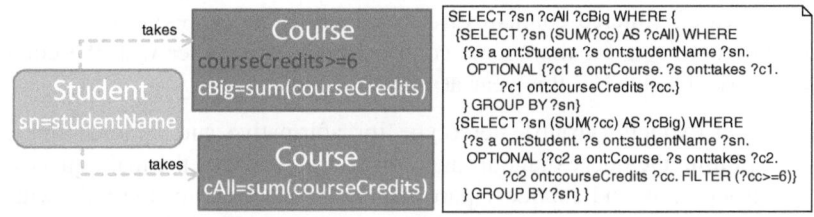

Fig. 7. Simple aggregation: optional links and multiple-class aggregates

box. The other example shows listing the different *courseCredits* values together with the count of courses corresponding to each of these values.

Figure 7 describes a query for finding student names together with both sum of credits for the student in all courses, and in "big" courses with at least 6 credit points each.

3 Explicit Grouping and Subqueries

The outlined basic query constructions cover a large range of practical queries that may arise in the exploration of the mini-University example, as well as in the practical use cases of query formulation over hospital information system and clinical records databases. There are, however, natural queries not fitting naturally the basic query pattern due to involving the aggregate-over-aggregate pattern, e.g.:

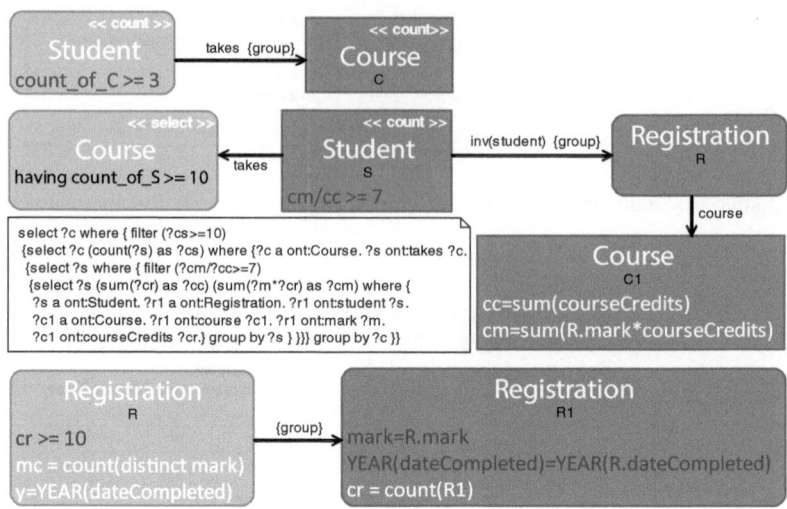

Fig. 8. Visual queries with explicit grouping.

A. Count all students taking at least three courses (count-over-counts).
B. Find all courses passed by at least 10 students with mean mark (over all passed courses) at least 7 (filtered counts over filtered aggregate expressions).
C. List all different years for the course completion dates together with the count of different marks received in this year at least 10 times.

We introduce an explicit {group} stereotype for affirmative and optional links. Its semantics is splitting the query diagram into "main" part towards the main query class side of the {group} link and subquery part behind the other end of the link, with the further design assumption that the URI of the instance on the "main" end of the link, as well as the link itself also participates in the subquery, making the "join condition" between the subquery and the main query. The {group} stereotype is not compatible with {condition} stereotype, nor is it to be used for negation links. The general query shape has to be a tree of simple components (i.e. components built with non-condition and non-group links), linked by {group}-links; the {condition}-links are allowed only within a single component, or from within a component to its incoming {group}-link source node. Figure 8 shows the A-C queries in the visual query notation.

There is also the option of introducing and using explicit named subqueries in the visual language. While the {group}-links in the query diagram may often appear to be an easier mechanism of involved query specification, the named subqueries would correspond to "derived concept" introduction and allow easier query reuse. Figure 9 shows the B example query definition and usage in the named subquery notation.

The visual query language provides also means for query result set limiting to a number of rows (the SPARQL LIMIT construction). Although one could easily add to the visual query language this notation also on the subquery level (including the inline and named subqueries), the SPARQL language the queries are translated into does not

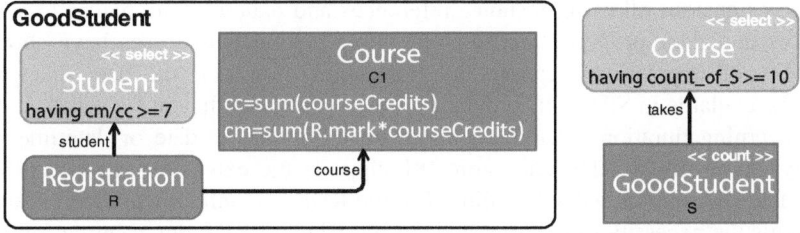

Fig. 9. A named subquery example

contain at least direct means for expressing this type of constructs. Therefore such an important query pattern as "find all x with their related most common y" (e.g. find all courses with the most often received marks in them) cannot be directly offered for practical usage. The practical workaround to this limitation would be to re-formulate the queries with LIMIT-bound subqueries in a way that they return larger result sets from which the needed results can easily be obtained e.g. in a spreadsheet.

4   Discussion and Conclusions

We aim at practical visual query formulation system creation over data via their conceptual structure view. As the initial experiments show, most of the practically interesting queries both in the hospital information system and clinical records data-base use cases can be formulated using the provided notation. The notation and tool polishing is certainly worth to be continued including the offering of the query tool to the domain experts. There would be need in a query creation methodology and initial training before the domain experts would be ready to use the query tool themselves.

The notation described in this paper has a prototype implementation in the Vizi-Quer tool.[3] The ViziQuer tool can be used for SPARQL query creation over any SPARQL endpoints with their data RDF schema available. The work in [14] discusses RDF schema extraction from a SPARQL endpoint. [17] outlines the possibility of using ViziQuer in the context of relational database semantic re-engineering, where a conceptual model of a relational database is created as an OWL ontology, then the mapping from the RDB to the ontology is described, enabling creation of the ontology-structured SPARQL endpoint that can accept queries created in ViziQuer. The limitation of SPARQL not allowing row-level aggregate subqueries with TOP/LIMIT restrictions (such queries would not be problematic e.g. in SQL) may lead to considerations of direct translations from the visual query language to SQL that would be well defined within the RDB semantic re-engineering framework.

A less considered query language aspect in this paper is the language of expressions allowed in conditions and query output definition. The idea of translating expressions into SPARQL is based on supporting SPARQL-like expression syntax in the language,

---

[3] http://viziquer.lumii.lv/.

with the extensions allowing instance references and data attribute names to stand for resources and their properties respectively. The practical use cases have shown the possibility of expression creation and translation, however, the date manipulation functions available in SPARQL standard [4] are clearly insufficient for practical queries e.g. concerning duration calculation based on the available date or datetime values. Notably, the Virtuoso RDF data store [8] supports the extensions allowing the necessary date and interval value handling. For the RDB semantic re-engineering use case this entails the necessity of creating and storing RDB-to-RDF dump into a triple store, instead of using an on-the-fly maintained SPARQL endpoint.

Acknowledgements. This work has been supported by European Union within the ERDF project 'Granular ontology tools for data analysis' (Project No. 2DP/2.1.1.1.0/14/APIA/VIAA/072) and Latvian State Research program NexIT project No.1 'Technologies of ontologies, semantic web and security'.

References

1. Resource Description Framework (RDF). http://www.w3.org/RDF/
2. RDF Schema [WWW]. http://www.w3.org/TR/rdf-schema/
3. Motik, B., Patel-Schneider P.F., Parsia B.: OWL 2 Web Ontology Language Structural Specification and Functional-Style Syntax (2009)
4. SPARQL 1.1 Overview. W3C Recommendation 21 March 2013 [WWW] http://www.w3.org/TR/sparql11-overview/
5. Linked Data. http://linkeddata.org
6. Berners-Lee, T., Hendler, J., Lassila, O.: The Semantic Web. Sci. Am. **122**(10), 29–37 (2001)
7. R2RML: RDB to RDF Mapping Language. http://www.w3.org/TR/r2rml/
8. Blakeley, C.: RDF Views of SQL Data (Declarative SQL Schema to RDF Mapping), OpenLink Software (2007)
9. D2RQ Platform. Treating Non-RDF Relational Databases as Virtual RDF Graphs. http://www4.wiwiss.fu-berlin.de/bizer/D2RQ/spec/
10. Bagosi, T., Calvanese, D., Hardi, J., Komla-Ebri, S., Lanti, D., Rezk, M., Rodriguez-Muro, M., Slusnys, M., Xiao, G.: The ontop framework for ontology based data access. In: Zhao, D., Du, J., Wang, H., Wang, P., Ji, D., Pan, J.Z. (eds.) CSWS 2014. CCIS, vol. 480, pp. 67–77. Springer, Heidelberg (2014)
11. Čerāns, K., Būmans, G.: RDB2OWL: a RDB-to-RDF/OWL Mapping Specification Language. In: Barzdins, J., Kirikova, M. (eds.) Databases and Information Systems VI, pp. 139–152. IOS Press, Amsterdam (2011)
12. Stardog. http://stardog.com/
13. Barzdins, G., Liepins, E., Veilande, M., Zviedris, M.: Semantic Latvia approach in the medical domain. In: Haav, H.M., Kalja, A. (eds.) Proceedings of the 8th International Baltic Conference on Databases and Information Systems., pp. 89–102. TUT Press (2008)
14. Zviedris, M., Barzdins, G.: ViziQuer: a tool to explore and query SPARQL endpoints. In: Antoniou, G., Grobelnik, M., Simperl, E., Parsia, B., Plexousakis, D., De Leenheer, P., Pan, J. (eds.) ESWC 2011, Part II. LNCS, vol. 6644, pp. 441–445. Springer, Heidelberg (2011)

15. Soylu, A., Giese, M., Jiménez-Ruiz, E., Kharlamov, E., Zheleznyakov, D., Horrocks, I.: OptiqueVQS: Towards an ontology based visual query system for big data. In: MEDES (2013)
16. Barzdins, J., Cerans, K., Liepins, R., Sprogis, A.: UML style graphical notation and editor for owl 2. In: Forbrig, P., Günther, H. (eds.) BIR 2010. LNBIP, vol. 64, pp. 102–114. Springer, Heidelberg (2010)
17. Cerans, K., Barzdins, G., Bumans, G., Ovcinnikova, J., Rikacovs, S., Romane, A., Zviedris, M.: A relational database semantic re-engineering technology and tools. Baltic J. Mod. Comput. (BJMC) 3(3), 183–198 (2014)

Conceptualizing a Network Process Model Based Production Platform

Thomas Knothe, Adrian Zoch$^{(\boxtimes)}$, and Malte Meißner

Corporate Management, Fraunhofer IPK, Berlin, Germany
{thomas.knothe,adrian.zoch,
malte.meissner}@ipk.fraunhofer.de

Abstract. First tier system suppliers play a key role in every economy. However, in a lot of European regions there is a lack of these kinds of business players even though OEM production is established, mostly due to political reasons. Based on nearly 25 years of experience in supplier network research, this paper proposes a model based platform that can support the establishment of a supplier based system through a network of SMEs. This platform streamlines requirements, orders and tasks and provides the ability to utilize a network's collective production capabilities more efficiently to comply with complex OEM system product requirements and remain competitive in a global market space. An underlying network process model allows for an efficient and flexible alignment of interfaces between network participants while a competence mapping helps allocating automatically fragmented production tasks to producers based on available production capacity and technological resources.

Keywords: Business process management · Supply chain integration · Supply chain platform

1 Introduction

Regions that have profound structural disadvantages in their economic set-up can never be revived with easy solutions. There are historical, political, economic and geographical reasons for a region's economic (mis-)fortune and trying to change such a fate requires a large tapestry of solutions which go far beyond the scope of this paper. Rather, this production platform seeks to be one cog in the wheel of a greater machinery to rejuvenate a struggling region's economy. More specifically, the aim of the current research project is the development of a regional tier 1 supplier platform in a region that has economic, social and structural deficits. The platform is designed to support the coordination of an integrated and robust supplier network that adheres to the needs of small and mid-sized enterprises (SMEs) while also offering OEMs the necessary flexibility, rapid response times, innovative product solutions and economic incentives required to compete in a global market space.

The rest of this paper is structured as follows: Sect. 2 will accentuate the need for a regional supplier platform by presenting the systemic economic challenges in the focused geographic region. Section 3 is going to take a brief look at state-of-the-art solutions and current academic research followed by a detailed presentation of the

© Springer International Publishing Switzerland 2015
R. Matulevičius and M. Dumas (Eds.): BIR 2015, LNBIP 229, pp. 282–289, 2015.
DOI: 10.1007/978-3-319-21915-8_20

concept of the production platform in Sect. 4. Finally, Sect. 5 concludes the paper by providing an outlook on the scalability and transferability of the proposed platform to other, more geographically dispersed actors from different industrial sectors.

2   Challenges and Goals for a Regional Supplier Platform

The region in question is characterized by a low level of economic productivity and a strong economic fragmentation compared to other regions that share the same legal framework. The average firm size is smaller than that of their counterparts, which results in the industry competitors being able to benefit from economies of scale and scope. The dominant structural economic limitation of the region is the absolute number of regional system suppliers (tier 1), as well as their technological capabilities and production capacities. Furthermore, the degree of innovation of complex components in the studied region lacks that of otherwise comparable locations. Value-adding activities that sustain the long term economic competitiveness of the region, such as research and development (R&D), are either deficient in their technical capabilities, the level of expertise or are missing completely. Cooperative industry networks of suppliers, OEMs and existing research institutions are largely non-existent. Figure 1 illustrates the structural economic deficits present in the studied region.

The main challenges that present themselves are a sluggish process in terms of suppliers aligning themselves and creating an offering and the trust between OEMs and suppliers. The first challenge that can be observed is that while there is a steady demand from OEMs, the number of suppliers (especially tier 1) that can deliver the required components is not enough to meet the demand. This in turn prompts OEMs to look elsewhere for suppliers, increasing the costs of their supply chains, prolonging delivery times and placing a strain on the logistical resources compared to resorting to local suppliers, as well as fragmenting the trust they have in the suppliers. However, this not only poses a major economic problem to OEMs, but further worsens the socioeconomic conditions in the region by forcing highly qualified personnel to migrate to other, more economic sound regions resulting in a so called "brain drain".

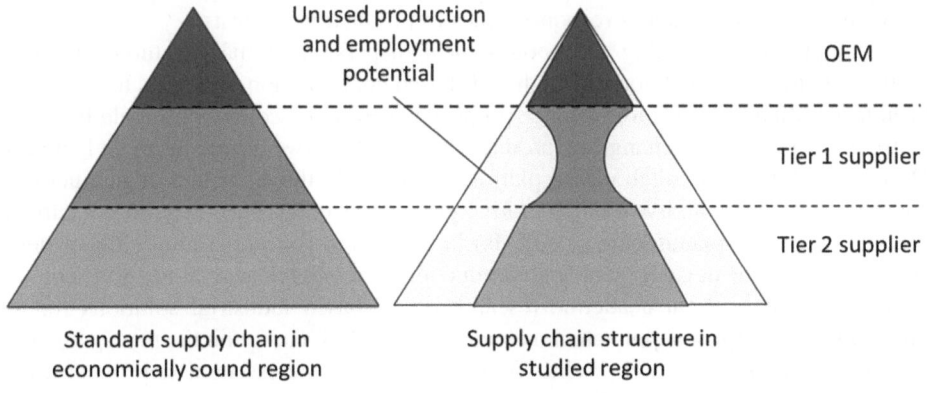

Fig. 1. - Graphical presentation of the studied region's structural economic deficits

The mechanisms of supplier coordination and supplier platforms are often too individually specified or not open enough to facilitate multilateral relationships. What is required is a system that provides a structured and systemic approach to efficiently connecting suppliers and OEMs within an extended production network to fully utilize available technological resources and local competences. The platform should provide OEMs with the ability to automatically fragment their complex and multicomponent production orders into more manageable tasks and delegate these to the most competent suppliers for the task within an open, non-static and transparent network.

3 State of the Art Solutions and Current Research

The focus of the supply chain management (SCM) literature has long shifted away from the traditional view of supplier relations conceptualized as chains to more network based approaches [1]. Improvements in communication and informational technology have allowed multilateral networks of suppliers to respond more quickly to volatile market conditions, shortening product life cycles and increasing rates of innovation. This is a departure from more static chains of up and downstream suppliers that were predominantly coordinated by the activities of one dominant OEM and were only as strong as their weakest link. Through coordinating research and development, as well as production activities between them, suppliers within this so-called "extended enterprise" are able to develop new synergies, complement their competences and reduce time-to-market periods substantially and thus compete more effectively for OEM orders [2]. However, while the ever increasing wealth of data and increasing flow of information and capital between economic actors has largely facilitated the growth of supplier networks, there are still a large number of barriers for small and medium sized suppliers. These barriers include limited technological and informational resources which are essential in order to gain access to extended supplier networks and to coordinate value adding activities between them. Some of these have already been addressed in various research projects. The project "Fluid-Win" for instance already developed concepts of dynamic business models and accompanying e-commerce applications that enable clusters of manufacturers to function as single business entities [3]. Hereby, independent suppliers could form a consortium of bidders more quickly and compete more effectively by reducing response times to production requests.

Attempts at overcoming the geographical dispersion of manufacturers within a global manufacturing network through web-based collaboration platforms have already been made. Zhan et al. [4] for instance propose a web-based collaboration platform that simplifies the secure exchange of product data (EDI) between remote manufacturers. However, while such collaborative platforms do enable the exchange of product data and reduce the complexity of collaborative product design (CPD), they do not support original enterprise manufacturers (OEMs) in the search for and commission of tier 1 suppliers with the development and production of complex and innovative components. Similarly, current academic research on IT based industrial solutions for the integration of complex supply chain networks primarily focusses on the management of information, knowledge and product flows, but neglect the essential step of matching OEM requirements with supplier competences. State of the art B2B search platforms, such as "europages.com" [5] or the German "Wer-liefert-was.de" [6] merely provide companies with a database to research potential suppliers in different industrial sectors and only support bilateral relations between two companies. They do not support more complex process chains, nor do these platforms take into account the highly individualized component requirements by manufacturing OEMs nor do they provide information about current production possibilities and capacities of small and medium sized suppliers. Current academic research also does not provide sufficient governance mechanisms to coordinate extended networks of small suppliers and larger OEMs. Additionally, it lacks the tier 1 specific focus which is essential to the presented topic.

The current collaborative research project thus focuses on this gap in the SCM literature and industrial applications and aims to develop and implement a regional supplier platform based on a business process network model that may easily be extended to connect global suppliers with OEMs, while maintaining the necessary flexibility, rapid response times and low costs of an agile and competitive supply chain.

4   A Network Process Model Based Production Platform

The underlying basis of the production platform is an inter-organizational enterprise network model of the regional supplier network. Enterprise/network models are an abstraction of the relations between products, organizations, roles and resources systems in organizations. One of the many advantages of such a simplified representation of an enterprise or network and their business objects and processes is the efficient management of interfaces between internal and external customers. The Integrated Enterprise Modelling (IEM) [7] method will be used to define and depict cross-enterprise business process models and interfaces in the extended enterprise model. Although various frameworks for the standardization of supply chain management processes have existed for a long time they have not been universally implemented, especially with regard to SMEs. The Supply Chain Operations Reference (SCOR) model for instance provides a cross industry supply chain framework advocating best practice processes and performance metrics in inter-organizational supplier networks to further "improve the alignment between the marketplace and the strategic response of a supply chain" [8]. A flexible and modular network process model that is at the heart of the proposed supply chain management platform will allow for such an alignment of interfaces between various tiers within the network and support regional actors in the following four ways: Fig. 2.

4.1   Technology Chain Configuration

The main feature of the production portal is an automated technology chain configurator. This will enable the decomposition of complex production orders into smaller, more manageable tasks/modules to be executed by (multiple) small and medium sized tier 1 suppliers based on available capacity, resources and skills within the supplier network as specified by the competence map. In case of a lack of available production technologies within the network the system will further provide advice on the substitution of alternative

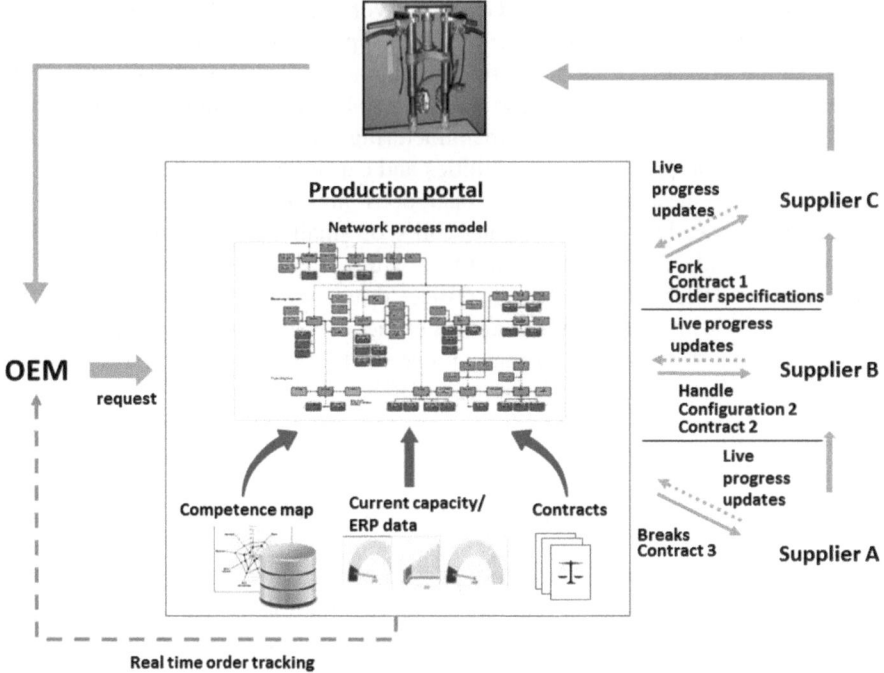

Fig. 2. Network process model at the core of the production portal

manufacturing technologies and intercompany line configurations to ensure the timely and economic fulfillment of OEM requirements. The platform will then facilitate the electronic interchange of product data via a central web based platform. This solution for the multilateral exchange of business documents will improve data accuracy and contribute to the use of universal data standards for the exchange of product specifications within the network. The use of a standardized format for the exchange of product data not only lowers the cost and improves upon the accuracy of the data transferred between different suppliers' software products, but also allows for the real time update of product and order specifications in case of order changes between supply chain actors [9]. SMEs especially are often confronted with a lack of competences in the implementation of sophisticated IT support systems. Missing universal data standards further represent a major obstacle in the implementation of autonomous production facilities. Existing industry data standards, such as e-business standards (e.g. EDIFACT, webXML or VDA standards) and industrial data exchange standards, like the "Standard for the Exchange of Product model data" (STEP), are rarely implemented in SMEs. This is either due to the costs involved in adopting such standards (e.g. through adapting hard-/software), interoperability issues or disagreements between networks and their constituents. Standardization in product data exchange may significantly reduce time-to-market for OEMs - in part through the reduction of set-up times - and improve the effectiveness with which networks can respond to changing demand conditions.

In addition, the platform as well as the underlying process model will be conceptualized to offer flexible interfaces to allow new suppliers to be connected to the production network. The concept of "plug and produce" allows firms to join the production network, contribute their manufacturing capabilities to the network and start producing almost immediately, greatly reducing search and configuration times. A major research focus here is on how to ensure universal quality and process standards of new suppliers to reduce the risk OEMs take with new supply structures to an acceptable level. In order to test existing platform functionalities and reduce quality issues in large production orders, an intermediate stage of only processing small volume prototyping orders is also possible.

4.2   Competence and Capacity Mapping

Competence mapping enables the automated allocation of technology elements and their requirements to the competences of regional actors within the network. The repository of available competencies within the network is essential for the configuration of possible technology chains, as modules of more complex components will be automatically assigned to manufacturers according to production facilities, product-specific competences and available capacity. The profound lack of sophisticated enterprise resource planning (ERP) systems, the lack of standardized data interfaces of manufacturing equipment and missing machine communication with centralized databases present a major challenge in the unification of data standards. Current research projects attempt to address this problem, by, for instance, retrospectively applying cyber physical systems (CPS) to non-smart manufacturing equipment (see CoCos [10], piCASSO [11]). However, more research is required to provide SMEs with a simple and standardized tool to communicate real time capacities to the platform.

4.3   Contract Generator

An automated contract generator will further improve the efficiency of administrative tasks surrounding the production order and thus reduce the organizational burden on limited SME resources. This will support SMEs through the generation of required documents of the assigned production order based on the inherent network process model, its processes and their parameters, product specifications, responsibilities and financial agreements. The basis of the contract generator is the supply chain production model including all foreseen exceptions. The AIAG inventory visibility and interoperability model is a good example [12].

4.4   Real Time Order Tracking

OEMs will be able to track the current status of their production orders throughout all stages of the supply chain including the transport activities between intermediate suppliers and the OEMs production facilities. This process transparency will allow all supply chain actors to plan more efficiently and adjust their manufacturing process in case of schedule deviations. Severe production difficulties that compromise order fulfillment with regards to quality, quantity or cost can be communicated almost instantly. Hereby, the results of the project "SPIDER-WIN" will be taken into account [13]. Based on an asynchronous data exchange of order status changes between the platform and enterprises, supply chain partners can be notified of schedule deviations through an alert function. Furthermore, alternative production scenarios within the networks capabilities may be devised to prevent a complete halt of the OEMs production line.

Overall integration. The presented platform functionalities will systemize and integrate already existing business processes in participating SMEs. While the automatic allocation of production orders to the supplier with the right competences will reduce acquisition and search efforts, the exchange of product data via the platform will further reduce unnecessary communication and transferability issues. Automated order tracking will further support SMEs by systemizing the processes with which OEMs are being informed of the current order status. In addition to faster response times, OEMs will further benefit from a diversification of their supply chain by breaking up existing single sourcing arrangements, thereby reducing their dependence on monopolistic market structures.

5   Conclusion and Future Research

The platform introduced in this paper is still in its early conception stage. Our hope is that it manages to contribute to a larger endeavor that aims at rejuvenating an economically weak region that specifically suffers from a lack of tier 1 suppliers. Future research will deal with its implementation in the region as well as its effectiveness. Specifically a use case scenario will be added which will further validate the platform. The platform needs to be tested in terms of accessibility as well as longevity.

Additionally, there are other factors that, once the project enters its implementation stage, need to be analyzed. Questions relating to the applicability of this project to other regions or its scalability concerning smaller or larger regions need to be studied. Furthermore, the current conception of the production platform illustrated above will be complemented by a number of additional features in a second stage to address the challenges regarding the lack of innovative capabilities shown in Sect. 2. Open innovation approaches and new collaborative forms of product design and development will be supported to improve the local economic competitiveness in the global market space.

References

1. Rice, J.B., Hoppe, R.M.: Supply chain vs. supply chain. The Hype & The Reality. Supply chain management review Sept/ Oct 2001

2. Accenture: Digital Supply Network—The New Standard for Modern Supply Chain Management. http://www.accenture.com/us-en/Pages/insight-digital-supply-network-modern-supply-chain-management.aspx
3. FLUID-WIN Consortium: FLUID-WIN. Finance, Logistics and Production Integration Domain by Web-based Interaction Network. FP6-IST-4-027 083. http://www.fluid-win.de/
4. Zhan, H.F., Lee, W.B., Cheung, C.F., Kwok, S.K., Gu, X.J.: A web-based collaborative product design platform for dispersed network manufacturing. J. Mater. Process. Technol. **138**, 600–604 (2003)
5. EUROPAGES SA.: EUROPAGES. Internationale Suche von Firmen, Produkten und b2b-Dienstleistungen. http://www.europages.de/
6. Wer liefert was? GmbH: Wer Liefert was. https://www.wlw.de
7. Mertins, K., Jochem, R.: Quality-oriented design of business processes. Kluwer Academic Publishers, Boston (1999)
8. Huan, S.H., Sheoran, S.K., Wang, G.: A review and analysis of supply chain operations reference (SCOR) model. Supp. Chain. Manag. **9**, 23–29 (2004)
9. Gao, J., Aziz, H., Maropoulos, P., Cheung, W.: Application of product data management technologies for enterprise integration. Int. J. Comput. Integr. Manuf. **16**, 491–500 (2003)
10. CoCos Consortium: CoCos Project. Context-Aware Connectivity and Service Infrastructure for Cyber-Physical Production Systems (CoCoS). http://www.cocos-project.de/index.html
11. pICASSO Consortium: pICASSO. Industrielle CloudbASierte Steuerungsplattform für eine Produktion mit cyber-physischen Systemen. http://www.projekt-picasso.de/index
12. Jankovic, M., Ivezic, N., Knothe, T., Marjanovic, Z., Snack, P.: A case study in enterprise modelling for interoperable cross-enterprise data exchange. In: Gonçalves, R.J., Müller, J.P., Mertins, K., Zelm, M. (eds.) Enterprise Interoperability II, pp. 541–552. Springer, London, London (2007)
13. Rabe, M.: Methods for the Analysis of Supply Network Processes at European SMEs. http://interop-esa05.unige.ch/INTEROP/Proceedings/Industrial/IND4_Abstract.pdf

Author Index